# CHEROKEE CITIZENSHIP COMMISSION DOCKETS 1880-1884 AND 1887-1889 VOLUME V

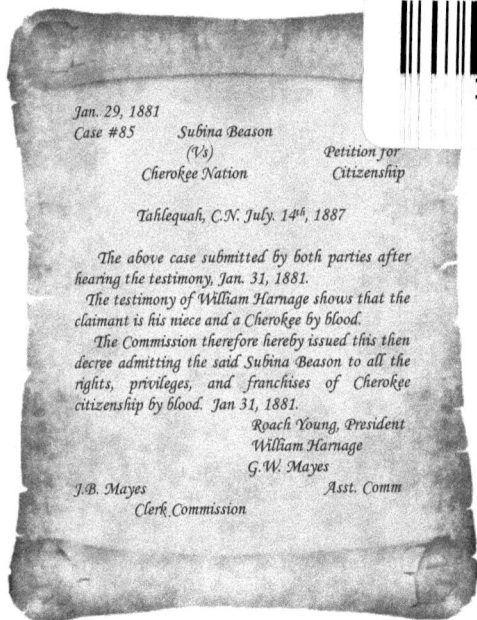

## TRANSCRIBED BY
## JEFF BOWEN

### NATIVE STUDY
**Gallipolis, Ohio**
**USA**

Originally published:
Baltimore, Maryland
2011


Reprinted by:

Native Study LLC
Gallipolis, OH
*www.nativestudy.com*
2020


Library of Congress Control Number: 2020916859

ISBN: 978-1-64968-062-4




*Made in the United States of America.*

# Other Books and Series by Jeff Bowen

*1901-1907 Native American Census  Seneca, Eastern Shawnee, Miami, Modoc, Ottawa, Peoria, Quapaw, and Wyandotte Indians  (Under Seneca School, Indian Territory)*

*1932 Census of The Standing Rock Sioux Reservation with Births And Deaths 1924-1932*

*Census of The Blackfeet, Montana, 1897- 1901  Expanded Edition*

*Eastern Cherokee by Blood, 1906-1910, Volumes I thru XIII*

*Choctaw of Mississippi Indian Census 1929-1932 with Births and Deaths 1924-1931     Volume I*
*Choctaw of Mississippi Indian Census 1933, 1934 & 1937, Supplemental Rolls to 1934 & 1935 with Births and Deaths 1932-1938, and Marriages 1936-1938 Volume II*

*Eastern Cherokee Census Cherokee, North Carolina 1930-1939*
*Census 1930-1931 with Births And Deaths 1924-1931 Taken By Agent L. W. Page Volume I*
*Eastern Cherokee Census  Cherokee, North Carolina 1930-1939*
*Census 1932-1933 with Births And Deaths 1930-1932 Taken By Agent R. L. Spalsbury    Volume II*
*Eastern Cherokee Census Cherokee, North Carolina 1930-1939*
*Census 1934-1937 with Births and Deaths 1925-1938 and Marriages 1936 & 1938 Taken by Agents R. L. Spalsbury And Harold W. Foght Volume III*

*Seminole of Florida Indian Census, 1930-1940 with Birth and Death Records, 1930-1938*

*Texas Cherokees 1820-1839  A Document For Litigation 1921*

*Choctaw By Blood Enrollment Cards 1898-1914 Volumes I thru XVII*

*Starr Roll 1894  (Cherokee Payment Rolls)  Districts: Canadian, Cooweescoowee, and Delaware  Volume One*
*Starr Roll 1894 (Cherokee Payment Rolls) Districts: Flint, Going Snake, and Illinois    Volume Two*
*Starr Roll 1894 (Cherokee Payment Rolls) Districts: Saline, Sequoyah, and Tahlequah; Including Orphan Roll   Volume Three*

*Cherokee Intruder Cases  Dockets of Hearings 1901-1909  Volumes I & II*

*Indian Wills, 1911-1921  Records of the Bureau of Indian Affairs*
*Books One thru Seven;*
*Native American Wills & Probate Records 1911-1921*

# Other Books and Series by Jeff Bowen

*Turtle Mountain Reservation Chippewa Indians 1932 Census with Births & Deaths, 1924-1932*

*Chickasaw By Blood Enrollment Cards 1898-1914 Volume I thru V*

*Cherokee Descendants East An Index to the Guion Miller Applications Volume I*
*Cherokee Descendants West An Index to the Guion Miller Applications Volume II (A-M)*
*Cherokee Descendants West An Index to the Guion Miller Applications Volume III (N-Z)*

*Applications for Enrollment of Seminole Newborn Freedmen, Act of 1905*

*Eastern Cherokee Census, Cherokee, North Carolina, 1915-1922, Taken by Agent James E. Henderson*      *Volume I (1915-1916)*
*Volume II (1917-1918)*
*Volume III (1919-1920)*
*Volume IV (1921-1922)*

*Complete Delaware Roll of 1898*

*Eastern Cherokee Census, Cherokee, North Carolina, 1923-1929, Taken by Agent James E. Henderson*      *Volume I (1923-1924)*
*Volume II (1925-1926)*
*Volume III (1927-1929)*

*Applications for Enrollment of Seminole Newborn  Act of 1905  Volumes I & II*

*North Carolina Eastern Cherokee Indian Census 1898-1899, 1904, 1906, 1909-1912, 1914  Revised and Expanded Edition*

*1932 Hopi and Navajo Native American Census with Birth & Death Rolls (1925-1931) Volume 1 - Hopi*
*1932 Hopi and Navajo Native American Census with Birth & Death Rolls (1930-1932) Volume 2 - Navajo*

*Western Navajo Reservation Navajo, Hopi and Paiute 1933 Census with Birth & Death Rolls 1925-1933*

*Cherokee Citizenship Commission Dockets 1880-1884 and 1887-1889 Volumes I,  II, III & IV*

Visit our website at **www.nativestudy.com** to learn more about these
and other books and series by Jeff Bowen

# INTRODUCTION

This publication was previously published by another publisher in 2009 and has now been reproduced by Native Study LLC. There are five volumes in this series concerning the Cherokee Citizenship Commission Dockets 1880 to 1889. This is material that was never before transcribed containing 2,288 Cherokee docket decisions.

This is somewhat of an explanation concerning the reasoning behind the proceedings that led the Cherokee tribal courts to take charge of these docket hearings.

The Cherokee relied upon their leaders to guide them but they ended up hanging in the balance after the Civil War, with their loyalties split worse than ever and their country ravished. Fathers and brothers were off fighting a war that didn't even concern them. By the time the war was over the Cherokee people had lost any form of stability. The men fighting the war came back to the same old political hatreds and in-fighting. The Nation was being over run with many that claimed they were Cherokee, hoping to benefit from false claims of citizenship. These people, known as intruders, did nothing but make it more difficult for the Cherokees because of the pressures from the Government to control their boundaries. The blood Cherokees that were seeking their homeland were again in question as to who they were. They found nothing but scrutiny and distrust, the war had made them choose a side, and the U.S. Government didn't care for the choice of the majority.

Intruder after intruder was encroaching on Cherokee land and what was to seem like a never ending battle. Many Cherokee citizens had lost their rights while intruders that didn't belong stayed using up what little resources there were. The government was telling the Cherokee leaders to settle their own intruder problems or else they would have to intercede. In an effort to clarify who were true Cherokee citizens and who were not, or who had been wrongfully taken off of the rolls, was a problem.

There were part-bloods, full-bloods, and no bloods along with mass confusion, prejudice, vendettas, and deceptions. The intruders wanted a free ride and were willing to use the confusion as a camouflage to achieve their purpose and greed.

v

This was a situation where the government was threatening to come in and turn the Cherokee Nation into a Federal Territory because it appeared to them that the Tribal Council would not be able to organize an effort to control the problem. But this wasn't the issue at hand as far as the Cherokee were concerned. They felt as if, according to their treaty stipulations, the United States was responsible for intruder removal. They felt as if the United States had let things get out of hand and that the government had not lived up to its contractual agreement. According to treaty stipulations this was true, but, they were told to either come up with a solution or lose their rights as a sovereign nation.

From William G. McLoughlin's book , *After the Trail of Tears, The Cherokees Struggle for Sovereignty 1839-1880*, it references on page 354, "Still, the Nation remained very uneasy about the fundamental question of its right to define who were its own citizens and its right to expect the United States to remove those who the Nation judged were not. Ever since 1872, federal agents had refused to expel from the Nation those former slaves whom the Nation considered 'aliens' and since 1874, federal agents had been under instructions from the Bureau of Indian Affairs to compile their own list of black or white persons who, in their opinion, had some claim to citizenship despite previous rulings of the Cherokee Courts on their claims."

On page 355-356, "On the basis of the affidavits and reports submitted, the Secretary of Interior, Zachariah Chandler, sent E.C. Watkins to the Nation in 1875, to investigate the citizenship problem and gather information that Chandler could use to ask Congress to take action on behalf of these 'men without a country'. Watkins reported in February, 1876, that many of those on Ingall's list were 'clearly entitled' to Cherokee citizenship. Oochalata denied it. He counter charged that Ingalls was meddling in Cherokee affairs and wrote to the Bureau of Indian Affairs to complain. Receiving no satisfactory response, he wrote directly to President Grant on November 13, 1876, enclosing a petition from the Cherokees Cooweescoowee District, complaining that the agent had not removed thousands of intruders in their area though ordered to do so by the Council. Some of these intruders were former slaves from the Deep South, but most were white U.S. citizens from Kansas, Missouri, and Arkansas.

Grant referred this letter to Commissioner J.Q. Smith. Annoyed that Oochalata had gone over the head of the Interior Department to the President, on December 8, Smith wrote Oochalata a long, assertive, and highly provocative letter outlining for the first time the department's position on this question. Smith said that from the evidence he had received, both from various federal agents and from the investigations of E.C. Watkins, the Cherokee Nation had failed to deal consistently and impartially with the problems of former slaves and others who claimed Cherokee citizenship. Therefore, the Bureau of Indian Affairs would continue to compile its own list of those who had 'prima facie' evidence for citizenship [whether the Cherokee courts had acted negatively on their claims or not], and it would take no action to remove them until the Cherokees carried four stipulations to resolve the issue. First, the Council must establish a clear, legal procedure providing due process for adjudicating all prima facie claims. Second, the rules by which such cases were decided must be approved by the Secretary of the Interior to ensure their impartiality. Third, he suggested that the Cherokee Circuit Courts be designated as the appropriate bodies for such hearings. Finally, claimants' appeals of the decisions of the Cherokee Circuit Courts must be forwarded to the Secretary of the Interior, and no claimant for citizenship should be removed from the Nation until the Secretary had made his own ruling. In effect, Smith asserted the right of the Bureau of Indian Affairs to decide who was and was not a Cherokee citizen. A crucial decision concerning the issue of the sovereignty of Indian nations was about to be reached.

Oochalata was stunned and wrote a 139-page letter to Smith explaining why this procedure was totally unacceptable and contrary to law, treaties, precedent, and the U.S. Constitution."

On page 357, "Acting on instructions from Oochalata, the Cherokee Delegation sent another letter to President Grant on Jan. 9, 1877, insisting that treaty rights, the Trade and Intercourse Act, and precedent gave the Nation the right 'to determine the question as to who are and who are not intruders.' The president referred their letter to Secretary of the Interior, Carl Schurz, who, on April 21, 1877, told the delegation that he supported Smith's four stipulations for settling the matter. Oochalata ignored this

vii

response and in August, 1877, sent to the new Commissioner of Indian Affairs, Ezra A. Hayt, a list of all the intruders whom the Cherokees wished to be immediately removed. On Nov. 7, Hayt replied flatly that the Bureau of Indian Affairs would not do so: 'while the department reserves to itself the right to finally determine who are and are not intruders under the law, **it expects the Cherokee Nation Council to enact some general and uniform law by which the Cherokee courts shall hear and determine the rights of claimants to citizenship,** subject only to the review of the Secretary of Interior after a final adjudication has been reached.'"

On page 358-9, "The department's claim that it had the right to judge intruders was, in Oochalata's opinion, 'a new doctrine for construing treaty or contracts in writing, to add to it verbally, a new clause, after the expiration of 92 years from date of that compact or treaty and without the consent of [one] party. . . . It is a dangerous doctrine to which I can never agree.'

While he urged the Council to send a protest through its delegation, Oochalata also asked it to enact a law that would establish a court to decide citizenship claims in a legal and uniform manner. The Council complied on Dec. 5, 1877, but the compromise was fatally weakened by the Council's failure to address two aspects of the law governing the Citizenship Court's actions.

First, the law provided no guidelines for deciding cases that would meet the demands of the Bureau of Indian Affairs, and consequently, in cases involving former slaves, the Citizenship Court relied, as the Cherokee Supreme Court had in 1870-71, simply on the wording in the Treaty of 1866. Second, the Council explicitly refused to allow the right of the Secretary of the Interior to review the decisions of the Court, stating that the Cherokee Citizenship Court was 'a tribunal of last resort'. The three persons appointed to the court, were John Chambers, O.P. Brewer, and George Downing. Also referred to as the Chamber's Commission, the Court began to hold hearings early in 1878. All persons claiming to have grounds for citizenship were required to present them or be declared intruders."

On pages 359-360, McLoughlin continues, "By the end of 1878, Oochalata struggling to find some new approach to the problem. On Dec. 3, he went over the head of the Bureau of Indian Affairs again, and wrote to Pres. Rutherford B. Hayes, forwarding a complete account of all of the cases adjudicated by the Citizenship Court and asking him to order the expulsion of those rejected and all other intruders. He told Hayes that the Cherokee Nation had an 'inherent national right' to define its own citizens, while the United States had a well-established obligation to expel non-citizens. Suspecting that Hayes would reject this request, Oochalata approached Commissioner Ezra A. Hayt and tried to work out a compromise. He said that the Cherokees would stop confiscating the property of those former slaves judged to be intruders pending the appointment of a joint commission of Cherokees and members of the Bureau to review the rejected claims. Hayt agreed only on the condition that decisions of this commission must be unanimous or the Bureau would retain the right to make its own decision in each case. Oochalata and the delegation could not accept such a condition, and the negotiations broke down. Finally, as a last resort, the council decided to submit a series of questions to the Secretary of Interior, Carl Schurz, about their right to determine citizenship and the obligation of the United States to accept their determinations. They asked Schurz to present their questions to Attorney General Charles Devens for his opinion. They sent the letter on March 3, 1879, and after Hayt informed Devens of his views on the matter, Devens held hearings at which both sides presented their views. Realizing the importance of the decision, the Cherokees spent the money necessary to hire the best lawyers they could find to assist them. Hayt said that the status of at least one-thousand persons was at issue, the Council argued that there were over twice that many intruders whom the Department was refusing to move.

Throughout the dispute, the Bureau of Indian Affairs declined to act against intruding squatters from Kansas who made no pretense to citizenship.

"The three questions that the Council asked Devens to answer were: Did the Cherokee Nation have the right to determine its own citizenship? Did the former slaves who were citizens have any share in the use of Cherokee land or in the money derived from the sale of the Cherokee land? Was it, or was it not, the duty of the Federal government to remove intruders under treaty stipulations and Trade and Intercourse Act? By the time Devens sent his reply, the Citizenship Court had heard 416 claims for citizenship and rejected 338."

Devens' opinion was clearly in the negative as far as the Cherokee Nation's sovereignty and decision processes were concerned. On page 364, McLoughlin observes, "Clearly, as since the days of Andrew Jackson, Federal refusal to honor the requirement of removing intruders was to be the means of forcing the Indian nations to do what they did not want to do." Ochalata would not run again as the election of August 1879 neared and Dennis W. Bushyhead became the new chief on August 4, 1879 but in the end it didn't matter who was chief the fight to keep Cherokee sovereignty along with self government was all but lost by 1880. On pages 365-366, McLoughlin wrote, "The turning point was reached in 1887 when Congress passed the Dawes Severalty Act. The act expressed what was now the national consensus among white voters (including Indian reformers, railroad magnates, and entrepreneurs) -that the solution to "'the Indian question'" was to denationalize the tribes in the Indian Territory, survey and allot their land in severalty, and establish a white-dominated territorial government over "'Oklahoma'" the Choctaw word for "'red man.'"

The sovereignty of the Western Cherokee tribe was taken, and to this day they still don't have a true land base as a nation. Even though others were able to take away the land that was promised to remain theirs forever; nobody was able to take away their right and ability to choose who was a true citizen and who was not. The dockets transcribed within this series are exactly as they appeared on the microfilm copies from the original court records involving citizenship during the time periods of 1880-1889.

These dockets were referenced and transcribed from microfilm series; 7RA25-0001 (American Genealogical Lending Library), Cherokee Citizenship Commission Docket Books, 1880-1884 and 1887-1889.


Jeff Bowen
Gallipolis, Ohio
NativeStudy.com

## WEBB

**DOCKET #1841**
CENSUS ROLLS 1835

APPLICANT FOR CHEROKEE CITIZENSHIP

| POST OFFICE: Whitner[sic] Ark | | ATTORNEY: C.H. Taylor | |
|---|---|---|---|
| No | NAMES | AGE | SEX |
| 1 | Ada S. Webb | 30 | Female |
| 2 | George W. Webb | 8 | Male |
| 3 | Cescil C. Webb | 6 | " |
| 4 | Charles C. Webb | 3 | " |
| 5 | Hettie A. Webb | 1 | Female |

ANCESTOR: Femby Vaughn

Office Commission on Citizenship
Tahlequah I.T. July 2$^{nd}$ 1889

There being no evidence in support of the above named case the Commission decide that Ada S. Webb aged 30 years, and the following named children George W aged 8 years, Cescil C aged 6 years, Charles C aged 3 years and Hettie A. Webb aged 1 year are not Cherokees by blood.
Attest

EG Ross
Clerk Commission

Will.P. Ross
Chairman
J.E. Gunter    Com

## KELTON

**DOCKET #1842**
CENSUS ROLLS 1835

APPLICANT FOR CHEROKEE CITIZENSHIP

| POST OFFICE: Sulphur Springs Tex | | ATTORNEY: C.H. Taylor | |
|---|---|---|---|
| No | NAMES | AGE | SEX |
| 1 | Sarah A Kelton | 29 | Female |
| 2 | Clint Kelton | 10 | Male |
| 3 | Benjamin Kelton | 7 | " |
| 4 | Angeline Kelton | 1 | Female |

ANCESTOR: Angeline Chambers

1

# Cherokee Citizenship Commission Docket Books
# (1880-84, 1887-89) Volume V
# Tahlequah, Cherokee Nation

Rejected Sept 2$^{nd}$ 1889

Office Commission on Citizenship
Cherokee Nation Ind Ter
Tahlequah  Sept 3$^{rd}$ 1889

The above applicant was called 3 times & no answer & there being no evidence on file in support of the application we decide that applicant Sarah A Kelton age 29 yrs and children Clint Kelton age 10 yrs. Benjamin Kelton age 7 yrs, Angeline Kelton age 1 yr are not Cherokees by blood. P.O. Sulphur Springs, Ark.

Will.P. Ross
Attest                                   Chairman
    D.S. Williams           J.E. Gunter   Com
    Asst  Clk  Com.

## KIRK

**DOCKET #1843**
CENSUS ROLLS  1835, '48, '51, & '52

APPLICANT FOR CHEROKEE CITIZENSHIP

| POST OFFICE: Canthron[sic] Ark | | ATTORNEY: Wm A. Thompson | |
|---|---|---|---|
| No | NAMES | AGE | SEX |
| 1 | Wm R Kirk | 24 | Male |

ANCESTOR: Rhoda Gideon

Rejected Sept 3$^{rd}$ 1889

Office Commission on Citizenship
Cherokee Nation Ind Ter
Tahlequah  Sept 3$^{rd}$ 1889

The application in the above case was this day submitted by Attorney for claimant Wm A Thompson[sic] without proof.  The Commission therefore decide that the applicant Wm R. Kirk 24 years old is not of Cherokee blood. P.O. Canthron Arkansas.

Will.P. Ross
Attest                                   Chairman
    D.S. Williams           J.E. Gunter   Com
    Asst  Clk  Com.

## KIRK

**DOCKET #1844**

CENSUS ROLLS 1835, '51 & '52

APPLICANT FOR CHEROKEE CITIZENSHIP

| POST OFFICE: Canthron[sic] Ark | | ATTORNEY: Wm A Thompson | |
|---|---|---|---|
| NO | NAMES | AGE | SEX |
| 1 | Emma May Kirk | 19 | Female |

ANCESTOR: Rhoda Gideon

Rejected Sept 3rd 1889

Office Commission on Citizenship
Cherokee Nation Ind Ter
Tahlequah Sept 3rd 1889

The application in the above case was submitted this day by Attorney for claimant Wm A Thompson without proof. The Commission therefore decide that the claimant Emma May Kirk age 19 years is not of Cherokee blood and not entitled to citizenship in the Cherokee Nation. P.O. Cothran[sic] Arkansas.

|  | Will.P. Ross |
|---|---|
| Attest | Chairman |
| D.S. Williams | J.E. Gunter   Com |
| Asst   Clk  Com. | |

## KING

**DOCKET #1845**

CENSUS ROLLS

APPLICANT FOR CHEROKEE CITIZENSHIP

| POST OFFICE: Bridgeport Texas | | ATTORNEY: C.H. Taylor | |
|---|---|---|---|
| NO | NAMES | AGE | SEX |
| 1 | Jane King | 34 | Female |
| 2 | Luther King | 14 | Male |
| 3 | Lonzo King | 12 | " |
| 4 | Lennie King | 9 | " |
| 5 | Lillie King | 7 | Female |
| 6 | Lou King | 5 | " |

ANCESTOR: Mary Ray, nee Taylor

3

# Cherokee Citizenship Commission Docket Books
## (1880-84, 1887-89) Volume V
## Tahlequah, Cherokee Nation

Rejected Sept 3rd 1889

Office Commission on Citizenship
Cherokee Nation Ind Ter
Tahlequah  Sept 3rd 1889

The above case was called and submitted by J.M. Taylor Atty.  The Commission decide that Jane King age 34 yrs and the following children Luther male 14 yrs, Lonzo male 12 yrs, Lennie male 9 yrs, Lillie Female 7 yrs, Lou King, Female 5 yrs are not Cherokees by blood.  Post Office Bridgeport Texas.

Attest
    D.S. Williams
    Asst  Clk  Com.

Will.P. Ross
Chairman
J.E. Gunter   Com

---

## KIRK

**DOCKET #1846**

CENSUS ROLLS  1835, '51 & '52

APPLICANT FOR CHEROKEE CITIZENSHIP

| POST OFFICE: Canthron[sic] Ark | | ATTORNEY: Wm A. Thompson | |
|---|---|---|---|
| NO | NAMES | AGE | SEX |
| 1 | Elizabeth Kirk | 44 | Female |
| 2 | Ester[sic] V. Kirk | 7 | " |
| 3 | Leander R. Kirk | 14 | Male |
| 4 | Randolph Kirk | 11 | " |
| 5 | Thomas J. Kirk | 8 | " |
| 6 | Lulu L. Kirk | 6 | Female |

ANCESTOR:  Rhoda Gideon

Rejected Sept 3rd 1889

Office Commission on Citizenship
Cherokee Nation Ind Ter
Tahlequah  Sept. 3rd 1889

The above named case was this day submitted by Attorney for claimant Wm A. Thompson without proof.  The Commission therefore decide that Elizabeth Kirk 44 years old and her daughters Esther V. Kirk 17 yrs, Lulu L. Kirk 6 yrs and

4

sons Leander R. Kirk 14 yrs, Randolph Kirk 11 yrs and Thomas J. Kirk 8 yrs are not Cherokee Indian by blood.  P.O. address Canthron[sic] Ark.

Will.P. Ross
Attest                      Chairman
   D.S. Williams         J.E. Gunter   Com
   Asst  Clk  Com.

## KIDD

**DOCKET #1847**
CENSUS ROLLS

APPLICANT FOR CHEROKEE CITIZENSHIP

| POST OFFICE: Grape Creek N.C. || ATTORNEY: C.H. Taylor ||
|---|---|---|---|
| NO | NAMES | AGE | SEX |
| 1 | Alrida Kidd | 40 | Female |

ANCESTOR:  Catharine McDonold[sic]

Re-admitted Sept 25th 1889

Office Commission on Citizenship
Cherokee Nation Ind Ter
Tahlequah  Sept. 25th 1889

The evidence of John M. Taylor of Tahlequah in the above case proves that the applicant is the daughter of his Sister Catherine the name of whose first husband was Felix Panther and of the second husband was McDaniel and whose name are[sic] found on the census rolls of Cherokees by blood taken and made by the United States in the years 1851 and 1852.  The Commission therefore decide that Alrilda[sic] Kidd 40 years of age is entitled to re-admission to citizenship in the Cherokee Nation in accordance with the constitution and laws thereof.  The names of children not given.  P.O. Grape Creek North Carolina.

Will.P. Ross
Attest                      Chairman
   D.S. Williams         J.E. Gunter   Com
   Asst  Clk  Com.

5

# Cherokee Citizenship Commission Docket Books
# (1880-84, 1887-89) Volume V
# Tahlequah, Cherokee Nation

## KIRK

**DOCKET #1848**

CENSUS ROLLS 1835

APPLICANT FOR CHEROKEE CITIZENSHIP

| POST OFFICE: Chetopa, Kansas | | ATTORNEY: C.H. Taylor | |
|---|---|---|---|
| No | NAMES | AGE | SEX |
| 1 | Nancy Kirk | 21 | Female |
| 2 | Jasper Kirk | 7 mos | Male |

ANCESTOR: John Monteath

Rejected Sept 3rd 1889.

Office Commission on Citizenship
Cherokee Nation Ind Ter
Tahlequah Sept 3rd 1889

The above case was called and submitted by Atty A.E. Ivey without evidence. The Commission therefore decide that Nancy Kirk age 21 yrs and her child Jasper Kirk male age 7 months are not Cherokees by blood. Post Office Chetopa Kansas.

Attest

D.S. Williams
Asst Clk Com.

Will.P. Ross
Chairman
J.E. Gunter Com

## KEYS

**DOCKET #1849**

CENSUS ROLLS 1835, '48, '51, & '52

APPLICANT FOR CHEROKEE CITIZENSHIP

| POST OFFICE: | | ATTORNEY: Cochran & Butler | |
|---|---|---|---|
| No | NAMES | AGE | SEX |
| 1 | Henry J.M. Keys | 48 | Male |
| 2 | Leander Keys | | " |
| 3 | Lewis Keys | | |
| 4 | John Keys | | |
| 5 | Thomas Keys | | " |
| 6 | Charles Keys | | " |

6

| 7 | Minnie Keys | | Female |
|---|---|---|---|

**ANCESTOR:** Benjamin Reynolds

Rejected Sept 3rd 1889

Office Commission on Citizenship
Cherokee Nation Ind Ter
Tahlequah  Sept 3rd 1889

The application in the above case is filed without proof and having been this day called three times without answer.  The Commission decide that the claimant Henry J.M. Keys age 48 and sons Leander Keys, Lewis Keys, John Keys, Thomas Keys, and Charles Keys, and daughters Minnie Keys and one other name not given are not of Cherokee blood and not entitled to citizenship in the Cherokee Nation.

Attest

D.S. Williams
Asst  Clk  Com.

Will.P. Ross
Chairman
J.E. Gunter   Com

---

## KEY

**DOCKET #1850**

CENSUS ROLLS  1835 to 1852

APPLICANT FOR CHEROKEE CITIZENSHIP

| POST OFFICE: Denton Texas | | ATTORNEY: A.E. Ivey | |
|---|---|---|---|
| NO | NAMES | AGE | SEX |
| 1 | Benj A. Key | 36 | Male |

**ANCESTOR:** John Looney

Rejected Sept 3rd 1889

Office Commission on Citizenship
Cherokee Nation Ind Ter
Tahlequah  Sept 3rd 1889

The above case was called and submitted by Atty A.E. Ivey without evidence. The Commission decide that Benj A. Key age 36 yrs is not a Cherokee by blood. Post Office Denton Tex.

Attest

D.S. Williams
Asst  Clk  Com.

Will.P. Ross
Chairman
J.E. Gunter   Com

## KESTERSON

**DOCKET #1851**

CENSUS ROLLS  1835 to 1852

APPLICANT FOR CHEROKEE CITIZENSHIP

| POST OFFICE: Mineral Springs Ark | | ATTORNEY: A.E. Ivey | |
|---|---|---|---|
| No | NAMES | AGE | SEX |
| 1 | William Kesterson | 590 | Male |

ANCESTOR: Mary Gauf

The Commission decide adversly[sic] to claimant William Kesterson in the above case. See decision in case of Annie Kesterson Docket 1865 Book D, Page 351. P.O. Mineral Springs, Texas[sic].

Will.P. Ross
Chairman
Jno E. Gunter   Com

## KESTERSON

**DOCKET #1852**

CENSUS ROLLS  1832[sic] to 1852

APPLICANT FOR CHEROKEE CITIZENSHIP

| POST OFFICE: Mineral Springs Ark | | ATTORNEY: A.E. Ivey | |
|---|---|---|---|
| No | NAMES | AGE | SEX |
| 1 | Nancy Kesterson | 54 | Female |

ANCESTOR: Mary Gauf

The Commission decide adversly[sic] to claimant. See decision in the case of Annie Kesterson Docket 1865, Book D, Page 351. P.O. Mineral Springs, Texas[sic].

Will.P. Ross
Chairman
Jno E. Gunter   Com

## KESTERSON

**DOCKET #1853**

CENSUS ROLLS 1835 to 1852

APPLICANT FOR CHEROKEE CITIZENSHIP

| POST OFFICE: Mineral Springs Ark | | ATTORNEY: A.E. Ivey | |
|---|---|---|---|
| No | NAMES | AGE | SEX |
| 1 | Mary Kesterson | 56 | Female |

ANCESTOR: Mary Gauf

Office Commission on Citizenship
Cherokee Nation Ind Ter
Tahlequah  Sept 4[th] 1889

The Commission decide <u>Adversely</u> to claimant in the above case.  See case of Annie Kesterson Docket 1865, Book D, Page 351.   P.O. Mineral Springs, Texas[sic].

Will.P. Ross
Chairman
Jno E. Gunter
Com

## KESTERSON

**DOCKET #1854**

CENSUS ROLLS 1835 to 1852

APPLICANT FOR CHEROKEE CITIZENSHIP

| POST OFFICE: Mineral Springs Ark | | ATTORNEY: A.E. Ivey | |
|---|---|---|---|
| No | NAMES | AGE | SEX |
| 1 | Lucindy Kesterson | 52 | Female |

ANCESTOR: Mary Gauf

The Commission decide against claimant.  See decision in the case of Annie Kesterson Docket 1865 Book D, Page 351.
P.O. Mineral Springs Texas[sic].

Will.P. Ross
Chairman
Jno. E. Gunter    Com

9

## RAKESTRAW

**DOCKET #1855**

CENSUS ROLLS

APPLICANT FOR CHEROKEE CITIZENSHIP

| POST OFFICE: Hickory Ga | | ATTORNEY: A.E. Ivey | |
|---|---|---|---|
| **NO** | **NAMES** | **AGE** | **SEX** |
| 1 | Malicia Rakestraw | 41 | Female |
| 2 | L.S. Sanders Rakestraw | 24 | Male |
| 3 | Aasba[sic] B. Rakestraw | 22 | Female |
| 4 | Jack B. Rakestraw | 18 | Male |
| 5 | Jas. N. Rakestraw | 16 | " |
| 6 | Tuscane Rakestraw | 14 | " |
| 7 | Elsa C. Rakestraw | 12 | " |
| 8 | Julas S. Rakestraw | 10 | " |

**ANCESTOR:** Fannie Ranes

Rejected Sept 3rd 1889

Office Commission on Citizenship
Cherokee Nation Ind Ter
Tahlequah Sept. 3rd 1889

The above case was called and submitted by Atty A.E. Ivey without evidence. The Commission decide that applicant Malicia Rakestraw age 41 yrs and the following children L.L. Male 24 yrs, Aasha B. Female 22 yrs, Jack B. Male 18 yrs, Jas. N. Male 16 yrs, Tuscane Male 14 yrs, Elsa C. Male 12 yrs, and Julas S. Rakestraw Male 10 yrs are not Cherokees by blood. Post Office Hickory Ga.

Will.P. Ross
Attest                       Chairman
     D.S. Williams        J.E. Gunter    Com
     Asst   Clk   Com.

## KESTERSON

**DOCKET #1856**

CENSUS ROLLS 1835 to 1852

APPLICANT FOR CHEROKEE CITIZENSHIP

| POST OFFICE: Mineral Springs, Ark | | ATTORNEY: A.E. Ivey | |
|---|---|---|---|
| NO | NAMES | AGE | SEX |
| 1 | Becky Kesterson | 54 | Female |

ANCESTOR: Mary Gauf

The Commission decide adversly[sic] to claimant in the above case. See decision in the case of Annie Kesterson Docket 1865 Book D, Page 351.

Will.P. Ross
Chairman
Jno. E. Gunter    Com

## KESTERSON

**DOCKET #1857**

CENSUS ROLLS 1835 to 1852

APPLICANT FOR CHEROKEE CITIZENSHIP

| POST OFFICE: Mineral Springs, Ark | | ATTORNEY: A.E. Ivey | |
|---|---|---|---|
| NO | NAMES | AGE | SEX |
| 1 | Sam'l Kesterson | 48 | Male |

ANCESTOR: Mary Gauf

The Commission decide adversly[sic] to claimant. See decision in the case of Annie Kesterson Docket 1865 Book D, Page 351. P.O. Mineral Springs Texas[sic].

Will.P. Ross
Chairman
Jno. E. Gunter
Com

11

## KESTERSON

**DOCKET #1858**

CENSUS ROLLS 1835 to 1852

APPLICANT FOR CHEROKEE CITIZENSHIP

| POST OFFICE: Mineral Springs Ark | | ATTORNEY: A.E. Ivey | |
|---|---|---|---|
| No | NAMES | AGE | SEX |
| 1 | V. L. Kesterson | 38 | Female |

ANCESTOR: Mary Gauf

Rejected Sept 4th 1889

Office Commission on Citizenship
Cherokee Nation Ind Ter
Tahlequah Sept 4th 1889

The Commission decide against claimant. See decision in the case of Annie Kesterson Docket 1865 Book D, Page 351. P.O. Mineral Springs, Ark.

Attest

D.S. Williams
Asst Clk Com.

Will.P. Ross
Chairman
J.E. Gunter Com

## KIDD

**DOCKET #1859**

CENSUS ROLLS 1835 to 1852

APPLICANT FOR CHEROKEE CITIZENSHIP

| POST OFFICE: Van Buren Ark. | | ATTORNEY: A.E. Ivey | |
|---|---|---|---|
| No | NAMES | AGE | SEX |
| 1 | Ellis Kidd | 27 | Male |
| 2 | Oscar Kidd | 6 | " |

ANCESTOR: Tiller Rately

Rejected Sept 3rd 1889

Office Commission on Citizenship
Cherokee Nation Sept 3rd 1889
Tahlequah Ind. Ter.

12

# Cherokee Citizenship Commission Docket Books
## (1880-84, 1887-89) Volume V
## Tahlequah, Cherokee Nation

The above case was submitted by applicants Attorney without any evidence. therefore we decide that applicant Ellis Kidd age 27 yrs and child Oscar Kidd age 6 yrs are not Cherokee by blood. P.O. Van Buren Ark.

Will.P. Ross<br>Chairman

Attest

    D.S. Williams

    Asst   Clerk Commission

J.E. Gunter   Com

---

## KESTERSON

**DOCKET #1860**

CENSUS ROLLS 1835 to 1852

APPLICANT FOR CHEROKEE CITIZENSHIP

| POST OFFICE: Mineral Springs Ark | | ATTORNEY: A.E. Ivey | |
|---|---|---|---|
| NO | NAMES | AGE | SEX |
| 1 | C.P. Kesterson | 36 | Female |

ANCESTOR: Mary Gauf

The Commission decide against claimant. See decision in the case of Annie Kesterson Docket 1865 Book D, Page 351.

Will.P. Ross<br>Chairman

Sept. 4th 1889

Jno. E. Gunter<br>Com

---

## KESTERSON

**DOCKET #1861**

CENSUS ROLLS 1835 to 1852

APPLICANT FOR CHEROKEE CITIZENSHIP

| POST OFFICE: Mineral Springs, Ark | | ATTORNEY: A.E. Ivey | |
|---|---|---|---|
| NO | NAMES | AGE | SEX |
| 1 | F.P. Kesterson | 34 | Male |

ANCESTOR: Mary Gauf

13

The Commission decide adversly[sic] to claimant. See decision in the case of Annie Kesterson Docket 1865 Book D, Page 351. P.O. Mineral Springs, Tex[sic].

Attest                                Will.P. Ross

    EG Ross                             Chairman

      Clerk Commission                  Jno. E. Gunter   Com

## KESTERSON

**DOCKET #1862**

CENSUS ROLLS 1835 to 1852

APPLICANT FOR CHEROKEE CITIZENSHIP

| POST OFFICE: Mineral Springs, Ark. | | ATTORNEY: A.E. Ivey | |
|---|---|---|---|
| **NO** | **NAMES** | **AGE** | **SEX** |
| 1 | J.K.P. Kesterson | 40 | |

ANCESTOR: Mary Gauf

Rejected Sept. 4[th] 1889

                                Office Commission on Citizenship

                                Cherokee Nation Ind Ter

                                Tahlequah Sept. 4[th] 1889

The Commission decide <u>Adversely</u> to claimant. See decision in the case of Annie Kesterson Docket 1865 Book D, Page 351. P.O. Mineral Springs, Ark.

Attest                                Will.P. Ross

    D.S. Williams                        Chairman

    Asst   Clk   Com.                     J. E. Gunter   Com

## KESTERSON

**DOCKET #1863**

CENSUS ROLLS 1835 to 1852

APPLICANT FOR CHEROKEE CITIZENSHIP

| POST OFFICE: Mineral Springs, Ark | | ATTORNEY: A.E. Ivey | |
|---|---|---|---|
| **NO** | **NAMES** | **AGE** | **SEX** |
| 1 | T.J. Kesterson | 42 | Male |

ANCESTOR: Mary Gauf

Rejected Sept. 4[th] 1889

The Commission decide against claimant. See decision in the case of Annie Kesterson Docket 1865 Book D, Page 351.

Will.P. Ross

Attest   D.S. Williams                                           Chairman

Asst   Clk Com.                              J.E. Gunter   Com

## KAY

**DOCKET #1864**

CENSUS ROLLS 1835 to 1852

APPLICANT FOR CHEROKEE CITIZENSHIP

| POST OFFICE: Springtown Ark | | ATTORNEY: A.E. Ivey | |
|---|---|---|---|
| NO | NAMES | AGE | SEX |
| 1 | Emily Kay | 59 | Female |
| 2 | Lealyear A Kay | 14 | " |
| 3 | Ollie P. Kay | 3 | " |

ANCESTOR: Sarah or Nancy M Cannon

Now on this the 31$^{st}$ day of March, 1888, comes the above case up for final disposition, they having made application pursuant to the provisions of an Act of the National Council, approved Dec. 8$^{th}$ 1886, and all the evidence being duly considered, it is adjudged and determined by the Commission that and determined by the Commission that Emily Kay, Lealyear A. Kay and Ollie P. Kay are not Cherokee citizens, and not entitled to the rights and privileges of such on account of Cherokee blood. The decision in this case will be found at length in the case of William Deese, in Docket "C", page 147, and the testimony on Journal pages governing this case.

Chairman Commission

Commissioner

Commissioner

The testimony in the Joseph Snow case found on Journal page 351 to 353 governs this case.

# Cherokee Citizenship Commission Docket Books
## (1880-84, 1887-89) Volume V
### Tahlequah, Cherokee Nation

## KESTERSON

**DOCKET #1865**

CENSUS ROLLS 1835 to 1852

APPLICANT FOR CHEROKEE CITIZENSHIP

| POST OFFICE: Mineral Springs, Ark | | ATTORNEY: A.E. Ivey | |
|---|---|---|---|
| **NO** | **NAMES** | **AGE** | **SEX** |
| 1 | Annie Kesterson | 59 | Female |

ANCESTOR:

Rejected Sept. 3rd 1889

*Commission on Citizenship.*

CHEROKEE NATION, IND. TER.

*Tahlequah,* Septr 3rd 1889

Annie Kesterson
    vs        Application for Cherokee Citizenship
The Cherokee Nation

      The applicant in the above case Claims her Cherokee Indian descent from one Mary Gauf whose name she believes was enrolled on the census rolls of Cherokees by blood taken and made by the United States in the years 1835 and 1852. The evidence offered ~~in~~ by claimant consists of exparte affidavits taken before John B. Hester, a Justice of the Peace and before Jno. H. Somerville, Clerk of the Circuit Court for Howard County, State of Arkansas. In substance their statements are as follows, J.J. Whitmore knew John Kesterson 25 years and he claims to be part Cherokee, John M. Somerville the clerk aforesaid certifies to the high character of John Kesterson, James Young, age 77 years, who claims to be part Indian himself, knew John Kesterson for more than fifty years and also his Mother, Mary Goff. This witness makes his mark (X) in signing his name without attesting witnesses, John Walden who states that he is 63 yrs old and knew John Kesterson ~~and his Mother~~ more than 40 years and also his Mother, and that they claimed to have Indian blood, subscribes his name in like manner, Benjamin Stephens 74 yrs old knew John Kesterson upwards of fifty years and often hear him say he was part Indian, and also had seen his mother who looked like a half breed and frequently heard her called Indian, Reese H.

16

Henry, 60 yrs old knew John Kesterson for more than 30 yrs and he often told him he had Indian blood and it came through his mother. The testimony of these witnesses is based upon statements alleged to have been made by John Kesterson and his mother Mary Goff and not upon personal knowledge of the source whence they derived their Cherokee blood. Sam Kesterson 48 yrs old and who is himself an applicant for citizenship gives the names and ages of the children of John Kesterson who was the son of Mary Gauf or Goff who he says was a Cherokee Indian by blood. This affidavit, which is not signed but bears the signature of John B. Hester, Justice of the Peace before whom it was made 23$^{rd}$ day of September 1887, and the official certificate of the before named John M. Somerville Clk. also states that the children of John Kesterson *(illegible)* now in the ~~state of Georgia~~ in the Cherokee Nation in the state of Georgia by Indians, Parchcow, Tooneye, Kyhoost Parchcow, Old (Illegible) Gunter, John Gunter, Squirreltail, *(Cherokee letters) (illegible...)* denies their Indian blood and have always claimed the blood as such." These witnesses fail to prove that John Kesterson of Mary Gauf were of Cherokee Indian blood nor are their names to be found on the rolls of Cherokees as they would have been in all probability, if they had been known and recognized as Cherokee Indians, when the names of the Indians enumerated above were enrolled in the state of Alabama then in the Cherokee Nation near Gunters Landing on the Tennessee river. The Commission therefore decide that the claimant Mary Kesterson is not of Cherokee blood and is not entitled to citizenship in the Cherokee Nation. P.O. Mineral Springs, Arkansas.

Will.P. Ross
Chairman
J.E. Gunter    Com

## KIMBROUGH

**DOCKET #1866**
CENSUS ROLLS 1835 to 1852

APPLICANT FOR CHEROKEE CITIZENSHIP

| POST OFFICE: Van Buren Ark | | ATTORNEY: J.P. Muller | |
|---|---|---|---|
| NO | NAMES | AGE | SEX |
| 1 | Nancy C Kimbrough | 31 | Female |
| 2 | Nester Duke Kimbrough | 12 | Male |
| 3 | Dora Kimbrough | 6 | Female |
| 4 | Hollis S. Kimbrough | 10 | Male |

| 5 | Joseph A Kimbrough | 4 | " |
|---|---|---|---|
| 6 | Ivey F. Kimbrough | 2 | " |

**ANCESTOR:** Angelina Foster

Rejected Sept 16<sup>th</sup> 1889

Office Commission on Citizenship
Cherokee Nation Ind Ter
Tahlequah Sept 16<sup>th</sup> 1889

The above applicant was called three times & no answer and there being no evidence on file in support of the application the Commission decide that applicant Nancy C. Kimbrough age 31 yrs & children Nester Duke age 12 yrs, Dora age 6 yrs, Hollis age 10 yrs, Joseph age 4 yrs, Ivey Kimbrough age 2 yrs are not Cherokees by blood.
P.O. Van Buren Ark.

Will.P. Ross

Attest                                     Chairman
    D.S. Williams               J.E. Gunter   Com
    Asst  Clk Com.

---

## KEY

**DOCKET #1867**
CENSUS ROLLS 1835 to 1852

APPLICANT FOR CHEROKEE CITIZENSHIP

| POST OFFICE: Denton, Texas | | ATTORNEY: A.E. Ivey | |
|---|---|---|---|
| **No** | **NAMES** | **AGE** | **SEX** |
| 1 | Mrs. Maranda A. Key | 33 | Female |
| 2 | Ben A. Key | 12 | Male |
| 3 | Thomas W. Key | 10 | " |
| 4 | Edward Key | 8 | " |
| 5 | Carrie May Key | 6 | Female |

**ANCESTOR:** Robert J. Jackson

Rejected Sept 3<sup>rd</sup> 1889

Office Commission on Citizenship
Cherokee Nation Ind Ter
Tahlequah Sept. 3<sup>rd</sup> 1889

The above case was submitted by Attorney A.E. Ivey without any evidence. Therefore we decide that applicant Mrs. Maranda A. Key age 33 yrs, Ben A. Key age 12 yrs, Thomas W. Key age 10 yrs, Edward Key age 8 yrs, Carrie May Key age 6 yrs are not Cherokees by blood. P.O. Denton Tex.

Will.P. Ross<br>Chairman

Attest
    D.S. Williams          J.E. Gunter    Com
    Asst   Clk   Com.

---

## KEENE

**DOCKET #1868**

CENSUS ROLLS 1835 to 1852

APPLICANT FOR CHEROKEE CITIZENSHIP

| POST OFFICE: Ivenhoe[sic] Texas | | ATTORNEY: A.E. Ivey | |
|---|---|---|---|
| NO | NAMES | AGE | SEX |
| 1 | S.A. Keene | | Female |
| 2 | Eugene Keene | 12 | Male |
| 3 | Arthur Keene | 9 | " |
| 4 | Leona Keene | 7 | Female |
| 5 | Bell Keene | 5 | " |
| 6 | Robt Keene | 2 | Male |

ANCESTOR: Jeremiah Ward

Adverse

Embraced in decision in Book A,
in John Ward case Page 231.

Attest
    EG Ross          Will.P. Ross
        Clerk Com          Chairman
            J.E. Gunter    Com

---

# Cherokee Citizenship Commission Docket Books
## (1880-84, 1887-89) Volume V
## Tahlequah, Cherokee Nation

### KELL

**DOCKET #1869**

CENSUS ROLLS 1851

APPLICANT FOR CHEROKEE CITIZENSHIP

| POST OFFICE: Ellijay Ga | | ATTORNEY: A.E. Ivey | |
|---|---|---|---|
| No | NAMES | AGE | SEX |
| 1 | Elkin Kell | 62 | |

ANCESTOR: Ellie Kell

Rejected Sept 3rd 1889

Office Commission on Citizenship
Cherokee Nation Ind Ter
Tahlequah Sept. 3rd 1889

The above case was called and submitted by Atty A.E. Ivey without evidence. The Commission therefore decide Elkin Kell age 62 yrs. yrs.[sic] is not a Cherokee by blood. P.O. Ellijay Ga.

Attest

    D.S. Williams
Asst. Clerk Commission

Will.P. Ross
Chairman
J.E. Gunter   Com

### KELLY

**DOCKET #1870**

CENSUS ROLLS

APPLICANT FOR CHEROKEE CITIZENSHIP

| POST OFFICE: Yeakly[sic] Mo | | ATTORNEY: A.E. Ivey | |
|---|---|---|---|
| No | NAMES | AGE | SEX |
| 1 | Viola O. Kelly | 19 | Female |
| 2 | Maude Bell O Kelly | 1 | " |

ANCESTOR: Silas Keatton

The above case was called & submitted by Atty A.E. Ivey without evidence. The Commission now in view of these facts decide that Viola O. Kelly are[sic] not Cherokees by blood. P.O. Yaukly[sic] Mo.

20

# Cherokee Citizenship Commission Docket Books
## (1880-84, 1887-89) Volume V
## Tahlequah, Cherokee Nation

Will.P. Ross
Chairman
Jno. E. Gunter   Com

---

## KELL

**DOCKET #1871**

CENSUS ROLLS 1851

APPLICANT FOR CHEROKEE CITIZENSHIP

| POST OFFICE: Clinton, Georgia | | ATTORNEY: A.E. Ivey | |
|---|---|---|---|
| **NO** | **NAMES** | **AGE** | **SEX** |
| 1 | John Kell | 35 | Male |

ANCESTOR: Elkin Kell

The above case was called & submitted by A.E. Ivey without evidence. The Commission therefore decide Jno Kell age 35 yrs is not a Cherokee by blood, are[sic] not entitled to citizenship in the Cherokee Nation. P.O. Clinton Ga.

Will.P. Ross
Chairman
Jno. E. Gunter   Com

---

## KELL

**DOCKET #1872**

CENSUS ROLLS 1851

APPLICANT FOR CHEROKEE CITIZENSHIP

| POST OFFICE: Pots Station, Ga. | | ATTORNEY: A.E. Ivey | |
|---|---|---|---|
| **NO** | **NAMES** | **AGE** | **SEX** |
| 1 | James Kell | 23 | Male |

ANCESTOR:

The above case was called and and[sic] submitted by Atty A.E. Ivey without evidence. The Commission therefore decide that James Kell age 23 yrs is not a Cherokee by blood. P.O. Pots Station Ga.

Will.P. Ross
Chairman
J.E. Gunter   Com

## KEEN

**DOCKET #1873**
CENSUS ROLLS 1835 to 1852

APPLICANT FOR CHEROKEE CITIZENSHIP

| POST OFFICE: Fort Smith Ark | | ATTORNEY: A.E. Ivey | |
|---|---|---|---|
| No | NAMES | AGE | SEX |
| 1 | Jennie B. Keen | 20 | Female |

ANCESTOR:

Embraced in the decision in the
John Ward case Book A, Page 231.

Attest                            Will.P. Ross
    E.G. Ross                      Chairman
    Clk Com                    J.E. Gunter    Com

## KERNES

**DOCKET #1874**
CENSUS ROLLS 1835 to 1852

APPLICANT FOR CHEROKEE CITIZENSHIP

| POST OFFICE: Norwalk Mo | | ATTORNEY: A.E. Ivey | |
|---|---|---|---|
| No | NAMES | AGE | SEX |
| 1 | Ellen E. Kernes | 29 | Female |
| 2 | Jasper F. Kernes | 8 | Male |
| 3 | V.E. Kernes | 7 | Female |

ANCESTOR: Patsy Barnes

The above case was called & submitted by Atty A.E. Ivey without evidence. The Commission now in view of these facts, decide that Ellen E. Kernes age 29 yrs & the following named persons *(Illegible)* F. Kernes Male 8 yrs & V.E. Kernes Female are not Cherokees by blood. Post Office Norwood[sic] Mo.

22

# Cherokee Citizenship Commission Docket Books
## (1880-84, 1887-89) Volume V
## Tahlequah, Cherokee Nation

Will.P. Ross
Chairman
Sept. 6<sup>th</sup>            Jno. E. Gunter   Com

---

### KEYS

**DOCKET #1875**
CENSUS ROLLS 1835 to 1852

APPLICANT FOR CHEREKEE CITIZENSHIP

| POST OFFICE: | | ATTORNEY: A.E. Ivey | |
|---|---|---|---|
| NO | NAMES | AGE | SEX |
| 1 | W.S. Keys | 42 | Male |
| 2 | Debora Keys | 10 | Female |
| 3 | Willie Maud Keys | 6 | " |
| 4 | Reed M Keys | 4 | Male |

ANCESTOR: James M Keys

Rejected Sept 16<sup>th</sup> 1889

Office Commission on Citizenship
Cherokee Nation Ind Ter
Tahlequah Sept. 16<sup>th</sup> 1889

The above case was filed on the 4<sup>th</sup> Oct. 1887, and being called was set for Sept 16<sup>th</sup> 1889 for a hearing and according to the time set the case was again called but no one responding and there being no evidence on file in support of application, the Commission are of the opinion and they so decide that W.S. Keys age 42 yrs and the following children Debora Keys Female 10 yrs. Willie Maud Keys Female 6 yrs. Reed M Keys male 4 yrs are not Cherokees by blood.

Will.P. Ross
Chairman
Attest            J.E. Gunter   Com
     D.S. Williams
     Asst   Clk   Com.

---

# Cherokee Citizenship Commission Docket Books
## (1880-84, 1887-89) Volume V
## Tahlequah, Cherokee Nation

### KINNEY

**DOCKET #1876**
CENSUS ROLLS 1835 to 1852

APPLICANT FOR CHEROKEE CITIZENSHIP

| POST OFFICE: | | ATTORNEY: A.E. Ivey | |
|---|---|---|---|
| No | NAMES | AGE | SEX |
| 1 | Charles Kinney | 35 | Male |

ANCESTOR: Caroline & John Williams

The above case coming up for final hearing, and the names of the ancestors appearing on the rolls of Cherokees, mentioned in the 7[th] Sec of the Act of Dec. 8[th] 1886 in relation to citizenship, and proving a straight descent from their ancestors, Caroline & John Williams, it is adjudged and determined by the Commission on Citizenship that Charles Kinney is a Cherokee by blood, and we do hereby so declare as provided under the provisions of the Act in relation to citizenship, approved Dec. 8[th] 1886.

> J. T. Adair    Chairman Commission
> H.C. Barnes   Commissioner

Office Com on Citizenship
Tahlequah, I.T.  Oct 8[th] 1888.

---

### KEYS

**DOCKET #1877**
CENSUS ROLLS 1835 to 1852

APPLICANT FOR CHEROKEE CITIZENSHIP

| POST OFFICE: Chelsea, Ind. Ter. | | ATTORNEY: A.E. Ivey | |
|---|---|---|---|
| No | NAMES | AGE | SEX |
| 1 | H.J.M. Keys | 34 | Male |

ANCESTOR:

Rejected Sept. 16[th] 1889

> Office Commission on Citizenship
> Cherokee Nation Ind Ter
> Tahlequah  Sept 16[th] 1889

The above case was filed on the 5[th] day of Oct. 1887 and was called and set for the 16[th] day of Sept. 1889 for a final hearing and no one answering for applicant

and there being no evidence in support of claim the Commission are of the opinion and so decide that H.J.M. Keys is not a Cherokee by blood.
P.O. Chelsea I.T.

|                        | Will.P. Ross          |
|------------------------|-----------------------|
| Attest                 | Chairman              |
| D.S. Williams          | J.E. Gunter    Com    |
| Asst  Clk  Com.        |                       |

---

## KEYS

**DOCKET #1878**

CENSUS ROLLS  1835 to 1852

APPLICANT FOR CHEROKEE CITIZENSHIP

| POST OFFICE: Fabius, Ala | | ATTORNEY: A.E. Ivey | |
|------|------------------|------|--------|
| NO   | NAMES            | AGE  | SEX    |
| 1    | Richard Keys     | 74   | Male   |
| 2    | Sarah keys       | 32   | Female |
| 3    | John Keys        | 12   | Male   |

ANCESTOR: Sam Keys

Rejected Sept. 16th 1889

Office Commission on Citizenship
Cherokee Nation Ind Ter
Tahlequah  Sept. 16th 1889

The above case was filed on the 3rd day of Oct 188? and it being called was set for Sept 16th 1889 for a hearing and according to the time set the case was again called and no one responding and there being no evidence on file in support of application the Commission are of the opinion and they so decide that Richard Keys age 74 yrs and his Daughter Sarah Keys, 32 yrs and his grand son John Keys 12 yrs are not Cherokees by blood.

|                        | Will.P. Ross          |
|------------------------|-----------------------|
| Attest                 | Chairman              |
| D.S. Williams          | J.E. Gunter    Com    |
| Asst  Clk  Com.        |                       |

---

# Cherokee Citizenship Commission Docket Books (1880-84, 1887-89) Volume V
## Tahlequah, Cherokee Nation

### ADAMS

**DOCKET #1879**

CENSUS ROLLS 1835 to 1852

APPLICANT FOR CHEROKEE CITIZENSHIP

| POST OFFICE: Mt. Carmel, Ill. | | ATTORNEY: Boudinot & Rasmus | |
|---|---|---|---|
| NO | NAMES | AGE | SEX |
| 1 | Wiley B. Adams | 35 | Male |

ANCESTOR: Wm Sevier

Rejected Sept 17th 1889

Office Commission on Citizenship
Cherokee Nation Ind Ter
Tahlequah Sept 17th 1889

The above case was called and submitted by Atty without evidence. The Commission therefore decide that Wiley B. Adams age 35 yrs is not a Cherokee by blood. P.O. Mt. Carmel Ill.

Attest

D.S. Williams
Asst Clk Com.

Will.P. Ross
Chairman
J.E. Gunter   Com

### ADAMS

**DOCKET #1880**

CENSUS ROLLS 1835 to 1852

APPLICANT FOR CHEROKEE CITIZENSHIP

| POST OFFICE: Mt. Carmel Ill. | | ATTORNEY: Boudinot & Ras. | |
|---|---|---|---|
| NO | NAMES | AGE | SEX |
| 1 | Willis J Adams | 36 | Male |

ANCESTOR: Wm Sevier

Rejected Sept 17th 1889

Office Commission on Citizenship
Cherokee Nation Ind Ter
Tahlequah Sept 17th 1889

The above case was submitted by Atty without evidence. The Commission therefore decide that Willis J. Adams age 36 yrs. is not a Cherokee by blood. P.O. Mt. Carmel Ill.

# Cherokee Citizenship Commission Docket Books
## (1880-84, 1887-89) Volume V
## Tahlequah, Cherokee Nation

|  |  |
|---|---|
| | Will.P. Ross |
| Attest | Chairman |
| D.S. Williams | J.E. Gunter    Com |
| Asst   Clk Com. | |

## SKIDMORE

**DOCKET #1881**

CENSUS ROLLS  1835, '48, '51, & '52

APPLICANT FOR CHEROKEE CITIZENSHIP

| POST OFFICE:  Gonzallis[sic] Texas | | ATTORNEY: Boudinot & Rasmus | |
|---|---|---|---|
| NO | NAMES | AGE | SEX |
| 1 | Annie Skidmore, nee Price | 28 | Female |
| 2 | Eugene O. Skidmore | 4 | Male |
| 3 | Otis T. Skidmore | 2 | " |
| 4 | Annie E. Skidmore | 4 mo | Female |

ANCESTOR:  Jane Coody, nee Ross

Now on this the 29[th] day of June 1888, comes the above case up for final hearing, and the Commission say, "We the Commission on Citizenship after examining the evidence in the above named case, and also the Old Settler pay rolls taken in the year 1851, find the applicants, Annie Skidmore and her three children, Eugene O. – Otis T. – and Annie E. Skidmore are Cherokees by blood and are hereby re-admitted to all the rights & privileges of Cherokee citizens by blood is in compliance with an Act of the National Council dated Febry 7th 1888 with an Act of the National Council, dated Febry. 7[th] 1888."

|  |  |
|---|---|
| J. T. Adair | Chairman Commission |
| D.W. Lipe | Commissioner |

## SMITH

**DOCKET #1882**

CENSUS ROLLS  1835, '48, '51, & 52

APPLICANT FOR CHEROKEE CITIZENSHIP

| POST OFFICE:  Dardanelle Ark | | ATTORNEY: Boudinot & Rasmus | |
|---|---|---|---|
| NO | NAMES | AGE | SEX |
| 1 | Mahala Smith | 55 | Female |
| 2 | Frank Smith | | Male |

| 3 | George Smith | 15 | " |
|---|---|---|---|

**ANCESTOR:** John Britton

Rejected Aug. 27<sup>th</sup> 1889

Office Commission on Citizenship
Cherokee Nation Ind Ter
Tahlequah  Aug 27<sup>th</sup> 1889

The above applicant was called three times & no answer and there being no evidence on file in support of the application We decide that applicant Mahala Smith age 55 yrs and her children, Frank Smith and George Smith age 13[sic] yrs are not Cherokees by blood and not entitled to citizenship in the Cherokee Nation. P.O. Dardanelle Ark.

Will.P. Ross
Attest                                          Chairman
    D.S. Williams                    J.E. Gunter   Com
    Asst  Clk  Com.

See the same case on Page 66 this book.

---

## SMITH

**DOCKET #1883**
CENSUS ROLLS  1835

APPLICANT FOR CHEROKEE CITIZENSHIP

| POST OFFICE: Lead Hill, Ark. | | ATTORNEY: C.H. Taylor | |
|---|---|---|---|
| NO | NAMES | AGE | SEX |
| 1 | C.J. Smith | 28 | |

**ANCESTOR:** Sela Brown

Docketed twice once on
page 75 and once on page 369 –

See decision in this case on page 75
in this Book Docket 1589.

Will.P. Ross
Chairman
Attest                                      J.E. Gunter   Com
    D.S. Williams
    Asst  Clk  Com.

28

## STEPHENS

**DOCKET #1884**

CENSUS ROLLS

APPLICANT FOR CHEROKEE CITIZENSHIP

| POST OFFICE: Indianapolis, Ind. | | ATTORNEY: L.B. Bell | |
|------|------------------|-----|-----|
| NO | NAMES | AGE | SEX |
| 1 | Jesse B Stephens | 21 | Male |
| 2 | Raymond Stephens | 2 | " |

ANCESTOR: Ann Crews

The Commission decide against claimant. See decision in the case of Andrew Meredith Docket 2180 Book E, Page 26 and John Henly Docket 1250, Book C Page 376.

Will.P. Ross    Chairman

John E. Gunter    Com

## STOUT

**DOCKET #1885**

CENSUS ROLLS

APPLICANT FOR CHEROKEE CITIZENSHIP

| POST OFFICE: New London, Ind | | ATTORNEY: L.B. Bell | |
|------|------------------|-----|-----|
| NO | NAMES | AGE | SEX |
| 1 | Emma Stout | 28 | female |

ANCESTOR: Ann Crews

The Commission decide against claimant. See decision in the case of Andrew Meredith Docket 2180 Book E, Page 26 And John Henly Docket 1250, Book C Page 376.

Will.P. Ross    Chairman

John E. Gunter    Com

# Cherokee Citizenship Commission Docket Books
## (1880-84, 1887-89) Volume V
## Tahlequah, Cherokee Nation

### STEED

**DOCKET #1886**

CENSUS ROLLS

APPLICANT FOR CHEROKEE CITIZENSHIP

| POST OFFICE: Independence, Kan. | | ATTORNEY: C.H. Taylor | |
|---|---|---|---|
| **No** | **NAMES** | **AGE** | **SEX** |
| 1 | T.L. Steed | 47 | Male |
| 2 | Hester Steed | 19 | Female |
| 3 | Rutha Steed | 16 | " |
| 4 | Anna Steed | 13 | " |
| 5 | Nora Steed | 8 | " |
| 6 | Lula Steed | 1 | " |

ANCESTOR: Margaret Bowlin

Rejected Sept 4th 1889

Office Commission on Citizenship
Cherokee Nation Ind Ter
Tahlequah Setp 4th 1889

The above case was called 3 several times and no response from applicant or by Atty. The Commission now decide that T.L. Steed age 47 yrs is not Cherokee by blood as there is no evidence in support of his claim with the following children Hester Female 19 yrs, Rutha Female 16 yrs, Anna Female 13 yrs, Nora Female 8 yrs and Lula Female 1 yr. Post Office Independence Kans.

Will.P. Ross
Attest          Chairman
    D.S. Williams       J.E. Gunter    Com
    Asst Clk Com.

---

### SMITH

**DOCKET #1887**

CENSUS ROLLS 1835

APPLICANT FOR CHEROKEE CITIZENSHIP

| POST OFFICE: Hindsville Ark | | ATTORNEY: C.H. Taylor | |
|---|---|---|---|
| **No** | **NAMES** | **AGE** | **SEX** |
| 1 | Florence E Smith | 20 | Female |

# Cherokee Citizenship Commission Docket Books
## (1880-84, 1887-89) Volume V
## Tahlequah, Cherokee Nation

| 2 | Belle Smith | 4 | " |
| 3 | Andrew C. Smith | 2 | "[sic] |
| 4 | Annis Smith | 1 | " |

ANCESTOR: Feraby Vaught

Office Commission on Citizenship
Tahlequah July 2$^{nd}$ 1889

The above case having been presented to the Commission without evidence to support it the Commission decide against the applicant and her children, Belle Smith daughter aged 4 years, Andrew aged 2 years, and Annis Smith aged 1 year. Post Office Hindsville Ark.

Attest                 Will.P. Ross
    E.G. Ross                               Chairman
       Clerk Commission                J.E. Gunter   Com

---

## STOCKSTILL

**DOCKET #1888**
CENSUS ROLLS 1835

APPLICANT FOR CHEROKEE CITIZENSHIP

| POST OFFICE: Decatur | | ATTORNEY: C.H. Taylor | |
|---|---|---|---|
| NO | NAMES | AGE | SEX |
| 1 | Eli Stockstill | 30 | Male |

ANCESTOR: William & Absolom Christen

Rejected Sept. 4$^{th}$ 1889

Office Commission on Citizenship
Cherokee Nation Ind Ter
Tahlequah Sept. 4$^{th}$ 1889

The applicant in the above named case having been called three times at intervals of not less than one hour without response wither by person or Attorney and there being no evidence in the case the Commission decide that Eli Stockstill is not of Cherokee blood. P.O. Decatur Texas.

                               Will.P. Ross
Attest                            Chairman
    D.S. Williams                  J.E. Gunter   Com
      Asst Clk Com.

## SMITH

**DOCKET #1889**
CENSUS ROLLS  1835

APPLICANT FOR CHEROKEE CITIZENSHIP

| POST OFFICE: Lead Hill, Ark. | | ATTORNEY: C.H. Taylor | |
|---|---|---|---|
| NO | NAMES | AGE | SEX |
| 1 | James Smith | 26 | Male |

ANCESTOR: Sela Brown

Office Commission on Citizenship
Tahlequah Ind Ter  July 2nd 1889

The above case having been submitted without evidence the Commission decide against the claimant.  Post Office Lead Hill, Ark.
Attest

E.G. Ross                         Will.P. Ross
   Clerk Commission                    Chairman
                                  J.E. Gunter   Com

## SPEARS

**DOCKET #1890**
CENSUS ROLLS  1835 to 1852

APPLICANT FOR CHEROKEE CITIZENSHIP

| POST OFFICE: Mountainburg Ark | | ATTORNEY: A.E. Ivey | |
|---|---|---|---|
| NO | NAMES | AGE | SEX |
| 1 | Mrs. Rebecca Spears | 19 | Female |
| 2 | Infant child | 2 wks | Male |

ANCESTOR: Minnie Franklin

Now on this the 9th day of January, 1888, comes the above case up for final hearing.  The applicant having made application pursuant to the provisions of an Act of the National Council approved Dec. 8th 1886, and all the evidence being fully considered in the Mary A. Couch case, which was made a test one of all the cases claiming a direct lineage from this same ancestor, Mima Edwards, it is adjudged and determined by the Commission that Rebecca Spears and her infant child are not Cherokees by blood, and not entitled to the rights of such.

The decision in the Mary A Couch case found on Docket "A", Page 100 governs this case.

> J. T. Adair    Chairman Commission
> D.W. Lipe    Commissioner

## STAMPS

**DOCKET #1891**
CENSUS ROLLS

APPLICANT FOR CHEROKEE CITIZENSHIP

| POST OFFICE: Galena, Ark | | ATTORNEY: A.E. Ivey | |
|---|---|---|---|
| NO | NAMES | AGE | SEX |
| 1 | Mary A. Stamps | 60 | Female |

ANCESTOR: Wholde Brooks

Rejected Sept 4th 1889

> Office Commission on Citizenship
> Cherokee Nation Ind Ter
> Tahlequah Sept 4th 1889

The above case was called 3 several times and submitted by Atty A.E. Ivey without evidence. The Commission therefore decide that Mary A. Stamps age 60 yrs is not a Cherokee by blood. P.O. Galena Ark.

> Will.P. Ross
Attest                 Chairman
> D.S. Williams       J.E. Gunter   Com
> Asst Clk Com.

# Cherokee Citizenship Commission Docket Books
## (1880-84, 1887-89) Volume V
## Tahlequah, Cherokee Nation

### STAMPS

**DOCKET #1892**

CENSUS ROLLS 1835 to 1852

APPLICANT FOR CHEROKEE CITIZENSHIP

| POST OFFICE: Galena Ark | | ATTORNEY: A.E. Ivey | |
|---|---|---|---|
| No | NAMES | AGE | SEX |
| 1 | John A. Stamps | 35 | Male |

ANCESTOR: Wholde Brooks

Rejected Sept 4th 1889

Office Commission on Citizenship
Cherokee Nation Ind Ter
Tahlequah Sept. 4th 1889

The above application was filed the 5th day of Oct. 1887, and was submitted on the 4th day of Sept. 1889, by Atty A.E. Ivey without evidence, the Commission in view of these facts decide that John A. Stamps age 35 yrs is not a Cherokee by blood. Post Office Galena Ark.

Will.P. Ross

Attest                  Chairman

    D.S. Williams          J.E. Gunter   Com

    Asst   Clk   Com.

### STAMPS

**DOCKET #1893**

CENSUS ROLLS 1835 to 1852

APPLICANT FOR CHEROKEE CITIZENSHIP

| POST OFFICE: Galena, Ark. | | ATTORNEY: A.E. Ivey | |
|---|---|---|---|
| No | NAMES | AGE | SEX |
| 1 | Adolph Stamps | 24 | Male |

ANCESTOR: Wholde Brooks

Rejected Sept 4th 1889

Office Commission on Citizenship
Cherokee Nation Ind Ter
Tahlequah Sept. 4th 1889

The above case was called and submitted by Atty A.E. Ivey without evidence. The Commission therefore in view of the facts decide that Adolph Stamps age 24 yrs. is not a Cherokee by blood. P.O. Galena Ark.

Will.P. Ross

Chairman

Attest

    D.S. Williams           J.E. Gunter   Com

    Asst  Clk  Com.

---

## SEDGLY

**DOCKET #1894**

CENSUS ROLLS 1835 to 1852

APPLICANT FOR CHEREKEE CITIZENSHIP

| POST OFFICE: Claremore, Ind. Ter. | | ATTORNEY: A.E. Ivey | |
|---|---|---|---|
| No | NAMES | AGE | SEX |
| 1 | S.J. Sedgly | 45 | Female |
| 2 | Bima V. Sedgly | 16 | |
| 3 | M.V. Sedgly | 14 | |
| 4 | Harry Sedgly | 12 | |

ANCESTOR: Mrs. Badson

Rejected Sept 4th 1889

Office Commission on Citizenship

Cherokee Nation Ind Ter

Tahlequah Sept. 4th 1889

The above case was called and submitted by Atty A.E. Ivey without evidence. The Commission therefore decide that S.J. Sedgly age 45 yrs and the following children Bima V. 16 yrs, M.V. 14 yrs, and Harry Sedgly 12 yrs. are not Cherokees by blood. Post Office Claremore I.T.

Will.P. Ross

Chairman

Attest

    D.S. Williams           J.E. Gunter   Com

    Asst  Clk  Com.

---

# Cherokee Citizenship Commission Docket Books
## (1880-84, 1887-89) Volume V
## Tahlequah, Cherokee Nation

### STERLING

**DOCKET #1895**

CENSUS ROLLS  1835 to 1852

APPLICANT FOR CHEROKEE CITIZENSHIP

| POST OFFICE: Montague Texas | | ATTORNEY: A.E. Ivey | |
|---|---|---|---|
| **NO** | **NAMES** | **AGE** | **SEX** |
| 1 | C.M. Sterling | 55 | Male |

ANCESTOR:  Wheeler

*Commission on Citizenship.*

CHEROKEE NATION, IND. TER.

*Tahlequah,* Sept. 17[th] 1889

C.M. Sterling

    vs           Application for Cherokee Citizenship

The Cherokee Nation

In the above named case the Commission decide there is nothing in the evidence submitted to show that the applicant C.M. Sterling claims to be of Cherokee blood but that his wife Ida Sterling does altho[sic] the names of her husband instead of her own is entered as applying for citizenship.  The Commission so regard the case, Ida Sterling therefore claims her right to citizenship in the Cherokee Nation by blood because she is the Daughter of J.B. Haney and wife Sarah Haney who was the daughter of James R. Wheeler who was the son of John B. Wheeler and his wife Tabitha *(Illegible)* who it is alleged was of both Cherokee and Choctaw descent.  The witness *(illegible)* upon to prove the Cherokee descent of J.R. Wheeler is one George W. Sims in an exparte affidavit sworn to before J.P. Mullen a Notary Public in Crawford County, State of Arkansas on the 4[th] day of September 1888.  Mr. Sims states that he was born in Mecklenburg County, State of Virginia in 1777 and and[sic] was at the time of making it one hundred and eleven (111) years old.  Giving his long life he spent several years in Georgia and Tennessee.  He knew Jerome Wheeler while he lived in Georgia.  Wheeler lived on Chickamauga Creek near the Georgia line in the Old Cherokee Nation.  He saw him frequently at *(illegible)* and other places public and private and he was known and treated as of Cherokee blood.  About 1851 witness moved from Hall County, Georgia to Bedford County, Tennessee and left Wheeler living on Chickamauga Creek.  He also knew the *(Illegible)* who resided in the Cherokee Country adjoining Hall County Georgia and they were also known and treated as Cherokee Indians. Wheeler did not emigrate with the Cherokees when they removed West but remained on Chickamauga Creek and lived there after most of them had left. James R. Wheeler identifies C.M. Sterling as the husband of Ida Sterling and his grandson by *(illegible)*. The ~~details~~ statements of these witnesses given with much detail induce the ~~Com~~ the[sic] belief that is the Wheelers referred to by them and the *(Illegible)* had been Cherokees residing in the Country at the time the census of Cherokees by blood was taken by the United States in 1835 not only would their names have been enrolled with their people, but that some members of the families would have their names entered on subsequent rolls as recipients of ~~part~~ their proportionate share per capita of funds paid to the Cherokees by the agents of the United States and whose special duty it was to avoid far as possible the omission from the census rolls of the Cherokee people of a single Cherokee Indian. But since the names of Jerome Wheeler and Tabitha Warrenton are not found on either of said rolls 1835 and 52, the Commission decide that Ida Sterling aged 35 years and her children as identified by her grand father James R. Wheeler to wit, Emma Alice 4 yrs, Linna May 2 yrs and Ida Lee Sterling about 5 months are not of Cherokee blood.

P.O. Montague, Texas

Will.P. Ross
Chairman
J.E. Gunter    Com

---

## SPELD

**DOCKET #1896**
CENSUS ROLLS 1835 to 1852

APPLICANT FOR CHEROKEE CITIZENSHIP

| POST OFFICE: Crawford Co, Ark. | | ATTORNEY: A.E. Ivey | |
|---|---|---|---|
| NO | NAMES | AGE | SEX |
| 1 | John T. Speld | 16 | Male |
| 2 | William D. Speld | 14 | " |
| 3 | Pat Speld | 11 | " |
| 4 | Robert B. Speld | 8 | " |
| 5 | Columbus Speld | 6 | " |

ANCESTOR: Minnie Edwards

# Cherokee Citizenship Commission Docket Books
## (1880-84, 1887-89) Volume V
## Tahlequah, Cherokee Nation

Now on this the 9th day of January, 1888, comes the above case up for final hearing. The applicants having made application pursuant to the provisions of an Act of the National Council approved Dec. 8th 1886, and all the evidence not being fully considered in the Mary A. Couch case, which was made a test one of all the cases claiming a direct lineage from the same ancestor, Mima Edwards, it is adjudged and determined by the Commission that John T. Speld – Wm. D. – Pat – Robt B. – and Columbus Speld are not Cherokees by blood, and in consequence not entitled to the rights and privileges of such.

The decision in the Mary A Couch case found on Docket "A", Page 100 governs the above case.

J. T. Adair    Chairman Commission

D.W. Lipe    Commissioner

## QUARLES

**DOCKET #1897**

CENSUS ROLLS 1851

APPLICANT FOR CHEREKEE CITIZENSHIP

| POST OFFICE: Tailes[sic] Creek, Ga. | | ATTORNEY: A.E. Ivey | |
|---|---|---|---|
| NO | NAMES | AGE | SEX |
| 1 | Mary A. Quarles | 36 | Female |
| 2 | James C. Quarles | 15 | Male |
| 3 | Sarah M. Quarles | 13 | Female |
| 4 | Henry B. Quarles | 12 | Male |
| 5 | Joseph Quarles | 9 | " |
| 6 | Mary Quarles | 7 | Female |
| 7 | Ella N. Quarles | 5 | " |
| 8 | El Dorah Quarles | 3 | " |
| 9 | Thomas A. Quarles | 1 | Male |

ANCESTOR: Nancy Goble

Rejected Oct. 4th 1889

Office Commission on Citizenship

Cherokee Nation Ind Ter

Tahlequah Oct. 4th 1889

38

# Cherokee Citizenship Commission Docket Books (1880-84, 1887-89) Volume V
## Tahlequah, Cherokee Nation

The application in the above case was submitted by Attorney for claimant A.E. Ivey for the action of the Commission on the 6th day of March. The evidence not being satisfactory to the Commission, their decision has been withheld awaiting evidence for the proper identification of Mary A. Quarles as the daughter of Nancy Goble, but it not having been presented. The Commission decide against the claimant as having failed to establish her Cherokee Indian blood. This decision includes the daughters of Mary A. Quarles 36 years of age Viz Sarah M. Quarles 13 yrs, Mary Quarles 7 yrs, Ella M Quarles 5 yrs, Eldora Quarles 3 yrs, and sons James C. Quarles 15 yrs, Henry B. Quarles 12 yrs, Joseph Quarles 9 yrs, Thomas A. Quarles 1 year. P.O. Tails Creek Georgia.

|  | Will.P. Ross |
|---|---|
| Attest | Chairman |
| D.S. Williams | J.E. Gunter   Com |
| Asst   Clk   Com. | |

---

## ZODEN

**DOCKET #1898**

CENSUS ROLLS 1835, '51, & 52

APPLICANT FOR CHEROKEE CITIZENSHIP

| POST OFFICE: McKinney, Texas | | ATTORNEY: W.A. Thompson | |
|---|---|---|---|
| **NO** | **NAMES** | **AGE** | **SEX** |
| 1 | Mrs. Caroline Zoden | 35 | Female |
| 2 | Julia A. Zoden | 15 | " |
| 3 | Ellen Zoden | 13 | " |
| 4 | Owen Zoden | 8 | Male |
| 5 | Thomas Zoden | 6 | " |
| 6 | Catharine Zoden | 3 | Female |
| 7 | Martha Zoden | 1 | " |
| 8 | *(Blank on microfilm)* | | |
| 9 | Abbie Rice (Old, helpless & crazy) | 75 | Female |

ANCESTOR: Ed. Fallen

The above case was called three several times & no response from applicant or by Attorney the Commission therefore decide that Mrs. Caroline Zoden age 35

39

yrs, Ellen 13 yrs, Owen male 8 yrs, Thomas male 6 yrs, Catharine Female 3 yrs, and Martha Zoden daughter are not Cherokees by blood. P.O. McKinney Texas.

Sept. 4<sup>th</sup>

Will.P. Ross
Chairman
Jno. E. Gunter   Com

## TAYLOR

**DOCKET #1899**
CENSUS ROLLS

APPLICANT FOR CHEROKEE CITIZENSHIP

| POST OFFICE: Darden, Texas | | ATTORNEY: C.H. Taylor | |
|---|---|---|---|
| No | NAMES | AGE | SEX |
| 1 | Pone Taylor | 40 | Male |

ANCESTOR: William Taylor

The above named case having been this day called three several times at intervals of not less than one hour apart without response from the claimant or his attorney and there being no evidence in support of the application the Commission decide that Pone Taylor age 40 yrs is not of Cherokee blood. P.O. Darden Texas.

Will.P. Ross
Chairman
Jno. E. Gunter   Com

## TANKSLEY

**DOCKET #1900**
CENSUS ROLLS

APPLICANT FOR CHEROKEE CITIZENSHIP

| POST OFFICE: Auroria[sic], Ga | | ATTORNEY: C.H. Taylor | |
|---|---|---|---|
| No | NAMES | AGE | SEX |
| 1 | Charley Tanksley | 22 | Male |
| 2 | Elizabeth Tanksley | 2 | Female |
| 3 | Boney Tanksley | 8 mos | Male |

ANCESTOR: N.C. Tanksley

Rejected Sept. 4<sup>th</sup> 1889

40

# Cherokee Citizenship Commission Docket Books
## (1880-84, 1887-89) Volume V
## Tahlequah, Cherokee Nation

Office Commission on Citizenship
Cherokee Nation Ind Ter
Tahlequah Sept 4[th] 1889

The above case was called 3 and no response from applicant or by Atty. The Commission decide that Charley Tanksley age 22 yrs and the following children Elizabeth Female 2 yrs and Boney Tanksley male 8 months are not Cherokees by blood. Post Office Auroria[sic] Ga.

Attest                    Will.P. Ross
     D.S. Williams                            Chairman
     Asst Clk Com.             J.E. Gunter    Com

## TANKSLEY

**DOCKET #1901**
CENSUS ROLLS

APPLICANT FOR CHEROKEE CITIZENSHIP

| POST OFFICE: Auroria[sic], Ga | | ATTORNEY: C.H. Taylor | |
|---|---|---|---|
| No | NAMES | AGE | SEX |
| 1 | N.C. Tansley[sic] | 48 | Male |
| 2 | Matilda Tanksley | 15 | Female |
| 3 | Andrew Tanksley | 12 | Male |
| 4 | Emery Tanksley | 6 | " |
| 5 | Bell Tanksley | 2 | Female |
| 6 | Mollie Tanksley | 8 | " |

ANCESTOR: Sarah Tanksley

Rejected Sept. 4[th] 1889

Office Commission on Citizenship
Cherokee Nation Ind Ter
Tahlequah Sept. 4[th] 1889

The above named case having been called three several times at intervals of not less than one hour without response by claimant either in person or by Attorney and there being no evidence in support of the application, the Commission decide that N.C. Tanksley age 48 years and his sons Andrew 12 yrs, Belle[sic] 2 yrs and Molly[sic] Tanksley 8 yrs are not of Cherokee blood. P.O. Auroria[sic], Ga.

# Cherokee Citizenship Commission Docket Books
## (1880-84, 1887-89) Volume V
## Tahlequah, Cherokee Nation

Attest
    D.S. Williams
    Asst Clk Com.

Will.P. Ross
Chairman
J.E. Gunter   Com

---

## TALBERT

**DOCKET #1902**

CENSUS ROLLS

APPLICANT FOR CHEROKEE CITIZENSHIP

| POST OFFICE: Carthage, Indiana | | ATTORNEY: L.B. Bell | |
|---|---|---|---|
| **NO** | **NAMES** | **AGE** | **SEX** |
| 1 | Maria Delphina Talbert | | Female |
| 2 | Rhoda A. Talbert | 18 | " |
| 3 | Paris Clark Talbert | 11 | Male |
| 4 | Lucy V. Talbert | 8 | Female |
| 5 | George S.S. Talbert | 6 | Male |

ANCESTOR: Martha Elmore

The Commission decide against claimant. See decision in case Lible[sic] J Bogue, Docket 2183, Book E, Page 29.

    Will.P. Ross   Chairman
    John E. Gunter   Com

---

## TODD

**DOCKET #1903**

CENSUS ROLLS   1835

APPLICANT FOR CHEROKEE CITIZENSHIP

| POST OFFICE: Clifton, Ark | | ATTORNEY: C.H. Taylor | |
|---|---|---|---|
| **NO** | **NAMES** | **AGE** | **SEX** |
| 1 | Mary J. Todd | 50 | Female |
| 2 | John A. Todd | 19 | Male |
| 3 | Zirri Todd | 16 | " |
| 4 | Andrew Todd | 14 | " |
| 5 | Edwin Todd | 11 | " |

ANCESTOR: Feraby Vaughn

42

# Cherokee Citizenship Commission Docket Books
## (1880-84, 1887-89) Volume V
## Tahlequah, Cherokee Nation

Office Commission on Citizenship
Cherokee Nation Ind Ter
Tahlequah July 2$^{nd}$ 1889

There being no evidence in support of the above named case the Commission decide that Mary J Todd aged 50 years and her children John A aged 19 years, Zirri aged 16 years, Andrew aged 14 years, and Edwin Todd aged 11 years. are not Cherokees by blood.

Attest                      Will.P. Ross

   EG Ross                            Chairman
   Clerk Commission             J.E. Gunter    Com

---

## TODD

**DOCKET #1904**
CENSUS ROLLS

APPLICANT FOR CHEROKEE CITIZENSHIP

| POST OFFICE: Clifty Ark | | ATTORNEY: C.H. Taylor | |
|---|---|---|---|
| No | NAMES | AGE | SEX |
| 1 | Elizabeth Todd | 46 | Female |
| 2 | Nancy A. Todd | 21 | " |
| 3 | B.F. Todd | 17 | Male |
| 4 | Albert Todd | 15 | " |
| 5 | Lafayette Todd | 12 | " |
| 6 | Manolia[sic] Todd | 10 | Female |
| 7 | Lizzie F. Todd | 7 | " |

ANCESTOR: Feraby Vaughn

Office Commission on Citizenship
Tahlequah CN July 2$^{nd}$ 1889

No evidence accompanies the above application. The Commission therefore decide <u>against</u> the applicant for admission to citizenship in the Cherokee Nation as Cherokees by blood, to wit, Elizabeth Todd aged 46 years and her children Nancy A. aged 21 years, B.F. Todd (son) 17 years, Albert 15 years, Lafayette 12 years, Mgnolia[sic] 10 years, Lizzie F. Todd 7 years. Post Office address Clifty Arkansas.

# Cherokee Citizenship Commission Docket Books
## (1880-84, 1887-89) Volume V
## Tahlequah, Cherokee Nation

Attest                       Will.P. Ross

     EG Ross                     Chairman

        Clerk Commission          J.E. Gunter    Com

---

## TODD

**DOCKET #1905**

CENSUS ROLLS 1835

APPLICANT FOR CHEROKEE CITIZENSHIP

| POST OFFICE: Clifty Ark | | ATTORNEY: C.H. Taylor | |
|---|---|---|---|
| NO | NAMES | AGE | SEX |
| 1 | George W Todd | 30 | Male |
| 2 | B.F. Todd | 8 | " |
| 3 | Nettie Todd | 6 | Female |

ANCESTOR: Feraby Vaughn

Office Commission on Citizenship

Cherokee Nation Ind Ter

Tahlequah July 2nd 1889

The above case was submitted without evidence to support it. The Commission therefore decide against the applicant George W. Todd aged 30 years and his son B.F. Todd aged 8 years and daughter Nettie Todd aged 6 years. Post Office address Clifty Arkansas.

Attest                       Will.P. Ross

     EG Ross                     Chairman

        Clerk Commission          J.E. Gunter    Com

---

## TODD

**DOCKET #1906**

CENSUS ROLLS 1835

APPLICANT FOR CHEROKEE CITIZENSHIP

| POST OFFICE: Clifty Ark | | ATTORNEY: C.H. Taylor | |
|---|---|---|---|
| NO | NAMES | AGE | SEX |
| 1 | J.W. Todd | 28 | Male |
| 2 | Maggie Todd | 6 | Female |

| 3 | David L. Todd | 4 | Male |
|---|---|---|---|

**ANCESTOR:** Feraby Vaughn

Office Commission on Citizenship
Cherokee Nation Ind Ter
Tahlequah  July 2[nd] 1889

There being no evidence presented in support of the above application, the Commission decide that J.W. Todd aged 28 years and daughter Maggie aged 6 years and son, David L. Todd aged 4 years are not entitled to citizenship in the Cherokee Nation as Cherokees by blood.

Attest            Will.P. Ross

    E.G. Ross                         Chairman

      Clerk Commission          J.E. Gunter   Com

---

## THOMAS

**DOCKET #1907**

CENSUS ROLLS

APPLICANT FOR CHEROKEE CITIZENSHIP

| POST OFFICE: Webbers Falls, Ind. Ter. | | ATTORNEY: C.H. Taylor | |
|---|---|---|---|
| **NO** | **NAMES** | **AGE** | **SEX** |
| 1 | Malinda E. Thomas | 60 | Female |
| 2 | Alonzo Musser | 40 | Male |

**ANCESTOR:** Margaret Robertson

Rejected Sept 4[th] 1889.

Office Commission on Citizenship
Cherokee Nation Ind Ter
Tahlequah  Sept. 4[th] 1889

The above case was called 3 several times and no response from applicant or by Atty. The Commission therefore decide that Malinda B. Thomas age 60 yrs. and her son Alonzo Musser male age 40 yrs are not Cherokees by blood. Post Office Webbers falls I.T.

                     Will.P. Ross

Attest               Chairman

    D.S. Williams       J.E. Gunter   Com

    Asst  Clk  Com.

# Cherokee Citizenship Commission Docket Books
## (1880-84, 1887-89) Volume V
## Tahlequah, Cherokee Nation

## TAYLOR

**DOCKET #1908**

CENSUS ROLLS 1835, '48, '51, & '52

APPLICANT FOR CHEROKEE CITIZENSHIP

| POST OFFICE: Sheffield, Ill. | | ATTORNEY: Boudinot & Rasmus | |
|---|---|---|---|
| No | NAMES | AGE | SEX |
| 1 | Zack Taylor | 39 | Male |
| 2 | Flora B. Taylor | 11 | Female |
| 3 | F.J. Taylor | 9 | Male |
| 4 | Willie J Taylor | 7 | " |
| 5 | Tom Taylor | 2 | " |

ANCESTOR: T.F. Taylor

Rejected Aug 27th 1889

Office Commission on Citizenship
Cherokee Nation Ind Ter
Tahlequah  Aug 27th 1889

In the above named case the Commission decide against the claim of Zack Taylor, age 39 years and his daughter Flora B. Taylor age 11 years and his sons L.J.[sic] Taylor age 9 years, Willie J. Taylor age 7 years, and Tom Taylor age 2 years for reasons set forth in their decision in the case of George W. Taylor, Docket 1909, Book D, Page 395.  P.O. Sheffield Illinois.

Will.P. Ross

Attest                                                                 Chairman

D.S. Williams                              J.E. Gunter   Com

Asst   Clk  Com.

## TAYLOR

**DOCKET #1909**

CENSUS ROLLS 1835 to 1852

APPLICANT FOR CHEROKEE CITIZENSHIP

| POST OFFICE: Baxter Springs, Kan | | ATTORNEY: Boudinot and Rasmus | |
|---|---|---|---|
| No | NAMES | AGE | SEX |
| 1 | George W. Taylor | 36 | Male |

46

# Cherokee Citizenship Commission Docket Books
## (1880-84, 1887-89) Volume V
## Tahlequah, Cherokee Nation

| 2 | Martin B Taylor | 8 | male |
|---|---|---|---|
| 3 | Leona D. Taylor | 5 | female |
| 4 | Charles Taylor | 1 | male |

ANCESTOR: T.F. Taylor

*Commission on Citizenship.*

CHEROKEE NATION, IND. TER.

*Tahlequah,* August 27th 1889

George W. Taylor
    vs            Application for Cherokee Citizenship
The Cherokee Nation

The application in the above case was filed the 1st day of October, A.D. 1887, alleging that applicant is the son of one T.J. Taylor whose name he believes was enrolled on the census rolls of Cherokees by blood, citizens of the Cherokee Nation taken and male in the years 1835, 48, 51, & 52. In his declaration made before J.A. Whitcraft, Clerk of the District Court ~~and~~ in and for the County of Cherokee and State of Kansas on the 9th day of October, A.D. 1884 and filed before the Department of the Interior, at Washington D.C. the Claimant represents that he is a person of Cherokee blood was born in the County of Guernsey, State of Ohio and is 32 years of age, that he is the son of one Jeff Taylor a person of Cherokee Indian descent who it ~~was~~ is said was born in Caroline County State of Virginia in the year 1809 and died in the same county and state in the year 1861. And that Jeff Taylor was the son of one Fanny Taylor a Cherokee Indian woman who is said to have been born in the Cherokee Nation East of the Mississippi river[sic] in the year 1783 and whose whereabouts since 1861 are unknown. The only evidence in support of these allegations is the <u>exparte</u> affidavit of one Adalide Taylor made and taken before J.A. Whitcraft Clerk of the District Court in and for the County of Cherokee and state of Kansas, on the 9th day of February 1884, who says that she was born in Caroline County Virginia and is 74 years of age and who corroborates the facts alleged in the declaration of claimant and has heard Cherokee Indian members of the tribe East of the Mississippi river[sic] acknowledge Jeff Taylor and Fanny Taylor to be Cherokee Indians and members of the tribe. This affidavit is not sufficient to establish the allegations set forth by claimant. It is not shown that

47

either the claimant of Jeff Taylor or Fanny Taylor were at any time citizens of the Cherokee Nation or that they enjoyed any Cherokee rights or privileges, altho[sic] Fanny Taylor was known to be alive as late as 1861. Nor is her name or that of Jeff Taylor, or of T.J. Taylor or of claimant to be found on any of the rolls referred to in the 7[th] Section of the Act of December 8[th] 1886 creating the Commission on Citizenship. The Commission therefore decide that George W. Taylor and his daughter Leona B. Taylor and sons Martin B. Taylor age 8 years and Charles age one year are not of Cherokee blood and not entitled to Cherokee Citizenship. P.O. Baxter Springs, Kansas

Will.P. Ross

Chairman

J.E. Gunter   Com

---

## TANSEY

**DOCKET #1910**
CENSUS ROLLS

APPLICANT FOR CHEROKEE CITIZENSHIP

| POST OFFICE: Afton, I.T. | | ATTORNEY: L.B. Bell | |
|---|---|---|---|
| **No** | **NAMES** | **AGE** | **SEX** |
| 1 | Albert C. Tansey | | Male |

ANCESTOR: Mary Crews

The Commission decide against claimant.   See decision in case Andrew Meredith Docket 2180 Book E, Page 26 and case John Henly Docket 1250, Book C Page 376.

Will.P. Ross   Chairman

John E. Gunter   Com

---

## TANSEY

**DOCKET #1911**
CENSUS ROLLS

APPLICANT FOR CHEROKEE CITIZENSHIP

| POST OFFICE: Afton I.T. | | ATTORNEY: L.B. Bell | |
|---|---|---|---|
| **No** | **NAMES** | **AGE** | **SEX** |
| 1 | Ellsion[sic] E. Tansey | | Male |

ANCESTOR: Mary Crews

The Commission decide against claimant. See decision in case Andrew Meredith Docket 2180 Book E, Page 26 and case John Henly Docket 1250, Book C Page 376.

Will.P. Ross    Chairman

John E. Gunter    Com

## THOMPSON

**DOCKET #1912**
CENSUS ROLLS

APPLICANT FOR CHEROKEE CITIZENSHIP

| POST OFFICE: Valley Mills, Kans | | ATTORNEY: L.B. Bell | |
|---|---|---|---|
| No | NAMES | AGE | SEX |
| 1 | Libby L Thompson | 30 | female |
| 2 | Rolph[sic] Thompson | 3 | male |
| 3 | Norman Thompson | 1 | " |

ANCESTOR: Sarah Morgan

Rejected July 2nd 1889

Office Commission on Citizenship<br>Cherokee Nation Ind Ter<br>Tahlequah   July 2nd 1889

Application for Cherokee Citizenship.

The above applicant was called 3 times & no answer either in person or by Attorney & there being no evidence on file in support of the application, we decide that applicant Libby Thompson age 30 yrs & children Norman Thompson age W.[sic] & Rolph Thompson age 3 yrs are not Cherokees by blood. P.O. Valey[sic] Mills Kans.

Attest                      Will.P. Ross
    D.S. Williams                 Chairman
    Asst   Clk   Com.           J.E. Gunter    Com

## THOMPSON

**DOCKET #1913**

CENSUS ROLLS

APPLICANT FOR CHEROKEE CITIZENSHIP

| POST OFFICE: Valley Mills Kans | | ATTORNEY: L.B. Bell | |
|---|---|---|---|
| **No** | **NAMES** | **AGE** | **SEX** |
| 1 | Sarah Thompson | 41 | female |
| 2 | Ella Q. Thompson | 15 | " |
| 3 | Arthur W. Thompson | 13 | male |
| 4 | Daisy M. Thompson | 10 | female |
| 5 | Myrtle L. Thompson | 8 | " |
| 6 | Braskill Thompson | 6 | " |
| 7 | Annie M. Thompson | 5 | " |

ANCESTOR: Sarah Morgan

Rejected July 2nd 1889

Office Commission on Citizenship
Cherokee Nation Ind Ter
Tahlequah  July 2nd 1889

Application for Cherokee Citizenship

The above applicant was called 3 times & no answer & there being no evidence on file in support of the application, we  decide that applicant Sarah Thompson age 41 yrs and children Ella Q, Arthur W, Daisy M, Myrtle L, Braskill, Anna M. Thompson are not Cherokees by blood. P.O. Valley Mills Kans.

Will.P. Ross

Attest                                          Chairman
   D.S. Williams                    J.E. Gunter    Com
   Asst  Clk  Com.

## TAYLOR

**DOCKET #1914**

CENSUS ROLLS 1835 to 1852

APPLICANT FOR CHEROKEE CITIZENSHIP

| POST OFFICE: Claremore I.T. | | ATTORNEY: A.E. Ivey | |
|---|---|---|---|
| **No** | **NAMES** | **AGE** | **SEX** |
| 1 | E.D. Taylor | 23 | female |
| 2 | O.A. Taylor | 23 | |
| 3 | W.E. Taylor | 1 | |

ANCESTOR: Mrs. Bradson

Rejected Sept 4th 1889

Office Commission on Citizenship
Cherokee Nation Ind Ter
Tahlequah Sept. 4th 1889

The above case was called and submitted by Atty A.E. Ivey without evidence. The Commission therefore in view of these facts decide that E.D. Taylor age 23 yrs and W.E. Taylor age 1 yr are not Cherokees by blood. Post Office Claremore I.T.

Will.P. Ross

Attest            Chairman

     D.S. Williams      J.E. Gunter    Com

     Asst   Clk   Com.

## THOMPSON

**DOCKET #1915**

CENSUS ROLLS 1835 to 1852

APPLICANT FOR CHEROKEE CITIZENSHIP

| POST OFFICE: Alma Ark | | ATTORNEY: A.E. Ivey | |
|---|---|---|---|
| **No** | **NAMES** | **AGE** | **SEX** |
| 1 | B.F. Thompson | 36 | male |
| 2 | Martha L. Thompson | 17 | female |
| 3 | George H. Thompson | 15 | male |
| 4 | William L. Thompson | 13 | " |
| 5 | Mary F. Thompson | 11 | female |
| 6 | E.B. Thompson | 7 | male |

| 7 | James F. Thompson | 2 | " |
|---|---|---|---|

**ANCESTOR:** Patsy Thompson

Rejected Sept 4<sup>th</sup> 1889

The above case was called three several times & no response by applicant or by Attorney the Commission ~~decide~~ therefore decide that Luther Terrel[sic] age 35 yrs is not a Cherokee by blood. P.O. Mulberry Ark.[sic]

Will.P. Ross
Chairman
J.E. Gunter   Com

---

## TONEY

**DOCKET #1916**

CENSUS ROLLS 1835 to 1852

APPLICANT FOR CHEROKEE CITIZENSHIP

| POST OFFICE: Van Buren Ark | | ATTORNEY: A.E. Ivey | |
|---|---|---|---|
| No | NAMES | AGE | SEX |
| 1 | Sarah M. Toney | 29 | female |

**ANCESTOR:** John Graham

The above case was called and submitted by Atty A.E. Ivey without evidence. The Commission therefore decide that Sarah M. Toney age 29 yrs is <u>not</u> a Cherokee by blood. P.O. Van Buren Ark.

Will.P. Ross
Chairman
Jno. E. Gunter   Com

---

## THOMAS

**DOCKET #1917**

CENSUS ROLLS

APPLICANT FOR CHEROKEE CITIZENSHIP

| POST OFFICE: Afton, I.T. | | ATTORNEY: L.B. Bell | |
|---|---|---|---|
| No | NAMES | AGE | SEX |
| 1 | Sarah A. Thomas | 21 | female |

**ANCESTOR:** Ann Crews

# Cherokee Citizenship Commission Docket Books
## (1880-84, 1887-89) Volume V
## Tahlequah, Cherokee Nation

The Commission ~~on~~ decide against the claimant. See decision in the Andrew Meredith Case Docket 2180 Book E, Page 26 and John Henly Docket 1250, Book C Page 376.

Will.P. Ross    Chairman

John E. Gunter    Com

---

## TANSY

**DOCKET #1918**
CENSUS ROLLS

APPLICANT FOR CHEROKEE CITIZENSHIP

| POST OFFICE: Richmond Ind | | ATTORNEY: L.B. Bell | |
|---|---|---|---|
| No | NAMES | AGE | SEX |
| 1 | Pamelia C. Tansy | 58 | female |

ANCESTOR: Mary Crews

The Commission decide <u>against</u> claimant. See decision in case Andrew Meredith Docket 2180 Book E, Page 26 and case John Henly Docket 1250, Book C Page 376.

Will.P. Ross    Chairman

J. E. Gunter    Com

---

## TIDWELL

**DOCKET #1919**
CENSUS ROLLS  1851

APPLICANT FOR CHEROKEE CITIZENSHIP

| POST OFFICE: Dallas, Ga | | ATTORNEY: A.E. Ivey | |
|---|---|---|---|
| No | NAMES | AGE | SEX |
| 1 | William E. Tidwell | 29 | male |
| 2 | John W. Tidwell | 5 | " |

ANCESTOR: John Tidwell

John W. Tidwell, son of William E. Tidwell, now deceased, is five years old. We the Commission find him to be a descendant of John Tidwell (Sen.) who was his grand-father and a Cherokee by blood, as has been proven by the evidence taken in his case.

Therefore we the Commission on Citizenship unanimously agree and decide that John W. Tidwell is a Cherokee by blood and he is hereby re-admitted to all the rights and privileges of a Cherokee citizen by blood.

> J. T. Adair   Chairman Commission
> D.W. Lipe   Commissioner
> H.C. Barnes  Commissioner

Office Com on Citizenship
Tahlequah I.T. Sept 21ˢᵗ 1888.

## TIDWELL

**DOCKET #1920**
CENSUS ROLLS 1851

APPLICANT FOR CHEROKEE CITIZENSHIP

| POST OFFICE: Dallas, Ga. | | ATTORNEY: A.E. Ivey | |
|---|---|---|---|
| **NO** | **NAMES** | **AGE** | **SEX** |
| 1 | Mancil Tidwell | 51 | male |
| 2 | Sarah E. Tidwell | 27 | female |
| 3 | Andy W. Tidwell | 12 | male |
| 4 | Oleana E. Tidwell | 8 | female |
| 5 | Carry M. Tidwell | 6 | " |
| 6 | Miney L Tidwell | 4 | " |
| 7 | Lenner E. Tidwell | 1 | " |

ANCESTOR: John Tidwell

In the matter of the above applicants, We the Commission on Citizenship, find that Mancil Tidwell is a son of John Tidwell who was a half-bred Cherokee Indian, and was so enrolled on the Siler Roll of 1851, and under the law passed by the National Council creating this Commission, dated Dec. 8ᵗʰ 1886, We the Commission decide that Mancil Tidwell and his six children are of Cherokee blood and under the law are hereby re-admitted to all the rights and privileges of Cherokee citizens by blood. The names of his children are as follows: Sarah E, Andy W, Oleana E, Carry M, Miney L, and Lenner E. Tidwell.

> J. T. Adair   Chairman Commission
> D.W. Lipe   Commissioner
> H.C. Barnes  Commissioner

# Cherokee Citizenship Commission Docket Books
## (1880-84, 1887-89) Volume V
## Tahlequah, Cherokee Nation

Office Com on Citizenship
Tahlequah I.T. Sept 21<sup>st</sup> 1888.

---

### TERRELL

**DOCKET #1921**

CENSUS ROLLS

APPLICANT FOR CHEROKEE CITIZENSHIP

| POST OFFICE: Mulbery[sic] Ark. | | ATTORNEY: L.B. Bell | |
| --- | --- | --- | --- |
| NO | NAMES | AGE | SEX |
| 1 | Luther Terrell | 35 | male |

ANCESTOR: Terrell

Rejected Sept. 4<sup>th</sup> 1889

Office Commission on Citizenship
Cherokee Nation Ind Ter
Tahlequah Sept. 4<sup>th</sup> 1889

The above case was called 3 times and no response from applicant or by Atty. The Commission therefore decide that Luther Terrell age 35 yrs is not a Cherokee by blood. P.O. Mulbery[sic] Ark.

Will.P. Ross

Attest

Chairman

D.S. Williams

J.E. Gunter   Com

Asst   Clk   Com.

---

### THOMPSON

**DOCKET #1922**

CENSUS ROLLS  1835 to 1852

APPLICANT FOR CHEROKEE CITIZENSHIP

| POST OFFICE: Clarksville Ark | | ATTORNEY: A.E. Ivey | |
| --- | --- | --- | --- |
| NO | NAMES | AGE | SEX |
| 1 | Nancy V. Thompson | 31 | female |
| 2 | Frank M. Thompson | 9 | male |
| 3 | Martha E Thompson | 6 | female |
| 4 | Virginia Thompson | 3 | " |
| 5 | Augustus P. Thompson | 11 m | male |

ANCESTOR: Louisa Bowen

55

# Cherokee Citizenship Commission Docket Books
## (1880-84, 1887-89) Volume V
### Tahlequah, Cherokee Nation

Office Commission on Citizenship Aug. 9th 1888

The above entitled case being submitted by plaintiffs Atty. on the 7th *(illegible)*. It was taken up and duly considered by the Commission, also the rolls mentioned in the 7th Sec. of the Act of Dec. 8th 1886 in relation thereto as well as those mentioned in the 7th amendment of Febry 7th 1888, but fail to find the name of Louisa Bowen, nee Smith, or that of Nancy V. Thompson enrolled thereon. In the absence of which, notwithstanding the testimony, this Commission cannot admit them to citizenship; therefore, declare Nancy V. Thompson and her four children, viz: now residing in Arkansas, Frank M, Martha E, Virginia E. and Augustus P. Thompson not to be Cherokees by blood and not entitled to the rights and privileges of such on account of their blood.

J. T. Adair    Chairman Commission
H.C. Barnes  Commissioner

## JOLLY

**DOCKET #1923**
CENSUS ROLLS 1835, '48, '51 to 1852

APPLICANT FOR CHEROKEE CITIZENSHIP

| POST OFFICE: Honey Grove, Texas | | ATTORNEY: Boudinot and Rasmus | |
|---|---|---|---|
| **NO** | **NAMES** | **AGE** | **SEX** |
| 1 | W.L. Jolly | 27 | Male |

ANCESTOR: Mrs. A.M. Jolly

Adverse
Embraced in decision in Book "A"
Page 231, in the John Ward case.

Attest              Will.P. Ross
   EG Ross                              Chairman
   Clerk Commission          J.E. Gunter  Com

# Cherokee Citizenship Commission Docket Books
## (1880-84, 1887-89) Volume V
## Tahlequah, Cherokee Nation

### JOHNSTON

**DOCKET #1924**

CENSUS ROLLS 1835 to 1852

APPLICANT FOR CHEROKEE CITIZENSHIP

| POST OFFICE: Fayetteville, Ark | | ATTORNEY: L.S. Sanders | |
|---|---|---|---|
| NO | NAMES | AGE | SEX |
| 1 | Mary C. Johnston | 32 | Female |
| 2 | Thurston L. Johnston | 10 | Male |
| 3 | Henry E. Johnston | 7 | " |
| 4 | Eskerin E. Johnston | 5 | " |
| 5 | Marian E. Johnston | 2 | " |

ANCESTOR: Houston F. Gilmore

Rejected Sept. 5th 1889

> Office Commission on Citizenship
> Cherokee Nation Ind Ter
> Tahlequah Sept. 5th 1889

This case having been submitted by the Attys without evidence the Commission decide that Mary C. Johnston age 32 years, Thurston L. age 10 years, Henry E, Eskerin E. age 5 years and Marian E. Johnston are not Cherokees by blood and not entitled to Cherokee citizenship. P.O. Fayetteville Ark.

Attest

    D.S. Williams

    Asst Clk Com.

              Will.P. Ross

              Chairman

              J.E. Gunter   Com

### JONES

**DOCKET #1925**

CENSUS ROLLS 1835

APPLICANT FOR CHEROKEE CITIZENSHIP

| POST OFFICE: McKinny[sic] Texas | | ATTORNEY: W.A. Thompson | |
|---|---|---|---|
| NO | NAMES | AGE | SEX |
| 1 | Leilsa E. Jones | 9 | Female |
| 2 | Glennie E. Jones | 5 | " |

ANCESTOR: Jack McGarrah

57

Rejected Sept. 5<sup>th</sup> 1889

Office Commission on Citizenship
Cherokee Nation Ind Ter
Tahlequah  Sept. 5<sup>th</sup> 1889

This case having been submitted by the Atty without evidence the Commission decide that Leilsa E. Jones age 7 yrs and Glennie E. Jones age 5 years, are not Cherokees by blood and are not entitled to Cherokee citizenship.   P.O. McKinny[sic] Texas.

Will.P. Ross

Attest
Chairman

D.S. Williams
J.E. Gunter   Com

Asst   Clk   Com.

---

## JACKSON

**DOCKET #1926**
CENSUS ROLLS  1835 to 1852

APPLICANT FOR CHEROKEE CITIZENSHIP

| POST OFFICE: Siloam Spring, Ark | | ATTORNEY: L.S. Sanders | |
|---|---|---|---|
| No | NAMES | AGE | SEX |
| 1 | Moses Jackson | 46 | Male |
| 2 | Dartha J Jackson | 22 | Female |
| 3 | Margaret E.D. Jackson | 18 | " |
| 4 | Henry W. Jackson | 15 | Male |
| 5 | Arrara E. Jackson | 10 | Female |
| 6 | Ollie L. Jackson | 7 | " |
| 7 | William L. Jackson | 5 | Male |
| 8 | Moses K. Jackson, Jr. | 2 | " |

ANCESTOR: George W. Jackson

Rejected Sept 5<sup>th</sup> 1889

Office Commission on Citizenship
Cherokee Nation Ind Ter
Tahlequah  Sept. 5<sup>th</sup> 1889

This case having been submitted by Attys without evidence the Commission decide that Moses Jackson age 46 years and his children Dartha J. age 22 years,

# Cherokee Citizenship Commission Docket Books
## (1880-84, 1887-89) Volume V
## Tahlequah, Cherokee Nation

Margaret E.D. age 18 years, Henry W. Jackson, Arrara E, Ollie L, William L age 5 years and Moses K. age 2 years are not Cherokees by blood and not entitled to Cherokee citizenship. P.O. Siloam Springs, Ark.

<table>
<tr><td></td><td>Will.P. Ross</td></tr>
<tr><td>Attest</td><td>Chairman</td></tr>
<tr><td>D.S. Williams</td><td>J.E. Gunter   Com</td></tr>
<tr><td>Asst  Clk Com.</td><td></td></tr>
</table>

---

## JENKINS

**DOCKET #1927**
CENSUS ROLLS 1835 to 1852

APPLICANT FOR CHEROKEE CITIZENSHIP

| POST OFFICE: Charleston, N.C. | | ATTORNEY: L.S. Sanders | |
|---|---|---|---|
| **NO** | **NAMES** | **AGE** | **SEX** |
| 1 | Rutha A. Jenkins | 41 | Female |
| 2 | Amanda Patterson | 18 | " |
| 3 | William Jenkins | 14 | "[sic] |
| 4 | Walker Jenkins | 11 | Male |
| 5 | Mary Jenkins | 8 | Female |
| 6 | Carrie M. Jenkins | 6 | " |
| 7 | 1 not named | 1 | Male |

ANCESTOR: Elizabeth Leatherwood

Rejected May 27ᵗʰ 1889

In the above named case the Commission this day decide that Ruth A. Jenkins age 41 years and her children whose names are as follows, Amanda C Walker Female age 11 years, William male age 14 years, Mary Female age 8 years, Carrie M. Female age 6 years, Lassie Jenkins Female age 4 years, & one babe not named male age 1 year, are not of Cherokee blood. See decision in case of Nancy Ann Thompson Docket 2008 Book D, Page 494.

<table>
<tr><td>Attest</td><td>Will.P. Ross</td></tr>
<tr><td>D.S. Williams</td><td>Chairman</td></tr>
<tr><td>Asst  Clk Com.</td><td>J.E. Gunter   Com</td></tr>
</table>

---

## JOLLY

**DOCKET #1928**

CENSUS ROLLS 1835, '48, '51 & '52

APPLICANT FOR CHEROKEE CITIZENSHIP

| POST OFFICE: Honey Grove Texas | | ATTORNEY: Boudinot & Rasmus | |
|---|---|---|---|
| No | NAMES | AGE | SEX |
| 1 | Lella Jolly | 22 | Female |

ANCESTOR: A.M. Jolly

Adverse

Embraced in decision in Book A
Page 231 in John Ward case.

Will.P. Ross
Chairman

Attest                          J.E. Gunter    Com
   EG Ross
   Clerk Com

## JONES

**DOCKET #1929**

CENSUS ROLLS

APPLICANT FOR CHEROKEE CITIZENSHIP

| POST OFFICE: Afton Ind. Ter | | ATTORNEY: L.B. Bell | |
|---|---|---|---|
| No | NAMES | AGE | SEX |
| 1 | Martha H. Jones | 55 | Female |

ANCESTOR: Ann Crews

The Commission decide against claimant. See decision in the case of Andrew
Meredith Docket 2180 Book E, Page 26 and John Henly Docket 1250, Book C
Page 376.

Will.P. Ross    Chairman
John E. Gunter    Com

# Cherokee Citizenship Commission Docket Books (1880-84, 1887-89) Volume V
## Tahlequah, Cherokee Nation

## JACKSON

**DOCKET #1930**
CENSUS ROLLS

APPLICANT FOR CHEROKEE CITIZENSHIP

| POST OFFICE: Afton Ind. Ter. | | ATTORNEY: L.B. Bell | |
|---|---|---|---|
| NO | NAMES | AGE | SEX |
| 1 | Lydia A. Jackson | 33 | Female |

ANCESTOR: Ann Crews

The Commission decide against claimant. See decision in the case of Andrew Meredith Docket 2180 Book E, Page 26 and John Henly Docket 1250, Book C Page 376.

Will.P. Ross    Chairman
John E. Gunter    Com

---

## JONES

**DOCKET #1931**
CENSUS ROLLS

APPLICANT FOR CHEROKEE CITIZENSHIP

| POST OFFICE: Macdowl[sic] Mo. | | ATTORNEY: L.B. Bell | |
|---|---|---|---|
| NO | NAMES | AGE | SEX |
| 1 | William T. Jones | | |

ANCESTOR: Sarah Elmore

Adverse. See decision of the Commission in case John R. Henly Docket 553, Book B, Page 266.

Will.P. Ross    Chairman

J.E. Gunter    Com

61

## JONES

**DOCKET #1932**

CENSUS ROLLS

APPLICANT FOR CHEROKEE CITIZENSHIP

| POST OFFICE: Lebo, Kansas | | ATTORNEY: L.B. Bell | |
|---|---|---|---|
| No | NAMES | AGE | SEX |
| 1 | Albert Jones | | Male |
| 2 | Killie E. Jones | 17 | Female |
| 3 | Lillie A. Jones | 15 | " |
| 4 | Mattie W. Jones | 13 | " |

ANCESTOR: Sarah Elmore

Rejected July 2nd 1889

Adversely

See decision of Commission in the case of John R. Henly Docket 553, Book B, Page 266. Also see the same case in this Book on Page 446.

Will.P. Ross

Attest                                          Chairman

D.S. Williams                    J.E. Gunter   Com

Asst   Clk   Com.

## JONES

**DOCKET #1933**

CENSUS ROLLS

APPLICANT FOR CHEROKEE CITIZENSHIP

| POST OFFICE: Strawn, Kansas | | ATTORNEY: L.B. Bell | |
|---|---|---|---|
| No | NAMES | AGE | SEX |
| 1 | Milton Jones | | Male |
| 2 | Orlee C. Jones | 12 | " |
| 3 | Stella May Jones | 10 | Female |
| 4 | Frank Milton Jones | 8 | Male |
| 5 | Thomas Elmore Jones | 2 | " |

ANCESTOR: Sarah Elmore

Adverse.  See decision of Commission in case John R. Henly Docket 553, Book B, Page 266.

# Cherokee Citizenship Commission Docket Books
# (1880-84, 1887-89) Volume V
# Tahlequah, Cherokee Nation

Will.P. Ross     Chairman

J.E. Gunter   Com

---

## JONES

**DOCKET #1934**

CENSUS ROLLS

APPLICANT FOR CHEROKEE CITIZENSHIP

| POST OFFICE: Blue Jacket, I.T. | | ATTORNEY: L.B. Bell | |
|---|---|---|---|
| NO | NAMES | AGE | SEX |
| 1 | Thomas N Jones | 46 | Male |
| 2 | Alfred M. Jones | 23 | " |
| 3 | Lundley M Jones | 20 | " |
| 4 | Lucinda Jones | 18 | Female |
| 5 | John J. Jones | 16 | Male |
| 6 | Hatta Jones | 14 | Female |
| 7 | Mary Jones | 9 | " |

ANCESTOR: Sarah Elmore

Adverse. See decision of Commission in case John R. Henly Docket 553, Book B, Page 266.

Will.P. Ross     Chairman

J.E. Gunter   Com

---

## JACKSON

**DOCKET #1935**

CENSUS ROLLS 1835 to 1852

APPLICANT FOR CHEROKEE CITIZENSHIP

| POST OFFICE: Coldwater, Kan. | | ATTORNEY: L.B. Bell | |
|---|---|---|---|
| NO | NAMES | AGE | SEX |
| 1 | Martha Jackson | 34 | Female |

ANCESTOR: Mary Crews

The Commission decide against claimant. See decision in case Andrew Meredith Docket 2180 Book E, Page 26 and case John Henly Docket 1250, Book C Page 376.

63

# Cherokee Citizenship Commission Docket Books
## (1880-84, 1887-89) Volume V
## Tahlequah, Cherokee Nation

Will.P. Ross
Chairman
John E. Gunter   Com

---

## JOLLY

**DOCKET #1936**

CENSUS ROLLS  1835, '48, '51, & '52

APPLICANT FOR CHEROKEE CITIZENSHIP

| POST OFFICE: Honey Grove, Texas | | ATTORNEY: Boudinot & Rasmus | |
|---|---|---|---|
| No | NAMES | AGE | SEX |
| 1 | Mrs. A. M. Jolly | 44 | Female |
| 2 | Jennie Jolly | 18 | " |

ANCESTOR:  Ward

See decision in the John Ward case.
Book A, Page 231.
See the same case in Book A. 268.

Attest
D.S. Williams
Asst  Clk  Com.

Will.P. Ross
Chairman
J.E. Gunter   Com

---

## JOHNSON

**DOCKET #1937**

CENSUS ROLLS  1835, '46

APPLICANT FOR CHEROKEE CITIZENSHIP

| POST OFFICE: | | ATTORNEY: A.E. Ivey | |
|---|---|---|---|
| No | NAMES | AGE | SEX |
| 1 | Nancy C. Johnson | 37 | Female |
| 2 | Horrace A. Johnson | 19 | Male |
| 3 | May F. Johnson | 14 | Female |
| 4 | William V. Johnson | 12 | Male |
| 5 | Samuel H. Johnson | 9 | " |
| 6 | Perle E. Johnson | 5 | Female |

ANCESTOR:

64

# Cherokee Citizenship Commission Docket Books
## (1880-84, 1887-89) Volume V
## Tahlequah, Cherokee Nation

*Commission on Citizenship.*

CHEROKEE NATION, IND. TER.

*Tahlequah,* August 28[th] 1889

Nancy C Johnson  
    VS.        Application for Cherokee Citizenship  
Cherokee Nation

    The above applicant claims to derive her Cherokee blood through her father and mother Henry and Polly Gibson whose names she believes will appear upon the Cherokee census roll taken in the year 1835. To sustain the allegations in claimant's application, she submits as evidence four affidavits, all of which are "exparte" also affiants know nothing of claimant's Cherokee blood, from their own personal knowledge, but gain this information from other persons. This evidence is not sufficient to establish applicant's claim of Cherokee blood while ~~also~~ the names of Henry and Polly Gibson, applicant's ancestors, does not appear upon the census roll of 1835.

    Therefore in view of these facts, we decide that applicant Nancy C. Johnson age 37 yrs and her children Horrace Johnson age 19 yrs, May F. Johnson age 14 yrs, William F[sic] Johnson age 12 yrs, Samuel Johnson age 9 yrs and Pearl E. Johnson age 5 yrs are not Cherokees by blood and not entitled to citizenship in the Cherokee Nation. Post Office *(no address given)*

                        Will.P. Ross  
                        Chairman  
                        J.E. Gunter    Com

## JACOBS

**DOCKET #1938**  
CENSUS ROLLS 1835 to 1852

APPLICANT FOR CHEROKEE CITIZENSHIP

| POST OFFICE: Mountainburg, Ark | | ATTORNEY: A.E. Ivey | |
|---|---|---|---|
| NO | NAMES | AGE | SEX |
| 1 | Mary Jacobs | 26 | Female |

65

| 2 | Eddie M. Jacobs | 9 | Male |
|---|---|---|---|

**ANCESTOR:** Rachel Gibson

Office Commission on Citizenship
Tahlequah C.N.  June 20[th] 1889

There being no evidence in support of the above named case the Commission decide that Mary Jacobs aged 26 years and her son Eddie M. Jacobs aged 9 years are not Cherokees by blood.

Attest                                      Will.P. Ross
  EG Ross                                            Chairman
    Clerk Commission                    J.E. Gunter   Com

## JONES

**DOCKET #1939**
CENSUS ROLLS  1835

APPLICANT FOR CHEROKEE CITIZENSHIP

| POST OFFICE: Barclay, Kan. | | ATTORNEY: A.E. Ivey | |
|---|---|---|---|
| NO | NAMES | AGE | SEX |
| 1 | Elie E. Jones | 41 | Male |
| 2 | Allison Jones | | |
| 3 | Harry Jones | | |

**ANCESTOR:** Jesse Hutchins

Rejected Sept 5[th] 1889

Office Commission on Citizenship
Cherokee Nation Ind Ter
Tahlequah  Sept. 5[th] 1889

The above case was submitted by Atty A.E. Ivey without evidence.  The Commission therefore decide that Elie E. Jones age 41 yrs and Addison[sic] Jones, Harry Jones are not Cherokees by blood. P.O. Barclay Kans.

Attest                                      Will.P. Ross
  D.S. Williams                                  Chairman
  Asst  Clk Com.                        J.E. Gunter   Com

# Cherokee Citizenship Commission Docket Books (1880-84, 1887-89) Volume V
## Tahlequah, Cherokee Nation

## JONES

**DOCKET #1940**

CENSUS ROLLS 1835

APPLICANT FOR CHEROKEE CITIZENSHIP

| POST OFFICE: Columbus, Kan. | | ATTORNEY: A.E. Ivey | |
|---|---|---|---|
| NO | NAMES | AGE | SEX |
| 1 | Leander H. Jones | 45 | Male |
| 2 | Mamie L. Jones | 3 | Female |
| 3 | Lola F. Jones | 2 | " |

ANCESTOR: Jesse Hutchins

Rejected Sept 5<sup>th</sup> 1889

Office Commission on Citizenship
Cherokee Nation Ind Ter
Tahlequah Sept. 5<sup>th</sup> 1889

The above case was called and submitted by Atty A.E. Ivey without evidence. Therefore the Commission decide that Leander H. Jones age 45 yrs and the following children Mamie L. Jones 3 yrs, Lola F. Jones Female 2 yrs are not Cherokees by blood. P.O. Columbus, Kans.

Will.P. Ross

Attest            Chairman

     D.S. Williams         J.E. Gunter    Com

     Asst   Clk   Com.

---

## JONES

**DOCKET #1941**

CENSUS ROLLS 1835

APPLICANT FOR CHEROKEE CITIZENSHIP

| POST OFFICE: Burlington, Kansas | | ATTORNEY: A.E. Ivey | |
|---|---|---|---|
| NO | NAMES | AGE | SEX |
| 1 | Franklin D. Jones | 38 | Male |
| 2 | Glenn H. Jones | 8 | " |
| 3 | Josie L. Jones | 6 | Female |
| 4 | Edgar F. Jones | 3 | Male |

ANCESTOR: Jesse Hutchins

Rejected Sept 5<sup>th</sup> 1889

# Cherokee Citizenship Commission Docket Books
## (1880-84, 1887-89) Volume V
## Tahlequah, Cherokee Nation

Office Commission on Citizenship
Cherokee Nation Ind Ter
Tahlequah  Sept. 5<sup>th</sup> 1889

The above case was called and submitted by Atty A.E. Ivey without evidence. The Commission therefore decide that Franklin D. Jones age 38 yrs and the following children Glenn H. Jones male 8 yrs, Josie L. Jones Female 6 yrs, Edgar F. Jones male 3 yrs are not Cherokees by blood.
P.O. Burlington, Kans.

                                    Will.P. Ross
Attest                                  Chairman
    D.S. Williams                    J.E. Gunter   Com
    Asst  Clk  Com.

---

## JOHNSON

**DOCKET #1942**
CENSUS ROLLS  1835

APPLICANT FOR CHEROKEE CITIZENSHIP

| POST OFFICE: Flint, C.N. | | ATTORNEY: Ivey & Welch | |
|---|---|---|---|
| No | NAMES | AGE | SEX |
| 1 | Charles Johnson | 39 | Male |
| 2 | Andrew Johnson | 1 | " |

ANCESTOR: Nannie Oo-yah-sis-tah

Rejected Sept. 5<sup>th</sup> 1889

Office Commission on Citizenship
Cherokee Nation Ind Ter
Tahlequah  Sept. 6<sup>th</sup> 1889

The Commission decide against the applicant in the above named case. Charles Johnson age 39 yrs and his Son Andrew Johnson age one year, for reasons set forth in the case of Jaily Johnson, Docket 1947, Book D, Page 433. P.O. Flint Ind. Ter.

                                    Will.P. Ross
Attest                                  Chairman
    D.S. Williams                    J.E. Gunter   Com
    Asst  Clk  Com.

---

# Cherokee Citizenship Commission Docket Books
## (1880-84, 1887-89) Volume V
## Tahlequah, Cherokee Nation

## JOHNSON

**DOCKET #1943**

CENSUS ROLLS 1835

APPLICANT FOR CHEROKEE CITIZENSHIP

| POST OFFICE: Salisaw[sic], Ind. Ter. | | ATTORNEY: Ivey & Welch | |
|---|---|---|---|
| No | NAMES | AGE | SEX |
| 1 | James Johnson | 39 | Male |
| 2 | Alexander Bowlen | 6 | " |
| 3 | Emanda[sic] Bowlen | 4 | Female |
| 4 | Tell A. Bowlen | 1 | Male |

ANCESTOR: Nannie Oo-yah-sis-tah

Rejected Sept. 5[th] 1889

Office Commission on Citizenship
Cherokee Nation Ind Ter
Tahlequah Sept. 6[th] 1889

The Commission decide against the applicant in the above named case. James Johnson age 39 years and his daughter Amanda age 4 years, and sons Alexander Bowlen aage[sic] 6 yrs and Tell A. Johnson age 1 year, fo reasons set forth in the case of Jaily Johnson, Docket 1947, Book D, Page 433. P.O. Sallisaw Ind. Ter.

Will.P. Ross

Attest                                         Chairman

    D.S. Williams               J.E. Gunter   Com

    Asst  Clk  Com.

---

## JONES

**DOCKET #1944**

CENSUS ROLLS 1851

APPLICANT FOR CHEROKEE CITIZENSHIP

| POST OFFICE: Talking Rock, Ga. | | ATTORNEY: A.E. Ivey | |
|---|---|---|---|
| No | NAMES | AGE | SEX |
| 1 | Josephine Jones | 30 | Female |
| 2 | Mollie Jones | 12 | " |
| 3 | David Jones | 11 | Male |
| 4 | William Jones | 9 | " |

| 5 | Victoria Jones | 7 | Female |
|---|---|---|---|
| 6 | Mattie Jones | 6 | " |
| 7 | Thomas Jones | 4 | Male |
| 8 | Violet A. Jones | 2 | Female |

**ANCESTOR:** Mary Arwood

Rejected Sept. 5th 1889

Office Commission on Citizenship
Cherokee Nation Ind Ter
Tahlequah Sept. 5th 1889

The above case was called and submitted by Atty A.E. Ivey without evidence. The Commission decide that Josephine Jones age 30 yrs and the following children, Mollie Female 12, David male 11, William 9, Victora[sic] Female 7, Mathis[sic] Female 6 yrs, Thomas male 4, and Violet A. Jones Female 2 yrs. are not Cherokees by blood. P.O. Talking Rock, Ga.

Attest
    D.S. Williams
    Asst Clk Com.

Will.P. Ross
Chairman
J.E. Gunter   Com

---

## JOBE

**DOCKET #1945**

CENSUS ROLLS 1835

APPLICANT FOR CHEROKEE CITIZENSHIP

| POST OFFICE: Bentonville, Ark. | | ATTORNEY: Ivey & Welch | |
|---|---|---|---|
| NO | NAMES | AGE | SEX |
| 1 | A.P. and H.B. Jobe | 28<br>20 | Male |

**ANCESTOR:** Nannie Oo-yah-sis-tah

Rejected Sept. 5th 1889

Office Commission on Citizenship
Cherokee Nation Ind Ter
Tahlequah Sept. 6th 1889

The Commission decide against the claimants in the above named case. A.P. Jobe age 28 years and H.B. Jobe age 20 yrs for reasons stated in the case of Jaily Johnson Docket 1947, B.D. Page 433. P.O. Bentonville Arkansas.

# Cherokee Citizenship Commission Docket Books (1880-84, 1887-89) Volume V
## Tahlequah, Cherokee Nation

Will.P. Ross

Attest               Chairman

    D.S. Williams        J.E. Gunter   Com

    Asst   Clk   Com.

---

## JONES

**DOCKET #1946**

CENSUS ROLLS 1835

APPLICANT FOR CHEROKEE CITIZENSHIP

| POST OFFICE: Wau-hil-lah, Ind. Ter. | | ATTORNEY: A.E. Ivey | |
|---|---|---|---|
| No | NAMES | AGE | SEX |
| 1 | Jesse P. Jones | 33 | Male |
| 2 | Rachel Jones (Mother) | 70 | Female |
| 3 | Sallie Woodall | 52 | " |
| 4 | Mary Jones | 50 | " |
| 5 | William Jones | 46 | Male |
| 6 | Elias Jones | 42 | " |
| 7 | Joseph Jones | 35 | " |
| 8 | Jesse Jones | 33 | " |
| 9 | Amanda Wadkins | 30 | Female |

ANCESTOR: Rachel Jones

Rejected Sept. 5th 1889

Office Commission on Citizenship

Cherokee Nation Ind Ter

Tahlequah Sept. 5th 1889

The above case was called and submitted by Atty A.E. Ivey without evidence. The Commission therefore decide that Jesse P. Jones age 33 yrs and his wife[sic] Rachel Jones Female age 70 yrs and the following children, Sallie Woodard age 52 yrs. Daughter, and Mary Jones Female age 50 yrs, and William male 46 yrs, Elias male 42 yrs, Joseph male 35 yrs, Jesse Jones male 33 yrs and Amanda Wadkins Daughter 30 yrs are not Cherokees by blood.

P.O. Wau-hil-lah, Ind. Ter.

# Cherokee Citizenship Commission Docket Books
## (1880-84, 1887-89) Volume V
## Tahlequah, Cherokee Nation

Will.P. Ross

Chairman

Attest                                J.E. Gunter   Com

D.S. Williams

Asst  Clk  Com.

---

## JOHNSON

**DOCKET #1947**

CENSUS ROLLS  1835

APPLICANT FOR CHEROKEE CITIZENSHIP

| POST OFFICE: Salisaw[sic], I.T. | | ATTORNEY: Ivey & Welch | |
|---|---|---|---|
| No | NAMES | AGE | SEX |
| 1 | Jaily Johnson | 52 | Male[sic] |

**ANCESTOR:** Nannie Oo-yah-sis-tah

Rejected Sept. 5[th] 1889

Office Commission on Citizenship

Cherokee Nation Ind Ter

Tahlequah  Sept. 5[th] 1889

The application in this case was filed Oct. 4[th] 1887.  The applicant set fourth[sic] in her application that she is the grand daughter of one Wannie[sic] Oo-yah-sis-ter[sic], whose name will be found on the census rolls of Cherokees by blood taken and made in the year 1835.  in support of this statement the applicant offers the testimony of John Ross, alone, which does not establish the Cherokee blood of Oo-yah-sis-ter, nor does it establish the fact that the applicant is the grand daughter of the aforesaid Oo-yah-sis-ter and on examination of the census rolls of Cherokees by blood taken and made in the year 1835, the Commission fails to find the name of Oo-yah-sis-ter.  Therefore the Commission decide that Jaily Johnson age 52 years is not of Cherokee blood and not entitled to Cherokee citizenship. P.O. Salisaw[sic] I.T.

Will.P. Ross

Attest                                Chairman

D.S. Williams                  J.E. Gunter   Com

Asst  Clk  Com.

---

5

72

# Cherokee Citizenship Commission Docket Books
## (1880-84, 1887-89) Volume V
## Tahlequah, Cherokee Nation

## JAMES

**DOCKET #1948**

CENSUS ROLLS  1835 to 1852

APPLICANT FOR CHEROKEE CITIZENSHIP

| POST OFFICE: Mulberry, Ark. | | ATTORNEY: A.E. Ivey | |
|---|---|---|---|
| No | NAMES | AGE | SEX |
| 1 | J.T. James | 33 | Male |
| 2 | Nora James | 11 | Female |
| 3 | Eula James | 9 | " |
| 4 | Warren James | 3 | Male |

ANCESTOR: Prather

Rejected Sept. 5th 1889

Office Commission on Citizenship
Cherokee Nation Ind Ter
Tahlequah  Sept. 5th 1889

The above case was called and submitted by Atty A.E. Ivey without evidence. The Commission decide that J.T. James age 33 yrs and the following children Nora James Female 11 yrs, Eula 9 yrs, & Warner[sic] James male 3 yrs are not Cherokees by blood.  P.O. Mulberry Ark.

Will.P. Ross
Chairman
Attest
D.S. Williams                              J.E. Gunter   Com
Asst  Clk  Com.

## JOHNSON

**DOCKET #1949**

CENSUS ROLLS  1835 to 1852

APPLICANT FOR CHEROKEE CITIZENSHIP

| POST OFFICE: Van Alstyne, Tex | | ATTORNEY: A.E. Ivey | |
|---|---|---|---|
| No | NAMES | AGE | SEX |
| 1 | S.M. Johnson | 26 | Female |

ANCESTOR: Henry Kent

Rejected Sept. 5th 1889

Office Commission on Citizenship
Cherokee Nation Ind Ter
Tahlequah  Sept. 5th 1889

The above case was called and submitted by Atty A.E. Ivey without evidence. The Commission decide that S.M. Johnson age 26 yrs. is not a Cherokee by blood. P.O. Van Alstyne Tex.

|  | Will.P. Ross |
| --- | --- |
| Attest | Chairman |
| D.S. Williams | J.E. Gunter   Com |
| Asst  Clk  Com. | |

## JAMES

**DOCKET #1950**

CENSUS ROLLS  1835 to 1852

APPLICANT FOR CHEROKEE CITIZENSHIP

| POST OFFICE: Little River, Texas | | ATTORNEY: A.E. Ivey | |
| --- | --- | --- | --- |
| NO | NAMES | AGE | SEX |
| 1 | W.M. James | 26 | Female |

ANCESTOR: Mrs. Tatum

Rejected Sept. 5th 1889

Office Commission on Citizenship
Cherokee Nation Ind Ter
Tahlequah Sept. 5th 1889

The above case was called and submitted by Atty A.E. Ivey without evidence. The Commission therefore decide that W.M. James age 26 yrs. is not a Cherokee by blood. P.O. Little River, Texas.

|  | Will.P. Ross |
| --- | --- |
| Attest | Chairman |
| D.S. Williams | J.E. Gunter   Com |
| Asst  Clk  Com. | |

# Cherokee Citizenship Commission Docket Books
## (1880-84, 1887-89) Volume V
## Tahlequah, Cherokee Nation

## JOHNSON

**DOCKET #1951**

CENSUS ROLLS 1835

APPLICANT FOR CHEROKEE CITIZENSHIP

| POST OFFICE: Van Buren, Ark. | | ATTORNEY: Ivey & Welch | |
|---|---|---|---|
| **NO** | **NAMES** | **AGE** | **SEX** |
| 1 | Alander[sic] Johnson | 43 | Male |
| 2 | Sarah J. Johnson | 36 | Female |
| 3 | Sidney Johnson | 17 | Male |
| 4 | Florenda Johnson | 15 | Female |
| 5 | Marian Johnson | 13 | Male |
| 6 | Richard Johnson | 10 | " |
| 7 | Rollie Johnson | 6 | " |

ANCESTOR: Oyah Sistah

Rejected Sept. 5th 1889

Office Commission on Citizenship
Cherokee Nation Ind Ter
Tahlequah Sept. 6th 1889

In the above named case the Commission decide that the claimant Alexander Johnson age 43 years and his wife Sarah J. Johnson and daughter Florenca Johnson 15 yrs, Richard Johnson 10 yrs and Rollie Johnson 6 yrs for reasons given in the case of Jaily Johnson Docket 1947, Book D, Page 433. P.O. Van Buren Arkansas.

Will.P. Ross

Attest

Chairman

D.S. Williams

J.E. Gunter   Com

Asst  Clk  Com.

---

## JONES

**DOCKET #1952**

CENSUS ROLLS

APPLICANT FOR CHEROKEE CITIZENSHIP

| POST OFFICE: Burlington, Kan. | | ATTORNEY: A.E. Ivey | |
|---|---|---|---|
| **NO** | **NAMES** | **AGE** | **SEX** |
| 1 | James I. Jones | 44 | Male |

| 2 | Horrace Greeley Jones | 18 | " |
| 3 | Grace Jones | 15 | Female |
| 4 | J.W. Jones | 10 | Male |
| 5 | Eugenia Jones | 4 | Female |
| 6 | Chas. Ogan Jones | 2 | Male |

**ANCESTOR:** Jim Jones

Rejected Sept. 13th 1889

Office Commission on Citizenship
Cherokee Nation Ind Ter
Tahlequah Sept. 5th 1889

The above case was called and submitted by Atty A.E. Ivey without evidence. The Commission therefore decide that James I. Jones age 33 yrs. and the following children Horrace Greeley male 18 yrs, Gracie female 15 yrs, J.W. male 10 yrs, Eugenia female 4 yrs and Chas Ogan Jones male 2 years are not Cherokees by blood. P.O. Burlington Kans.

Will.P. Ross
Chairman
Attest                                    R. Bunch      Com
    D.S. Williams                         J.E. Gunter   Com
Asst  Clk  Com.

---

## JONES

**DOCKET #1953**

CENSUS ROLLS

APPLICANT FOR CHEROKEE CITIZENSHIP

| POST OFFICE: Burlington Kan. | | ATTORNEY: A.E. Ivey | |
|---|---|---|---|
| NO | NAMES | AGE | SEX |
| 1 | Isaac C. Jones | 37 | Male |

**ANCESTOR:** Jim Jones

Rejected Sept. 5th 1889

Office Commission on Citizenship
Cherokee Nation Ind Ter
Tahlequah Sept. 5th 1889

The above case was called and submitted by Atty A.E. Ivey without evidence. The Commission therefore decide that Isaac C. Jones age 37 yrs is not a Cherokee by blood. P.O. Burlington, Kan.

76

# Cherokee Citizenship Commission Docket Books
## (1880-84, 1887-89) Volume V
## Tahlequah, Cherokee Nation

Will.P. Ross
Chairman

Attest

D.S. Williams

Asst   Clk   Com.

J.E. Gunter   Com

---

## JONES

**DOCKET #1954**

CENSUS ROLLS

APPLICANT FOR CHEROKEE CITIZENSHIP

| POST OFFICE: Lebo, Kan. | | ATTORNEY: | |
|---|---|---|---|
| NO | NAMES | AGE | SEX |
| 1 | Albert Jones | 49 | Male |
| 2 | Kittie E. Jones | 17 | Female |
| 3 | Lillie A. Jones | 15 | " |
| 4 | Mattie M. Jones | 13 | " |

ANCESTOR:  Sarah Elmore

Adverse.  See decision of the Commission in case
John R. Henly Docket 553, Book B, Page 266.

Will.P. Ross     Chairman

R. Bunch     Com

J.E. Gunter     Com

---

## JOHNSON

**DOCKET #1955**

CENSUS ROLLS  1835 to 1852

APPLICANT FOR CHEROKEE CITIZENSHIP

| POST OFFICE: Van Buren Ark | | ATTORNEY: A.E. Ivey | |
|---|---|---|---|
| NO | NAMES | AGE | SEX |
| 1 | Younger Johnson | 40 | Male |
| 2 | Fielden H. Johnson | 14 | Male |
| 3 | Henry C. Johnson | 14 | " |
| 4 | Wm M. Johnson | 11 | " |
| 5 | George W. Johnson | 8 | " |

twins

| 6 | Mary S. Johnson | 6 | Female |

**ANCESTOR:** Ross Azbell

Rejected Sept. 5<sup>th</sup> 1889

Office Commission on Citizenship
Cherokee Nation Ind Ter
Tahlequah Sept. 6<sup>th</sup> 1889

The Commission decide against the applicant in the above named case because it is presented without evidence. Younger Johnson age 40 yrs, Fielden H. Johnson and twin brother Henry C. Johnson age 14 yrs, Wm M. Johnson 11 yrs and Geo. W. Johnson 8 yrs and Mary S. Johnson age 6 years.
P.O. Van Buren Arkansas.

Will.P. Ross

Attest
    D.S. Williams
    Asst Clk Com.

Chairman
J.E. Gunter   Com

## JOHNSON

**DOCKET #1956**
CENSUS ROLLS 1835 to 1852

APPLICANT FOR CHEROKEE CITIZENSHIP

| POST OFFICE: Wau-hilla, Ind. Ter. | | ATTORNEY: A.E. Ivey | |
|---|---|---|---|
| NO | NAMES | AGE | SEX |
| 1 | Jaley Johnson | 55 | Female |

**ANCESTOR:** Ross Azbill

The above case coming up for final hearing on this day, the 11<sup>th</sup> day of Oct 1888, and all the testimony as well as the rolls mentioned in the 7th Sec. of the Act of Dec. 8th 1886, being duly duly[sic] examined, it is adjudged and determined by the Commission on Citizenship, in the absence of the name of Ross Azbill, the alleged Cherokee ancestor, appearing on some of these rolls mentioned in the 7th Sec. of said Act of Dec. 8th 1886, or the name of the applicant herself, that she is not of Cherokee descent, and not entitled to any of the rights and privileges of Cherokee citizens on account of her blood, and Jaley Johnson is therefore declared to be an intruder upon the public domain of the Cherokee Nation.

# Cherokee Citizenship Commission Docket Books
## (1880-84, 1887-89) Volume V
## Tahlequah, Cherokee Nation

J. T. Adair    Chairman Commission
H.C. Barnes   Commissioner

Office Commission on Citizenship
   Tahlequah I.T.  Oct. 11<sup>th</sup> 1888

## JONES

**DOCKET #1957**
CENSUS ROLLS

APPLICANT FOR CHEROKEE CITIZENSHIP

| POST OFFICE: Strawn, Kan. | | ATTORNEY: | |
|---|---|---|---|
| **NO** | **NAMES** | **AGE** | **SEX** |
| 1 | Milton Jones | 34 | Male |
| 2 | Orla Cope Jones | 12 | Female |
| 3 | Stella May Jones | 10 | " |
| 4 | Frank Melton Jones | 8 | Male |
| 5 | Thomas Elmer Jones | 2 | " |

ANCESTOR: Sarah Elmore

Adverse. See decision of the Commission in case John
R. Henly Docket 553, Book B, Page 266.

Will.P. Ross    Chairman
R. Bunch    Com
J.E. Gunter    Com

## JONES

**DOCKET #1958**
CENSUS ROLLS

APPLICANT FOR CHEROKEE CITIZENSHIP

| POST OFFICE: Blue Jacket, Ind. Ter. | | ATTORNEY: | |
|---|---|---|---|
| **NO** | **NAMES** | **AGE** | **SEX** |
| 1 | Thomas N. Jones | 46 | Male |
| 2 | Alfred M. Jones | 23 | " |
| 3 | Lyndley M. Jones | 20 | " |
| 4 | Lucinda Jones | 18 | Female |
| 5 | John J Jones | 16 | Male |

79

| 6 | Hattie Jones | 14 | Female |
|---|---|---|---|
| 7 | Mary Jones | 9 | " |

**ANCESTOR:** Sarah Elmore

Adverse. See decision of the Commission in case
John R. Henly Docket 553, Book B, Page 266.

|  | Will.P. Ross    Chairman |
|---|---|
| Attest | R. Bunch    Com |
| D.S. Williams | J.E. Gunter    Com |
| Asst   Clk   Com. |  |

---

## JOHNSON

**DOCKET #1959**
CENSUS ROLLS  1835 to 1852

APPLICANT FOR CHEREKEE CITIZENSHIP

| POST OFFICE: Salisaw[sic], I.T. | | ATTORNEY: A.E. Ivey | |
|---|---|---|---|
| **NO** | **NAMES** | **AGE** | **SEX** |
| 1 | Stephen Johnson | 26 | Male |
| 2 | Jesse Johnson | 1 | " |

**ANCESTOR:** Rose Azbill

Rejected Sept. 5th 1889

Office Commission on Citizenship
Cherokee Nation Ind Ter
Tahlequah  Sept. 6th 1889

The above named case having been submitted by Attorney without evidence,
The Commission decide against the claimant Stephen Johnson age 26 years, and
his son Jesse Johnson age one year. P.O. Indian Territory.

|  | Will.P. Ross |
|---|---|
| Attest | Chairman |
| D.S. Williams | J.E. Gunter    Com |
| Asst   Clk   Com. |  |

---

80

# Cherokee Citizenship Commission Docket Books (1880-84, 1887-89) Volume V Tahlequah, Cherokee Nation

## JARNAGIN

**DOCKET #1960**

CENSUS ROLLS

APPLICANT FOR CHEROKEE CITIZENSHIP

| POST OFFICE: Mossy Creek | | ATTORNEY: L.B. Bell | |
|---|---|---|---|
| NO | NAMES | AGE | SEX |
| 1 | Kate D. Jarnagin | 34 | Female |
| 2 | Esbelle S. Jarnagin | 10 | " |

ANCESTOR: Ann Crews

The Commission decide against claimant. See decision in the case of Andrew Meredith Docket 2180 Book E, Page 26 and John Henly Docket 1250, Book C Page 376.

Will.P. Ross  Chairman

John E. Gunter  Com

---

## JOURDAN

**DOCKET #1961**

CENSUS ROLLS

APPLICANT FOR CHEROKEE CITIZENSHIP

| POST OFFICE: Cincinnati, Ark | | ATTORNEY: C.H. Taylor | |
|---|---|---|---|
| NO | NAMES | AGE | SEX |
| 1 | Jessy Jourdan (Guardian) | 70 | Male |
| 2 | Emma J. Dickson | 11 | Female |
| 3 | Jesse H. Dickson | 9 | Male |

ANCESTOR: River Jourdan

Rejected April 30, 1889

April 30th 1889

The above case Jessey[sic] Jourdan is an application filed Oct. 5th 1887 by a guardian for the re-admission of his grand children Emma J. Dickson aged eleven years and Jesse H. Dickson aged nine years for admission as the grand children of one River Jourdan whose names would be found on the census rolls of Cherokees by blood taken in the year 1835. It is submitted by Attorney without evidence and the Commission decide that the said Jesse H. Dickson and Emma J. Dickson are not Cherokees by blood.

81

Will.P. Ross

This May 1<sup>st</sup> 1889                                    Chairman
D.S. Williams                          John E. Gunter   Com
Clk. Com
Tah. I.T.

---

### JONES

**DOCKET #1962**
CENSUS ROLLS  1851 to 1852

APPLICANT FOR CHEROKEE CITIZENSHIP

| POST OFFICE: Green Forest, Ark. | | ATTORNEY: L.B. Bell | |
|---|---|---|---|
| **No** | **NAMES** | **AGE** | **SEX** |
| 1 | Theodore Jones | 21 | Male |
| 2 | Elizabeth Jones | 19 | Female |
| 3 | Caledonia Jones | 16 | " |
| 4 | Margaret A. Jones | 10 | " |

ANCESTOR:  Elizabeth Hampton

Rejected Sept. 5<sup>th</sup> 1889

Office Commission on Citizenship
Cherokee Nation Ind Ter
Tahlequah  Sept. 5<sup>th</sup> 1889

This case having been submitted without evidence by the Attys, the Commission decide that Theodore Jones & Sister Elizabeth, Caledonia and Margaret Jones age 21, 19, 16 & 10 years, respectfully, are not Cherokees by blood and not entitled to Cherokee citizenship. P.O. Green Forest Ark.

Will.P. Ross
Attest                                          Chairman
D.S. Williams                          J.E. Gunter   Com
Asst  Clk  Com.

---

82

# Cherokee Citizenship Commission Docket Books
# (1880-84, 1887-89) Volume V
# Tahlequah, Cherokee Nation

## JOBE

**DOCKET #1963**

CENSUS ROLLS 1835, '48, '51, & '52

APPLICANT FOR CHEROKEE CITIZENSHIP

| POST OFFICE: Russelville[sic], Ark | | ATTORNEY: Boudinot & Rasmus | |
|---|---|---|---|
| NO | NAMES | AGE | SEX |
| 1 | Sallie F. Jobe | 32 | Female |
| 2 | Cora Edna Jobe | 13 | " |
| 3 | Floy Bessie Jobe | 11 | " |

ANCESTOR:

Office Commission on Citizenship
Cherokee Nation June 20[th] 1889

There being no evidence in support of the above named case the Commission decide that Sallie F. Jobe aged 32 years and the following children Cora Edna aged 13 years and Floy Bessie Jobe aged 11 years are not Cherokees by blood.

Attest                                      Will.P. Ross
  E.G. Ross                                   Chairman
    Clerk Commission                    J.E. Gunter   Com

## JACKSON

**DOCKET #1964**

CENSUS ROLLS 1835, '48, '51, & '52

APPLICANT FOR CHEROKEE CITIZENSHIP

| POST OFFICE: Ladonia Texas | | ATTORNEY: Boudinot & Rasmus | |
|---|---|---|---|
| NO | NAMES | AGE | SEX |
| 1 | J.E. Jackson | 52 | Male |
| 2 | Fannie Jackson | 17 | Female |
| 3 | James Jackson | | Male |
| 4 | Charley Jackson | 20 | " |
| 5 | Brodie Jackson | 18 | " |
| 6 | Rosa Jackson | 16 | "[sic] |

ANCESTOR: D. Caldwell

Rejected Sept. 5[th] 1889

83

# Cherokee Citizenship Commission Docket Books
# (1880-84, 1887-89) Volume V
# Tahlequah, Cherokee Nation

Office Commission on Citizenship
Cherokee Nation Ind Ter
Tahlequah  Sept. 5<sup>th</sup> 1889

The Commission decide against the applicant in the above named case.  James E. Jackson age 52 years and his daughters Fannie 17 yrs and Rosa 16 yrs and sons, James Jackson, Charley Jackson 20 yrs, Brodie Jackson 18 yrs and four other children whose names are not given for reasons set forth in their decision in the case of Eliza M. Black.  See Docket 678 Book B, Page 393.

Will.P. Ross
Attest                                          Chairman
   D.S. Williams                        R. Bunch    Com
   Asst  Clk  Com.                    J.E. Gunter   Com

---

## JACKSON

**DOCKET #1965**
CENSUS ROLLS 1835 to 1852

APPLICANT FOR CHEROKEE CITIZENSHIP

| POST OFFICE: Siloam Springs, Ark | | ATTORNEY: L.S. Sanders | |
|---|---|---|---|
| No | NAMES | AGE | SEX |
| 1 | George W. Jackson | 57 | Male |
| 2 | Lida Ann Jackson | 30 | Female |
| 3 | George C. Jackson, Jr. | 17 | Male |

ANCESTOR: Thomas Jackson

Rejected June 3<sup>rd</sup> 1889

Office Commission on Citizenship
Cherokee Nation Ind Ter
Tahlequah  June 3<sup>rd</sup> 1889

The application in the above case was filed the 28<sup>th</sup> day of September 1887 and alleges that George W. Jackson is the son of Thomas Jasckson[sic] whose name should appear on the rolls of Cherokees by blood taken and made in 1835 to 1852.   The name of Thomas Jackson the Father and Burrell Jackson and Winniford Jackson nee Cook are not found on said rolls while the two affidavits of Moses Jackson and Hattie E. Simpson taken before D. Shafer, Notary Public of Benton County Arkansas the 30<sup>th</sup> day of August 1887 do not even allege that the applicant is of Cherokee blood. The Commission therefore decide that George W. Jackson aged 57 years and his daughter Lida Ann Jackson aged 30 years and son George C. Jackson, Jr. aged 17 years are not of Cherokee blood.

|  |  |  |
|---|---|---|
|  | Will.P. Ross | Chairman |
| Attest | J.E. Gunter | Com |
| D.S. Williams | R. Bunch | " |
| Asst  Clk  Com. |  |  |

---

## JOHNSON

**DOCKET #1966**

CENSUS ROLLS  1835, '48, '51, & '52

APPLICANT FOR CHEROKEE CITIZENSHIP

| POST OFFICE: Farmer, Ark | | ATTORNEY: Boudinot & Rasmus | |
|---|---|---|---|
| NO | NAMES | AGE | SEX |
| 1 | Mrs. N.M. Johnson | 55 | Female |
| 2 | R.M. Johnson | 17 | Male |
| 3 | Thomas ? Johnson | 14 | " |
| 4 | Leora A. Johnson | 10 | Female |

ANCESTOR: Leah Reeves

Rejected Aug. 28th 1889

Office Commission on Citizenship
Cherokee Nation Ind Ter
Tahlequah  Aug. 28th 1889

The above case was this day submitted by Attorney Rasmus without evidence. The Commission therefore decide that Mrs. N.M. Johnson nee Miles who claims to be the daughter of Leah Reeves and her sons R.M. Johnson age 17 yrs & Thomas W. Johnson age 14 yrs and daughter Leora Johnson age 10 years are not of Cherokee blood. P.O. Farmer Ark.

|  |  |
|---|---|
|  | Will.P. Ross |
| Attest | Chairman |
| D.S. Williams | J.E. Gunter  Com |
| Asst  Clk  Com. |  |

---

# Cherokee Citizenship Commission Docket Books
## (1880-84, 1887-89) Volume V
## Tahlequah, Cherokee Nation

## JACKSON

**DOCKET #1967**

CENSUS ROLLS 1835, '48, '58[sic], & '52

APPLICANT FOR CHEROKEE CITIZENSHIP

| POST OFFICE: Ladonia, Texas | | ATTORNEY: Boudinot & Rasmus | |
|---|---|---|---|
| No | NAMES | AGE | SEX |
| 1 | Andrew C. Jackson | 48 | Male |
| 2 | Mollie Jackson | | Female |
| 3 | Laura Jackson | | " |

ANCESTOR: D. Caldwell

Rejected Sept 5th 1889

Office Commission on Citizenship
Cherokee Nation Ind Ter
Tahlequah Sept. 5th 1889

The Commission decide against the claimant Andrew C. Jackson and his daughters Mollie Jackson, Laura Jackson, and one other whose name is not given in the above case for reasons set forth in their decision in the case of Eliza M. Jackson. See Docket 678, Book B, Page 393. P.O. Ladonia Texas.

Will.P. Ross
Chairman

Attest

   D.S. Williams

   Asst Clk Com.

R. Bunch   Com

J.E. Gunter   Com

## JOHNSON

**DOCKET #1968**

CENSUS ROLLS 1835 to 1852

APPLICANT FOR CHEROKEE CITIZENSHIP

| POST OFFICE: | | ATTORNEY: L.B. Bell | |
|---|---|---|---|
| No | NAMES | AGE | SEX |
| 1 | Louisa Johnson | | Female |

ANCESTOR: Ann Crews

The Commission decide against claimant. See decision in the case of Andrew Meredith Docket 2180 Book E, Page 26 and John Henly Docket 1250, Book C Page 376.

86

# Cherokee Citizenship Commission Docket Books (1880-84, 1887-89) Volume V
## Tahlequah, Cherokee Nation

Attest                  Will.P. Ross
    EG Ross                         Chairman
       Clerk Commission        John E. Gunter    Com

---

## JAMISON

**DOCKET #1969**
CENSUS ROLLS

APPLICANT FOR CHEROKEE CITIZENSHIP

| POST OFFICE: Anneville[sic] Texas now near Garfield I.T. July 28 '88 || ATTORNEY: C.H. Taylor ||
|---|---|---|---|
| NO | NAMES | AGE | SEX |
| 1 | Sidney R. Jamison | 45 | Female |

ANCESTOR: Mary Ray, Family Taylor

*Commission on Citizenship.*

CHEROKEE NATION, IND. TER.

Sidney R. Jamison and        *Tahlequah,* July 28th 1888
William H. Drake
     ( VS )          Applicants for Citizenship
Cherokee Nation

The above case being submitted by Plaintiffs Atty. C.H. Taylor, Esq. and the Nation's Atty. Hon. R.F. Wyly, agreeing to the same, submits as evidence the Rolls mentioned in the 7th Sec. of the Act creating and empowering this Commission, Approved Dec. 8th 1886.

All the evidence on part of the Plaintiffs goes to show that Sidney A. Jamison and William H. Drake are the grand children of William Taylor, whom they allege is or was of Cherokee Indian descent, and that he resided in Tennessee and Alabama, then part of the Old Nation, prior to and after the year 1835, and that his name should appear on the rolls of 1835 as a Cherokee Indian by blood. -     Now in summing up the evidence in this cause, as well as all others, it is useless to go further until we find out, by reference to the rolls laid down in the law, the name of the ancestor from whom the parties are trying to prove a lineal descent, or their own names. The name of William Taylor does

87

not appear on the census rolls of Cherokees made in the year 1835, but the Siler Roll, of 1851 does contain the name of one William Taylor, a son of David Taylor, at that time – 1851 – aged 20 years. He was a brother of John M. Taylor, who gave evidence in this case in which he says: that the William Taylor mentioned in the letter of the Hon. Commissioner of Indian Affairs under date of April 9[th] 1888, addressed to H.N. Jamison, Esq. Garfield, Ind. Ter. was his brother and that he died in this country in the year 1864, and that he left no family. Neither do the rolls mentioned in the law, the rolls of 1835 – 1848 – 1851 and 1852 contain the name of Mary Ray, nee Taylor. Therefore: We the Commission on Citizenship after examining carefully the evidence in this case and the census and pay rolls mentioned in the law, are of the opinion, in the absence of conclusive testimony, and the Rolls of Cherokees not setting the fact forth, that Sidney R. Jamison and William H. Drake and Jim M. Drake are not Cherokees by blood and are not entitled to the rights of such by virtue of their blood and are pronounced and declared to be intruders upon the public domain of the Cherokee Nation.

> J. T. Adair    Chairman Commission
> H.C. Barnes   Commissioner

---

## JARVIS

**DOCKET #1970**
CENSUS ROLLS  1835

APPLICANT FOR CHEROKEE CITIZENSHIP

| POST OFFICE: Erie, Kansas | | ATTORNEY: L.B. Bell | |
|---|---|---|---|
| No | NAMES | AGE | SEX |
| 1 | Allie Jarvis | 21 | Female |
| 2 | Quida Jones | 4 | " |

ANCESTOR:  W.T. England

Rejected Sept. 6[th] 1889

> Office Commission on Citizenship
> Cherokee Nation Ind Ter
> Tahlequah  Sept. 6[th] 1889

The above case was called and submitted by Atty without evidence. The Commission therefore decide that Allie Jarvis age 21 yrs and Quida Jarvis[sic] Female 4 yrs are not Cherokees by blood. P.O. Erie Kansas.

# Cherokee Citizenship Commission Docket Books (1880-84, 1887-89) Volume V
# Tahlequah, Cherokee Nation

Will.P. Ross
Chairman

Attest
D.S. Williams
Asst Clk Com.

J.E. Gunter Com

---

## JOHNSON

**DOCKET #1971**

CENSUS ROLLS 1835 to 1852

APPLICANT FOR CHEROKEE CITIZENSHIP

| POST OFFICE: Farmington Kan | | ATTORNEY: L.S. Sanders | |
|---|---|---|---|
| No | NAMES | AGE | SEX |
| 1 | Kate Johnson | 41 | Female |
| 2 | Luna T. Johnson | 21 | " |
| 3 | Dibrell C. Johnson | 18 | Male |
| 4 | Orris S. Johnson | 17 | " |
| 5 | Medley O. Johnson | 15 | " |
| 6 | Richard C. Johnson | 13 | " |
| 7 | Walter S. Johnson | 11 | " |
| 8 | Alley G. Johnson | 9 | " |
| 9 | Jesse D. Johnson | 7 | " |

ANCESTOR: Isaac N. Miller

Rejected Sept. 6th 1889

Office Commission on Citizenship
Cherokee Nation Ind Ter
Tahlequah Sept. 6th 1889

The above case was called 3 times and submitted by Atty without evidence. The Commission therefore decide that Kate Johnson age 41 yrs, Luna T. Daughter female 21 yrs, Dibrell C. Johnson male 18 yrs, Orris S. male 17 yrs, Medley O. male 15 yrs son, Richard C. male 13 yrs, Walter S. male 11 yrs, Alley G. male 9 yrs & Jesse D. Johnson male 7 yrs are not Cherokees by blood. Post Office Farmington Kansas.

Will.P. Ross
Chairman

Attest
D.S. Williams
Asst Clk Com.

J.E. Gunter Com

89

## JESSUP

**DOCKET #1972**

CENSUS ROLLS  1835, '48, '51, & '52

APPLICANT FOR CHEROKEE CITIZENSHIP

| POST OFFICE: Plainfield, Indiana | | ATTORNEY: Boudinot & Rasmus | |
|---|---|---|---|
| NO | NAMES | AGE | SEX |
| 1 | Massey Jessup | 55 | Male |

ANCESTOR:

*Commission on Citizenship.*

CHEROKEE NATION, IND. TER.

*Tahlequah,* Sept. 6th 1889

Massy Jessup
    vs.           Application for Cherokee Citizenship
Cherokee Nation

     The above named applicant filed his claim of Cherokee blood, before the Interior Department at Washington D.C. and by the Secretary of the Interior. The application was transmitted to this Commission. In claimant's declaration taken before the U.S. clerk of the state of Indiana on the ? day of March 1885, says that she is a Cherokee by blood, that she derived said blood through her mother Massy Sanders who was a Cherokee by descent & was born in the state of South Carolina on the 7th day of Oct. ~~18~~ 1789 & died in Hendricks County, state of Indiana on the 23rd day of May 1854.

     The burden of proof is always on the Plaintiff in any suit & so the same principals of law governs this case & as the claimant submits only his own affidavits in support of his case we do not decree it sufficient to admit him to Cherokee citizenship. The applicant *(illegible)* fails to name any of the census rolls of Cherokees taken by the U.S. Gov't in the years 1835, 48, 51 & 1852 where the name of his ancestor might be found. In consideration of these facts, The Commission ~~we~~ decide & so declare, that applicant Massey Jessup & her children, Sarah A. Jessup age 34 yrs & Lydia A. Jessup age 27 yrs are not Cherokees by blood. P.O. Plainfield, Indiana.

# Cherokee Citizenship Commission Docket Books (1880-84, 1887-89) Volume V
## Tahlequah, Cherokee Nation

Will.P. Ross
Chairman
J.E. Gunter   Com

---

## NELSON

**DOCKET #1973**

CENSUS ROLLS  1835 to 1852

APPLICANT FOR CHEROKEE CITIZENSHIP

| POST OFFICE: Lewisville, Texas | | ATTORNEY: A.E. Ivey | |
|---|---|---|---|
| NO | NAMES | AGE | SEX |
| 1 | E.M. Nelson | | Male |

ANCESTOR: Wein

Rejected Sept. 6[th] 1889

Office Commission on Citizenship
Cherokee Nation Ind Ter
Tahlequah  Sept. 6[th] 1889

The above case was submitted by Atty without evidence.  The Commission therefore decide that E.M. Nelson is not a Cherokee by blood. P.O. Lewisville Texas.

Will.P. Ross
Chairman

Attest

D.S. Williams
Asst  Clk  Com.

J.E. Gunter   Com

---

## NELSON

**DOCKET #1974**

CENSUS ROLLS  1835

APPLICANT FOR CHEROKEE CITIZENSHIP

| POST OFFICE: Dyer Station, Ark | | ATTORNEY: A.E. Ivey | |
|---|---|---|---|
| NO | NAMES | AGE | SEX |
| 1 | Columbus F. Nelson | 17 | Male |
| 2 | Monro[sic] L. Nelson | | " |

ANCESTOR:  John Rogers

Now on this the 17[th] day of March 1888, comes the above case for a final hearing. The parties having made application pursuant to the provisions of an Act of the National Council approved December 8[th] 1886, and all the evidence being duly considered and found to be insufficient and unsatisfactory, it is adjudged and declared by the Commission that

Columbus F. Nelson and Monroe L. Nelson not Cherokees and are not entitled to the rights, privileges and immunities of Cherokee citizens by blood.

J. T. Adair     Chairman Commission
John E. Gunter    Commissioner
D.W. Lipe     Commissioner

Attest
    C.C. Lipe
    Clerk Com

The decision in the James C.C. Rogers case found in Book C, page 627, and Journal pages 325 to 333 governs this case.

---

## NEWHOUSE

**DOCKET #1975**
CENSUS ROLLS 1835

APPLICANT FOR CHEROKEE CITIZENSHIP

| POST OFFICE: Oo wa la I.T. | | ATTORNEY: C.H. Taylor | |
|---|---|---|---|
| No | NAMES | AGE | SEX |
| 1 | A.E. Newhouse | 24 | Female |
| 2 | A.M. Newhouse | 6 | Male |
| 3 | Thomas Newhouse | 3 | " |

ANCESTOR: John Bryant

Rejected March 18[th] 1889

### Adverse

Embraced in decision on page 431.
Book B. in the Aaron Bellew case
Rendered March 18[th] 1889.

# Cherokee Citizenship Commission Docket Books
## (1880-84, 1887-89) Volume V
## Tahlequah, Cherokee Nation

Will.P. Ross
Chairman Com
John E. Gunter    Com

Office Commission on Citizenship
Tahlequah I.T.  March 18<sup>th</sup> 1889
D.S. Williams
Clk Com.

---

## NEWHOUSE

**DOCKET #1976**
CENSUS ROLLS 1835

APPLICANT FOR CHEROKEE CITIZENSHIP

| POST OFFICE: Oo-wa-la, I.T. | | ATTORNEY: C.H. Taylor | |
|---|---|---|---|
| NO | NAMES | AGE | SEX |
| 1 | Z.B. Newhouse | 24 | Male |

ANCESTOR: John Bryant

Rejected March 18<sup>th</sup> 1889

Adverse

Embraced in decision on page 431.
Book B. in the Aaron Bellew case
Rendered March 18<sup>th</sup> 1889.

Will.P. Ross
Chairman Com
John E. Gunter    Com
Office Commission on Citizenship
Tahlequah I.T.  March 18<sup>th</sup> 1889
D.S. Williams
Clk Com.

---

93

## NEAL

**DOCKET #1977**

CENSUS ROLLS 1835 to 1852

APPLICANT FOR CHEROKEE CITIZENSHIP

| POST OFFICE: Brownstown, Ark. | | ATTORNEY: A.E. Ivey | |
|---|---|---|---|
| NO | NAMES | AGE | SEX |
| 1 | Paul B. Neal | 30 | Male |
| 2 | Noel G. Neal | 54 | " |
| 3 | Rufus D. Neal | 48 | " |
| 4 | Mrs. Sarah Williams | 50 | Female |
| 5 | " Bamma Brown | 40 | " |

ANCESTOR: Noel O. Neal

Rejected Sept. 6th 1889

Office Commission on Citizenship
Cherokee Nation Ind Ter
Tahlequah Sept. 6th 1889

The above case was submitted by Atty without evidence. The Commission therefore decide that Paul B. Neal age 30 yrs and the following named persons Noel G. Neal male 54 yrs. Father, Rufus D. Neal male 48 yrs Uncle, Mrs. Sarah Williams Female 50 yrs Aunt, Mrs Bamma Brown 40 yrs. Aunt are not Cherokees by blood. P.O. Brownstown Ark.

Will.P. Ross

Attest                                          Chairman

D.S. Williams                    J.E. Gunter   Com
Asst  Clk  Com.

## NEAL

**DOCKET #1978**

CENSUS ROLLS 1835 to 1852

APPLICANT FOR CHEROKEE CITIZENSHIP

| POST OFFICE: Mulberry, Ark | | ATTORNEY: A.E. Ivey | |
|---|---|---|---|
| NO | NAMES | AGE | SEX |
| 1 | Sarah M. Neal | 24 | Female |
| 2 | Lizzie Neal | 3 | " |
| 3 | Bell Neal | 2 | " |

ANCESTOR: Richard Henson

94

Rejected Sept. 6[th] 1889

Office Commission on Citizenship
Cherokee Nation Ind Ter
Tahlequah Sept. 6[th] 1889

The above case was submitted by Atty without evidence. The Commission therefore decide that Sarah M Neal age 24 yrs and the following children Lizzie Neal Female 3 yrs, Bell Neal Female 2 yrs. are not Cherokees by blood and are not entitled to citizenship in the Cherokee Nation. P.O. Mulberry, Ark.

Will.P. Ross

Attest                                                    Chairman

D.S. Williams                          J.E. Gunter   Com

Asst  Clk  Com.

## NEWMAN

**DOCKET #1979**

CENSUS ROLLS  1835 to 1852

APPLICANT FOR CHEROKEE CITIZENSHIP

| POST OFFICE: Fort Worth, Texas | | ATTORNEY: A.E. Ivey | |
|---|---|---|---|
| NO | NAMES | AGE | SEX |
| 1 | William A. Newman | 22 | Male |

ANCESTOR:  Ward

Rejected Sept. 6[th] 1889

Office Commission on Citizenship
Cherokee Nation Ind Ter
Tahlequah Sept. 6[th] 1889

The above case was submitted by Atty without evidence. The Commission therefore decide that William A. Newman age 22 yrs. is not a Cherokee by blood. P.O. Fort Smith[sic], Ark.[sic]

Will.P. Ross

Attest                                                    Chairman

D.S. Williams                          J.E. Gunter   Com

Asst  Clk  Com.

# Cherokee Citizenship Commission Docket Books
## (1880-84, 1887-89) Volume V
## Tahlequah, Cherokee Nation

### NEWMAN

**DOCKET #1980**

CENSUS ROLLS 1835 to 1852

APPLICANT FOR CHEROKEE CITIZENSHIP

| POST OFFICE: Fort Worth, Texas | | ATTORNEY: A.E. Ivey | |
|---|---|---|---|
| No | NAMES | AGE | SEX |
| 1 | Lou Vicey B. Newman | 42 | Female |
| 2 | Charley Newman | 13 | Male |

ANCESTOR: Ward

Rejected Sept. 6th 1889

Office Commission on Citizenship
Cherokee Nation Ind Ter
Tahlequah Sept. 6th 1889

The above case was submitted by Atty without evidence. The Commission therefore decide that Lou Vicey B. Newman age 42 yrs. and Charley Newman male 13 yrs. are not Cherokees by blood. P.O. Fort Worth Tex.

Will.P. Ross
Attest                                                   Chairman
   D.S. Williams                          J.E. Gunter   Com
   Asst  Clk  Com.

---

### NEAL

**DOCKET #1981**

CENSUS ROLLS 1835

APPLICANT FOR CHEROKEE CITIZENSHIP

| POST OFFICE: | | ATTORNEY: A.E. Ivey | |
|---|---|---|---|
| No | NAMES | AGE | SEX |
| 1 | Mary L. Neal | 26 | Female |
| 2 | Ollie Neal | 4 | " |

ANCESTOR: Mima Franklin

Now on this the 9th day of January 1888, comes the above case up for final hearing. The applicants having made application pursuant to the provisions of an Act of the National Council approved Dec. 8th 1886, and all the evidence being fully examined in the Mary A. Couch case, which was made a test one of

96

all cases, claiming a direct lineage from this same ancestor, Mima Edwards, it is adjudged and determined by the Commission that Mary L. Neal and Ollie Neal are not Cherokees by blood and in consequence not entitled to the rights of such.

The decision in the Mary A Couch case found in Docket "A", Page 100 governs this case.

|  |  |
|---|---|
| J. T. Adair | Chairman Commission |
| D.W. Lipe | Commissioner |

## NEELEY

**DOCKET #1982**

CENSUS ROLLS 1835, '48, '51, & '52

APPLICANT FOR CHEROKEE CITIZENSHIP

| POST OFFICE: Baxter Springs, Kan | | ATTORNEY: Boudinot & Rasmus | |
|---|---|---|---|
| NO | NAMES | AGE | SEX |
| 1 | Benjamin F. Neeley | 53 | Male |

ANCESTOR: Rachel Pugh

*Commission on Citizenship.*

CHEROKEE NATION, IND. TER.

*Tahlequah,* Sept. 6[th] 1889

Benjamin F. Neeley
vs                     Application for Cherokee Citizenship
Cherokee Nation

The above applicant filed his claim of Cherokee blood ~~through~~ before the Interior Department at Washington D.C. and which was transmitted by the Secty of the Interior to the Commission. On claimant's application, he claims to derive his Cherokee blood from his grand mother, Rachel Pugh, whose name applicant believes is enrolled upon some of the census rolls of Cherokees taken in the years of 1835, 48, 51 & 2. In proof of claimant's application, he submits as evidence the affidavits of Rebecca Borden & Leah P. Small taken before a "Notary Public" on the 14[th] day of August 1884, in the state of Ohio. Affiants affirm that they are well acquainted with applicant & know that he is a reputed Cherokee Indian and that Rachel Pugh was his grand mother. This evidence is "exparte" and affiants gain this knowledge through other persons & the Commission does not deem it sufficient to establish applicant's claim of Cherokee blood. But *(illegible)* this fact, the Commission fails to find the name of Rachel Pugh upon any of the Cherokee census rolls referred to by applicant. Sec. 7th of the law that governs this Commission in its decisions providing that applicant's name or that of their ancestor *(illegible)* appear upon some of the census rolls, taken in the years 1835, 48, 51 & 52. In consideration of these facts, the Commission decide that applicant Benjamin F. Neeley is not a Cherokee by blood. P.O. Baxter Springs, Kans.

Will.P. Ross

Chairman

J.E. Gunter    Com

---

## NALLY

**DOCKET #1983**

CENSUS ROLLS  1835

APPLICANT FOR CHEROKEE CITIZENSHIP

| POST OFFICE: Cherokee City | | ATTORNEY: C.H. Taylor | |
|---|---|---|---|
| NO | NAMES | AGE | SEX |
| 1 | Lucritia[sic] Nally | 41 | female |
| 2 | Elizabeth Nally | 22 | " |
| 3 | Ida Bell Nally | 20 | " |
| 4 | Jasper Nally | 16 | male |
| 5 | Jessie Nally | 13 | " |
| 6 | George Nally | 6 | " |
| 7 | Vinittia Nally | 3 | female |
| 8 | Edward B. Nally | 1 | male |

ANCESTOR: Arch Miller

Rejected Sept. 6th 1889

Office Commission on Citizenship
Cherokee Nation Ind Ter
Tahlequah  Sept. 6th 1889

The above case was called 3 times and submitted by Atty without evidence. The Commission therefore decide that Lucretia Nally age 41 yrs. and the following children Elizabeth Female 22 yrs., Ida Bell Female 20 yrs., Jasper male 16 yrs.,

# Cherokee Citizenship Commission Docket Books
## (1880-84, 1887-89) Volume V
## Tahlequah, Cherokee Nation

Jessie male 13 yrs., George male 6 yrs., Vinittia Female 3 yrs., and Edward B. Nally male 1 yr. are not Cherokees by blood. P.O. Cherokee City, Ark.

Will.P. Ross

Attest                                  Chairman
    D.S. Williams                  J.E. Gunter   Com
    Asst  Clk Com.

## NEELEY

**DOCKET #1984**
CENSUS ROLLS 1835 to 1852

APPLICANT FOR CHEROKEE CITIZENSHIP

| POST OFFICE: Colton, Cal. | | ATTORNEY: Boudinot and Rasmus | |
|---|---|---|---|
| NO | NAMES | AGE | SEX |
| 1 | John F. Neeley | 27 | Male |

ANCESTOR: Rachel Pugh

Rejected Sept. 6th 1889

Office Commission on Citizenship<br>Cherokee Nation Ind Ter<br>Tahlequah Sept. 6th 1889

The above named case having been submitted by Attorney without proof the Commission decide that John F. Neely[sic] of Colton California 27 yrs. old at the filing of his application on the 29th day of September A.D. 1887, is not of Cherokee blood.

Will.P. Ross

Attest                                  Chairman
    D.S. Williams                  J.E. Gunter   Com
    Asst  Clk Com.

99

## NEELEY

**DOCKET #1985**

CENSUS ROLLS 1835 to 1852

APPLICANT FOR CHEROKEE CITIZENSHIP

| POST OFFICE: Colton, Cal. | | ATTORNEY: Boudinot and Rasmus | |
|---|---|---|---|
| No | NAMES | AGE | SEX |
| 1 | Ella F. Neeley | 28 | female |

ANCESTOR: Rachel Pugh

Rejected Sept. 6<sup>th</sup> 1889

Office Commission on Citizenship
Cherokee Nation Ind Ter
Tahlequah Sept. 6<sup>th</sup> 1889

No evidence on file in support of the above application. We decide that applicant Ella F. Neely[sic] age 28 yrs. is not a Cherokee by blood. P.O. Colton Cal.

Will.P. Ross

Attest                                            Chairman
    D.S. Williams           J.E. Gunter   Com
    Asst  Clk  Com.

---

## NEELEY

**DOCKET #1986**

CENSUS ROLLS 1835 to 1852

APPLICANT FOR CHEROKEE CITIZENSHIP

| POST OFFICE: Colton, Cal. | | ATTORNEY: Boudinot and Rasmus | |
|---|---|---|---|
| No | NAMES | AGE | SEX |
| 1 | Carrie B. Neeley | 23 | female |

ANCESTOR: Rachel Pugh

Rejected Sept. 6<sup>th</sup> 1889

Office Commission on Citizenship
Cherokee Nation Ind Ter
Tahlequah Sept. 6<sup>th</sup> 1889

# Cherokee Citizenship Commission Docket Books
## (1880-84, 1887-89) Volume V
## Tahlequah, Cherokee Nation

The application in the above case having been submitted by Attorney Rasmus without proof, the Commission decide that the claimant Carrie B. Neeley of Colton California is not of Cherokee blood.

Will.P. Ross<br>Chairman

Attest

  D.S. Williams       J.E. Gunter   Com

  Asst   Clk   Com.

---

## NIX

**DOCKET #1987**

CENSUS ROLLS  1835

APPLICANT FOR CHEROKEE CITIZENSHIP

| POST OFFICE: Locus Grove, I.T. | | ATTORNEY: C.H. Taylor | |
|---|---|---|---|
| NO | NAMES | AGE | SEX |
| 1 | Rachel F. Nix | 47 | female |
| 2 | Marion F. Nix | 22 | male |
| 3 | John C. Nix | 10 | " |
| 4 | Susie A. Nix | 6 | female |

ANCESTOR: Robin Taylor

On this date, the 16th day of Oct, 1888, comes the above case up for final disposition. This case was rejected by the Commission on Citizenship under date of Sept. 28th 1882. – The evidence was duly considered on part of the applicant, who alleges she is the grand-daughter of Robin Taylor, whose name should appear on the rolls of Cherokees of the year 1835. The name of Robin Taylor does not appear on any of the rolls mentioned in the 7th Sec. of Act of Dec. 8th 1886 in relation to citizenship, nor those of the applicants themselves. Therefore under the law, Rachel F. Nix, Marion F. Nix, John C. Nix and Susie A. Nix, not Cherokees and are not entitled to any of the rights and privileges of citizens of the Cherokee Nation, and are intruders upon the public domain thereof.

      J. T. Adair   Chairman Commission

      H.C. Barnes   Commissioner

---

# Cherokee Citizenship Commission Docket Books
## (1880-84, 1887-89) Volume V
## Tahlequah, Cherokee Nation

## NIXON

**DOCKET #1988**

CENSUS ROLLS

APPLICANT FOR CHEROKEE CITIZENSHIP

| POST OFFICE: Chicago, Ill | | ATTORNEY: L.B. Bell | |
|---|---|---|---|
| NO | NAMES | AGE | SEX |
| 1 | Charles Nixon | 30 | Male |

ANCESTOR: Annie Crews

The Commission decide against claimant. See decision in case of Andrew Meredith Docket 2180 Book E, Page 26 and case John Henly Docket 1250, Book C Page 376.

Will.P. Ross    Chairman
R. Bunch    Com
J.E. Gunter    Com

## NEWBY

**DOCKET #1989**

CENSUS ROLLS

APPLICANT FOR CHEROKEE CITIZENSHIP

| POST OFFICE: Spiceland, Ind. | | ATTORNEY: L.B. Bell | |
|---|---|---|---|
| NO | NAMES | AGE | SEX |
| 1 | Caroline Newby | 52 | female |
| 2 | Emma Newby | 27 | " |
| 3 | Luther Newby | 20 | male |
| 4 | Henry Newby | 18 | " |
| 5 | Albert Newby | 15 | " |

ANCESTOR: Anna Crews

The Commission decide against claimant. See decision in the case of Andrew Meredith Docket 2180 Book E, Page 26 and John Henly Docket 1250, Book C Page 376.

Will.P. Ross    Chairman
R. Bunch    Com
John E. Gunter    Com

# Cherokee Citizenship Commission Docket Books
## (1880-84, 1887-89) Volume V
## Tahlequah, Cherokee Nation

## NIXON

**DOCKET #1990**

CENSUS ROLLS

APPLICANT FOR CHEROKEE CITIZENSHIP

| POST OFFICE: Chicago, Ill | | ATTORNEY: L.B. Bell | |
|---|---|---|---|
| NO | NAMES | AGE | SEX |
| 1 | O.W. Nixon | 62 | male |

ANCESTOR: Ann Crews

The Commission decide against claimant. See decision in case Andrew Meredith Docket 2180 Book E, Page 26 and case John Henly Docket 1250, Book C Page 376.

Will.P. Ross   Chairman
R. Bunch   Com
J.E. Gunter   Com

---

## NIXON

**DOCKET #1991**

CENSUS ROLLS

APPLICANT FOR CHEROKEE CITIZENSHIP

| POST OFFICE: Afton, I.T. | | ATTORNEY: L.B. Bell | |
|---|---|---|---|
| NO | NAMES | AGE | SEX |
| 1 | W.P. Nixon | 65 | male |

ANCESTOR: Ann Crews

The Commission decide against claimant. See decision in case Andrew Meredith Docket 2180 Book E, Page 26 and case John Henly Docket 1250, Book C Page 376.

Will.P. Ross   Chairman
R. Bunch   Com
J.E. Gunter   Com

---

# Cherokee Citizenship Commission Docket Books
## (1880-84, 1887-89) Volume V
## Tahlequah, Cherokee Nation

## NATHAN

**DOCKET #1992**

CENSUS ROLLS  1835 to 1852

APPLICANT FOR CHEROKEE CITIZENSHIP

| POST OFFICE: Siloam Springs, Ark. | | ATTORNEY: L.S. Sanders | |
|---|---|---|---|
| No | NAMES | AGE | SEX |
| 1 | Charlotte Nation | 23 | female |

ANCESTOR:  George Cline

Rejected Sept. 6th 1889

Office Commission on Citizenship
Cherokee Nation Ind Ter
Tahlequah Sept. 6th 1889

The above case was called 3 times and submitted by Atty without evidence. The Commission therefore decide that Charlotte Nathan age 23 yrs. is not a Cherokee by blood.  P.O. Siloam Springs Ark.

Attest

D.S. Williams
Asst  Clk  Com.

Will.P. Ross
Chairman
J.E. Gunter   Com

---

## NELSON

**DOCKET #1993**

CENSUS ROLLS  1835 to 1852

APPLICANT FOR CHEROKEE CITIZENSHIP

| POST OFFICE: Cedarville, Crawford Co, Ark. | | ATTORNEY: Wm A. Thompson | |
|---|---|---|---|
| No | NAMES | AGE | SEX |
| 1 | Dennis M Nelson | 44 | Male |
| 2 | Robert A. Nelson | 15 | " |
| 3 | Samuel Nelson | 13 | " |
| 4 | Robert Nelson | 10 | " |
| 5 | George Nelson | 8 | " |

ANCESTOR:  Several Meeks

Rejected Sept. 6th 1889

# Cherokee Citizenship Commission Docket Books
## (1880-84, 1887-89) Volume V
## Tahlequah, Cherokee Nation

The above case was called 3 times and submitted by Atty without evidence. The Commission therefore decide that Dennis M. Nelson age 44 yrs. and the following children Robert A. Nelson male 15 son, Samuel male 13 yrs. son, Robert male 10 son and George Nelson male 8 son, are not Cherokees by blood. Post Office Cedarville, Crawford Co, Ark.

Will.P. Ross

Attest                                    Chairman

    D.S. Williams              J.E. Gunter   Com

    Asst  Clk  Com.

---

## NEALEY

**DOCKET #1994**

CENSUS ROLLS  1835 to 1852

APPLICANT FOR CHEROKEE CITIZENSHIP

| POST OFFICE: Fort Graham | | ATTORNEY: A.E. Ivey | |
|---|---|---|---|
| **NO** | **NAMES** | **AGE** | **SEX** |
| 1 | Mrs. L.J. Nealey | 35 | female |
| 2 | L.C. Nealey | 12 | " |
| 3 | E.A. Nealey | 6 | " |
| 4 | E.C. Nealey | 3 | male |

ANCESTOR: Johnson Hembre

Rejected Sept. 6<sup>th</sup> 1889

The above case was submitted by Atty without evidence.  The Commission therefore decide that Mrs. L.J. Nealy[sic] age 35 yrs. and the following children L.C. Nealy Female 12 daughter, A.E. Ivey Nealy Female 6 daughter, E.C. Nealy male 3 son are not Cherokees by blood. P.O. Fort Graham.

# Cherokee Citizenship Commission Docket Books
## (1880-84, 1887-89) Volume V
## Tahlequah, Cherokee Nation

Will.P. Ross

Attest                  Chairman

    D.S. Williams           J.E. Gunter   Com

    Asst  Clk  Com.

---

## OLIVER

**DOCKET #1995**

CENSUS ROLLS 1835 to 1852

APPLICANT FOR CHEROKEE CITIZENSHIP

| POST OFFICE: Union Town, Ark. | | ATTORNEY: A.E. Ivey | |
|---|---|---|---|
| No | NAMES | AGE | SEX |
| 1 | Kittie A. Oliver | 38 | Female |
| 2 | Heiram C. Oliver | 17 | Male |
| 3 | Nancy M. Oliver | 15 | Female |
| 4 | Lilly Oliver | 13 | " |
| 5 | James Henry Oliver | 10 | Male |
| 6 | Harriet E. Oliver | 7 | Female |
| 7 | Louis Tucker Oliver | 4 | Male |
| 8 | Sarah A. Oliver | 2 | Female |

ANCESTOR: Elizabeth Baker

Rejected Sept. 6th 1889

Office Commission on Citizenship
Cherokee Nation Ind Ter
Tahlequah Sept. 6th 1889

This case was submitted by Atty without evidence. The Commission therefore decide that Kittie A. Oliver age 38 yrs. and the following children Heiram C. Oliver male 17 yrs., Nancy M. Female 15 yrs. Lilly Female 13 yrs. James Henry male 10 yrs. Harriet E. Female 7 yrs. Louis Tucker male 4 yrs. & Sarah A. Oliver Female 2 yrs. are not Cherokees by blood. P.O. Union Town Ark.

Will.P. Ross

Attest                  Chairman

    D.S. Williams           J.E. Gunter   Com

    Asst  Clk  Com.

---

# Cherokee Citizenship Commission Docket Books
# (1880-84, 1887-89) Volume V
# Tahlequah, Cherokee Nation

## ONEAL

**DOCKET #1996**

CENSUS ROLLS

APPLICANT FOR CHEROKEE CITIZENSHIP

| POST OFFICE: Richmond Ind. | | ATTORNEY: L.B. Bell | |
|---|---|---|---|
| **NO** | **NAMES** | **AGE** | **SEX** |
| 1 | Mary Oneal | 23 | Female |
| 2 | Laura Oneal | 12 | " |

ANCESTOR: Ann Crews

The Commission decide against claimant. See decision in the case of Andrew Meredith Docket 2180 Book E, Page 26 and John Henly Docket 1250, Book C Page 376.

> Will.P. Ross    Chairman
> R. Bunch    Com
> John E. Gunter    Com

## OSTEEN

**DOCKET #1997**

CENSUS ROLLS 1835, '48, '51, & '52

APPLICANT FOR CHEROKEE CITIZENSHIP

| POST OFFICE: Farmer, Ark | | ATTORNEY: Boudinot & Rasmus | |
|---|---|---|---|
| **NO** | **NAMES** | **AGE** | **SEX** |
| 1 | Samuel H. Osteen | 28 | Male |
| 2 | Zephne Osteen | 4 | " |
| 3 | Okly Osteen | 2 | " |
| 4 | Opie Osteen (Infant) | | " |

ANCESTOR: Leah Reeves

Rejected Aug. 28th 1889

> Office Commission on Citizenship
> Cherokee Nation Ind Ter
> Tahlequah  Aug. 28th 1889

The above named case having been submitted this day by W.F. Rasmus Attorney without evidence, the Commission decide against the applicant Samuel H. Osteen age 28 yrs. and his son, Zephne Osteen age 4 yrs. Okly Osteen age 2 yrs. and Opie Osteen Infant as not entitled to citizenship in the Cherokee Nation. P.O. Farmer Ark.

Will.P. Ross

Attest                                        Chairman

    D.S. Williams                J.E. Gunter   Com

    Asst  Clk Com.

## ORVIS

**DOCKET #1998**

CENSUS ROLLS  1835 to 1852

APPLICANT FOR CHEROKEE CITIZENSHIP

| POST OFFICE: Coffeyville, Kans | | ATTORNEY: Boudinot and Rasmus | |
|---|---|---|---|
| NO | NAMES | AGE | SEX |
| 1 | William B. Orvis | 37 | male |
| 2 | Elnor B Orvis | 12 | female |
| 3 | Nora G Orvis | 8 | " |
| 4 | Joel Orvis | 1 | male |

ANCESTOR:  Emeline Orvis

Rejected Aug. 28<sup>th</sup> 1889

Office Commission on Citizenship
Cherokee Nation Ind Ter
Tahlequah  Aug. 28<sup>th</sup> 1889

The above case was this day submitted by W.F. Rasmus Attorney for claimant without evidence. The Commission therefore decide that Wm B. Orvis age 37 years and daughters Elnor E. Orvis age 12 yrs. & Nora F. Orvis age 8 years & son Joel Orvis age 1 year are not of Cherokee blood. Post Office Coffyville[sic] Kans.

Will.P. Ross

Attest                                        Chairman

    D.S. Williams                J.E. Gunter   Com

    Asst  Clk Com.

## ONEAL

**DOCKET #1999**

CENSUS ROLLS 1835 to 1852

APPLICANT FOR CHEROKEE CITIZENSHIP

| POST OFFICE: Fabius, Ala. | | ATTORNEY: A.E. Ivey | |
|---|---|---|---|
| NO | NAMES | AGE | SEX |
| 1 | Eliza K Oneal | 30 | female |
| 2 | Mary Oneal | 6 | " |
| 3 | Rhoda Oneal | 4 | " |
| 4 | Addie Oneal | 2 | " |

ANCESTOR: Richard Keyes

Rejected Sept. 6<sup>th</sup> 1889

Office Commission on Citizenship
Cherokee Nation Ind Ter
Tahlequah Sept. 6<sup>th</sup> 1889

The above case was called and submitted by Atty without evidence. The Commission therefore decide that Eliza K. Oneal age 30 yrs. and the following children Mary Oneal Female 6 yrs. Rhoda Oneal Female 4 yrs. Adie[sic] Oneal Female age 2 yrs. are not Cherokees by blood. Post Office Fabius Ala.

Will.P. Ross

Attest                                          Chairman

    D.S. Williams                    J.E. Gunter   Com

    Asst  Clk  Com.

## OAKES

**DOCKET #2000**

CENSUS ROLLS 1835 to 1852

APPLICANT FOR CHEROKEE CITIZENSHIP

| POST OFFICE: Blue Jacket, I.T. | | ATTORNEY: A.E. Ivey | |
|---|---|---|---|
| NO | NAMES | AGE | SEX |
| 1 | Rachel J. Oakes | 39 | female |
| 2 | Miles W. Oakes | 20 | male |
| 3 | Dela J Oakes | 11 | female |
| 4 | John Henry Oakes | 6 | male |

ANCESTOR: Isham Sizemore

# Cherokee Citizenship Commission Docket Books (1880-84, 1887-89) Volume V Tahlequah, Cherokee Nation

Rejected Sept. 6[th] 1889

Office Commission on Citizenship
Cherokee Nation Ind Ter
Tahlequah Sept. 6[th] 1889

This case was submitted by Atty without evidence. The Commission therefore decide that Rachel J. Oaks[sic] age 39 yrs. and the following children Miles W. Oaks male 20 yrs. son, Dela J. Oaks Female Daughter 11 yrs. and John Henry Oaks 6 son are not Cherokees by blood. Post Office Blue Jacket I.T.

|  | Will.P. Ross |
|---|---|
| Attest | Chairman |
| D.S. Williams | J.E. Gunter   Com |
| Asst   Clk  Com. |  |

---

## OBERGANT

**DOCKET #2001**
CENSUS ROLLS  1835 to 1852

APPLICANT FOR CHEROKEE CITIZENSHIP

| POST OFFICE: Alma, Ark. | | ATTORNEY: A.E. Ivey | |
|---|---|---|---|
| NO | NAMES | AGE | SEX |
| 1 | Sarah Obergant | 36 | female |
| 2 | William Obergant | 17 | male |
| 3 | John Obergant | 15 | " |
| 4 | Anna Obergant | 12 | female |
| 5 | Jackson Obergant | 10 | male |
| 6 | Cornelia Obergant | 8 | female |
| 7 | Ada Obergant | 6 | " |

ANCESTOR: Sarah Thomas

Rejected Sept. 6[th] 1889

Office Commission on Citizenship
Cherokee Nation Ind Ter
Tahlequah Sept. 6[th] 1889

The above case was submitted without evidence. The Commission therefore decide that Sarah Obergant age 36 yrs. Wm  Obergant male 17 son, John male 15, Anna Female 12 Daughter, Jackson male 10 son, Cornelia Female 8 yrs. and Ada Obergant 6 daughter are not Cherokees by blood. P.O. Alma Ark.

# Cherokee Citizenship Commission Docket Books
# (1880-84, 1887-89) Volume V
# Tahlequah, Cherokee Nation

Will.P. Ross

Attest                    Chairman

     D.S. Williams             J.E. Gunter   Com

     Asst   Clk   Com.

## OWENS

**DOCKET #2002**

CENSUS ROLLS 1835 to 1852

APPLICANT FOR CHEROKEE CITIZENSHIP

| POST OFFICE: Fort Graham, Tex | | ATTORNEY: A.E. Ivey | |
|---|---|---|---|
| NO | NAMES | AGE | SEX |
| 1 | James Owens | 23 | male |

ANCESTOR: Johnson Hembre

See decision in this case in that of Mrs. G.W. Curtis in Book "C" page 51 – Adverse to claimant.

Cornell Rogers
Clk Com. on Citizenship

Office Com on Citizenship
Tahlequah I.T. Oct. 23$^{rd}$ '88

## OWENS

**DOCKET #2003**

CENSUS ROLLS 1835 to 1852

APPLICANT FOR CHEROKEE CITIZENSHIP

| POST OFFICE: Fort Graham, Tex | | ATTORNEY: A.E. Ivey | |
|---|---|---|---|
| NO | NAMES | AGE | SEX |
| 1 | Mary W. Owens | 50 | female |
| 2 | *(Illegible)* Owens | 19 | male |
| 3 | Effie Owens | 17 | female |
| 4 | Julis Owens | 14 | male |
| 5 | Newton Owens | 20 | " |

ANCESTOR: Johnson Hembre

The decision in this case will be found in that of Mrs. G.W. Curtis in Book "C" page 51 – Adverse to claimant.

Cornell Rogers
Clk Com. on Citizenship

Office Com on Citizenship
Tahlequah I.T.  Oct. 23rd '88

---

## OWENS

**DOCKET #2004**

CENSUS ROLLS  1835 to 1852

APPLICANT FOR CHEROKEE CITIZENSHIP

| POST OFFICE: Fort Graham, Tex | | ATTORNEY: A.E. Ivey | |
|---|---|---|---|
| NO | NAMES | AGE | SEX |
| 1 | G.W. Owens | 25 | male |

ANCESTOR:  Johnson Hembre

See decision in this case in that of Mrs. G.W. Curtis in Book "C" page 51 – Adverse to claimant.

Cornell Rogers
Clk Com. on Citizenship

Office Com on Citizenship
Tahlequah I.T.  Oct. 23rd '88

---

## TAYLOR

**DOCKET #2005**

CENSUS ROLLS  1851 & 1852

APPLICANT FOR CHEROKEE CITIZENSHIP

| POST OFFICE: Lenore Station Tenn | | ATTORNEY: C.H. Taylor | |
|---|---|---|---|
| NO | NAMES | AGE | SEX |
| 1 | Andrew J. Taylor | 63 | male |

ANCESTOR:  Polly Taylor

Now on this the 30th day of July 1888, the demandant[sic] submits this case by Atty C.H. Taylor, and after a careful examination of the evidene and pay rolls and census rolls of Cherokees made in the years 1835, 1848, 1851 and 1852. find that Andrew J. Taylor is a Cherokee by blood and entitled to all the rights of and benefits of citizens of the Cherokee Nation by virtue of such blood and is therefore;

Re-admitted to all the rights and privileges of Cherokee citizens by blood in accordance with the provisions of Section of 7 of the Act of Dec. 8[th] 1886.

J. T. Adair    Chairman Commission
H.C. Barnes  Commissioner

## TRACY

**DOCKET #2006**
CENSUS ROLLS 1835 to 1852

APPLICANT FOR CHEROKEE CITIZENSHIP

| POST OFFICE: Salem, Ill | | ATTORNEY: Wm A. Thompson | |
|---|---|---|---|
| No | NAMES | AGE | SEX |
| 1 | D.E. Tracy | | male |

ANCESTOR: Grant

Rejected May 20 – 89

Office Commission on Citizenship Cher Nat I.T.
Tahlequah May 20[th] 1889

The application in the above case was filed on the 5[th] day of October 1887, and is supported by no evidence. The Commission therefore decide that D.E. Tracy is not of Cherokee blood and are[sic] not entitled to citizenship in the Cherokee Nation, whose post office was Salem Illinois, at the time of filing.

Attest

D.S. Williams                 Will.P. Ross
Asst  Clk  Com.                Chairman
                            J.E. Gunter  Com

# Cherokee Citizenship Commission Docket Books (1880-84, 1887-89) Volume V
## Tahlequah, Cherokee Nation

## TRACY

**DOCKET #2007**

CENSUS ROLLS 1835 to 1852

APPLICANT FOR CHEROKEE CITIZENSHIP

| POST OFFICE: Salem, Ill | | ATTORNEY: Wm A. Thompson | |
|---|---|---|---|
| No | NAMES | AGE | SEX |
| 1 | Dwyer Tracy | | male |

ANCESTOR: Grant

Rejected May 20 – 89

Office Commission on Citizenship Cher Nat I.T.

Tahlequah May 20th 1889

The application in the above case was filed on the 5th day of Oct. 1887, and is supported by no evidence.

The Commission therefore decide that D.E. Tracy is not of Cherokee blood and is not entitled to citizenship in the Cherokee Nation, whose Post Office was Salem Illinois, at the time of filing.

Attest

D.S. Williams
Asst  Clk  Com.

Will.P. Ross
Chairman
J.E. Gunter    Com

## THOMPSON

**DOCKET #2008**

CENSUS ROLLS 1835 to 1852

APPLICANT FOR CHEROKEE CIIZENSHIP

| POST OFFICE: Charleston, N.C. | | ATTORNEY: L.S. Sanders | |
|---|---|---|---|
| No | NAMES | AGE | SEX |
| 1 | Nancy Ann Thompson | 61 | female |
| 2 | Samantha Thompson | 39 | " |
| 3 | Sarah J. Thompson | 37 | " |
| 4 | Nathan B. Thompson | 35 | male |
| 5 | Justamah Thompson | 33 | female |
| 6 | Alice B. Thompson | 30 | " |
| 7 | John W. Thompson | 28 | male |

| 8 | James A.L. Thompson | 25 | " |
|---|---|---|---|
| 9 | Julia A.E. Ivey Thompson | 23 | female |
| 10 | Carry R. Thompson | 19 | " |

ANCESTOR: Mrs. F.M. Millsaps

Office Commission on Citizenship
Tahlequah C.N. May 23$^{rd}$ 1889

The applicant in this case alleges that she is own cousin to one Mrs. F.M. Millsaps whose name will be found on the census rolls of Cherokees by blood taken and made in the years 1835 – 1852. Mrs. F.M. Millsap, it is alleged derives her Cherokee blood from Elizabeth Hide nee Elizabeth Leatherwood. The preponderance of the evidence shows that Mrs. Hide, nee Leatherwood, the Mother of Mrs. F.M. Millsaps and Grandmother of Nancy Ann Thompson was a white woman and her husband Hide, a white man, while neither the names of Leatherwood, Hide, nor Millsaps is found on the rolls of 1835 or 1852. The Commission therefore adjudged that Nancy Ann Thompson Battle age 61 years and her daughters, Samantha Jane, aged 39 years, Sarah Jane Thompson 37, Justamah, 33 years, Alice Barthama 30 years, Julia A.E. Ivey 23 years, Carry Ruth 19 years and sons, Nathan B. aged 35 years, John Wesly[sic] 28 years, James A. Lee 25 years, are not of Cherokee blood and not entitled to citizenship in the Cherokee Nation.

Will.P. Ross    Chairman
Attest                                    J.E. Gunter    Com
    EG Ross
    Clerk Com

## TURNER

**DOCKET #2009**
CENSUS ROLLS 1835 to 1852

APPLICANT FOR CHEROKEE CITIZENSHIP

| POST OFFICE: Clarksville Ark | | ATTORNEY: Boudinot and Rasmus | |
|---|---|---|---|
| NO | NAMES | AGE | SEX |
| 1 | John D. Turner | 42 | Male |
| 2 | D.M. Turner | 19 | " |
| 3 | Jesse S. Turner | 16 | Twins |
| 4 | W.J. Turner | 16 | |

| 5 | M.J. Turner | 14 | |
|---|---|---|---|
| 6 | L.E. Turner | 12 | |
| 7 | T.J. Turner | 10 | |
| 8 | L.M. Turner | 7 | |
| 9 | N.C. Turner | 5 | |
| 10 | G.C. Turner | 3 | |

**ANCESTOR:** Barsheba Goodrich

Office Commission on Citizenship
Cherokee Nation
Tahlequah June 20, 1889

There being no evidence in support of the above named case, the Commission decide that John D. Turner aged 42 years and the following named children D.M. Turner male aged 19 years, Jessie S. female aged 16 years, W.J. male aged 16 years, M.J. male aged 14 years, L.E. aged 12 years, T.J. aged 10 years, L.M. aged 7 years, H.[sic]C. aged 5 years. and G.C. Turner aged 3 years are not Cherokees by blood.

Attest                                  Will.P. Ross

  EG Ross                                              Chairman
    Clerk Commission              J.E. Gunter   Com

---

## TAYLOR

**DOCKET #2010**
CENSUS ROLLS 1851 & 1852

APPLICANT FOR CHEROKEE CITIZENSHIP

| POST OFFICE: Lenore Station | | ATTORNEY: C.H. Taylor | |
|---|---|---|---|
| **No** | **NAMES** | **AGE** | **SEX** |
| 1 | Wyly Taylor | 58 | male |
| 2 | John D. Taylor | 28 | " |

**ANCESTOR:** Polly Taylor

Now on this the 30[th] day of *(Illegible)* 1888, comes the above case, it being submitted by demandants Atty Mr. C.H. Taylor, and all the evidence being carefully examined as well as the rolls mentioned in the 7th Section of the Act creating this Commission. It is adjudged and determined by the Commission on Citizenship that Wiley Taylor and his son John D. Taylor, are Cherokees by blood and as such entitled to all the rights and privileges of Cherokee citizens. Therefore,

We the Commission on Citizenship re-admit Wiley Taylor and John D. Taylor to all the rights and privileges of Cherokee citizens and do hereby so declare.

J. T. Adair    Chairman Commission
H.C. Barnes   Commissioner

---

## THOMAS

**DOCKET #2011**
CENSUS ROLLS 1835 to 1852

APPLICANT FOR CHEROKEE CITIZENSHIP

| POST OFFICE: Carroll Co, Ark. | | ATTORNEY: Boudinot and Rasmus | |
|---|---|---|---|
| NO | NAMES | AGE | SEX |
| 1 | Absolom M. Thomas | 60 | Male |

ANCESTOR: Nesyphones Stanlee

Rejected Sept. 6<sup>th</sup> 1889

Office Commission on Citizenship
Cherokee Nation Ind Ter
Tahlequah Sept. 6<sup>th</sup> 1889

The application in the above case was filed on the 1<sup>st</sup> day of October A.D. 1887, and was this day submitted by the Attorneys for both parties for decision to the Commission. The claimant alleges that he is 60 years old and derives his Cherokee Indian blood from Nesyphones Stanlee who was of Cherokee blood and whose name he believes was enrolled on the rolls of Cherokees taken and made by the United States in the years 1835 – 48 – 51 – 52. The evidence in the case consists of the affidavits exparte of John H. Jones 56 yrs. old and Nathan J. Hill taken before H.H. Moore Clk of Circuit Court for Carroll County State of Arkansas on the 16<sup>th</sup> day of July 1887, and A.A. Baker and Aaron Baker taken before same on the 18 and 19<sup>th</sup> of May 1887. These affiants have no knowledge of the claimants further than that derived from statements of the parties, claimant and from common report. It appears that Absolom Thomas and his grand Father Stanlee resided in Arkansas for many years not far from the Cherokee Country and doubtless had years of *(illegible)* extending through a period of many years to avail themselves if of Cherokee Indian descent to the rights and privileges common to the Cherokee people. There is no evidence that

117

they ever did so or sought to do so and as neither the name of Absolom M. Thomas nor Nesyphones Stanlee is to be found on either of the census rolls of Cherokees by blood named in the application, the Commission decide that Absolom Marshal Thomas and his children whose names are not given are not of Cherokee blood and not entitled to citizenship in the Cherokee Nation. P.O. Carroll County Arkansas.

Will.P. Ross

Attest                        Chairman

    D.S. Williams          J.E. Gunter   Com

    Asst Clk Com.

## TAYLOR

**DOCKET #2012**

CENSUS ROLLS 1835 to 1852

APPLICANT FOR CHEROKEE CITIZENSHIP

| POST OFFICE: Baxter Springs, Kans. | | ATTORNEY: Boudinot and Rasmus | |
|---|---|---|---|
| No | NAMES | AGE | SEX |
| 1 | James W. Taylor | 56 | male |
| 2 | Henry E. Taylor | 16 | " |
| 3 | Addie E. Taylor | 10 | female |
| 4 | Bertha M. Taylor | 5 | " |

ANCESTOR: T.J. Taylor

Rejected Aug. 27th 1889

Office Commission on Citizenship
Cherokee Nation Ind Ter
Tahlequah Aug. 27th 1889

The Commission in the above case decide that applicant James W. Taylor age 56 years and his son Henry E. Taylor age 16 years and daughters Addie Taylor age 10 years and Bertha M. Taylor age 5 years are not of Cherokee blood. See decision in case of George W. Taylor Docket 1909 Book D Page 395. P.O. Baxter Springs, Kansas.

Will.P. Ross

Attest                   Chairman

    D.S. Williams        J.E. Gunter   Com

    Asst Clk Com.

## TERRY

**DOCKET #2013**

CENSUS ROLLS 1835

APPLICANT FOR CHEROKEE CITIZENSHIP

| POST OFFICE: Wolf City Tex | | ATTORNEY: Boudinot and Rasmus | |
|---|---|---|---|
| NO | NAMES | AGE | SEX |
| 1 | Cesena J. Terry | 50 | female |
| 2 | James Terry | | male |
| 3 | John Terry | | " |
| 4 | Lilly Terry | | female |

ANCESTOR: D. Caldwell

Rejected Sept 5<sup>th</sup> 1889

Office Commission on Citizenship
Cherokee Nation Ind Ter
Tahlequah Sept 5<sup>th</sup> 1889

The Commission decide against the claimant in the above named case. Cesena Terry and her four children James Terry, John Terry, Lilly Terry, and one other not named, for reasons set for in the case of Eliza M. Black. See Docket 678, Book B, Page 393.

Will.P. Ross

Attest                    Chairman

D.S. Williams        J.E. Gunter   Com

Asst  Clk  Com.

---

## TUCKER

**DOCKET #2014**

CENSUS ROLLS 1835

APPLICANT FOR CHEROKEE CITIZENSHIP

| POST OFFICE: Santaluga[sic], Ga. | | ATTORNEY: J.E. Welch | |
|---|---|---|---|
| NO | NAMES | AGE | SEX |
| 1 | M.L. Tucker | | |

ANCESTOR: John Tucker

Re-Admitted Oct. 22<sup>nd</sup> 1889

Office Commission on Citizenship
Cherokee Nation Ind Ter
Tahlequah  Oct. 21<sup>st</sup> 1889

119

# Cherokee Citizenship Commission Docket Books
## (1880-84, 1887-89) Volume V
## Tahlequah, Cherokee Nation

It having been proved to the satisfaction of the Commission that M.L. Tucker whose name is Lafayette Tucker is the son of Lewallen Tucker and grand son of John Tucker whose name is found on the census rolls of Cherokees taken by the United States in the year 1835 and is of Cherokee Indian blood, it is hereby adjudged and decreed that the said M.L. Tucker 39 yrs. old and daughters Amanda Elizabeth 11 yrs. and Deluie D. 6 yrs. and sons Louallen Adolphus 9 yrs. and Edward Tucker 3 yrs. are of Cherokee descent and entitled to re-admission to citizenship in the Cherokee Nation.
P.O. Santaluga[sic], Ga.

<table>
<tr><td></td><td>Will.P. Ross</td></tr>
<tr><td>Attest</td><td>Chairman</td></tr>
<tr><td>D.S. Williams</td><td>J.E. Gunter  Com</td></tr>
<tr><td>Asst  Clk Com.</td><td></td></tr>
</table>

Certificate delivered to J.E. Welch, Nov. 15[th] 1890

## TIMS

**DOCKET #2015**
CENSUS ROLLS 1835 to 1852

APPLICANT FOR CHEROKEE CITIZENSHIP

| POST OFFICE: Calhoun, Ga.q | | ATTORNEY: A.E. Ivey | |
|---|---|---|---|
| NO | NAMES | AGE | SEX |
| 1 | Mary J Tims | 35 | female |

ANCESTOR: Charles Gaus[sic]

Rejected Sept 6[th] 1889

Office Commission on Citizenship
Cherokee Nation Ind Ter
Tahlequah Sept. 6[th] 1889

The above case was submitted by Atty without evidence. The Commission therefore decide that Mary J Tims age 35 yrs. is not a Cherokee by blood. Post Office Calhoun Ga.

<table>
<tr><td></td><td>Will.P. Ross</td></tr>
<tr><td>Attest</td><td>Chairman</td></tr>
<tr><td>D.S. Williams</td><td>J.E. Gunter  Com</td></tr>
<tr><td>Asst  Clk Com.</td><td></td></tr>
</table>

## TAYLOR

**DOCKET #2016**

CENSUS ROLLS 1835 to 1852

APPLICANT FOR CHEROKEE CITIZENSHIP

| POST OFFICE: Missouri | | ATTORNEY: Boudinot and Rasmus | |
|---|---|---|---|
| **NO** | **NAMES** | **AGE** | **SEX** |
| 1 | Calidonia C. Taylor | 22 | female |

ANCESTOR: Susan Bracket

Reported Dead.

> The evidence in the above case is filed with John Thomas Mayfield. The applicant is reported (dead)
>
> This Oct. 5[th] 1889

Attest

D.S. Williams

Asst Clk Com.

---

## THOMAS

**DOCKET #2017**

CENSUS ROLLS 1835 to 1852

APPLICANT FOR CHEROKEE CITIZENSHIP

| POST OFFICE: Fountain City, Mo | | ATTORNEY: L.B. Bell | |
|---|---|---|---|
| **NO** | **NAMES** | **AGE** | **SEX** |
| 1 | Sarah J Thomas | 56 | female |

ANCESTOR: John Merideth

The Commission decide against the claimant in the above named case. It is accompanied by no evidence but is one of several cases which will be found to be covered by the decision of the Commission in the case of Andrew Meredith Docket 2180 Book E Page 26. P.O. Fountain City, Mo.

Will.P. Ross

Chairman

J.E. Gunter Com

---

# Cherokee Citizenship Commission Docket Books
## (1880-84, 1887-89) Volume V
## Tahlequah, Cherokee Nation

### TANSEY

**DOCKET #2018**

CENSUS ROLLS

APPLICANT FOR CHEROKEE CITIZENSHIP

| POST OFFICE: Afton I.T. | | ATTORNEY: L.B. Bell | |
|---|---|---|---|
| No | NAMES | AGE | SEX |
| 1 | L.J. Tansey | | male |

ANCESTOR: Mary Crews

The Commission decide against claimant. See decision in case Andrew Meredith Docket 2180 Book E, Page 26 and case of John Henly Docket 1250, Book C Page 376.

Will.P. Ross

Chairman

R. Bunch   Com

J. E. Gunter   Com

---

### TANKSLEY

**DOCKET #2019**

CENSUS ROLLS

APPLICANT FOR CHEROKEE CITIZENSHIP

| POST OFFICE: Valley Mills, Ga | | ATTORNEY: C.H. Taylor | |
|---|---|---|---|
| No | NAMES | AGE | SEX |
| 1 | Elizabeth B. Tanksley | 21 | female |
| 2 | Boney Tanksley | 3 | male |
| 3 | Nora Tanksley | 1 | female |

ANCESTOR: H.C. Tanksley

Rejected Sept. 6th 1889

Office Commission on Citizenship

Cherokee Nation Ind Ter

Tahlequah  Sept. 6th 1889

The above case was called 3 several times and submitted by Atty without evidence. The Commission therefore decide that Elizabeth Tanksley age 21 yrs. and the following children Boney Tanksley male 3 yrs. Nora Tanksley Female 1 yr. are not Cherokees by blood. Post Office Valley Mills, Ga.

# Cherokee Citizenship Commission Docket Books
## (1880-84, 1887-89) Volume V
## Tahlequah, Cherokee Nation

Will.P. Ross
Chairman
J.E. Gunter    Com

Attest
  D.S. Williams
  Asst  Clk  Com.

## TAYLOR

**DOCKET #2020**
CENSUS ROLLS  1835 to 1852

APPLICANT FOR CHEROKEE CITIZENSHIP

| POST OFFICE: Little River, Tex. | | ATTORNEY: A.E. Ivey | |
|---|---|---|---|
| NO | NAMES | AGE | SEX |
| 1 | L.A.M. Taylor | 30 | female |

ANCESTOR: Mrs. Tatum

Rejected Sept 6th 1889

Office Commission on Citizenship
Cherokee Nation Ind Ter
Tahlequah  Sept. 6th 1889

The above case was submitted by Atty without evidence.  The Commission therefore decide that L.A.M. Taylor age 39 yrs. is not a Cherokee by blood. Post Office Little River, Tex.

Will.P. Ross
Chairman
J.E. Gunter    Com

Attest
  D.S. Williams
  Asst  Clk  Com.

## TURNER

**DOCKET #2021**
CENSUS ROLLS  1835 to 1852

APPLICANT FOR CHEROKEE CITIZENSHIP

| POST OFFICE: Lousville[sic], Tex | | ATTORNEY: A.E. Ivey | |
|---|---|---|---|
| NO | NAMES | AGE | SEX |
| 1 | Samuel Turner | | male |
| 2 | E.V. Turner | | " |
| 3 | M.C. Turner and children | | " |
| 4 | Jennie Turner | 13 | female |

123

| 5 | Haley Turner | 10 | " |
|---|---|---|---|
| 6 | May Turner | 6 | " |
| 7 | Henry Turner | 4 | male |

**ANCESTOR:** Marshuck Green

Rejected Sept 6<sup>th</sup> 1889

Office Commission on Citizenship
Cherokee Nation Ind Ter
Tahlequah Sept. 6<sup>th</sup> 1889

The above case was submitted by Atty without evidence. The Commission decide that Samuel Turner et.al. 24, E.V. Turner male Turner[sic], and the following children Jennie Female 12 yrs. Haley Female 10 yrs. May Female 6 yrs. & Henry Turner male age 4 yrs. are not Cherokees by blood.
Post Office Louisville Texas.

Will.P. Ross

Attest                                            Chairman
    D.S. Williams                    J.E. Gunter   Com
    Asst   Clk   Com.

---

## TURNER

**DOCKET #2022**

CENSUS ROLLS 1851 & 1852

APPLICANT FOR CHEROKEE CITIZENSHIP

| POST OFFICE: Arkansas City, Kans. | | ATTORNEY: A.E. Ivey | |
|---|---|---|---|
| NO | NAMES | AGE | SEX |
| 1 | Julia A.E. Ivey Turner | 21 | female |

**ANCESTOR:** Pleas and Martha Haney

Rejected Sept. 6<sup>th</sup> 1889

Office Commission on Citizenship
Cherokee Nation Ind Ter
Tahlequah Sept. 6<sup>th</sup> 1889

The above case was submitted by Atty without evidence. The Commission therefore decide that Julia A.E. Ivey Turner age 21 yrs. and the following children Dan Gones[sic], Oliver Gones, Joseph Haney, Nelson Winters, Luther Winters, are not Cherokees by blood. P.O. Arkansas City, Kansas.

# Cherokee Citizenship Commission Docket Books
## (1880-84, 1887-89) Volume V
### Tahlequah, Cherokee Nation

<table>
<tr><td>Attest</td><td>Will.P. Ross<br>Chairman</td></tr>
<tr><td>D.S. Williams</td><td>J.E. Gunter   Com</td></tr>
</table>

---

## THOMAS

**DOCKET #2023**

CENSUS ROLLS 1835 to 1852

APPLICANT FOR CHEREE CITIZENSHIP

| POST OFFICE: Little River, Tex | | ATTORNEY: A.E. Ivey | |
|---|---|---|---|
| NO | NAMES | AGE | SEX |
| 1 | T.W. Thomas | 40 | male |

ANCESTOR: Mrs. Tatum

Rejected Sept. 7th 1889

Office Commission on Citizenship
Cherokee Nation Ind Ter
Tahlequah Sept. 7th 1889

The above application was submitted by claimant's Attorney A.E. Ivey without evidence. Therefore the Commission decide that applicant T.W. Thomas age 40 yrs. is not a Cherokee by blood and he is hereby rejected. P.O. Little River Texas.

<table>
<tr><td>Attest</td><td>Will.P. Ross<br>Chairman</td></tr>
<tr><td>D.S. Williams<br>Asst Clk Com.</td><td>J.E. Gunter   Com</td></tr>
</table>

---

## THOMAS

**DOCKET #2024**

CENSUS ROLLS 1835 to 1852

APPLICANT FOR CHEREE CITIZENSHIP

| POST OFFICE: Little River Tex | | ATTORNEY: A.E. Ivey | |
|---|---|---|---|
| NO | NAMES | AGE | SEX |
| 1 | E.G. Ross Thomas | 30 | male |

ANCESTOR: Mrs. Tatum

Rejected Sept. 7th 1889

125

Office Commission on Citizenship
Cherokee Nation Ind Ter
Tahlequah  Sept. 7[th] 1889

The above application was submitted by claimant's Attorney A.E. Ivey without evidence. Therefore we decide that claimant E.G. Ross Thomas age 30 yrs. is not a Cherokee by blood. P.O. Little River Texas.

Will.P. Ross

Attest                                    Chairman

    D.S. Williams                 J.E. Gunter   Com

    Asst  Clk  Com.

---

## TALLY

**DOCKET #2025**

CENSUS ROLLS  1851

APPLICANT FOR CHEROKEE CITIZENSHIP

| POST OFFICE: Jasper, Mo | | ATTORNEY: A.E. Ivey | |
|---|---|---|---|
| No | NAMES | AGE | SEX |
| 1 | Abram Tally | 61 | male |
| 2 | John Tally, Jr. | 31 | " |

ANCESTOR: Horatio Tally

Now on this the 17[th] day of May 1888, comes the above case up for final hearing, and the Commission says: "We the Commission on Citizenship after "carefully examining the evidence in the case of the above applicants, and also "the rolls of 1851, fail to show their ancestors as alleged; the testimony taken in "their behalf fail to ~~show~~ prove they are Cherokees by blood, but only state they "are related to Cherokees. The testimony of G.W. Morris who at one time "resided in the same locality in Georgia, goes to show that none of Talleys "family were recognized as being Cherokees by blood, but they were recognized "as being mixed with Cataba[sic] blood.

"    The Commission therefore decide that Abram and John Talley[sic] are not "Cherokees by blood and not entitled to any rights & privileges of the Cherokee "Nation, and hereby rejected.

J. T. Adair    Chairman Commission

D.W. Lipe    Commissioner

# Cherokee Citizenship Commission Docket Books (1880-84, 1887-89) Volume V
## Tahlequah, Cherokee Nation

---

## THURSTON

**DOCKET #2026**

CENSUS ROLLS 1835 to 1852

APPLICANT FOR CHEROKEE CITIZENSHIP

| POST OFFICE: Alma. Ark. | | ATTORNEY: A.E. Ivey | |
|---|---|---|---|
| **No** | **NAMES** | **AGE** | **SEX** |
| 1 | Garland A. Thurston | 24 | male |

ANCESTOR: Andrew Moton

Rejected Sept. 7th 1889

Office Commission on Citizenship
Cherokee Nation Ind Ter
Tahlequah Sept. 7th 1889

The above application was submitted by claimant's Attorney A.E. Ivey without evidence. Therefore the Commission that applicant Garland A. Thurston age 24 yrs. is not a Cherokee by blood. P.O. Alma, Ark.

Attest
    D.S. Williams
    Asst Clk Com.

Will.P. Ross
    Chairman
J.E. Gunter   Com

---

## THURSTON

**DOCKET #2027**

CENSUS ROLLS 1835 to 1852

APPLICANT FOR CHEROKEE CITIZENSHIP

| POST OFFICE: Alma, Ark. | | ATTORNEY: A.E. Ivey | |
|---|---|---|---|
| **No** | **NAMES** | **AGE** | **SEX** |
| 1 | Richard M. Thurston | 29 | male |
| 2 | Rosa Thurston | 20 | female |
| 3 | Hugh F. Thurston | 18 | male |
| 4 | Anna A. Thurston | 14 | female |

ANCESTOR: Andrew Moton

Rejected Sept. 7th 1889

127

# Cherokee Citizenship Commission Docket Books
## (1880-84, 1887-89) Volume V
## Tahlequah, Cherokee Nation

Office Commission on Citizenship
Cherokee Nation Ind Ter
Tahlequah  Sept. 7[th] 1889

The above application was submitted by claimant's Attorney A.E. Ivey without evidence. Therefore the Commission decide that applicant Richard M. Thurston age 29 yrs. and children Rosa Thurston age 20 yrs. Hugh F. Thurston age 18 yrs. and Anna A. Thurston, are not Cherokees by blood and are hereby rejected.

Will.P. Ross
Chairman
J.E. Gunter   Com

Attest
    D.S. Williams
    Asst  Clk  Com.

---

## THURSTON

**DOCKET #2028**
CENSUS ROLLS  1835 to 1852

APPLICANT FOR CHEROKEE CITIZENSHIP

| POST OFFICE: Dyer, Ark. | | ATTORNEY: A.E. Ivey | |
|---|---|---|---|
| NO | NAMES | AGE | SEX |
| 1 | Richard Thurston | 22 | male |

ANCESTOR:  Richard Thurston

Rejected Sept. 7[th] 1889

Office Commission on Citizenship
Cherokee Nation Ind Ter
Tahlequah  Sept. 7[th] 1889

The above application was submitted by claimant's Attorney A.E. Ivey without evidence. Therefore the Commission decide that applicant Richard Thurston age 22 yrs. is not a Cherokee by blood. P.O. Dyer Ark.

Will.P. Ross
Chairman
J.E. Gunter   Com

Attest
    D.S. Williams
    Asst  Clk  Com.

---

128

# Cherokee Citizenship Commission Docket Books
## (1880-84, 1887-89) Volume V
## Tahlequah, Cherokee Nation

## TALLY

**DOCKET #2029**

CENSUS ROLLS 1851

APPLICANT FOR CHEROKEE CITIZENSHIP

| POST OFFICE: Jasper, Ga. | | ATTORNEY: A.E. Ivey | |
|---|---|---|---|
| **NO** | **NAMES** | **AGE** | **SEX** |
| 1 | Horatio Tally | 28 | male |
| 2 | Plonnie Tally | 5 | female |
| 3 | Bettie Tally | 4 | " |
| 4 | Maud A. Tally | 1 | " |

ANCESTOR: John Tally, Sr.

Now on this, the 17th day of May 1888, comes the above case up for final hearing, and the Commission say, "We the Commission on Citizenship after "carefully examining the evidence in the above case & also the census rolls of "1851, fail to find their ancestor, John Talley[sic], as alleged. The testimony "taken in the state of Georgia in their own behalf, fail to show that they are "Cherokees by blood. The evidence of G.W. Morris, who once resided in the "state of Georgia in the same locality where the applicants resided, show "conclusively that they are not Cherokees by blood, but they once claimed to be "Cataba[sic] Indians.

" The Commission therefore decide that Horatio Talley[sic] and his three "children, viz: Plonnie – Bettie – and Mauda[sic] Ann Talley are not Cherokees "by blood and are not entitled to any of the rights and privileges of the Cherokee "Nation, and are hereby rejected.

J. T. Adair     Chairman Commission

D.W. Lipe     Commissioner

## TALLY

**DOCKET #2030**

CENSUS ROLLS 1851

APPLICANT FOR CHEROKEE CITIZENSHIP

| POST OFFICE: Jasper, Ga. | | ATTORNEY: A.E. Ivey | |
|---|---|---|---|
| **NO** | **NAMES** | **AGE** | **SEX** |
| 1 | John Tally | 29 | male |

ANCESTOR: Horatio Tally

# Cherokee Citizenship Commission Docket Books
## (1880-84, 1887-89) Volume V
## Tahlequah, Cherokee Nation

Now on this, the 17[th] day of May 1888, comes the above case up for final hearing, and the Commission say, "We the Commission on Citizenship after "carefully examining the evidence in the case of the above applicant, and also "the census rolls, fail to find the ancestor as alleged. The testimony ~~of~~ taken in "his behalf fail to show that they[sic] are Cherokees by blood. The testimony of "G.W. Morris, taken on part of the Nation, shows conclusively that they are not "Cherokees by blood, but that they or their family once claimed to be part "Cataba[sic] Indian. The Commission therefore decide that said John Talley is "not a Cherokee by blood and are[sic] not entitled to any rights and privileges of "the Cherokee Nation, and stands rejected.

J. T. Adair    Chairman Commission
D.W. Lipe    Commissioner

## TIDWELL

**DOCKET #2031**
CENSUS ROLLS 1851

APPLICANT FOR CHEROKEE CITIZENSHIP

| POST OFFICE: Huntsville, Ark. | | ATTORNEY: A.E. Ivey | |
|---|---|---|---|
| **NO** | **NAMES** | **AGE** | **SEX** |
| 1 | John Tidwell | 72 | male |
| 2 | Verceney Tidwell | 37 | female |
| 3 | Marney C. Tidwell | 33 | " |
| 4 | Safronia C. Tidwell | 31 | " |
| 5 | Pennington W. Tidwell | 26 | male |
| 6 | Miner L. Tidwell | 22 | " |
| 7 | Ida Tidwell | 16 | female |
| 8 | James F. Tidwell | 13 | male |
| 9 | Charles M. Tidwell | 6 | " |
| 10 | John W. Tidwell | 1 | " |
| 11 | Lizzie Tidwell | 1 | female |

ANCESTOR: Young Deer

In the matter of the above applicant and his family, after examining all the evidence carefully, and also the census rolls taken in 1851 by Mr. Siler, of all the Cherokees east of the Mississippi river[sic], we find the name of John

# Cherokee Citizenship Commission Docket Books (1880-84, 1887-89) Volume V
## Tahlequah, Cherokee Nation

Tidwell enrolled as a Cherokee by blood, and Mr. Siler states under the head of remarks, that he "made diligent inquiry and from information gained from the most reliable persons in the vicinity where he resided, (he) was satisfied that John Tidwell was a half breed Cherokee" and taking the 1851 rolls as our guide, under the law passed Dec. 8[th] 1886, creating this Commission, together with the testimony submitted in this case, especially that of James R. Hendricks, a citizen of this Nation and a Cherokee by blood, who is also closely related to the applicant, we the Commission unanimously agree and adjudge, that John Tidwell, the above applicant is a Cherokee by blood, and <u>he</u> and his ten children mentioned in this application are hereby re-admitted to all the rights and privileges of Cherokee citizens by blood. The names of his children in this application are as follows, viz: Verceney, Marney C, Safronia C., Pennington W, Miner J[sic], Ida, James T., Chauney[sic] M., John W. and Lize[sic] Tidwell.

|  |  |
|---|---|
| J. T. Adair | Chairman Commission |
| D.W. Lipe | Commissioner |
| H.C. Barnes | Commissioner |

Office Com on Citizenship
  Tahlequah I.T. Sept. 21[st] 1888

---

## TIDWELL

**DOCKET #2032**
CENSUS ROLLS

APPLICANT FOR CHEROKEE CITIZENSHIP

| POST OFFICE: Dallas, Ga. | | ATTORNEY: A.E. Ivey | |
|---|---|---|---|
| NO | NAMES | AGE | SEX |
| 1 | Pleasant Tidwell | 44 | male |
| 2 | Mary M. Tidwell | 21 | female |
| 3 | Lucresa Tidwell | 17 | " |
| 4 | Martha V. Tidwell | 14 | " |
| 5 | Elsa J. Tidwell | 12 | " |
| 6 | James P. Tidwell | 10 | male |

ANCESTOR: John Tidwell

We the Commission on Citizenship after examining the evidence in the above case, find the applicants are descended from John Tidwell who has proven by the evidence of James Hendricks to be a relation of his and a

# Cherokee Citizenship Commission Docket Books
## (1880-84, 1887-89) Volume V
## Tahlequah, Cherokee Nation

Cherokee by blood. The Siler rolls taken East of the Mississippi river[sic] in the year 1851, shows that John Tidwell was recognized and enrolled as a Cherokee by blood. Therefore we the Commission, decide under the law creating this Commission dated Dec. 8[th] 1886, that Pleasant Tidwell and his five children, Mary M., Lucrecia[sic], Martha, Eliza[sic] S[sic] and James P. Tidwell are Cherokees by blood and are hereby re-admitted to all the rights & privileges of Cherokee citizens by blood.

|                  |                      |
|------------------|----------------------|
| J. T. Adair      | Chairman Commission  |
| D.W. Lipe        | Commissioner         |
| H C Barnes       | Commissioner         |

Office Com on Citizenship
Tahlequah, I.T. Sept. 21[st] 1888.

---

## TARPLEY

**DOCKET #2033**
CENSUS ROLLS 1835 to 1852

APPLICANT FOR CHEROKEE CITIZENSHIP

| POST OFFICE: Alma, Ark. | | ATTORNEY: A.E. Ivey | |
|------|--------------------|------|--------|
| **NO** | **NAMES** | **AGE** | **SEX** |
| 1 | S.S. Tarpley | 42 | male |
| 2 | John Tarpley | 16 | " |
| 3 | W.C. Tarpley | 14 | " |
| 4 | J.S. Tarpley | 12 | " |
| 5 | Sarah P. Tarpley | 10 | female |
| 6 | Virginia Tarpley | 8 | " |
| 7 | Lucretia Tarpley | 5 | " |
| 8 | Viola Tarpley | 3 | " |

ANCESTOR: Mary Davis

Rejected Sept. 7[th] 1889

Office Commission on Citizenship
Cherokee Nation Ind Ter
Tahlequah Sept. 7[th] 1889

The above application was submitted by claimant's Attorney A.E. Ivey without evidence. Therefore we decide that applicant S.S. Tarpley age 42 yrs. and children, John Tarpley age 16 yrs. W.C. Tarpley age 14 yrs. J.B. Tarpley age 12 yrs. Sarah P. Tarpley age 10 yrs. Virginia Tarpley 8 yrs. Lucretia Tarpley age 5 yrs. Viola Tarpley age 3 yrs. are not Cherokees by blood and are hereby rejected.

Will.P. Ross<br>
Chairman

Attest<br>
 D.S. Williams       J.E. Gunter   Com<br>
 Asst Clk Com.

---

## TERRY

**DOCKET #2034**
CENSUS ROLLS 1835

APPLICANT FOR CHEROKEE CITIZENSHIP

| POST OFFICE: Berryville, Ark. | | ATTORNEY: A.E. Ivey | |
|---|---|---|---|
| No | NAMES | AGE | SEX |
| 1 | Miles Terry | 36 | male |
| 2 | Rosetta Terry | 8 | female |

ANCESTOR: Hiram Bryant

Now on this the 26th day of June 1888, comes the above case for a final hearing, it being one of eleven applicants claiming a descent from Hiram Bryant. The testimony in this case will be found in application of Rachel Wilder & Isaac Terry. Also on Record pages 74 to 81.

The decision will also be found governing this case on page 311 of this Book in the Rachel Wilder case – Adverse to claimant.

     J. T. Adair   Chairman Commission<br>
     D.W. Lipe   Commissioner

---

## TERRY

**DOCKET #2035**
CENSUS ROLLS 1835

APPLICANT FOR CHEROKEE CITIZENSHIP

| POST OFFICE: Berryville, Ark | | ATTORNEY: A.E. Ivey | |
|---|---|---|---|
| No | NAMES | AGE | SEX |
| 1 | H.B. Terry | 28 | male |

| 2 | Pearly Terry | 4 | female |
|---|---|---|---|
| 3 | Effie Terry | 2 | " |
| 4 | Ada Terry | 1 | " |

**ANCESTOR:** Hiram Bryant

Now on this the 26<sup>th</sup> day of June 1888, comes the above case up for final hearing, it being one of eleven applicants claiming a descent from Hiram Bryant. Decision Adverse to claimant and will be found in the Rachel Wilder case in this book on page 311.

The testimony will be found on Record pages 74 to 81.

J. T. Adair    Chairman Commission
D.W. Lipe    Commissioner

---

## TERRY

**DOCKET #2036**
CENSUS ROLLS 1835

APPLICANT FOR CHEROKEE CITIZENSHIP

| POST OFFICE: Berryville, Ark. | | ATTORNEY: A.E. Ivey | |
|---|---|---|---|
| NO | NAMES | AGE | SEX |
| 1 | John Terry | 32 | male |
| 2 | Lucretia C. Terry | 13 | female |
| 3 | Rachel C. Terry | 10 | " |

**ANCESTOR:** Hiram Bryant

Now on this the 26<sup>th</sup> day of June 1888, comes the above case up for final hearing, it being one of eleven cases claiming a descent from one Hiram Bryant. Decision governing this case will be found in the Rachel Wilder, et. al. case found on page 311 of this book.

Testimony will be found in Rachel Wilder & Isaac Terry cases on Record pages 74 to 81. Adverse to claimant.

J. T. Adair    Chairman Commission
D.W. Lipe    Commissioner

---

# Cherokee Citizenship Commission Docket Books
# (1880-84, 1887-89) Volume V
# Tahlequah, Cherokee Nation

## TERRY

**DOCKET #2037**
CENSUS ROLLS 1835

APPLICANT FOR CHEROKEE CITIZENSHIP

| POST OFFICE: Berryville, Ark | | ATTORNEY: A.E. Ivey | |
|---|---|---|---|
| NO | NAMES | AGE | SEX |
| 1 | Joseph Terry | 35 | male |

ANCESTOR: Hiram Bryant

Now on this the 26th day of June 1888, comes the above case up for final hearing, it being one of eleven cases claiming a descent from one Hiram Bryant. Decision will be found governing this case in the Rachel Wilder case in this book on page 311.

Testimony will be found on Records pages 74 to 81. Adverse to claimant.

J. T. Adair      Chairman Commission
D.W. Lipe      Commissioner

---

## TERRY

**DOCKET #2038**
CENSUS ROLLS 1835

APPLICANT FOR CHEROKEE CITIZENSHIP

| POST OFFICE: Berryville, Ark. | | ATTORNEY: A.E. Ivey | |
|---|---|---|---|
| NO | NAMES | AGE | SEX |
| 1 | Samuel Terry | 19 | male |
| 2 | John Terry | 18 | " |
| 3 | Caloin Terry | 16 | " |
| 4 | Ausell D. Terry | 14 | " |

ANCESTOR: Hiram Bryant

Now on this the 26th day of June 1888, comes the above case up for final hearing, it being one of eleven cases claiming a descent from one Hiram Bryant. Testimony will be found on Record pages 74 to 81 in the Rachel Wilder case. Decision will be found in this same case, Rachel Wilder, et. al. in this book on page 311.

135

Adverse to claimant.

J. T. Adair    Chairman Commission
D.W. Lipe    Commissioner

## TIDWELL

**DOCKET #2039**
CENSUS ROLLS 1851

APPLICANT FOR CHEROKEE CITIZENSHIP

| POST OFFICE: Centree[sic], Ala. | | ATTORNEY: A.E. Ivey | |
|---|---|---|---|
| No | NAMES | AGE | SEX |
| 1 | John G. Tidwell | 35 | male |
| 2 | George P. Tidwell | 6 | " |
| 3 | Martha C. Tidwell | 4 | female |

ANCESTOR: John Tidwell

We the Commission on Citizenship after carefully examing[sic] into the above case, and also the census rolls of Cherokees taken East of the Mississippi river[sic] in the year 1851, and that the applicant and his children are of Cherokee blood, he being the son of John Tidwell a half breed Cherokee Indian.

Therefore we the Commission on Citizenship decide that John G. Tidwell and his two children George P. and Martha C. Tidwell are Cherokees by blood and are hereby re-admitted to all the rights and privileges of Cherokee citizens by blood.

J. T. Adair    Chairman Commission
D.W. Lipe    Commissioner
H.C. Barnes   Commissioner

Office Com on Citizenship
Tahlequah I.T. Sept 21$^{st}$ 1888.

## McFADDEN

**DOCKET #2040**
CENSUS ROLLS 1835 to 1852

APPLICANT FOR CHEROKEE CITIZENSHIP

| POST OFFICE: Russelville[sic], Ark. | | ATTORNEY: Boudinot and Rasmus | |
|---|---|---|---|
| No | NAMES | AGE | SEX |
| 1 | Nancy A. McFadden | 56 | female |

| 2 | Garland C. McFadden | 12 | male |
|---|---|---|---|

ANCESTOR: Barsheba Goodrich

Office Commission on Citizenship
Tahlequah Cherokee Nation IT
June 20[th] 1889

There being no evidence in support of the above named case the Commission decide that Nancy A. McFadden age 56 years and her son Garland C. McFadden age 12 years are not Cherokees by blood.

Attest                              Will.P. Ross
    EG Ross                                           Chairman
        Clerk Commission            J.E. Gunter    Com

## McDANIEL

**DOCKET #2041**
CENSUS ROLLS

APPLICANT FOR CHEROKEE CITIZENSHIP

| POST OFFICE: Science Hill, N.C. | | ATTORNEY: | |
|---|---|---|---|
| NO | NAMES | AGE | SEX |
| 1 | Jame McDaniel | 51 | female |
| 2 | Mary J. McDaniel | 24 | " |
| 3 | John H. McDaniel | 19 | male |
| 4 | Sarah C. McDaniel | 21 | female |
| 5 | Elizabeth J. Winslow | 19 | " |
| 6 | Edward J, Winslow | 17 | male |
| 7 | James Winslow | 15 | " |
| 8 | Nancy W. Winslow | 13 | female |

ANCESTOR: Sarah Elmore

Adverse. See decision of Commission in case John R. Henly Docket 553, Book B, Page 266.

Will.P. Ross
                                    Chairman
            R. Bunch    Com
                J.E. Gunter    Com

## McDONNALD

**DOCKET #2042**

CENSUS ROLLS 1851 & 1852

APPLICANT FOR CHEROKEE CITIZENSHIP

| POST OFFICE: Grape Creek, N.C. | | ATTORNEY: C.H. Taylor | |
|---|---|---|---|
| NO | NAMES | AGE | SEX |
| 1 | Mary McDonnald | 42 | female |

ANCESTOR: Catherine McDonnald

Rejected Sept. 7th 1889

Office Commission on Citizenship
Cherokee Nation Ind Ter
Tahlequah Sept. 7th 1889

The above case was called 3 times and no response from applicant or by Atty and there being no evidence on file in support of claim the Commission are of the opinion and so decide that Mary McDonnald age 43 yrs. is not a Cherokee by blood. P.O. Grape Creek, N.C.

Will.P. Ross
Attest                                    Chairman
   D.S. Williams                  J.E. Gunter   Com
   Asst   Clk   Com.

## McDANIEL

**DOCKET #2043**

CENSUS ROLLS

APPLICANT FOR CHEROKEE CITIZENSHIP

| POST OFFICE: Science Hill, N.C. | | ATTORNEY: L.B. Bell | |
|---|---|---|---|
| NO | NAMES | AGE | SEX |
| 1 | Jame McDaniel | | female |

ANCESTOR: Sarah Elmore

Adverse. See decision Commission in case John R. Henly Docket 553, Book B, Page 266.

Will.P. Ross   Chairman
J.E. Gunter   Com

# Cherokee Citizenship Commission Docket Books
## (1880-84, 1887-89) Volume V
## Tahlequah, Cherokee Nation

---

## MARTIN

**DOCKET #2044**

CENSUS ROLLS  1835 to 1852

APPLICANT FOR CHEROKEE CITIZENSHIP

| POST OFFICE: Fall River, Kans | | ATTORNEY: A.E. Ivey | |
|------|------|------|------|
| NO | NAMES | AGE | SEX |
| 1 | Benjamin L. Martin | 37 | male |

ANCESTOR: Lewis Martin

Rejected Sept 7th 1889

Office Commission on Citizenship
Cherokee Nation Ind Ter
Tahlequah  Sept. 7th 1889

The application in the above case having been submitted by Attorney A.E. Ivey for claimant without proof the Commission decide that Benj. L. Martin 37 years old of Fall River Kansas is not of Cherokee blood.

Will.P. Ross
Chairman

Attest

D.S. Williams
Asst  Clk  Com.

J.E. Gunter   Com

---

## MAXIEL

**DOCKET #2045**

CENSUS ROLLS  1835 to 1852

APPLICANT FOR CHEROKEE CITIZENSHIP

| POST OFFICE: Van Buren Ark. | | ATTORNEY: A.E. Ivey | |
|------|------|------|------|
| NO | NAMES | AGE | SEX |
| 1 | Corie Maxiel | 45 | female |

ANCESTOR: Siller Ratcliff

Rejected Sept. 7th 1889

Office Commission on Citizenship
Cherokee Nation Ind Ter
Tahlequah  Sept. 7th 1889

The above application having been submitted by Attorney A.E. Ivey without proof, the Commission decide that claimant is not of Cherokee blood.  P.O. Van Buren Ark.

|  |  |
|---|---|
| | Will.P. Ross |
| Attest | Chairman |
| D.S. Williams | J.E. Gunter   Com |
| Asst  Clk  Com. | |

## MOORE

**DOCKET #2046**

CENSUS ROLLS  1835 to 1852

APPLICANT FOR CHEROKEE CITIZENSHIP

| POST OFFICE: White Rock, Texas | | ATTORNEY: A.E. Ivey | |
|---|---|---|---|
| NO | NAMES | AGE | SEX |
| 1 | J.J. Moore | 54 | male |
| 2 | Beatrice Moore | 12 | female |
| 3 | Laura Moore | 8 | " |
| 4 | L.L. Moore | 6 | " |

ANCESTOR: William Moore

Office Commission on Citizenship
Tahlequah Ind Ter  July 2$^{nd}$ 1889

There being no evidence in support of the above named case the Commission decide that J.J. Moore aged 54 years, Beatrice aged 12 years, Laura aged 8 years, and L.L. Moore aged 6 years are not Cherokees by blood.

|  |  |
|---|---|
| Attest | Will.P. Ross |
| E.G. Ross | Chairman |
| Clerk Com. | J.E. Gunter   Com |

# Cherokee Citizenship Commission Docket Books
## (1880-84, 1887-89) Volume V
## Tahlequah, Cherokee Nation

### MELTON

**DOCKET #2047**

CENSUS ROLLS  1835 to 1851

APPLICANT FOR CHEROKEE CITIZENSHIP

| POST OFFICE: Claremore I.T. | | ATTORNEY: A.E. Ivey | |
|---|---|---|---|
| **No** | **NAMES** | **AGE** | **SEX** |
| 1 | Thompson Melton | 50 | male |
| 2 | William Melton | 20 | female[sic] |

ANCESTOR: Mrs. Badson

Rejected Sept. 7<sup>th</sup> 1889

Office Commission on Citizenship
Cherokee Nation Ind Ter
Tahlequah  Sept. 7<sup>th</sup> 1889

The above case was called 3 times and no response from Applicant or by Atty and there being no evidence on file in support of claim, The Commission are of the opinion and so decide that Thompson Melton age 50 yrs. and his son Wm Melton male 20 yrs. are not Cherokees by blood. P.O. Claremore I.T.

Will.P. Ross

Attest                                    Chairman
  D.S. Williams                         J.E. Gunter   Com
  Asst  Clk  Com.

---

### MELTON

**DOCKET #2048**

CENSUS ROLLS  1835 to 1852

APPLICANT FOR CHEROKEE CITIZENSHIP

| POST OFFICE: Claremore I.T. | | ATTORNEY: A.E. Ivey | |
|---|---|---|---|
| **No** | **NAMES** | **AGE** | **SEX** |
| 1 | Richard R. Melton | 25 | male |

ANCESTOR: Mrs. Badson

Rejected Sept. 7<sup>th</sup> 1889

Office Commission on Citizenship
Cherokee Nation Ind Ter
Tahlequah  Sept. 7<sup>th</sup> 1889

141

# Cherokee Citizenship Commission Docket Books
## (1880-84, 1887-89) Volume V
## Tahlequah, Cherokee Nation

The application in the above case having been submitted by Attorney for claimant A.E. Ivey without proof. The Commission decide that Richard R. Melton 25 years old is not of Cherokee blood. P.O. Claremore I.T.

Will.P. Ross

| Attest | Chairman |
|---|---|
| D.S. Williams | J.E. Gunter   Com |
| Asst  Clk  Com. | |

---

## MELTON

**DOCKET #2049**

CENSUS ROLLS  1835 to 1852

APPLICANT FOR CHEROKEE CITIZENSHIP

| POST OFFICE: Claremore I.T. | | ATTORNEY: A.E. Ivey | |
|---|---|---|---|
| **NO** | **NAMES** | **AGE** | **SEX** |
| 1 | Eliza Melton | 55 | female |

ANCESTOR: Mrs. Badson

Rejected Sept. 7th 1889

Office Commission on Citizenship<br>Cherokee Nation Ind Ter<br>Tahlequah  Sept. 7th 1889

The above case was called 3 times and no response from applicant or by Attorney. The Commission are of the opinion and so decide that Eliza Melton age 55 yrs. is not a Cherokee by blood. P.O. Claremore I.T.

Will.P. Ross

| Attest | Chairman |
|---|---|
| D.S. Williams | J.E. Gunter   Com |
| Asst  Clk  Com. | |

---

142

# Cherokee Citizenship Commission Docket Books
## (1880-84, 1887-89) Volume V
## Tahlequah, Cherokee Nation

## MELTON

**DOCKET #2050**

CENSUS ROLLS 1835 to 1852

APPLICANT FOR CHEROKEE CITIZENSHIP

| POST OFFICE: Claremore, I.T. | | ATTORNEY: A.E. Ivey | |
|---|---|---|---|
| NO | NAMES | AGE | SEX |
| 1 | E.R. Melton | 25 | male |

ANCESTOR: Mrs. Bradson

Rejected Sept. 7th 1889

Office Commission on Citizenship
Cherokee Nation Ind Ter
Tahlequah Sept. 7th 1889

The application in the above case having been submitted by Attorney A.E. Ivey for claimant without proof, the Commission decide that E.R. Melton is not of Cherokee blood. P.O. Claremore I.T.

Will.P. Ross

Attest
Chairman
   D.S. Williams
J.E. Gunter   Com
   Asst   Clk   Com.

## MELTON

**DOCKET #2051**

CENSUS ROLLS 1835 to 1852

APPLICANT FOR CHEROKEE CITIZENSHIP

| POST OFFICE: Claremore, I.T. | | ATTORNEY: A.E. Ivey | |
|---|---|---|---|
| NO | NAMES | AGE | SEX |
| 1 | W.T. Melton | 32 | male |

ANCESTOR: Mrs. Badson

Rejected Sept. 7th 1889

Office Commission on Citizenship
Cherokee Nation Ind Ter
Tahlequah Sept. 7th 1889

The above case was called 3 times and no response from applicant or by Atty and there being no evidence on file in support of claim the Commission are of the opinion and so decide that W.T. Melton age 32 yrs. is not a Cherokee by blood. P.O. Claremore, I.T.

Attest

D.S. Williams
Asst Clk Com.

Will.P. Ross
Chairman
J.E. Gunter    Com

---

## McCOY

**DOCKET #2052**

CENSUS ROLLS

APPLICANT FOR CHEROKEE CITIZENSHIP

| POST OFFICE: Mineral Springs, Ga. | | ATTORNEY: A.E. Ivey | |
|---|---|---|---|
| NO | NAMES | AGE | SEX |
| 1 | James W. McCoy | 21 | male |
| 2 | William M. McCoy | 1 | " |

ANCESTOR: Rosana McCoy

Now on this the 1st day of June, 1888, comes the above case up for final hearing and the Commission say: "We the Commission on Citizenship after examining the evidence and the rolls of 1852 find the above applicant to be Cherokee by blood and the above James W. McCoy and his son William McCoy are hereby re-admitted to all the rights and privileges of Cherokee citizens by blood."

J. T. Adair    Chairman Commission
John E. Gunter    Commissioner
D.W. Lipe    Commissioner

---

## McCOY

**DOCKET #2053**

CENSUS ROLLS 1851

APPLICANT FOR CHEROKEE CITIZENSHIP

| POST OFFICE: Mineral Springs, Ga. | | ATTORNEY: A.E. Ivey | |
|---|---|---|---|
| NO | NAMES | AGE | SEX |
| 1 | John W. McCoy | 26 | male |
| 2 | John W. McCoy | 6 | " |
| 3 | Josaphine McCoy | 5 | female |

| 4 | Martha McCoy | 4 | " |
| 5 | Lillie McCoy | 1 | " |

**ANCESTOR:** Rosana McCoy

Now on this the 1<sup>st</sup> day of June 1888, comes the above case up for final hearing and the Commission say: "We the Commission on Citizenship after examining the testimony in the above case, and also the rolls of 1852, find that the applicants are Cherokees by blood, and the above named John W. McCoy and his four children, John W. – Joseph[sic] – Martha and Lillie McCoy are hereby re-admitted to all the rights and privileges of Cherokee citizens by blood."

J. T. Adair    Chairman Commission
John E. Gunter    Commissioner
D.W. Lipe    Commissioner

---

## MISER

**DOCKET #2054**
CENSUS ROLLS 1835 to 1852

APPLICANT FOR CHEROKEE CITIZENSHIP

| POST OFFICE: Lattenet, Wash, Tex. | | ATTORNEY: A.E. Ivey | |
|---|---|---|---|
| NO | NAMES | AGE | SEX |
| 1 | Mary S. Miser | 42 | female |
| 2 | Annie Miser | 14 | " |
| 3 | Columbus Miser | 10 | male |
| 4 | James Miser | 8 | " |
| 5 | Garfield Miser | 6 | " |

**ANCESTOR:** Mary S. Bell

Rejected Sept. 7<sup>th</sup> 1889

Office Commission on Citizenship
Cherokee Nation Ind Ter
Tahlequah Sept. 7<sup>th</sup> 1889

The above application was submitted by claimant's Attorney A.E. Ivey without evidence. Therefore we decide that applicant Mary Susan Miser age 42 yrs. and children Annie Miser age 14 yrs. Columbus Miser age 10 yrs. James Miser age 8 yrs. Garfield Miser age 6 yrs. are not Cherokees by blood. P.O. *(Illegible)* Wash, Tex.

|                    | Will.P. Ross        |
| ------------------ | ------------------- |
| Attest             | Chairman            |
| D.S. Williams      | J.E. Gunter   Com   |
| Asst  Clk  Com.    |                     |

---

## MORRIS

**DOCKET #2055**

CENSUS ROLLS  1835 to 1852

APPLICANT FOR CHEROKEE CITIZENSHIP

| POST OFFICE:  Galena, Ark. | | ATTORNEY: A.E. Ivey | |
| --- | --- | --- | --- |
| No | NAMES | AGE | SEX |
| 1 | Bell Morris | 28 | female |
| 2 | Sarah Morris | 8 | " |
| 3 | Paden Morris | 5 | male |

ANCESTOR: John Thompson

Rejected Sept. 7th 1889

Office Commission on Citizenship
Cherokee Nation Ind Ter
Tahlequah  Sept. 7th 1889

The above application was submitted by Attorney A.E. Ivey without evidence. Therefore we decide that applicant Bell Morris age 28 yrs. and children Sarah Morris age 8 yrs. and Paden Morris age 5 yrs. are not Cherokees by blood. P.O. Galena Ark.

|                    | Will.P. Ross        |
| ------------------ | ------------------- |
| Attest             | Chairman            |
| D.S. Williams      | J.E. Gunter   Com   |
| Asst  Clk  Com.    |                     |

---

# Cherokee Citizenship Commission Docket Books
## (1880-84, 1887-89) Volume V
## Tahlequah, Cherokee Nation

## MOORE

**DOCKET #2056**

CENSUS ROLLS

APPLICANT FOR CHEROKEE CITIZENSHIP

| POST OFFICE: Afton, I.T. | | ATTORNEY: L.B. Bell | |
|---|---|---|---|
| **NO** | **NAMES** | **AGE** | **SEX** |
| 1 | Thomas A Moore | 44 | male |

ANCESTOR: Ann Crews

The Commission decide against claimant. See decision in case of Andrew Meredith Docket 2180 Book E, Page 26 and John Henly Docket 1250, Book C Page 376.

Will.P. Ross   Chairman
R. Bunch   Com
John E. Gunter   Com

## MUNROW

**DOCKET #2057**

CENSUS ROLLS

APPLICANT FOR CHEROKEE CITIZENSHIP

| POST OFFICE: Center, N.C. | | ATTORNEY: L.B. Bell | |
|---|---|---|---|
| **NO** | **NAMES** | **AGE** | **SEX** |
| 1 | Mary F. Munrow | 40 | female |

ANCESTOR: Ann Crews

The Commission decide against claimant. See decision in the Andrew Meredith case Docket 2180 Book E, Page 26 and John Henly Docket 1250, Book C Page 376.

Will.P. Ross   Chairman
R. Bunch   Com
John E. Gunter   Com

## MERIDETH

**DOCKET #2058**

CENSUS ROLLS

APPLICANT FOR CHEREOKEE CITIZENSHIP

| POST OFFICE: Spiceland, Ind. | | ATTORNEY: L.B. Bell | |
|---|---|---|---|
| NO | NAMES | AGE | SEX |
| 1 | J.H. Merideth | | male |

ANCESTOR: Mary Crews

The Commission decide against claimant. See decision in case Andrew Merideth Docket 2180 Book E, Page 26 and John Henly Docket 1250, Book C Page 376.

> Will.P. Ross   Chairman
> R. Bunch   Com
> J. E. Gunter   Com

---

## MORGAN

**DOCKET #2059**

CENSUS ROLLS  1835 to 1852

APPLICANT FOR CHEREOKEE CITIZENSHIP

| POST OFFICE: Washington, Kan | | ATTORNEY: L.B. Bell | |
|---|---|---|---|
| NO | NAMES | AGE | SEX |
| 1 | Webster M. Morgan | 29 | male |

ANCESTOR: John Merideth

The Commission decide against claimant. See decision in case of Andrew Merideth Docket 2180 Book E, Page 26 and John Henly Docket 1250, Book C Page 376.

> Will.P. Ross   Chairman
> R. Bunch   Com
> J.E. Gunter   Com

---

# Cherokee Citizenship Commission Docket Books
## (1880-84, 1887-89) Volume V
## Tahlequah, Cherokee Nation

### MERIDETH

**DOCKET #2060**

CENSUS ROLLS  1835 to 1852

APPLICANT FOR CHEROKEE CITIZENSHIP

| POST OFFICE: Huntington, Ind. | | ATTORNEY: L.B. Bell | |
|---|---|---|---|
| NO | NAMES | AGE | SEX |
| 1 | Oscar Merideth | 23 | male |

ANCESTOR:  Mary Crews

The Commission decide against claimant.  See decision in the case of Andrew Merideth Docket 2180 Book E, Page 26 and case John Henly Docket 1250, Book C Page 376.

Will.P. Ross    Chairman

R. Bunch    Com

J.E. Gunter    Com

---

### MERIDETH

**DOCKET #2061**

CENSUS ROLLS

APPLICANT FOR CHEROKEE CITIZENSHIP

| POST OFFICE: Afton, I.T. | | ATTORNEY: L.B. Bell | |
|---|---|---|---|
| NO | NAMES | AGE | SEX |
| 1 | Young B. Merideth | | male |

ANCESTOR:  Mary Crews

The Commission decide against claimant.  See decision in case Andrew Merideth Docket 2180 Book E, Page 26 and case John Henly Docket 1250, Book C Page 376.

Will.P. Ross    Chairman

R. Bunch    Com

J.E. Gunter    Com

---

149

## MERIDETH

**DOCKET #2062**

CENSUS ROLLS

APPLICANT FOR CHEROKEE CITIZENSHIP

| POST OFFICE: Lewis, Iowa | | ATTORNEY: L.B. Bell | |
|---|---|---|---|
| NO | NAMES | AGE | SEX |
| 1 | Wm H. Merideth | 41 | male |
| 2 | W. E. Merideth | 20 | " |
| 3 | Edward Merideth | 14 | " |
| 4 | Sarah E. Merideth | 10 | female |

ANCESTOR: Mary Crews

The Commission decide against claimant. See decision in case Andrew Merideth Docket 2180 Book E, Page 26 and case John Henly Docket 1250, Book C Page 376.

Will.P. Ross    Chairman
R. Bunch
Com
J.E. Gunter    Com

## MERIDETH

**DOCKET #2063**

CENSUS ROLLS

APPLICANT FOR CHEROKEE CITIZENSHIP

| POST OFFICE: Linnville, Iowa | | ATTORNEY: L.B. Bell | |
|---|---|---|---|
| NO | NAMES | AGE | SEX |
| 1 | C.O. Merideth | 43 | male |
| 2 | Ernest Merideth | 17 | " |
| 3 | Effie B. Merideth | 11 | female |
| 4 | Gertie Merideth | 7 | " |

ANCESTOR: Mary Crews

The Commission decide against claimant. See decision in case Andrew Merideth Docket 2180 Book E, Page 26 and case John Henly Docket 1250, Book C Page 376.

# Cherokee Citizenship Commission Docket Books (1880-84, 1887-89) Volume V
## Tahlequah, Cherokee Nation

Will.P. Ross    Chairman
R. Bunch    Com
J.E. Gunter    Com

---

## MOFFITT

**DOCKET #2064**
CENSUS ROLLS

APPLICANT FOR CHEROKEE CITIZENSHIP

| POST OFFICE: Thorntown, Iwa. | | ATTORNEY: L.B. Bell | |
|---|---|---|---|
| No | NAMES | AGE | SEX |
| 1 | Ascenith Moffitt | | female |

ANCESTOR: Martha Elmore

The Commission decide against claimant. See decision in case Lible[sic] J Bogue, Docket 2183, Book E, Page 29.

Will.P. Ross
Chairman
R. Bunch    Com
J.E. Gunter    Com

---

## MILLS

**DOCKET #2065**
CENSUS ROLLS

APPLICANT FOR CHEROKEE CITIZENSHIP

| POST OFFICE: Hartland, Kans. | | ATTORNEY: L.B. Bell | |
|---|---|---|---|
| No | NAMES | AGE | SEX |
| 1 | Daniel M Mills | | male |

ANCESTOR:

*Commission on Citizenship.*

CHEROKEE NATION, IND. TER.

*Tahlequah,* Sept. 9[th] 1889

Daniel M. Mills
    vs.                Application for Cherokee Citizenship
Cherokee Nation

151

# Cherokee Citizenship Commission Docket Books
## (1880-84, 1887-89) Volume V
## Tahlequah, Cherokee Nation

The above applicant affirms in his declaration taken before the Clerk of Marian County in & for the State of Indiana on the 27[th] day of March 1886 – that he is a Cherokee by blood, that he derived said blood through his mother Charity Mills who was born in Warren County, State of Ohio, 1806 & died in Marion County, State of Indiana on the 7[th] day of March 1840. This is all the evidence submitted by applicant to sustain his claim of Cherokee blood. This affidavit above is not sufficient to establish his Cherokee blood and also claimant fails to name any of the Cherokee census rolls where the name of his ancestor ~~name~~ might be found.

In consideration of these facts we ~~do not~~ decide that applicant Daniel M. Mills, age 59 yrs. and children, viz: Amanda M Powell, age 38 yrs., William A. Mills age 36 yrs., Lula A. Starbuck age 32 yrs. Lewis Mills age 22 yrs. Charity Bradford age 26 yrs. Cordelia Mills age 25 yrs. Gurney Mills age 23 yrs. Oscar L Mills age 17 yrs. and grand children, viz: Veman L. Powell age 16 yrs. Amanda E. Mills 13 yrs Magory L. Mills age 11 yrs. *(Illegible)* Mills age 8 yrs. Minnie L. Starbuck age 9 yrs. Flora Starbuck age 7 yrs. *(Illegible)* Starbuck age 1 yr., Clifford Starbuck age 7 yrs., Blanch Bradford 4 yrs. Rascal E. Mills age 4 months are not Cherokees by blood  P.O. Hartland Kans.

Will.P. Ross
Chairman
J.E. Gunter   Com

---

## MILLER

**DOCKET #2066**
CENSUS ROLLS

APPLICANT FOR CHEROKEE CITIZENSHIP

| POST OFFICE: Afton, I.T. | | ATTORNEY: L.B. Bell | |
|---|---|---|---|
| **No** | **NAMES** | **AGE** | **SEX** |
| 1 | Mamie C. Miller | 19 | female |

ANCESTOR: Ann Crews

The Commission decide against claimant.  See decision in case Andrew Meredith Docket 2180 Book E, Page 26 and John Henly Docket 1250, Book C Page 376.

Will.P. Ross   Chairman
R. Bunch   Com
John E. Gunter   Com

---

## MACEY

**DOCKET #2067**

CENSUS ROLLS

APPLICANT FOR CHEROKEE CITIZENSHIP

| POST OFFICE: Afton, I.T. | | ATTORNEY: L.B. Bell | |
|---|---|---|---|
| NO | NAMES | AGE | SEX |
| 1 | Lydia G. Macey | 2 | female |
| 2 | M.G. Macey | 1 | |

ANCESTOR: Ann Crews

The Commission decide against claimant. See decision in case of Andrew Meredith Docket 2180 Book E, Page 26 and John Henly Docket 1250, Book C Page 376.

> Will.P. Ross   Chairman
> R. Bunch   Com
> John E. Gunter   Com

## MORGAN

**DOCKET #2068**

CENSUS ROLLS

APPLICANT FOR CHEROKEE CITIZENSHIP

| POST OFFICE: Sommerset[sic], Ind. | | ATTORNEY: L.B. Bell | |
|---|---|---|---|
| NO | NAMES | AGE | SEX |
| 1 | Ella Morgan | 47 | female |
| 2 | Myrtle Morgan | 18 | " |

ANCESTOR: Mary Crews

The Commission decide against claimant. See decision in case Andrew Merideth Docket 2180 Book E, Page 26 and case John Henly Docket 1250, Book C Page 376.

> Will.P. Ross   Chairman
> R. Bunch   Com
> J.E. Gunter   Com

Cherokee Citizenship Commission Docket Books
(1880-84, 1887-89) Volume V
Tahlequah, Cherokee Nation

## MERIDETH

**DOCKET #2069**

CENSUS ROLLS

APPLICANT FOR CHEROKEE CITIZENSHIP

| POST OFFICE: Ollie, Iowa | | ATTORNEY: L.B. Bell | |
|---|---|---|---|
| **No** | **NAMES** | **AGE** | **SEX** |
| 1 | Thomas B. Merideth | 32 | male |
| 2 | Permelia A. Merideth | 19 | female |
| 3 | Sada E. Merideth | 16 | " |
| 4 | Samuel N. Merideth | 13 | male |
| 5 | Etta Merideth | 11 | female |
| 6 | Thomas B. Merideth | 8 | male |

ANCESTOR: Mary Crews

The Commission decide against claimant. See decision in case Andrew Merideth Docket 2180 Book E, Page 26 and case John Henly Docket 1250, Book C Page 376.

Will.P. Ross   Chairman
R. Bunch   Com
J.E. Gunter   Com

## MERIDETH

**DOCKET #2070**

CENSUS ROLLS

APPLICANT FOR CHEROKEE CITIZENSHIP

| POST OFFICE: Lewis, Iowa | | ATTORNEY: L.B. Bell | |
|---|---|---|---|
| **No** | **NAMES** | **AGE** | **SEX** |
| 1 | James M. Merideth | 33 | male |
| 2 | Preston Merideth | 12 | " |
| 3 | Lula E. Merideth | 5 | female |

ANCESTOR: Mary Crews

The Commission decide against claimant. See decision in case Andrew Merideth Docket 2180 Book E, Page 26 and case John Henly Docket 1250, Book C Page 376.

154

# Cherokee Citizenship Commission Docket Books
## (1880-84, 1887-89) Volume V
## Tahlequah, Cherokee Nation

Will.P. Ross   Chairman
R. Bunch   Com
J.E. Gunter   Com

## MARTIN

**DOCKET #2071**

CENSUS ROLLS 1835 to 1852

APPLICANT FOR CHEROKEE CITIZENSHIP

| POST OFFICE: Carlane, Mo | | ATTORNEY: L.S. Sanders | |
|---|---|---|---|
| No | NAMES | AGE | SEX |
| 1 | Margaret A Martin | 54 | female |
| 2 | John D. Noble | 36 | male |
| 3 | Sarah A. Noble | 34 | female |
| 4 | Mary F. Noble | 32 | " |
| 5 | Laura J. Martin | 30 | " |
| 6 | Delia J. Martin | 28 | " |
| 7 | Margaret L. Martin | 24 | " |

ANCESTOR: Emiline Boatright

Rejected Sept. 7[th] 1889

Office Commission on Citizenship
Cherokee Nation Ind Ter
Tahlequah  Sept. 7[th] 1889

The above case was called 3 times and no response from applicant or by Attorney and there being no evidence on file in support of claim the Commission decide that several times and no response from applicant or by Atty the Commission therefore decide that Margaret A. Martin age 54 yrs. and the following children, John D. male 36 yrs. son, Sarah Ann female 34 yrs. Mary Francis female 32 yrs. Daughter, Laura J. Martin 30 yrs. Daughter, Delia Jane Martin female 28 yrs. Daughter, Margaret L. 24 yrs. Daughter, are not Cherokees by blood. P.O. Carland[sic] Mo.

Attest
   D.S. Williams
   Asst  Clk  Com.

Will.P. Ross
   Chairman
J.E. Gunter   Com

155

# Cherokee Citizenship Commission Docket Books
## (1880-84, 1887-89) Volume V
## Tahlequah, Cherokee Nation

### MURRAY

**DOCKET #2072**

CENSUS ROLLS 1835 to 1852

APPLICANT FOR CHEROKEE CITIZENSHIP

| POST OFFICE: Siloam Springs, Ark. | | ATTORNEY: L.S. Sanders | |
|---|---|---|---|
| **NO** | **NAMES** | **AGE** | **SEX** |
| 1 | George W. Murray | 32 | male |
| 2 | Randolph Murray | 11 | " |
| 3 | Ansona E. Murray | 7 | female |

ANCESTOR: Eliza Murray

Rejected Sept. 9[th] 1889

Office Commission on Citizenship
Cherokee Nation Ind Ter
Tahlequah Sept. 9[th] 1889

Application for Cherokee Citizenship

The above applicant was called 3 times & no answer and there being no evidence on file in support of the application we decide that applicant George W. Murray age 32 yrs and children viz: Randolph Murray age 11 yrs. Ansona E. Murray age 7 yrs. are not Cherokees by blood & this application is hereby rejected. P.O. Siloam Springs.

Will.P. Ross

Attest                              Chairman

D.S. Williams          J.E. Gunter   Com

Asst Clk Com.

---

### MILLS

**DOCKET #2073**

CENSUS ROLLS 1835

APPLICANT FOR CHEROKEE CITIZENSHIP

| POST OFFICE: Natural Dam, Ark. | | ATTORNEY: J.E. Welch | |
|---|---|---|---|
| **NO** | **NAMES** | **AGE** | **SEX** |
| 1 | Alice F. Mills | 39 | female |
| 2 | Wm. H. Mills | 19 | male |
| 3 | John M. Mills | 19 | " |

156

# Cherokee Citizenship Commission Docket Books
## (1880-84, 1887-89) Volume V
### Tahlequah, Cherokee Nation

| 4 | James H. Mills | 11 | " |
|---|---|---|---|

**ANCESTOR:** Larkin Moton

Rejected Sept. 7<sup>th</sup> 1889

Office Commission on Citizenship
Cherokee Nation Ind Ter
Tahlequah Sept. 7<sup>th</sup> 1889

The above case was called 3 times and no response from applicant or by Atty the Commission therefore decide that Alice F. Mills age 29 yrs. and the following children William Mills male 19 yrs., John M. male 16[sic] yrs. James male 11 yrs. are not Cherokees by blood. P.O. Natural dam Ark.

Will.P. Ross
Chairman
Attest
D.S. Williams
Asst Clk Com.
J.E. Gunter Com

---

**Docket #2074**  *(Missing from archival records)*

---

**Docket #2075**  *(Missing from archival records)*

---

## MITCHEL

**DOCKET #2076**
CENSUS ROLLS 1835

APPLICANT FOR CHEROKEE CITIZENSHIP

| POST OFFICE: Carelton[sic], Ark. | | ATTORNEY: C.H. Taylor | |
|---|---|---|---|
| No | NAMES | AGE | SEX |
| 1 | Edward Mitchel | 35 | male |
| 2 | Alice Mitchel | 13 | female |
| 3 | Joel Mitchel | 6 | male |
| 4 | Robert Mitchel | 2 | " |

**ANCESTOR:** Joel Mitchel

Rejected May 23<sup>rd</sup> 1889

Office Commission on Citizenship
Cherokee Nation Ind Ter
Tahlequah May 23<sup>rd</sup> 1889

157

This case is decided adversely to applicant upon the grounds set forth in the decision against William M. Mitchell. See Docket 2075, Book D, Page 561 and includes Alice Mitchell age 13 yrs. Joel Mitchell 6 yrs. and Robert Mitchell 2 yrs.

|  | Will.P. Ross |
|---|---|
| Attest | Chairman |
| D.S. Williams | *(Cherokee letters)* |
| Asst Clk Com. | J.E. Gunter   Com |

## MOODY

**DOCKET #2077**

CENSUS ROLLS  1835

APPLICANT FOR CHEROKEE CITIZENSHIP

| POST OFFICE: South Sulphur, Tex. | | ATTORNEY: C.H. Taylor | |
|---|---|---|---|
| NO | NAMES | AGE | SEX |
| 1 | Sarah Moody | | female |

ANCESTOR: Newrony Mitchel

*Commission on Citizenship.*

CHEROKEE NATION, IND. TER.

*Tahlequah,* Sept. 9th *188*9

Sarah Moody  
VS                    Application for Cherokee Citizenship  
Cherokee Nation

The application in the above case was filed the 3rd day of October A.D. 1887. The claimant alleges that she derived her Cherokee blood from her Aunt Newrony Mitchell whose name she believes was enrolled on the census rolls of Cherokees by blood taken and made by the United States in the year 1835. The only witness in the case is *(Illegible)* Mitchell who made a statement before the Commission on Citizenship the 10th day of Aug. 1888. The father of Mrs. Moody was Abraham Guinn brother of witness and whose father was Alman Guinn. Alman Guinn left Polk County Tennessee about 49 years ago and died in Polk County Ark 31 or 32 years ago. The witness claims that she was admitted to citizenship in the Cherokee Nation by Judge John S. Vann in 1871

# Cherokee Citizenship Commission Docket Books
## (1880-84, 1887-89) Volume V
## Tahlequah, Cherokee Nation

but that she moved into Arkansas about 11 years previous to the making of her statement. She alleged admission to citizenship by Chief Justice Vann is not regarded as conclusive of the right to citizenship in the Cherokee Nation because he had no authority to admit the witness and there is no evidence before the Commission to show that he did so. The right of the Guinns to citizenship because of their Cherokee blood has not been recognized heretofore by any Commission or branch of the Cherokee government nor do their names or that of Newrony Mitchell appear upon the census roll of 1835 as they certainly would if Alman or Abraham Guinn who were then living in Polk County Tennessee. This fact taken in connection with the absence of proof as allegation that any of the persons named while residing among the Cherokees East of the Mississippi river[sic] or for many years as their border in Ark. establish their Cherokee blood or right to residence in the Cherokee Nation is conclusive to the minds of the Commission that the claimant Sarah Moody and her children whose names are not given are not Cherokees by blood and not entitled to citizenship in the Cherokee Nation.

P.O. South Sulphur Tex.

Will.P. Ross
Chairman
JE Gunter
Com

I hereby certify the 3 foregoing pages is a true copy of the original.

D.S. Williams
Asst Clk Com.

## McMELLEN

**DOCKET #2078**
CENSUS ROLLS 1835 to 1852

APPLICANT FOR CHEROKEE CITIZENSHIP

| POST OFFICE: Darlington, Mo. | | ATTORNEY: L.S. Sanders | |
|---|---|---|---|
| No | NAMES | AGE | SEX |
| 1 | Mary A. McMellen | 40 | female |
| 2 | Permelia N. McMellen | 22 | " |
| 3 | William McMellen | 20 | male |
| 4 | Burnna McMellen | 19 | female |
| 5 | Delsa McMellen | 13 | " |
| 6 | Francis McMellen | 9 | " |

159

| 7 | Jane McMellen | 17 | " |
|---|---|---|---|

**ANCESTOR:** Elizabeth Blackburn

Rejected Sept. 7th 1889

Office Commission on Citizenship
Cherokee Nation Ind Ter
Tahlequah Sept 7th 1889

The above case was called 3 times and no response from applicant or by Atty and there being no evidence on file in support of claim the Commission are of the opinion and so decide that Mary A. McMellen age 40 yrs. and the following children Permelia N. female 22 yrs. William male 20 son, Burnna female 19 Daughter, Jane McMellen female 17 yrs. Delsa female 13 yrs, and Francis McMellen age 9 yrs. are not Cherokees by blood.
P.O. Darlington Mo.

Attest

D.S. Williams
Asst Clk Com.

Will.P. Ross
Chairman
J.E. Gunter   Com

---

## MILLER

**DOCKET #2079**

CENSUS ROLLS 1835 to 1852

APPLICANT FOR CHEROKEE CITIZENSHIP

| POST OFFICE: Kellem, Tex | | ATTORNEY: L.S. Sanders | |
|---|---|---|---|
| No | NAMES | AGE | SEX |
| 1 | Cornelia A. Miller | 28 | female |
| 2 | Lili Miller | 5 | " |
| 3 | Margaret Miller | 3 | " |

**ANCESTOR:** Malissa Faust

Rejected Sept. 7th 1889

Office Commission on Citizenship
Cherokee Nation Ind Ter
Tahlequah Sept. 7th 1889

The above case was called 3 times and no response from applicant or by Atty and there being no evidence on file in support of claim the Commission therefore are of the opinion and so decide that Cornelia Miller age 28 yrs. and the following children Lili Miller female 5 yrs. Margaret Miller female 3 yrs. are not Cherokees by blood. P.O. Kellem Texas.

|  |  |
|---|---|
| | Will.P. Ross |
| Attest | Chairman |
| D.S. Williams | J.E. Gunter   Com |
| Asst  Clk  Com. | |

## MOUNT

**DOCKET #2080**
CENSUS ROLLS 1835

APPLICANT FOR CHEROKEE CITIZENSHIP

| POST OFFICE: Vinita, C.N. | | ATTORNEY: | |
|---|---|---|---|
| **NO** | **NAMES** | **AGE** | **SEX** |
| 1 | W.S. Mount | 37 | male |
| 2 | Kent R. Mount | 10 | " |
| 3 | Martha Mount | 8 | female |
| 4 | Grace E. Mount | 6 | " |
| 5 | John A. Mount | 3 | male |

ANCESTOR: Annie Foreman

Rejected Sept. 9th 1889

Office Commission on Citizenship
Cherokee Nation Ind Ter
Tahlequah  Sept. 9th 1889

Application for Cherokee Citizenship.

The above application was called 3 times & no answer & as there is no evidence on file in support of the claimant's case, We decide that applicant N.G.[sic] Mount age 37 yrs. and children Kent R. Mount age 10 yrs. Martha Anna Mount age 8 yrs. Gracie[sic] E Mount age 6 yrs. and John A. Mount age 3 yrs. are not Cherokees by blood.
P.O. Vinita I.T.

|  |  |
|---|---|
| | Will.P. Ross |
| Attest | Chairman |
| D.S. Williams | J.E. Gunter   Com |
| Asst  Clk  Com. | |

## McLARRY

**DOCKET #2081**
CENSUS ROLLS 1835

APPLICANT FOR CHEROKEE CITIZENSHIP

| POST OFFICE: McKinney, Tex. | | ATTORNEY: Wm A. Thompson | |
|---|---|---|---|
| **NO** | **NAMES** | **AGE** | **SEX** |
| 1 | Mary V. McLarry | 38 | female |
| 2 | Don McLarry | 9 | male |
| 3 | Sallie McLarry | 5 | female |

ANCESTOR: Jack McGarrah

Office Commission on Citizenship
Cherokee Nation June 26, 1889

There being no evidence in support of the above named case the Commission decide that Mary V. McLarry aged 38 years and her children Don McLarry aged 9 years and Sallie McLarry aged 5 years are not Cherokees by blood. Post Office McKinney Texas.

Attest                                    Will.P. Ross

EG Ross                                                    Chairman
    Clerk Commission                    J.E. Gunter   Com

## McGUIRE

**DOCKET #2082**
CENSUS ROLLS 1835

APPLICANT FOR CHEROKEE CITIZENSHIP

| POST OFFICE: Decatur, Tex. | | ATTORNEY: C.H. Taylor | |
|---|---|---|---|
| **NO** | **NAMES** | **AGE** | **SEX** |
| 1 | Mynervia McGuire | 40 | female |
| 2 | Molly McGuire | 20 | " |
| 3 | Eli McGuire | 22 | male |
| 4 | Charley McGuire | 18 | " |
| 5 | Lillie McGuire | 16 | female |
| 6 | Lorena McGuire | 14 | " |
| 7 | John F. McGuire | 12 | male |

162

# Cherokee Citizenship Commission Docket Books (1880-84, 1887-89) Volume V
## Tahlequah, Cherokee Nation

| 8 | Buster McGuire | 6 | " |
|---|---|---|---|

**ANCESTOR:** Wm Chysum

Rejected Sept. 7<sup>th</sup> 1889

Office Commission on Citizenship
Cherokee Nation Ind Ter
Tahlequah Sept. 7<sup>th</sup> 1889

The above named case was called three times this day without answer and being accompanied by no proof the Commission decide that claimant Minerva[sic] McGuire age 40 yrs. and her daughters Molly 20 yrs. Lillie 16 yrs. Lorence[sic] 14 yrs. and her sons Eli 22 yrs. Charley S. 18 yrs. John F. 12 yrs. and Buster McGuire 6 yrs. are not of Cherokee blood. P.O. Decatur, Texas.

Will.P. Ross
Chairman
J.E. Gunter    Com

Attest
    D.S. Williams
    Asst  Clk  Com.

---

## MONTEATH

**DOCKET #2083**
CENSUS ROLLS

APPLICANT FOR CHEROKEE CITIZENSHIP

| POST OFFICE: Hollowell[sic], Kane. | | ATTORNEY: C.H. Taylor | |
|---|---|---|---|
| NO | NAMES | AGE | SEX |
| 1 | William Monteath | 28 | male |

**ANCESTOR:** John Monteath

Rejected Sept. 7<sup>th</sup> 1889

Office Commission on Citizenship
Cherokee Nation Ind Ter
Tahlequah Sept. 7<sup>th</sup> 1889

The above case was called 3 times and no response from applicant or by Atty and there being no evidence on file in support of claim the Commission are of the opinion and they so decide that William Monteath age 28 yrs. is not a Cherokee by blood. P.O. Hollowell[sic], Kans.

# Cherokee Citizenship Commission Docket Books
## (1880-84, 1887-89) Volume V
## Tahlequah, Cherokee Nation

Will.P. Ross
Attest      Chairman
    D.S. Williams      J.E. Gunter   Com
    Asst  Clk  Com.

---

## MANLEY

**DOCKET #2084**
CENSUS ROLLS 1835

APPLICANT FOR CHEROKEE CITIZENSHIP

| POST OFFICE: Lead Hill, Ark. | | ATTORNEY: C.H. Taylor | |
|---|---|---|---|
| NO | NAMES | AGE | SEX |
| 1 | Isabella Manley | 23 | female |

ANCESTOR: Sela Brown

Office Commission on Citizenship
Tahlequah Ind Ter. July 2$^{nd}$ 1889

    The above case being submitted without evidence the Commission decide against the applicant.

Attest      Will.P. Ross
    EG Ross      Chairman
     Clerk Commission      J.E. Gunter   Com

---

## MOORE

**DOCKET #2085**
CENSUS ROLLS 1835

APPLICANT FOR CHEROKEE CITIZENSHIP

| POST OFFICE: White Rock, Tex. | | ATTORNEY: C.H. Taylor | |
|---|---|---|---|
| NO | NAMES | AGE | SEX |
| 1 | James J. Moore | 54 | male |
| 2 | Beatris Moore | 12 | female |
| 3 | Laura Moore | 8 | " |
| 4 | Luellen Moore | 6 | " |

ANCESTOR: William Moore

Rejected Sept. 19$^{th}$ 1889

# Cherokee Citizenship Commission Docket Books (1880-84, 1887-89) Volume V
## Tahlequah, Cherokee Nation

Office Commission on Citizenship
Cherokee Nation Ind Ter
Tahlequah Sept. 9th 1889

Application for Cherokee Citizenship.

The above case was called and submitted by Atty J.M. Taylor without evidence. The Commission therefore decide that James J. Moore age 54 yrs. and the following children Beatris Moore Female 12 yrs. Laura Moore Fem 8 yrs. Luellen Moore Female age 6 yrs. are not Cherokees by blood. P.O. White Rock Tex.

Will.P. Ross
Attest                                          Chairman
   D.S. Williams                    J.E. Gunter   Com
   Asst  Clk  Com.

---

## MOORE

**DOCKET #2086**

CENSUS ROLLS 1835

APPLICANT FOR CHEROKEE CITIZENSHIP

| POST OFFICE: Tahlequah, I.T. | | ATTORNEY: C.H. Taylor | |
|---|---|---|---|
| NO | NAMES | AGE | SEX |
| 1 | Joseph S. Moore | 23 | male |

ANCESTOR: William Moore

Office Commission on Citizenship
Tahlequah, July 2nd 1889

There being no evidence in support of the above named case the Commission decide that Joseph S. Moore aged 23 years is not a Cherokee by blood. Post Office Tahlequah I.T.

Attest                                          Will.P. Ross
   E.G. Ross                                    Chairman
   Clerk Commission                 J.E. Gunter   Com

---

# Cherokee Citizenship Commission Docket Books
## (1880-84, 1887-89) Volume V
## Tahlequah, Cherokee Nation

## MAY

**DOCKET #2087**

CENSUS ROLLS  1835

APPLICANT FOR CHEROKEE CITIZENSHIP

| POST OFFICE: Cherokee City, Ark. | | ATTORNEY: C.H. Taylor | |
|---|---|---|---|
| No | NAMES | AGE | SEX |
| 1 | E.M. May | 35 | female |

ANCESTOR: Sally May

Rejected Sept. 9th 1889

Office Commission on Citizenship
Cherokee Nation Ind Ter
Tahlequah Sept. 9th 1889

Application for Cherokee Citizenship

    The above case was called and submitted by Atty J.M. Taylor without evidence. The Commission therefore decide that E.M. May age 35 yrs. is not a Cherokee by blood. P.O. Cherokee City, Ark.

|  |  |
|---|---|
|  | Will.P. Ross |
| Attest | Chairman |
| D.S. Williams | J.E. Gunter   Com |
| Asst  Clk  Com. |  |

---

## MAYFIELD

**DOCKET #2088**

CENSUS ROLLS  1835 to 1852

APPLICANT FOR CHEROKEE CITIZENSHIP

| POST OFFICE: Vinita, C.N. | | ATTORNEY: Boudinot and Rasmus | |
|---|---|---|---|
| No | NAMES | AGE | SEX |
| 1 | Francis M. Mayfield | 20 | male |
| 2 | John Thomas Mayfield | 3 mos | " |

ANCESTOR: Susan Bracket

Re-admitted February 14th 1889

    Now on this the 14th day of February, 1889, comes the above case, to wit; Francis M. Mayfield & son John Thomas Mayfield, <u>versus</u>. the Cherokee Nation, for a final hearing, they having made application pursuant to the provisions of the Act of the National Council approved December 8th 1886, from

166

# Cherokee Citizenship Commission Docket Books
## (1880-84, 1887-89) Volume V
## Tahlequah, Cherokee Nation

an examination it appears that the name of Susan Bracket is found on the Silar roll of 1851 as a person of Cherokee blood and the applicant has established his identity as the son of Elijah Mayfield Sr, who is a white man, and Michel Mayfield nee Bracket, the daughter of Susan Bracket nee Susan Hubbard above mentioned and who was the sister of Wilkerson Hubbard who was admitted to citizenship as a Cherokee by blood on Nov. 1$^{st}$ 1888, Page 94, No. 93, Doc. A. by the Commission on Citizenship. It is therefore adjudged that Francis M. Mayfield & son John Thomas Mayfield are Cherokees by blood and they are therefore hereby re-admitted to the rights and privileges of native Cherokees.

|  | Will.P. Ross | Chairman |
|---|---|---|
| Attest | John E. Gunter | Com |

D.S. Williams
Asst Clk Com.

---

## MOORE

**DOCKET #2089**
CENSUS ROLLS

APPLICANT FOR CHEROKEE CITIZENSHIP

| POST OFFICE: Milton, Ind. | | ATTORNEY: L.B. Bell | |
|---|---|---|---|
| NO | NAMES | AGE | SEX |
| 1 | Richard W. Moore | 71 | male |
| 2 | Ellen Moore | 25 | female |
| 3 | Ollie Moore | 24 | " |

ANCESTOR: Ann Crews

The Commission decide against claimant. See decision in the case of Andrew Meredith Docket 2180 Book E, Page 26 and John Henly Docket 1250, Book C Page 376.

Will.P. Ross    Chairman
R. Bunch    Com
John E. Gunter    Com

---

167

## MOORE

**DOCKET #2090**
CENSUS ROLLS

APPLICANT FOR CHEROKEE CITIZENSHIP

| POST OFFICE: Milton, Ind. | | ATTORNEY: L.B. Bell | |
|---|---|---|---|
| No | NAMES | AGE | SEX |
| 1 | Marcus H. Moore | 42 | male |
| 2 | 5 children | | |

ANCESTOR:

The Commission decide against claimant. See decision in the case of Andrew Meredith Docket 2180 Book E, Page 26 and John Henly Docket 1250, Book C Page 376.

Will.P. Ross    Chairman
John E. Gunter    Com

## MORGAN

**DOCKET #2091**
CENSUS ROLLS

APPLICANT FOR CHEROKEE CITIZENSHIP

| POST OFFICE: Lowell, Kans. | | ATTORNEY: C.H. Taylor | |
|---|---|---|---|
| No | NAMES | AGE | SEX |
| 1 | Sarah H. Morgan | 57 | Female |
| 2 | William E. Morgan | 28 | Male |
| 3 | Jessy H. Morgan | 26 | " |

ANCESTOR: Sarah Henley formerly – Elmore

Rejected Sept. 9[th] 1889

Office Commission on Citizenship
Cherokee Nation Ind Ter
Tahlequah  Sept. 9[th] 1889

Application for Cherokee Citizenship

The above application was filed on the 4[th] Oct. 1887, and was called and submitted by Atty J.M. Taylor without evidence. Therefore the Commission are of the opinion and they so decide that Sarah H. Morgan age 57 yrs. and the following children William E. Morgan male 28 yrs. and Jessy Morgan male 26 yrs. are not Cherokees by blood. P.O. Lowell Kans.

# Cherokee Citizenship Commission Docket Books
## (1880-84, 1887-89) Volume V
## Tahlequah, Cherokee Nation

Attest                                      Chairman
   D.S. Williams                        J.E. Gunter    Com
   Asst   Clk   Com.

---

## MAY

**DOCKET #2092**
CENSUS ROLLS  1835-48-51-52
          or Old Settler    APPLICANT FOR CHEROKEE CITIZENSHIP

| POST OFFICE: Cherokee City Ark. | | ATTORNEY: Boudinot & Rasmus | |
|---|---|---|---|
| No | NAMES | AGE | SEX |
| 1 | E.M. May | | |

ANCESTOR:

Rejected Sept. 9th 1889

          Office Commission on Citizenship
             Cherokee Nation Ind Ter
             Tahlequah  Sept. 9th 1889

Application for Cherokee Citizenship
    The above named claimant was called 3 times & no answer and there being no evidence on file in support of the application the Commission decide that applicant E.M. May is not a Cherokee by blood and he is hereby rejected. P.O. Cherokee City Ark.

          Will.P. Ross
Attest                                      Chairman
   D.S. Williams                        J.E. Gunter    Com
   Asst   Clk   Com.

---

## MORRIS

**DOCKET #2093**
CENSUS ROLLS
                  APPLICANT FOR CHEROKEE CITIZENSHIP

| POST OFFICE: Indiana | | ATTORNEY: L.B. Bell | |
|---|---|---|---|
| No | NAMES | AGE | SEX |
| 1 | Susan Morris | | |
| 2 | 3 children | | |

ANCESTOR:  Ann Cruws – or Cran

169

The Commission decide against claimant. See decision in the case of Andrew Meredith Docket 2180 Book E, Page 26 and ~~that~~ John Henly Docket 1250, Book C Page 376.

Will.P. Ross   Chairman
John E. Gunter   Com

---

## MUNROW

**DOCKET #2094**
CENSUS ROLLS

APPLICANT FOR CHEROKEE CITIZENSHIP

| POST OFFICE: Center, N.C. | | ATTORNEY: | |
|---|---|---|---|
| NO | NAMES | AGE | SEX |
| 1 | Shabal Munrow | 24 | |

ANCESTOR: Ann Crews

The Commission decide against claimant. See decision in the case of Andrew Meredith Docket 2180 Book E, Page 26 and John Henly Docket 1250, Book C Page 376.

Will.P. Ross   Chairman
John E. Gunter   Com

---

## MEREDETH

**DOCKET #2095**
CENSUS ROLLS

APPLICANT FOR CHEROKEE CITIZENSHIP

| POST OFFICE: | | ATTORNEY: L.B. Bell | |
|---|---|---|---|
| NO | NAMES | AGE | SEX |
| 1 | Thomas P. Meredeth | | |

ANCESTOR: Mary Crews

The Commission decide against claimant. See decision in case ~~John Hanly~~ Andrew Meredith Docket 2180 Book E, Page 26 and John Hanly[sic] Docket 1250, Book C Page 376.

Will.P. Ross   Chairman
R. Bunch   Com
J.E. Gunter   Com

## MURROW

**DOCKET #2096**

CENSUS ROLLS

APPLICANT FOR CHEROKEE CITIZENSHIP

| | POST OFFICE: Center, N.C. | ATTORNEY: | |
|---|---|---|---|
| **NO** | **NAMES** | **AGE** | **SEX** |
| 1 | John Murrow | 38 | Male |
| 2 | Marvin Murrow | 9 | " |
| 3 | Joshua S. Murrow | 7 | " |
| 4 | Lillian Murrow | 5 | Female |
| 5 | Mozelle Murrow | 3 | " |

ANCESTOR: Ann Crews

The Commission decide against claimant. See decision in the case of Andrew Meredith Docket 2180 Book E, Page 26 and John Henly Docket 1250, Book C Page 376.

Attest              Will.P. Ross    Chairman

    E.G. Ross

       Clerk Commission       John E. Gunter    Com

## MURROW

**DOCKET #2097**

CENSUS ROLLS

APPLICANT FOR CHEROKEE CITIZENSHIP

| | POST OFFICE: Center, N.C. | ATTORNEY: | |
|---|---|---|---|
| **NO** | **NAMES** | **AGE** | **SEX** |
| 1 | Eugene C. Murrow | 29 | |

ANCESTOR: Ann Crews

The Commission decide against claimant. See decision in case Andrew Meredith Docket 2180 Book E, Page 26 and case John Hanly[sic] Docket 1250, Book C Page 376.

           Will.P. Ross    Chairman

         R. Bunch    Com

            J.E. Gunter    Com

## McGARRAH

**DOCKET #2098**

CENSUS ROLLS 1835 to 1852

APPLICANT FOR CHEROKEE CITIZENSHIP

| POST OFFICE: Red River Sta. Texas | | ATTORNEY: Wm A. Thompson | |
|---|---|---|---|
| No | NAMES | AGE | SEX |
| 1 | S G McGarrah | 52 | |
| 2 | John C. McGarrah | 20 | |
| 3 | Edward McGarrah | 18 | |

ANCESTOR: Jack McGarrah

Office Commission on Citizenship
Cherokee Nation June 26, 1889

There being no evidence in support of the above named case the Commission decide that L[sic] G. McGarrah aged 52 years and the children John C. age 20 years and Edward McGarrah male aged 18 years are not Cherokees by blood.

Attest                                    Will.P. Ross
  E.G. Ross                                    Chairman
    Clerk Commission                    J.E. Gunter   Com

## MAYFIELD

**DOCKET #2099**

CENSUS ROLLS 1835 to 1852

APPLICANT FOR CHEROKEE CITIZENSHIP

| POST OFFICE: Vinita, C.N. | | ATTORNEY: Boudinot and Rasmus | |
|---|---|---|---|
| No | NAMES | AGE | SEX |
| 1 | Eligah[sic] Mayfield, Jr. | 18 | Male |

ANCESTOR: Susan Bracket

Re-admitted February 14th 1889

Now on this the 14th day of February, 1889, comes the above case, to wit; Elijah Mayfield <u>versus</u> the Cherokee Nation, for a final he[sic] hearing. . . made application pursuant to the provisions of the Act of the National Council approved December 8[th] 1886, from an examination it appears that the name Susan Bracket is found on the Sila[sic] roll of 1851 as a person of Cherokee blood and the applicant has established his identity as the son of Elijah Mayfield, Sr. who is a white man and Michel Mayfield nee Bracket the daughter of Susan Bracket nee Susan Hubbard above mentioned and who was the sister of Wilkerson Hubbard, who was admitted to citizenship as a Cherokee by blood on Nov. 1[st] 1888, Page 94, No. 93, Docket A. by the Commission on Citizenship. It is therefore adjudged that Elijah Mayfield is a Cherokee by blood and he is therefore hereby re-admitted to the rights and privileges of a native Cherokee.

Will.P. Ross

Attest | Chairman

D.S. Williams | John E. Gunter   Com

Asst   Clk   Com.

---

## MURROW

**DOCKET #2100**
CENSUS ROLLS

APPLICANT FOR CHEROKEE CITIZENSHIP

| POST OFFICE: Center, N.C. | | ATTORNEY: | |
|---|---|---|---|
| NO | NAMES | AGE | SEX |
| 1 | Joshua L. Murrow | 36 | male |
| 2 | Roscoe C. Murrow | 9 | " |
| 3 | Gracie Murrow | 1 | female |

ANCESTOR:  Ann Crews

The Commission decide against claimant.  See decision in the case of Andrew Meredith Docket 2180 Book E, Page 26 and case John Henly Docket 1250, Book C Page 376.

Will.P. Ross   Chairman

John E. Gunter   Com

---

# Cherokee Citizenship Commission Docket Books
## (1880-84, 1887-89) Volume V
## Tahlequah, Cherokee Nation

## MAYFIELD

**DOCKET #2101**

CENSUS ROLLS 1835 to 1852

APPLICANT FOR CHEROKEE CITIZENSHIP

| POST OFFICE: Wyoming Cheyenne | | ATTORNEY: Boudinot and Rasmus | |
|---|---|---|---|
| No | NAMES | AGE | SEX |
| 1 | John Thomas Mayfield | 27 | male |

ANCESTOR: Susan Bracket

Re-admitted Sept. 6[th] 1889

Office Commission on Citizenship          Cher. Nat Ind Ter

Tahlequah  Sept. 6[th] 1889

In the above named case the Commission decide that the claimant John Thomas Mayfield age 27 years, at the filing of his application, the 3[rd] day of October 1887, has proven to the satisfaction of the Commission that he is of Cherokee blood having derived the same from Susan Bracket whose name is entered on the Sila[sic] roll of 1851 as a person of Cherokee blood and that he is entitled to re-admission to citizenship in the Cherokee Nation.  See decision of the Commission in the case of Francis M. Mayfield Docket 2088, Book D, Page 574. P.O. Cheyenne Wyoming Ter.

Will.P. Ross

Attest                                                          Chairman

D.S. Williams                                        J.E. Gunter   Com

Asst  Clk  Com.

## MERIDETH

**DOCKET #2102**

CENSUS ROLLS

APPLICANT FOR CHEROKEE CITIZENSHIP

| POST OFFICE: New Gorden, N.C. | | ATTORNEY: L.B. Bell | |
|---|---|---|---|
| No | NAMES | AGE | SEX |
| 1 | Jesse Merideth | 63 | male |
| 2 | Franklin Merideth | 41 | " |
| 3 | M.A. Merideth Davis | 39 | female |
| 4 | Anna J.M. Hibbs | 37 | " |
| 5 | John C. Merideth | 35 | male |
| 6 | James H. Merideth | 33 | " |

| 7  | Marshal Merideth     | 30 | "      |
|----|----------------------|----|--------|
| 8  | Elizabeth M. Merideth | 28 | female |
| 9  | Elvira Merideth      | 25 | "      |
| 10 | Clarkson Merideth    | 22 | male   |

ANCESTOR: Mary Crews

Rejected Aug. 21, 1889

*Commission on Citizenship.*

CHEROKEE NATION, IND. TER.

*Tahlequah,* August 21ˢᵗ *188*9

Jesse Merideth
    VS.          Application for Cherokee Citizenship
Cherokee Nation

The applicant in the above case states in his affidavit taken before the Clerk of the Superior Court of the State of North Carolina that he is a Cherokee by blood that he was born in *(Illegible)* County & State of North Carolina, his age is 60[sic] yrs. and the son of James Merideth whom applicant believes to be a Cherokee & a grand son of one Mary Crews. In further support of applicant case he submits as evidence the affidavit of Mary Merideth, who makes oath to the same facts as that of applicant. In our opion[sic] the evidence is not sufficient in enough to warrant us in deciding in applicant's favor, because our main & *(illegible...)* from the evidence, is that applicant is now a man of advance years, being now 60 years & not *(illegible)* until a year ago did he avail himself of the opportunity of applying for his alleged Cherokee citizenship, this privilege has been be ex extended by the natives for a number of years back. But *(illegible)* all these facts, the applicant fails to name any of the census rolls of Cherokees taken in the year 1835, 48, 51, 52, where his ancestor's name might be found thereby not complying with Sec. 7ᵗʰ of the law that governs this Commission in the provisions.

Therefore we decide that applicant Jesse Merideth age 60 & his children "to wit" *(Illegible)* O. Merideth age 41 yrs. Franklin Merideth age 39 yrs. Malissa M. Davis age 37, Anna J. Hill age 35 yrs. John C. Merideth age 34 yrs. James H. Merideth age 31 yrs. Marshal Merideth age 29 yrs. Elisabeth M. *(Illegible)* age 24 yrs. Elvira *(Illegible)* age 22 yrs. Clarkson D. Merideth age 20 yrs. Rachel N Merideth age 12 yrs. David R Merideth age 8 yrs. Jesse Q Merideth age 5 yrs. also his grand children, 'To wit' Ernest C. Merideth age 15 yrs. Effie B. Merideth age 10 yrs., Gertrude Merideth age 6 yrs. Lucreta *(Illegible)* age 4 yrs. Dwight Howerton age 1 yrs. Luzena M Davis age 8 yrs. Orland G. Davis age 6 yrs. Randolph R. Rily age 3 yrs. Elma Hibbs age 15 yrs., Estella Hibbs age 13 yrs. Lutha Hibbs age 12 yrs. Herman G. Hibbs age 5 yrs. and *(Illegible)* M. Hibbs age 1 yr. are not Cherokees by blood and are not ~~Cherokees b~~ entitled to Cherokee citizenship in the Cherokee Nation. The facts that govern this case are the same as those *(illegible)* & in the opion[sic] in the case of Herman Pitts. See Docket 2155, Book E, Page 1.

Attest ~~Chairman~~

E.G. Ross
  Clerk Commission

Will.P. Ross
  Chairman
John E. Gunter  Com

---

## MERIDETH

**DOCKET #2103**

CENSUS ROLLS

APPLICANT FOR CHEROKEE CITIZENSHIP

| POST OFFICE: Linnville[sic], Iowa | | ATTORNEY: L.B. Bell | |
|---|---|---|---|
| No | NAMES | AGE | SEX |
| 1 | Thomas J. Merideth | | |
| 2 | Robert Merideth | | |
| 3 | Alfred Merideth | | |
| 4 | David Merideth | | |

ANCESTOR: Mary Crews

The Commission decide against claimant. See decision in case Andrew Meredith Docket 2180 Book E, Page 26 and case John Henly Docket 1250, Book C Page 376.

Will.P. Ross  Chairman
R. Bunch  Com
John E. Gunter  Com

---

# Cherokee Citizenship Commission Docket Books (1880-84, 1887-89) Volume V Tahlequah, Cherokee Nation

## McONTICNEL

**DOCKET #2104**
CENSUS ROLLS

APPLICANT FOR CHEROKEE CITIZENSHIP

| POST OFFICE: Knightstown, Ind. | | ATTORNEY: L.B. Bell | |
|---|---|---|---|
| NO | NAMES | AGE | SEX |
| 1 | Izzie McOnticnel | | female |

ANCESTOR: Ann Crews

The Commission decide against claimant. See decision in the case of Andrew Meredith Docket 2180 Book E, Page 26 and John Henly Docket 1250, Book C Page 376.

Will.P. Ross    Chairman
John E. Gunter    Com

---

## MURROW

**DOCKET #2105**
CENSUS ROLLS

APPLICANT FOR CHEROKEE CITIZENSHIP

| POST OFFICE: Center, N.C. | | ATTORNEY: L.B. Bell | |
|---|---|---|---|
| NO | NAMES | AGE | SEX |
| 1 | Andrew Murrow | 68 | male |

ANCESTOR: Ann Crews

The Commission decide against claimant. See decision in the case of Andrew Meredith Docket 2180 Book E, Page 26 and John Henly Docket 1250, Book C Page 376.

Will.P. Ross    Chairman
John E. Gunter    Com

---

## MILLER

**DOCKET #2106**

CENSUS ROLLS

APPLICANT FOR CHEROKEE CITIZENSHIP

| POST OFFICE: Dallas, Tex. | | ATTORNEY: L.B. Bell | |
|---|---|---|---|
| No | NAMES | AGE | SEX |
| 1 | Emma Miller | | female |

ANCESTOR: Ann Crews

The Commission decide against claimant. See decision in the case of Andrew Meredith Docket 2180 Book E, Page 26 and John Henly Docket 1250, Book C Page 376.

Will.P. Ross
Chairman
John E. Gunter   Com

## MERIDETH

**DOCKET #2107**

CENSUS ROLLS

APPLICANT FOR CHEROKEE CITIZENSHIP

| POST OFFICE: Afton, I.T. | | ATTORNEY: L.B. Bell | |
|---|---|---|---|
| No | NAMES | AGE | SEX |
| 1 | David Merideth | 43 | male |
| 2 | Clarence Merideth | 19 | " |
| 3 | Meade Merideth | 8 | " |

ANCESTOR: Mary Crews

The Commission decide against claimant. See decision in the case of Andrew Meredith Docket 2180 Book E, Page 26 and John Henly Docket 1250, Book C Page 376.

Will.P. Ross
Chairman
John E. Gunter   Com

# Cherokee Citizenship Commission Docket Books (1880-84, 1887-89) Volume V
## Tahlequah, Cherokee Nation

## MOODY

**DOCKET #2108**
CENSUS ROLLS

APPLICANT FOR CHEROKEE CITIZENSHIP

| POST OFFICE: Afton, I.T. | | ATTORNEY: L.B. Bell | |
|---|---|---|---|
| **NO** | **NAMES** | **AGE** | **SEX** |
| 1 | Rhoda A. Moody | 41 | female |

ANCESTOR: Ann Crews

The Commission decide against claimant. See decision in the case of Andrew Meredith Docket 2180 Book E, Page 26 and John Henly Docket 1250, Book C Page 376.

Will.P. Ross    Chairman
John E. Gunter    Com

---

## MOORE

**DOCKET #2109**
CENSUS ROLLS

APPLICANT FOR CHEROKEE CITIZENSHIP

| POST OFFICE: Afton, I.T. | | ATTORNEY: L.B. Bell | |
|---|---|---|---|
| **NO** | **NAMES** | **AGE** | **SEX** |
| 1 | William H. Moore | 63 | male |

ANCESTOR: Ann Crews

The Commission decide against claimant. See decision in the case of Andrew Meredith Docket 2180 Book E, Page 26 and John Henly Docket 1250, Book C Page 376.

Will.P. Ross    Chairman
John E. Gunter    Com

179

## MACE

**DOCKET #2110**

CENSUS ROLLS

APPLICANT FOR CHEROKEE CITIZENSHIP

| POST OFFICE: Kansas | | ATTORNEY: L.B. Bell | |
|---|---|---|---|
| **NO** | **NAMES** | **AGE** | **SEX** |
| 1 | Thomas C. Mace | 55 | male |

ANCESTOR: Ann Crews

The Commission decide against claimant. See decision in the case of Andrew Meredith Docket 2180 Book E, Page 26 and John Henly Docket 1250, Book C Page 376.

Will.P. Ross
Chairman
John E. Gunter   Com

---

## MURROW

**DOCKET #2111**

CENSUS ROLLS

APPLICANT FOR CHEROKEE CITIZENSHIP

| POST OFFICE: Center, N.C. | | ATTORNEY: L.B. Bell | |
|---|---|---|---|
| **NO** | **NAMES** | **AGE** | **SEX** |
| 1 | Mary F. Murrow | | female |

ANCESTOR: Ann Crews

The Commission decide against claimant. See decision in the case of Andrew Meredith Docket 2180 Book E, Page 26 and John Henly Docket 1250, Book C Page 376.

Will.P. Ross
Chairman
John E. Gunter   Com

---

## COLLINS

**DOCKET #2112**

CENSUS ROLLS

APPLICANT FOR CHEROKEE CITIZENSHIP

| POST OFFICE: Green Grove, Kentucky | | ATTORNEY: forwarded from Interior Department | |
|---|---|---|---|
| No | NAMES | AGE | SEX |
| 1 | Davis Collins | 43 | male |
| 2 | William H.H. Collins | 23 | " |
| 3 | Julia A. James | 22 | female |
| 4 | Emily K. Collins | 20 | " |
| 5 | James T. Collins | 15 | male |
| 6 | Lawrentus F. Collins | 13 | " |
| 7 | Robert Collins | 12 | male |
| 8 | Allen B. Collins | 10 | " |
| 9 | Gordy L. Collins | 5 | " |
| 10 | Lewis H. Collins | 3 | " |

ANCESTOR: Zaechins Collins

Rejected Sept. 23rd 1889

Office Commission on Citizenship
Cherokee Nation Ind Ter
Tahlequah Sept. 23rd 1889

The Commission in this case decide that Davis Collins age 43 yrs. and the following children, Wm H.H. Collins age 23 yrs. Julia A. James age 22 yrs. Emily K. Collins age 20 yrs. James T. Collins age 15 yrs. Lawsentus[sic] F. Collins age 13 yrs. Robert Collins age 12 yrs. Allen B. Collins age 10 yrs, Gordy L. Collins age 5 yrs. and Lewis H. Collins age 3 yrs. are not Cherokees by blood. See Andrew J. Young Docket 2152, B.D. Page 638. P.O. Green Grove Kentucky.

Will.P. Ross

Attest        Chairman
 D.S. Williams     J.E. Gunter  Com
 Asst  Clk  Com.

## Cherokee Citizenship Commission Docket Books
## (1880-84, 1887-89) Volume V
## Tahlequah, Cherokee Nation

### COLLINS

**DOCKET #2113**

CENSUS ROLLS

APPLICANT FOR CHEROKEE CITIZENSHIP

| | | | |
|---|---|---|---|
| POST OFFICE: Caseyville, Ky | | ATTORNEY: Forwarded from Interior Department | |
| **NO** | **NAMES** | **AGE** | **SEX** |
| 1 | Jeremiah C. Collins | 40 | Male |
| 2 | Julia J. Collins | 14 | Female |
| 3 | *(Illegible)* C. Collins | 10 | |
| 4 | Delilah B. Collins | 6 | Female |
| 5 | Perlia M. Collins | 4 | |
| 6 | Emma C. Collins | 2 | Female |

ANCESTOR: Christopher G. Collins

Rejected Sept. 23rd 1889

Office Commission on Citizenship
Cherokee Nation Ind Ter
Tahlequah Sept. 23rd 1889

The Commission in this case decide that Jeremiah C. Collins age 40 yrs. Julia J. Collins age 14 yrs. *(Illegible)* C. Collins age 10 yrs. Delilah B. Collins age 6 yrs. Perlia M. Collins age 4 yrs. and Emma C. Collins age 2 yrs. are not Cherokees by blood. See decision in case of Andrew J. Young Docket 2152, Book D. Page 638. P.O. Caseyville Ky.

Attest

    D.S. Williams

    Asst  Clk  Com.

Will.P. Ross

Chairman

J.E. Gunter  Com

# Cherokee Citizenship Commission Docket Books
## (1880-84, 1887-89) Volume V
## Tahlequah, Cherokee Nation

### CHANDLER

**DOCKET #2114**

CENSUS ROLLS

APPLICANT FOR CHEROKEE CITIZENSHIP

| POST OFFICE: Mulvane, Kansas | | ATTORNEY: Forwarded from Interior Department | |
|---|---|---|---|
| No | NAMES | AGE | SEX |
| 1 | Henry T. Chandler | 27 | Male |

ANCESTOR: John Sanders

Rejected Sept. 20th 1889

Office Commission on Citizenship
Cherokee Nation Ind Ter
Tahlequah Sept. 20th 1889

The Commission in this case decide that Henry T. Chandler age 27 yrs. is not of Cherokee blood.

See decision in the case of David Elmore et.al. Docket 2279, B.E. Page 141. P.O. Mulvane Kansas.

Attest
    D.S. Williams
    Asst  Clk  Com.

Will.P. Ross
Chairman
J.E. Gunter   Com

---

### CHANDLER

**DOCKET #2115**

CENSUS ROLLS

APPLICANT FOR CHEROKEE CITIZENSHIP

| POST OFFICE: Mulvane, Kansas | | ATTORNEY: Forwarded from Interior Department | |
|---|---|---|---|
| No | NAMES | AGE | SEX |
| 1 | William P. Chandler | 34 | male |
| 2 | Fay Chandler | 1 | "[sic] |

ANCESTOR: John Sanders

Rejected Sept. 20th 1889

# Cherokee Citizenship Commission Docket Books
## (1880-84, 1887-89) Volume V
## Tahlequah, Cherokee Nation

Office Commission on Citizenship
Cherokee Nation Ind Ter
Tahlequah  Sept. 20th 1889

The Commission in this case decide that William P. Chandler age 34 yrs. is not a Cherokee by blood.  See decision in case of David Elmore, Docket 2279, B.E. Page 141.  P.O. Mulvane Kansas.

Will.P. Ross

Attest                                                     Chairman
   D.S. Williams                                    J.E. Gunter   Com
   Asst  Clk  Com.

---

## CHANDLER

**DOCKET #2116**
CENSUS ROLLS

APPLICANT FOR CHEROKEE CITIZENSHIP

| POST OFFICE: Norwood, Iowa | | ATTORNEY: Forwarded from Interior Department | |
|---|---|---|---|
| NO | NAMES | AGE | SEX |
| 1 | John H. Chandler | 39 | Male |
| 2 | Cynthia A. Chandler | 18 | Female |
| 3 | George E. Chandler | 13 | Male |
| 4 | Lewis C. Chandler | 3 | " |

ANCESTOR: John Sanders

Rejected Sept. 20th 1889

Office Commission on Citizenship
Cherokee Nation Ind Ter
Tahlequah  Sept. 20th 1889

The Commission in this case decide John H. Chandler age 39 yrs. and his children Cynthia A. Chandler age 18 yrs. George E. Chandler age 13 yrs. and Lewis C. Chandler age 3 yrs. are not Cherokees by blood.

See decision in the case of David
Elmore et.al. Docket 2279, B.E.  Page 141

P.O. Norwood Iowa

184

# Cherokee Citizenship Commission Docket Books
## (1880-84, 1887-89) Volume V
## Tahlequah, Cherokee Nation

Will.P. Ross
Chairman
Attest
D.S. Williams                J.E. Gunter    Com
Asst  Clk  Com.

## COOPER

**DOCKET #2117**

CENSUS ROLLS

APPLICANT FOR CHEREOKEE CITIZENSHIP

| POST OFFICE: Kokomo, Indiana | | ATTORNEY: Forwarded from Interior Department | |
|---|---|---|---|
| NO | NAMES | AGE | SEX |
| 1 | Mary L. Cooper | 39 | Female |
| 2 | Charles A.G. Cooper | 18 | Male |
| 3 | Addie E. Cooper | 16 | Female |
| 4 | Thomas J. Cooper | 13 | Male |
| 5 | Nellie B. Cooper | 11 | Female |
| 6 | Lena J. Cooper | 7 | " |
| 7 | Donald C. Cooper | 5 | Male |

ANCESTOR: Bethsheba Jay

Rejected Sept. 20th 1889

Office Commission on Citizenship
Cherokee Nation Ind Ter
Tahlequah  Sept. 24th 1889

The Commission in this case decide that Mary L. Cooper age 39 yrs. and her children Charles A.G. Cooper age 18 yrs. Addie E. Cooper age 16 yrs. Thomas J. Cooper age 13 yrs. Nellie B. Cooper age 11 yrs. Lena J. Cooper age 7 yrs. & Donald C. Cooper age 5 yrs. are not Cherokees by blood.

See decision in case of William A. Pugh Docket 2157, B.E. Page 3.

Will.P. Ross
Chairman
Attest
D.S. Williams                J.E. Gunter   Com
Asst  Clk  Com.

## COLLINS

**DOCKET #2118**

CENSUS ROLLS

APPLICANT FOR CHEROKEE CITIZENSHIP

| POST OFFICE: Caseyville, Ky | | ATTORNEY: From Interior Department Washington D.C. | |
|---|---|---|---|
| **NO** | **NAMES** | **AGE** | **SEX** |
| 1 | John D. Collins | 31 | Male |
| 2 | Roy Collins | 5 | " |
| 3 | Guy Collins | 3 | " |
| 4 | Mary K. Collins | 1 | Female |

ANCESTOR: Nancy Collins

Rejected Sept. 23rd 1889

Office Commission on Citizenship
Cherokee Nation Ind Ter
Tahlequah Sept. 23rd 1889

The Commission in this case decide that John D. Collins age 31 yrs. and the following children Roy Collins Born January 1st 1881 A.D. Guy Collins Born November 6th A.D. 1883, and Mary K. Collins Born January 8th A.D. 1885, are not Cherokees by blood.

See decision in case of Andrew J. Young Docket 2152 B.D. Page 638. P.O. Caseyville Ky.

Will.P. Ross
Attest                                          Chairman
   D.S. Williams                  J.E. Gunter   Com
   Asst  Clk  Com.

## COMMONS

**DOCKET #2119**

CENSUS ROLLS

APPLICANT FOR CHEROKEE CITIZENSHIP

| POST OFFICE: Nortonville, Indiana | | ATTORNEY: Forwarded from Washington City, D.C. | |
|---|---|---|---|
| **NO** | **NAMES** | **AGE** | **SEX** |
| 1 | Emily R. Commons | 43 | Female |

# Cherokee Citizenship Commission Docket Books
## (1880-84, 1887-89) Volume V
## Tahlequah, Cherokee Nation

| 2 | Mary L. Milliken | 23 | " |
|---|---|---|---|
| 3 | Jacob Commons | 27 | Male |
| 4 | Sarah J. Commons | 20 | Female |
| 5 | John M. Commons | 17 | Male |
| 6 | James C. Commons | 16 | " |
| 7 | Martha M. Commons | 13 | Female |
| 8 | Isaac L. Commons | 8 | Male |
| 9 | Bertha L. Commons | 5 | Female |

ANCESTOR: Jane Lass

Rejected Sept. 21<sup>st</sup> 1889

Office Commission on Citizenship
Cherokee Nation Ind Ter
Tahlequah Sept. 21<sup>st</sup> 1889

The Commission in this case decide that Emily R. Commons age 48 yrs. and her children, Mary L. Millikin age 23 yrs. Jacob Commons age 21 yrs. Sarah J. Commons age 20 yrs. John M. Commons age 17 yrs. James C. Commons age 16 yrs. Martha M. Commons age 13 yrs. Isaac L. Commons age 8 yrs. and Bertha L. Commons age 5 yrs. are not Cherokees by blood.

See decision in case of Thomas C. Dunbar Docket 2131 B.D. Page 617. P.O. Hortonville, Indiana.

Will.P. Ross

Attest                                    Chairman
    D.S. Williams                    J.E. Gunter    Com
    Asst  Clk  Com.

---

## ALLEN

**DOCKET #2120**
CENSUS ROLLS

APPLICANT FOR CHEROKEE CITIZENSHIP

| POST OFFICE: Tipton, Indiana | | ATTORNEY: Forwarded from Interior Department | |
|---|---|---|---|
| NO | NAMES | AGE | SEX |
| 1 | Nathan H. Allen | 46 | Male |
| 2 | William E. Allen | 14 | " |

187

| 3 | Grace M. Allen | 4 | Female |
|---|---|---|---|

**ANCESTOR:** Mary Clark

Rejected Sept. 18th 1889

Office Commission on Citizenship
Cherokee Nation Ind Ter
Tahlequah Sept. 18th 1889

The Commission in this case decide that Nathan H. Allen age 46 yrs. and his children William E. age 14 yrs. and Grace M. Allen age 4 yrs. are not Cherokees by blood. See decision in the case of Libbie J. Bogue Docket 2183, B.E. Page 29. P.O. Tipton Indiana.

Will.P. Ross

Attest                        Chairman

D.S. Williams            J.E. Gunter   Com

Asst  Clk  Com.

## ALLEN

**DOCKET #2121**

CENSUS ROLLS

APPLICANT FOR CHEROKEE CITIZENSHIP

| POST OFFICE: Fulton, Mo. | | ATTORNEY: Forwarded from Washington City | |
|---|---|---|---|
| **NO** | **NAMES** | **AGE** | **SEX** |
| 1 | Mary Allen | 56 | Female |
| 2 | Jon M. Herring | 32 | Male |
| 3 | Henry C. Sparks | 38 | " |
| 4 | John T. Sparks   et al | 35 | " |
| 5 | Hamilton G. Allen | 30 | " |
| 6 | Mary E. Allen | 28 | Female |
| 7 | Sarah Gough | 25 | " |
| 8 | John W. Allen | 22 | Male |

**ANCESTOR:**

# Cherokee Citizenship Commission Docket Books
## (1880-84, 1887-89) Volume V
### Tahlequah, Cherokee Nation

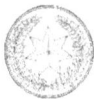

*Commission on Citizenship.*

CHEROKEE NATION, IND. TER.

*Tahlequah,*  September 21st *188*9

Mary Allen
    vs            Application for Cherokee Citizenship
The Cherokee Nation

      This case was referred from the Department of the Interior at Washington. The 13th day of September A.D. 1886 before James D. Henderson, Clerk of the Court of Caloway[sic] County State of Missouri, the applicant deposes that she ~~was~~ is a person of Cherokee Indian descent and was born in Claybourne[sic] County State of Tennessee, that she is 56 yrs. of age and is the daughter of one Elizabeth Walker a person of Cherokee Indian descent who was born in said county and state in 1811 and died in Calloway County, Missouri the 13th day of April 1861, that Elizabeth Walker was the daughter of one William ~~Walker~~ Langley a halfbreed Cherokee Indian born on the Cherokee reservation East of the Mississippi River and died in said Caloway[sic] County, Missouri in 1841 and that she is the daughter of one Thomas Walker who was born in Claybourne[sic] County, Tennessee in 1805 and abandoned his family in 1839 and that he was the son of one Thomas Walker a halfbreed Cherokee who died in said County in 1837. These allegations are supported by no proof. The applicant has at no time resided in the Cherokee Country nor does it appear that ~~they~~ she or her alleged ancestors are recorded on either of the census rolls of Cherokees by blood taken by the United States in 1835, 48, 51, 52. The Commission therefore decide that Mary Allen the claimant and her children Joe M. Herring 32 yrs. Henry C. Sparks 38 years, John F. Sparks 35 years, Hamilton G. Allen 30 yrs. Mary E. Allen 28 years, Sarah Gough age 25 yrs. John W. Allen 22 yrs. and her grandchildren viz: Perlie M. Sparks 12 years, Lester E. Sparks 10 yrs. Cora A. Sparks 8 yrs. Bruce B. Sparks 4 years, Maud M. Early 7 years, Dolar Herring 14 yrs. Clyor[sic] Herring 13 years, Seth Herring 10 yrs. Myrlie Herring 8 yrs. Marmie Herring 6 yrs. Brent Herring 4 yrs. Grover C. Herring ? yrs. Karah Gough 6 yrs. Cleveland E. Gough 1 yr. Nevel A. Allen 3 yrs. and Osie Allen are not of Cherokee blood and not entitled to citizenship in the Cherokee Nation. P.O. Fulton, Missouri.

                           Will.P. Ross
                           Chairman
                          J.E. Gunter    Com

# Cherokee Citizenship Commission Docket Books
## (1880-84, 1887-89) Volume V
## Tahlequah, Cherokee Nation

---

## ALLEN

**DOCKET #2122**

<small>CENSUS ROLLS</small>

<small>APPLICANT FOR CHEROKEE CITIZENSHIP</small>

| POST OFFICE: Thornton, Indiana | ATTORNEY: Forwarded from Washington City | | |
|---|---|---|---|
| No | NAMES | AGE | SEX |
| 1 | Harman H. Allen | 58 | Male |
| 2 | Elizabeth A. Hill | 34 | Female |
| 3 | Frank E. Allen | 32 | Male |

ANCESTOR: Mary Clark

Rejected Sept. 18th 1889

Office Commission on Citizenship
Cherokee Nation Ind Ter
Tahlequah Sept. 18th 1889

The Commission in this case decide that Harman H. Allen age 58 yrs. and his children Elizabeth A. Age 34 yrs. and Frank E. Allen are not of Cherokee blood. See decision in the case of Lible[sic] J Bogue, Docket 2183, Book E, Page 29. P.O. Thorntown[sic], Indiana.

Attest

D.S. Williams
Asst Clk Com.

Will.P. Ross
Chairman
J.E. Gunter   Com

---

## ALLEN

**DOCKET #2123**

<small>CENSUS ROLLS</small>

<small>APPLICANT FOR CHEROKEE CITIZENSHIP</small>

| POST OFFICE: Eagletown, Indiana | ATTORNEY: Forwarded from Washington City | | |
|---|---|---|---|
| No | NAMES | AGE | SEX |
| 1 | Samuel C. Allen | 69 | Male |
| 2 | Narcissie[sic] E. Allen } et al | 30 | Female |
| 3 | William P. Allen | 28 | Male |

| 4 | Asenath[sic] P. Allen | 23 | |
|---|---|---|---|

**ANCESTOR:**

*Commission on Citizenship.*

CHEROKEE NATION, IND. TER.

*Tahlequah,* August 20 *188*9

Samuel C. Allen
    VS.         Application for Cherokee Citizenship
Cherokee Nation

The applicant in the above case alleges that he is the grandson of Mary Clark, from whom he claims to have derived his Cherokee blood. In support of the above allegations claimant submits his own affidavit and that of Mary A. Henly taken by a Notary Public in and for Douglas County State of Kansas. ~~The affidavit of~~ Mary A. Henly claims to be of Cherokee blood and testifies that she is acquainted with ~~claimed~~ claimant & knows him to be of Cherokee descent being the said son of Mary Clark who was born in Guilford County & State of North Carolina in the year 1765 and died in Rush County and State of Indiana in the year 1854. The affidavit of Samuel C. Allen, the applicant in this case alleges the same as that of Mary A Hinly[sic].

These statements are not regarded by the Commission as being ~~could~~ conclusive as to the Cherokee blood of applicant because they state details which it is not probable that affiants came into possession from their own personal knowledge, and because there is nothing to show that Mary Clark, at any time resided in the Cherokee Nation and further the applicant does not allege any of the census rolls of Cherokees made in the year 1835, 48, 51 & 52 where his ancestor's name might be found, thereby not complying with the 7th Section of the law that governs the Commission in their action in ~~wh~~ the provisions. Therefore we decide that applicant Samuel C. Allen age 69 and his children "To wit" Narcissa E. Allen age 30 years, William P. Allen age 28 years Asnath[sic] P. Allen age 23 and his grand children "To wit" Armostella E. Allen age 7 years and *(Illegible)* Allen age 10 months are not Cherokees by blood and are not entitled to Cherokee citizenship in the Cherokee Nation.

# Cherokee Citizenship Commission Docket Books (1880-84, 1887-89) Volume V
## Tahlequah, Cherokee Nation

Will.P. Ross
Chairman

John E. Gunter    Commissioner

## ABERCROMBIE

**DOCKET #2124**
CENSUS ROLLS

APPLICANT FOR CHEROKEE CITIZENSHIP

| POST OFFICE: Rushville, Indiana | | ATTORNEY: Forwarded from Washington City | |
|---|---|---|---|
| NO | NAMES | AGE | SEX |
| 1 | Sarah W. Abercrombie | 42 | Female |
| 2 | Guy Abercrombie | 13 | Male |
| 3 | Ned Abercrombie | 12 | " |
| 4 | John ? Abercrombie | 10 | " |
| 5 | Roy Abercrombie | 4 | " |

ANCESTOR: Hannah Sexton

Rejected Sept. 24[th] 1889

Office Commission on Citizenship
Cherokee Nation Ind Ter
Tahlequah  Sept. 24[th] 1889

This case is brought here from the Department of the Interior Washington D.C.

The Commission decide against the applicant in the above case.  Sarah W. Abercrombie 42 yrs. of age of Russellville, Rush County Indiana and her children viz.  Guy Abercrombie age 14 years, Ned Abercrombie 10[sic] years and Roy Abercrombie 4 years are not entitled to citizenship in the Cherokee Nation.  See decision in case William A. Pugh Docket 2157, Book E, Page 3. P.O. Russellville Indiana

Attest
   D.S. Williams
   Asst  Clk Com.

Will.P. Ross
Chairman
J.E. Gunter   Com

# Cherokee Citizenship Commission Docket Books
## (1880-84, 1887-89) Volume V
## Tahlequah, Cherokee Nation

### AUMAN

**DOCKET #2125**
CENSUS ROLLS

APPLICANT FOR CHEROKEE CITIZENSHIP

| POST OFFICE: Pisgah, N. Carolina | | ATTORNEY: Forwarded from Washington City | |
|---|---|---|---|
| NO | NAMES | AGE | SEX |
| 1 | Franklin Auman | 60 | Male |
| 2 | Jason Auman | 36 | " |
| 3 | Jasper Auman | 34 | " |
| 4 | Braxton Auman | 29 | " |
| 5 | Leacy Auman | 22 | " |
| 6 | Elijah Auman | 21 | " |
| 7 | Rufus Auman | 19 | " |
| 8 | Sinah A. Auman | 16 | " |
| 9 | Thadeus Auman | 8 | " |
| 10 | Alphecis Auman | 6 | " |
| 11 | Franklin Auman | 4 | " |
| 12 | Lebems Auman | 2 | " |

ANCESTOR: Rebecca Auman

Rejected Sept. 24th 1889

Office Commission on Citizenship Cher. Nat. Ind. Ter. Tah. Sept. 24th 1889

The above case was refered[sic] here from the Department of the Interior. The applicant filed his declaration on the 13th day of December A.D. 1886 before George L. Bradshaw Clerk of the Supreme Court in and for Randolph County and State of North Carolina. In it he deposes that he is a person of Cherokee blood and is 60 years of age that he is the son of one Rebecca Auman a person of Cherokee Indian descent who was born in Randolph County North Carolina in the year A.D. 1793 and died there in 1854 and that she was the daughter of one John Steed who was born in the Cherokee Nation and died in the before named county and state in the year 1812 and has heard his Mothe in her life time claim to be of Cherokee blood. The only witness in support of the above claim is George Auman who in an exparte affidavit made before Ranson Lucas a Justice of the Peace in and for said county and state on the 13th day of December 1886, swears that he is 70 years of age, is a person of Cherokee

193

Indian descent and is a son of the before named Rebecca Auman and confirms the statement of his brother. Such proof is not sufficient to establish the facts alleged nor does the name of the applicant or one of his ancestors appear on the census rolls of Cherokees by blood taken by the United States in 1835-48-51-51. The Commission therefore decide that Franklin Auman 60 years of age and his children, viz: Jason Auman age 36, Jasper Auman 34 yrs. Braxton Auman 29 yrs. Leacy Auman 22 yrs. Elijah Auman 21 yrs., Rufus Auman 19 yrs. Sinah A. Auman 16 yrs. Thadeus Auman 8 yrs. Alphecis Auman 6 yrs., Franklin Auman, Jr. 4 yrs. and Lebems Auman 2 yrs. are not of Cherokee blood and not entitled to citizenship in the Cherokee Nation.

P.O. Pisgah North Carolina.

Attest

    D.S. Williams

    Asst Clk Com.

Will.P. Ross

    Chairman

J.E. Gunter    Com

---

## ALLEN

**DOCKET #2126**

CENSUS ROLLS

APPLICANT FOR CHEROKEE CITIZENSHIP

| POST OFFICE: Eagletown, Indiana | | ATTORNEY: Forwarded from Washington City | |
|---|---|---|---|
| **NO** | **NAMES** | **AGE** | **SEX** |
| 1 | Thomas C. Allen | 55 | Male |
| 2 | Samuel R. Allen | 20 | " |
| 3 | James E. Allen | 17 | " |
| 4 | Cora E. Allen | 14 | Female |
| 5 | Netty J. Allen | 11 | " |
| 6 | John R. Allen | 6 | Male |
| 7 | Charles A. Allen | 4 | " |

ANCESTOR: Mary Clark

Rejected Sept. 18th 1889

    Office Commission on Citizenship

    Cherokee Nation Ind Ter

    Tahlequah Sept. 18th 1889

The Commission in this case decide that Thomas C. Allen age 55 yrs. and his children Samuel R. Age 20 yrs. James E Age 17 yrs. Cora E. Age 14 yrs. Netty

J. age 11 yrs. John R. age 6 yrs. and Charles A. Allen are not of Cherokee blood. See decision in case Libbie J Bogue, Docket 2183, B. E, Page 29.

|  |  |
|---|---|
| | Will.P. Ross |
| Attest | Chairman |
| D.S. Williams | J.E. Gunter   Com |
| Asst   Clk   Com. | |

---

## ALLEN

**DOCKET #2127**
CENSUS ROLLS

APPLICANT FOR CHEREKEE CITIZENSHIP

| POST OFFICE: Emporia, Kansas | | ATTORNEY: Forwarded from Washington City | |
|---|---|---|---|
| **NO** | **NAMES** | **AGE** | **SEX** |
| 1 | Daniel E. Allen    et al | | Male |
| 2 | John Allen | 41 | " |
| 3 | Jobe D. Allen | 33 | " |

ANCESTOR: Mary Clark

Rejected Sept. 18th 1889

Office Commission on Citizenship
Cherokee Nation Ind Ter
Tahlequah  Sept. 18th 1889

The Commission in this case decide that Daniel E. Allen and his children John age 41 yrs. and Jobe D. Allen are not of Cherokee blood.

See decision in case Lible[sic] J Bogue, Docket 2183, Book E, Page 29.  P.O. Emporia Kans.

|  |  |
|---|---|
| | Will.P. Ross |
| Attest | Chairman |
| D.S. Williams | J.E. Gunter   Com |
| Asst   Clk   Com. | |

---

195

# Cherokee Citizenship Commission Docket Books
## (1880-84, 1887-89) Volume V
## Tahlequah, Cherokee Nation

## ALLEN

**DOCKET #2128**

CENSUS ROLLS

APPLICANT FOR CHEROKEE CITIZENSHIP

| POST OFFICE: Progress, N. Carolina | | ATTORNEY: Forwarded from Washington City | |
|---|---|---|---|
| NO | NAMES | AGE | SEX |
| 1 | James A. Allen | 41 | Male |
| 2 | John G. Allen | 11 | " |
| 3 | Nora L. Allen | 7 | Female |
| 4 | Fanny L. Allen | 5 | " |
| 5 | Emma J. Allen | 2 | " |

ANCESTOR: Mary Clark

Rejected Sept. 18th 1889

Office Commission on Citizenship
Cherokee Nation Ind Ter
Tahlequah Sept. 18th 1889

The Commission in this case decide that James A. Allen age 41 yrs. and his children John G. Age 11 yrs. Nora L. age 7 yrs. Fanny L. age 5 yrs. and Emma J. Allen age 2 yrs. are not of Cherokee blood.

See decision in the case of Libbe J Bogue, Docket 2183, Book E, Page 29. P.O. Progress N. Carolina.

Will.P. Ross
Attest                                            Chairman
    D.S. Williams                        J.E. Gunter   Com
    Asst   Clk  Com.

---

## ALLEN

**DOCKET #2029**

CENSUS ROLLS

APPLICANT FOR CHEROKEE CITIZENSHIP

| POST OFFICE: Richmond, Indiana | | ATTORNEY: Forwarded from Washington City | |
|---|---|---|---|
| NO | NAMES | AGE | SEX |
| 1 | Joseph M. Allen | 61 | Male |

# Cherokee Citizenship Commission Docket Books
## (1880-84, 1887-89) Volume V
## Tahlequah, Cherokee Nation

| 2 | Charles F. Allen | 32 | " |
|---|---|---|---|
| 3 | Ann E. Gaar | 30 | Female |
| 4 | Emma L. Allen | 28 | " |
| 5 | Mary A. Reed | 26 | " |
| 6 | George C. Allen | 23 | Male |
| 7 | Minnie M. Allen | 19 | Female |

ANCESTOR: Mary Clark

Rejected Sept. 18[th] 1889

Office Commission on Citizenship
Cherokee Nation Ind Ter
Tahlequah  Sept. 18[th] 1889

The Commission in this case decide that Joseph M. Allen age 61 yrs. and his children Charles F. Allen age 32 yrs. Ann E. Gaar age 30 yrs. Emma L. Allen age 28 yrs. Mary A. Reed age 26 yrs. Geo. C. Allen age 23 yrs. and Minnie M. Allen age 19 yrs. are not of Cherokee blood.

See decision in the case of Libbie J Bogue, Docket 2183, B. E, Page 29. P.O. Richmond, Indiana.

Will.P. Ross

Attest                                                  Chairman
D.S. Williams               J.E. Gunter   Com
Asst  Clk  Com.

---

## DUNBAR

**DOCKET #2030**
CENSUS ROLLS

APPLICANT FOR CHEROKEE CITIZENSHIP

| POST OFFICE: Lane Kansas | | ATTORNEY: From Washington City (forwarded) | |
|---|---|---|---|
| NO | NAMES | AGE | SEX |
| 1 | Leander Dunbar | 36 | Male |
| 2 | Mary L Dunbar | 12 | Female |
| 3 | Albert L. Dunbar | 10 | Male |
| 4 | John A. Dunbar | 8 | " |
| 5 | Charley A. Dunbar | 6 | " |

197

| 6 | Roy E. Dunbar | 4 | " |
|---|---|---|---|
| 7 | Clara E. Dunbar | 2 | Female |

**ANCESTOR:** Elizabeth Dunbar

Rejected Sept. 21st 1889

Office Commission on Citizenship
Cherokee Nation Ind Ter
Tahlequah Sept. 21st 1889

The Commission in this case decide that Leander Dunbar age 36 yrs. and the following children Mary L. Dunbar age 12 yrs. Albert L. Dunbar age 10 yrs. John A. Dunbar age 8 yrs. Charley A. Dunbar age 6 yrs. Roy E. Dunbar age 4 yrs. Clara E. Dunbar age 2 yrs. are not Cherokees by blood. See decision in case Thomas C. Dunbar Docket 2131 B.D. Page 617. P.O. Lane Kansas.

Will.P. Ross
Attest                   Chairman
   D.S. Williams          J.E. Gunter    Com
   Asst   Clk  Com.

---

### DUNBAR

**DOCKET #2131**

CENSUS ROLLS

APPLICANT FOR CHEROKEE CITIZENSHIP

| POST OFFICE: Varck[sic], Kansas | | ATTORNEY: Forwarded from Washington City | |
|---|---|---|---|
| **NO** | **NAMES** | **AGE** | **SEX** |
| 1 | Thomas C. Dunbar | 50 | Male |
| 2 | Sarah M. Watkins | 24 | Female |
| 3 | John H. Dunbar | 19 | Male |
| 4 | James A. Dunbar | 15 | " |
| 5 | William L. Dunbar | 12 | " |

**ANCESTOR:**

# Cherokee Citizenship Commission Docket Books
## (1880-84, 1887-89) Volume V
## Tahlequah, Cherokee Nation

*Commission on Citizenship.*

CHEROKEE NATION, IND. TER.

*Tahlequah,* Sept. 21[st] *188*9

Thomas C. Dunbar
    VS.            Application for Cherokee Citizenship
Cherokee Nation

The above applicant filed his claim of Cherokee citizenship before the Interior Department, Washington D.C. and his application was transmitted by the Secretary of the Interior to the Commission on Citizenship, for a final hearing. In claimant's declaration, affirmed on the 22[nd] day of October 1885, before J.A. Whitcraft, Clerk of the District Court in & for ~~Thomas~~ Cherokee County, State of Kansas, states that he is of Cherokee Indian descent & was born in Randolph County & State of North Carolina that his age is 50 yrs. and his Post Office is Varck, Cherokee County, State of Kansas, that he derives ~~the~~ his Cherokee blood from his father John Dunbar, who was born in the State of Virginia in the year 1794. In further sustaining the allegations set up in claimant's application the affidavit of Cyntha Scarlett, who affirms before a Justice of the Peace, to the same facts & incidents as that of claimant. In any case at law, the burden of proff[sic] is always on the Plaintiff to sustain every allegation set up & so it is in this case. All of claimant's evidence is "exparte" & not sufficient in any opion[sic] to establish the Cherokee blood of applicants. Another ~~rea~~ reason will justify this conclusion, is that claimant has never applied or sought to establish his claim of Cherokee blood until recently & has never lived within the limits of the Cherokee Nation. But *(illegible)* all this Sec. 7[th] of the law that governs this Commission says, "that ~~all~~ applicants names or that of their ancestor must appear upon some of the census rolls of Cherokees taken in the years 1835, 48, 51 & 52. The applicant in this case does not allege any rolls. Therefore the Commission decide that applicant Thomas C. Dunbar age 50 yrs. & children, viz: Sarah M. Watkins age 24 yrs. John H. Dunbar age 19 yrs. James A. Dunbar age 15 yrs. & William L. Dunbar age 12 yrs. & also, Louisa E. Nudergraff are not Cherokees by blood and they are hereby rejected. Post Office Varck, Kansas.

Will.P. Ross
Chairman
J.E. Gunter   Com

## DIAL

**DOCKET #2132**
CENSUS ROLLS

APPLICANT FOR CHEROKEE CITIZENSHIP

| POST OFFICE: Prairie City, Ind. Ter. | | ATTORNEY: Forwarded from Washington City | |
|---|---|---|---|
| No | NAMES | AGE | SEX |
| 1 | Marian A. Dial | 38 | Female |
| 2 | Lena L. Dial | 15 | " |
| 3 | John M. Dial | 13 | Male |
| 4 | Lula Dial | 6 | Female |
| 5 | Anna F. Dial | 3 | " |
| 6 | Ethel Dial | 6 mos | " |

ANCESTOR: America Clemants

Rejected Sept. 24th 1889

Office Commission on Citizenship
Cherokee Nation Ind Ter
Tahlequah Sept. 24th 1889

The Commission in this case decide that Marian A. Dial age 38 yrs. and her children Lena L. Dial age 15 yrs. John M. Dial age 13 yrs. Lula Dial age 6 yrs. Anna F. Dial age 3 yrs. and Ethel Dial age 6 months are not Cherokees by blood.

See decision in case Andrew J. Young Docket 2152 B.D. Page 638. P.O. Prairie City, Ind. Ter.

Will.P. Ross
Attest                                                            Chairman
   D.S. Williams                                   J.E. Gunter   Com
   Asst  Clk  Com.

# Cherokee Citizenship Commission Docket Books
## (1880-84, 1887-89) Volume V
## Tahlequah, Cherokee Nation

## DAVIS

**DOCKET #2133**

CENSUS ROLLS

APPLICANT FOR CHEROKEE CITIZENSHIP

| POST OFFICE: Kerneville[sic], N.Carolina | ATTORNEY: Forwarded from Washington City | | |
|---|---|---|---|
| NO | NAMES | AGE | SEX |
| 1 | Sarah D. Davis | 47 | Female |

ANCESTOR: William G. Beard

Rejected Sept. 24th 1889

Office Commission on Citizenship
Cherokee Nation Ind Ter
Tahlequah  Sept. 24th 1889

The Commission in this case decide that Sarah D. Davis age 47 yrs. is not a Cherokee by blood.

See decision in the case of Augustus H. F. Beard Docket 2193 B.E. Page 40. P.O. Kerneville[sic] N. Carolina.

Will.P. Ross
Attest                                                  Chairman
    D.S. Williams                          J.E. Gunter   Com
    Asst  Clk  Com.

---

## DICKS

**DOCKET #2134**

CENSUS ROLLS

APPLICANT FOR CHEROKEE CITIZENSHIP

| POST OFFICE: Spiceland, Indiana | ATTORNEY: Forwarded from Washington City | | |
|---|---|---|---|
| NO | NAMES | AGE | SEX |
| 1 | Nancy C. Dicks | 52 | Female |
| 2 | Eoline Lamb | 29 | " |
| 3 | Gurnsey H. Dicks | 25 | Male |
| 4 | Allen C. Dicks | 23 | " |

ANCESTOR: Mary Clark

Rejected Sept. 18th 1889

# Cherokee Citizenship Commission Docket Books
## (1880-84, 1887-89) Volume V
## Tahlequah, Cherokee Nation

Office Commission on Citizenship
Cherokee Nation Ind Ter
Tahlequah Sept. 18$^{th}$ 1889

The Commission in this case decide that Nancy C. Dicks age 52 yrs. and her children Eoline age 29 yrs. Gurnsey H. age 25 yrs. and Allen C. Dicks are not of Cherokee blood.

See decision in the case of Libbie J Bogue, Docket 2183, B. E. Page 29. P.O. Spiceland, Ind.

Will.P. Ross

Chairman

Attest

    D.S. Williams           J.E. Gunter   Com

    Asst  Clk  Com.

---

## DUFFIELD

**DOCKET #2135**

CENSUS ROLLS

APPLICANT FOR CHEROKEE CITIZENSHIP

| POST OFFICE: Emporia Kansas | ATTORNEY: Forwarded from Washington City | | |
|---|---|---|---|
| **NO** | **NAMES** | **AGE** | **SEX** |
| 1 | Land Duffield | 24 | Male |

ANCESTOR: George Duffield

*Commission on Citizenship.*

CHEROKEE NATION, IND. TER.

*Tahlequah,* September 19$^{th}$ *188*9

Land Duffield

    vs.         Application for Cherokee Citizenship

The Cherokee Nation

      The above case was referred ~~to the~~ from the Department of the Interior, Washington D.C. Land Duffield on the 4$^{th}$ day of June A.D. 1885 before J.G. *(Illegible)* Clerk of the District Court of Lyon County State of Kansas deposes that he is a person of Cherokee Indian descent, that he is 24 years old and was born in Carter County, Tennessee, that he is the reputed son of one Nathaniel Duffield a half breed Cherokee Indian who [sic] born in the last named county and state in the year 1838 and where[sic] whereabouts since he left to go in the Un Federal Army in 1864 is unknown to declarant that said Nathaniel Duffield was the acknowledge son of one George Duffield a full blood Cherokee Indian who was born on the Cherokee Reservation East in 1805 and died in said county and state in the year A.D. 1880. At the same time and before the same Clerk were sworn to the affidavits exparte of one Samuel W. Boyd and one C.C. Wilcox and who corroborates the statements of the claimant. They further state that they knew Charlotte Duffield the mother wh of Nathaniel Duffield and who was a mixed blood person of about one fourth Cherokee Indian. If the statements made by these persons are correct the name of George Duffield, Charlotte Duffield and Nathaniel Duffield should appear on one or more of the census rolls of Cherokees by blood taken by the United States in the years 1835, 48, 52, but such us bit the case and the Commission therefore decide that the applicant Land Duffield is not of Cherokee descent.

Will.P. Ross
Chairman
J.E. Gunter    Com

---

## SULIVAN

**DOCKET #2136**
CENSUS ROLLS

APPLICANT FOR CHEROKEE CITIZENSHIP

| POST OFFICE: Deep River, N. Carolina | | ATTORNEY: Forwarded from Washington City | |
|---|---|---|---|
| NO | NAMES | AGE | SEX |
| 1 | Emily Sulivan | 51 | Female |
| 2 | Clarinda Sulivan | 16 | " |
| 3 | Junius Sulivan | 14 | Male |
| 4 | Thomas A. Sulivan | 12 | " |
| 5 | Franklin G. Sulivan | 10 | " |
| 6 | Robert T. Sulivan | 8 | " |

ANCESTOR: Lucinda Starbuck

Rejected Sept. 20<sup>th</sup> 1889

# Cherokee Citizenship Commission Docket Books
## (1880-84, 1887-89) Volume V
## Tahlequah, Cherokee Nation

Office Commission on Citizenship
Cherokee Nation Ind Ter
Tahlequah  Sept. 20[th] 1889

The Commission in this case decide that Emily Suliven[sic] age 51 yrs. and her children, Clarinda age 16 yrs. Junius age 14 yrs. Thomas A. age 12 yrs. Franklin G. age 10 yrs. and Robert T. Suliven, are not of Cherokee blood. See decision in the case of Caleb Hubbard Docket 2145, B.D. Page 631. P.O. Deep River N. Carolina.

|                     | Will.P. Ross      |
|---------------------|-------------------|
| Attest              | Chairman          |
| D.S. Williams       | J.E. Gunter   Com |
| Asst   Cour. Clk. Citz. |               |

---

## SEXTON

**DOCKET #2137**

CENSUS ROLLS

APPLICANT FOR CHEROKEE CITIZENSHIP

| POST OFFICE: Rushville, N.Carolina | | ATTORNEY: Forwarded from Washington City | | |
|---|---|---|---|---|
| **NO** | **NAMES** | | **AGE** | **SEX** |
| 1 | Marshall Sexton | | 61 | Male |
| 2 | Louisa E. Havens | | 38 | Female |
| 3 | Rubie N. Sexton | et al | 33 | " |
| 4 | Sally M. Parsons | | 28 | " |
| 5 | John C. Sexton | | 25 | Male |

ANCESTOR: Hannah Sexton

Rejected Sept. 24[th] 1889

Office Commission on Citizenship
Cherokee Nation Ind Ter
Tahlequah  Sept. 24[th] 1889

The Commission in this case decide that Marshall Sexton age 61 yrs. and his children, Lousa[sic] E. Havens age 38 yrs. Rubie N. Sexton age 33 yrs. Sally M Parsons age 28 yrs. John C. Sexton age 25 yrs. and his grand children, Lewis M. Sexton age 17 yrs. Horatio C. Sexton age 15 yrs. Albert E. Sexton age 14 yrs. Thomas Sexton age 11 yrs. William H. Sexton age 9 yrs. Anna M. Havens age

15 yrs. Horatio G. Havens age 13 yrs. George W. Havens age 9 yrs. Ketty[sic] C. Havens age 7 yrs. and John Parsons age 3 yrs. are not Cherokees by blood.

See decision in case of William A. Pugh Docket 2157, B.E. Page 3. P.O. Russellville Indiana[sic]

|  | Will.P. Ross |
|---|---|
| Attest | Chairman |
| D.S. Williams | J.E. Gunter   Com |
| Asst   Clk   Com. | |

---

## SHUMARD

**DOCKET #2138**
CENSUS ROLLS

APPLICANT FOR CHEROKEE CITIZENSHIP

| POST OFFICE: Richmond, Indiana | | ATTORNEY: Forwarded from Washington City | |
|---|---|---|---|
| NO | NAMES | AGE | SEX |
| 1 | Sarah S. Shumard | 35 | Female |
| 2 | Elizabeth B. Shumard | 9 | " |
| 3 | Jane A. Shumard | 5 | " |

ANCESTOR: Jacob Sanders

Rejected Sept. 20<sup>th</sup> 1889

Office Commission on Citizenship
Cherokee Nation Ind Ter
Tahlequah  Sept. 20<sup>th</sup> 1889

The Commission in this case decide that Sarah S. Shumard age 35 yrs. and her children, Elizabeth B. age 9 yrs. and Jane A. Shumard are not of Cherokee blood.

See decision in the case of David Elmore et. al. Docket 2279, B.E. Page 141. P.O. North 11<sup>th</sup> Street
Richmond Indiana

205

# Cherokee Citizenship Commission Docket Books
## (1880-84, 1887-89) Volume V
## Tahlequah, Cherokee Nation

| | Will.P. Ross |
|---|---|
| Attest | Chairman |
| D.S. Williams | J.E. Gunter   Com |
| Asst   Clk   Com. | |

---

## <u>SCOTT</u>

**DOCKET #2139**

CENSUS ROLLS

APPLICANT FOR CHEROKEE CITIZENSHIP

| POST OFFICE: Valley Mills, Indiana | | ATTORNEY: Forwarded from Washington City | |
|---|---|---|---|
| **No** | **NAMES** | **AGE** | **SEX** |
| 1 | John Scott | 63 | Male |
| 2 | Edward Scott | 39 | " |
| 3 | William Scott | 38 | " |
| 4 | Sarah Burnett      et al | 35 | Female |
| 5 | Harriet Stokesberry | 33 | " |
| 6 | Ruth Surley | 31 | " |
| 7 | Marietta Barrett | 22 | " |

ANCESTOR: William Sanders

Rejected Sept. 20<sup>th</sup> 1889

Office Commission on Citizenship
Cherokee Nation Ind Ter
Tahlequah  Sept. 20<sup>th</sup> 1889

The Commission in this case decide that John Scott age 60 yrs. and his children, Edward age 39 yrs. William age 38 yrs. Sarah age 35 yrs. Harriet age 33 yrs. Ruth 31 yrs. & Martha[sic] age 22 yrs. and his grand children, Edgar L. age 14 yrs. Winfield age 13 yrs. Otwell age 12 yrs. Frank age 10 yrs. Halsey age 8 yrs. Arlee 5 yrs. Jasper L. Scott age 2 yrs. Minnie age 9 yrs. & Birtie Barrett age 4 yrs. Elizabeth age 9 yrs. and Maud Stokesberry and Jesse Surley age 6 yrs. are not Cherokees by blood.

See decision in the case of David Elmore et. al. Docket 2279, B.E. Page 141. (P.O. Valley Mills Indiana.)

# Cherokee Citizenship Commission Docket Books
## (1880-84, 1887-89) Volume V
## Tahlequah, Cherokee Nation

Attest
D.S. Williams
Asst Clk Com.

Will.P. Ross
Chairman
J.E. Gunter   Com

## SCOTT

**DOCKET #2140**

CENSUS ROLLS

APPLICANT FOR CHEROKEE CITIZENSHIP

| POST OFFICE: Valley Mills, Indiana | | ATTORNEY: Forwarded from Washington City | |
|---|---|---|---|
| No | NAMES | AGE | SEX |
| 1 | Isaam[sic] Scott | 62 | Male |
| 2 | Lucinda S. George | 38 | Female |
| 3 | Jobe Scott | 37 | Male |
| 4 | Lewis C. Scott   et al | 34 | " |
| 5 | Hannah C. Burke | 32 | Female |
| 6 | John W. Scott | 26 | Male |
| 7 | Calvin C. Scott | 25 | " |
| 8 | Ella J. Scott | 16 | Female |

ANCESTOR: William Sanders

Rejected Sept. 20th 1889

Office Commission on Citizenship
Cherokee Nation Ind Ter
Tahlequah  Sept. 20th 1889

The Commission in this case decide that Isam Scott age 62 yrs. and his children, Lucinda S. George age 38 yrs. Jobe Scott age 37 yrs. Lewis C. Scott age 34 yrs. Hannah C. Burk[sic] age 32 yrs. John W. Scott age 26 yrs. Calvin C. Scott age 25 yrs. Ella J. Scott age 16 yrs and his grand children Ida M. George age 13 yrs. Jesse E. George age 5 yrs. Clara L. George age 3 yrs. Thurlow W. George age 1 yr. Ivy S. Scott age 7 yrs. Dolphy Scott age 11 yrs. Lillian Scott age 8 yrs. Freddy Scott age 6 yrs. Elsee Lee Scott age 12 yrs. Nora C. Scott age 8 yrs. Leslie E. Scott age 3 yrs. Edgar R. Burke age 10 yrs. Vilena A. Burke age 9 yrs. Gilbert E. Burk[sic] age 8 yrs. Arthur D. Burke age 5 yrs. Martha S. Burke age 2 yrs. and Osia M. Burke age 1 yr. are not Cherokees by blood.  See decision in

case of David Elmore et. al. Docket 2279, B.E. Page 141.  P.O. Valley Mills
Indiana.

|  | Will.P. Ross |
|---|---|
| Attest | Chairman |
| D.S. Williams | J.E. Gunter   Com |
| Asst  Clk  Com. | |

## HUBBARD

**DOCKET #2141**

CENSUS ROLLS

APPLICANT FOR CHEROKEE CITIZENSHIP

| POST OFFICE: Alla[sic], Missouri | | ATTORNEY: From Washington City (forwarded) | |
|---|---|---|---|
| NO | NAMES | AGE | SEX |
| 1 | Joseph A. Hubbard | 33 | Male |
| 2 | Anna B. Hubbard | | Female |
| 3 | Jesse Hubbard | | Male |

ANCESTOR: Joseph Hubbard

Rejected Sept. 20<sup>th</sup> 1889

Office Commission on Citizenship
Cherokee Nation Ind Ter
Tahlequah  Sept. 20<sup>th</sup> 1889

The Commission in this case decide that Joseph A. Hubbard age 33 yrs. and his
children, Anna B. and Jesse Hubbard ages not given are not of Cherokee blood.

See decision in the case of Caleb Hubbard Docket 2145, B.D. Page 631.  P.O.
Alla Mo.

|  | Will.P. Ross |
|---|---|
| Attest | Chairman |
| D.S. Williams | J.E. Gunter   Com |
| Asst  Clk  Com. | |

# Cherokee Citizenship Commission Docket Books
## (1880-84, 1887-89) Volume V
## Tahlequah, Cherokee Nation

### HUBBARD

APPLICANT FOR CHEROKEE CITIZENSHIP

| POST OFFICE: Carthage, Mo. | | ATTORNEY: Forwarded from Washington City | |
|---|---|---|---|
| NO | NAMES | AGE | SEX |
| 1 | Woodson B. Hubbard | 45 | Male |
| 2 | Joseph W. Hubbard | 21 | " |
| 3 | Frank C. Hubbard | 20 | " |
| 4 | Earnest H. Hubbard | 12 | " |
| 5 | Ethel J. Hubbard | 3 | Female |
| 6 | Edith M. Hubbard | 1 | " |

ANCESTOR: Joseph Hubbard

Rejected Sept. 20th 1889

Office Commission on Citizenship
Cherokee Nation Ind Ter
Tahlequah Sept. 20th 1889

The Commission in this case decide that Woodson B. Hubbard age 45 yrs. and his children, Joseph W. age 21 yrs. Frank C. age 20 yrs. Earnest H. age 12 yrs. & Ethel M. Hubbard are not of Cherokee blood.

See decision in the case of Caleb Hubbard Docket 2145, B.D. Page 631. P.O. Carthage Mo.

Will.P. Ross
Chairman
Attest
D.S. Williams          J.E. Gunter   Com
Asst  Clk  Com.

# Cherokee Citizenship Commission Docket Books
## (1880-84, 1887-89) Volume V
## Tahlequah, Cherokee Nation

## HUBBARD

**DOCKET #2143**

CENSUS ROLLS

APPLICANT FOR CHEROKEE CITIZENSHIP

| POST OFFICE: Alla[sic], Mo. | | ATTORNEY: Forwarded from Washington City | |
|---|---|---|---|
| NO | NAMES | AGE | SEX |
| 1 | Gamaliel B. Hubbard | 37 | Male |
| 2 | Grace D. Hubbard | 6 | Female |
| 3 | Nellie S. Hubbard | 3 | " |
| 4 | Anabel Hubbard | 1 | |

ANCESTOR: Joseph Hubbard

Rejected Sept. 20th 1889

Office Commission on Citizenship
Cherokee Nation Ind Ter
Tahlequah Sept. 20th 1889

The Commission in this case decide that Gamaliel B. Hubbard age 37 yrs. and his children Grace D. age 6 yrs. Nellie S. age 3 yrs. and Anabel Hubbard age 1 year are not Cherokees by blood.

See decision in the case of Caleb Hubbard Docket 2145, B.D. Page 631. P.O. Alla, Mo.

Will.P. Ross

Attest
Chairman
D.S. Williams
J.E. Gunter   Com
Asst  Clk  Com.

---

## HUBBARD

**DOCKET #2144**

CENSUS ROLLS

APPLICANT FOR CHEROKEE CITIZENSHIP

| POST OFFICE: Alla[sic], Mo. | | ATTORNEY: From Washington City (forwarded) | |
|---|---|---|---|
| NO | NAMES | AGE | SEX |
| 1 | Henry Hubbard | 39 | Male |
| 2 | Woodson B. Hubbard | 14 | " |

# Cherokee Citizenship Commission Docket Books
# (1880-84, 1887-89) Volume V
# Tahlequah, Cherokee Nation

| 3 | Katie Hubbard | 12 | Female |
|---|---|---|---|
| 4 | Gurney Hubbard | 9 | |
| 5 | Earl Hubbard | 5 | Male |

ANCESTOR: Joseph Hubbard

Rejected Sept 20th 1889

Office Commission on Citizenship
Cherokee Nation Ind Ter
Tahlequah Sept. 20th 1889

The Commission in this case decide that Henry Hubbard age 39 yrs. and his children, Woodson B. age 14 yrs. Katie age 12 yrs Gurney age 9 yrs. and Earl Hubbard are not of Cherokee blood.

See decision in the case of Caleb Hubbard Docket 2145, B.D. Page 631. P.O. Alla[sic] Mo.

Will.P. Ross
Chairman
Attest
D.S. Williams     J.E. Gunter   Com
Asst  Clk  Com.

---

## HUBBARD

**DOCKET #2145**
CENSUS ROLLS

APPLICANT FOR CHEROKEE CITIZENSHIP

| POST OFFICE: Alla[sic], Mo | | ATTORNEY: Forwarded from Washington City | |
|---|---|---|---|
| NO | NAMES | AGE | SEX |
| 1 | Caleb Hubbard | 65 | Male |
| 2 | Martin Hubbard | 35 | " |
| 3 | Martha E. Baldwin | 33 | Female |
| 4 | Simeon Hubbard | 30 | Male |
| 5 | James Hubbard | 26 | " |
| 6 | Edgar Hubbard | 23 | " |
| 7 | Frank Hubbard | 19 | " |

ANCESTOR: Ann Crews

211

*Commission on Citizenship.*

CHEROKEE NATION, IND. TER.

July 2 owlth[sic]

~~Tahlequah, August 17~~ *188*9

Caleb Hubbard

vs

The Cherokee Nation

  The applicant in the above case alleges that he is of Cherokee descent that he was born in Guilford County, State of North Carolina and at the time of filing his declaration before the Clerk of the Circuit Court in and for Jasper County State of Missouri the 23$^{rd}$ day of March 1885 was 65 years of age that he is the reputed son of one Hardy Hubbard a halfbreed Cherokee Indian who it <u>is said</u> was born in Mecklenburg County State of Virginia in the year 1770 and died Howard County State of Indiana in the year 1864, that said Hardy Hubbard was the son of one Ann Hubbard whose maiden name was Ann Crews a Cherokee Indian woman who it is said was born on the Cherokee Indian reservation East of the Mississippi river[sic] and was taken when a child and educated by the Society of friends and died in Person County State of North Carolina in the year 1812.

  ~~The~~ Two <u>exparte</u> affidavits are presented in support of the facts alleged in the declaration namely those of Jemima Whitworth 85 years of age and Alexander Whitworth 82 years of age and affirmed before W.S. Reddick, Notary Public in Henry County, State of Indiana on the 30$^{th}$ day of April A.D. 1885.

  These witnesses testify that they ~~are natives of~~ were born in Guilford County North Carolina and at the date of testifying were residing in Henry County State of Indiana and they corroborate in form and manner the statement of the before ~~Caleb~~ named applicant Caleb Hubbard, and further that they have heard Cherokee Indians claim Jeremiah Hubbard, a brother of ~~Caleb~~ Hardy Hubbard and his mother Ann Hubbard to be Cherokees.

  As the decision of the Commission in this case will determine that of a large number of others in which the applicants base their claim to citizenship on the same special and similar statements of alleges facts, they have given the evidence before them the consideration which appeared to be due to it. It does not suffice to convince our minds that the applicant is a Cherokee Indian by

# Cherokee Citizenship Commission Docket Books (1880-84, 1887-89) Volume V Tahlequah, Cherokee Nation

blood. It is entirely exparte and so far as the main point is involved is based upon reputation as to the blood of Ann Crews. Nor does it appear that Ann Crews who died in 1812. Mr Hardy Hubbard who was born in 1770 and died in 1864, or any of his descendants have at any time resided among the Cherokees or heretofore sought to avail themselves of any of the rights, benefits and privileges to which if Cherokee they were entitled in common with other Cherokee Indians and which have been enjoyed by them whether residing on or off the reservation of the Cherokee Nation. Aside from these facts it is admitted by the Attorney ~~LB~~ for claimants, L.B. Bell Esqr. that ~~the names~~ neither the name of ~~the~~ Caleb Hubbard nor that of his reputed ancestors are entered upon the rolls of Cherokees by blood which define the jurisdiction of the Commission in re-admitting persons to citizenship in the Cherokee Nation. For these reasons the Commission decide ~~against~~ that the applicant is not of Cherokee blood and not entitled to citizenship in the Cherokee Nation.

Will.P. Ross
Chairman
John E. Gunter   Com

## HARRIS

**DOCKET #2146**

CENSUS ROLLS

APPLICANT FOR CHEROKEE CITIZENSHIP

| POST OFFICE: High Point, N.C. | | ATTORNEY: Forwarded from Washington City | |
|---|---|---|---|
| NO | NAMES | AGE | SEX |
| 1 | Lucella S. Harris | 68 | Female |
| 2 | Robert S. Harris | 42 | Male |
| 3 | Orlando Harris | 39 | " |
| 4 | Sarah E. Rush | 36 | Female |
| 5 | Nancy M. Hill | 34 | " |
| 6 | Mary L. Harris | 25 | " |

ANCESTOR: Nixon Henly

Rejected Sept. 20th 1889

Office Commission on Citizenship
Cherokee Nation Ind Ter
Tahlequah Sept. 20th 1889

The Commission in this case decide that Lucella S. Harris age 68 yrs. and her children, Robert S. Harris age 42 yrs. Orland[sic] Harris age 39 yrs. Sarah E. Rush age 36 yrs. Nancy M. Hill age 34 yrs. and Mary L. Harris age 25 yrs. are not Cherokees by blood.

See decision in the case of David Elmore et. al. Docket 2279, B.E. Page 141. P.O. High Point, N.C.

|  | Will.P. Ross |
| --- | --- |
| Attest | Chairman |
| D.S. Williams | J.E. Gunter   Com |
| Asst  Clk  Com. |  |

## HAMILTON

**DOCKET #2147**
CENSUS ROLLS

APPLICANT FOR CHEROKEE CITIZENSHIP

| POST OFFICE:  Columbus Kansas | | ATTORNEY: A.E. Ivey  Forwarded from Washington City | |
| --- | --- | --- | --- |
| NO | NAMES | AGE | SEX |
| 1 | Susan M. Hamilton | 32 | Female |
| 2 | Arthur B. Hamilton | 5 | Male |
| 3 | Alice P. Hamilton | 2 | Female |

ANCESTOR: William F. Howell

Rejected Sept. 19th 1889

Office Commission on Citizenship Cher. Nat. Ind. Ter.
Tahlequah Sept. 19th 1889

The above named case has been refered[sic] from the Department of the Interior at Washington D.C. The applicant in her declaration subscribed and sworn to the 22nd day of September A.D. 1886, before J.A. Whitcraft Clerk of the District Court for Cherokee County State of Kansas and which is the only paper connected with the case, alleges that she is the daughter of one William F. Howell a halfbreed Cherokee Indian who was born in the Cherokee Nation in the year 1812 and died at Fort Scott, Kansas Territory on the 10th day of March A.D. 1858 while on his way to the Cherokee Nation Indian Territory. While the statement of the claimant unsupported by other evidence is insufficient to establish the facts alleged, the Commission has caused a careful examination of

214

the rolls of Cherokees taken and made by the United States in the years 1835-48 and 52 to be made for the name of William F. Howell, but they fail to find it. The Commission therefore decide that the said claimant Susan M. Hamilton aged 32 years and her children, Arthur B. Hamilton age 5 years and Alice B. Hamilton age 2 years, are not of Cherokee blood and not entitled to citizenship in the Cherokee Nation. P.O. Columbus, Cherokee County, Kansas.

|  |  |
|---|---|
| | Will.P. Ross |
| Attest | Chairman |
| D.S. Williams | J.E. Gunter   Com |
| Asst  Clk  Com. | |

## JAY

**DOCKET #2148**
CENSUS ROLLS

APPLICANT FOR CHEROKEE CITIZENSHIP

| POST OFFICE: Kokomo, Indiana | | ATTORNEY: Forwarded from Washington City | |
|---|---|---|---|
| NO | NAMES | AGE | SEX |
| 1 | Charles A. Jay | 36 | Male |
| 2 | Joseph P. Jay | 4 | " |

ANCESTOR: Bathsheba Jay

Rejected Sept. 24th 1889

Office Commission on Citizenship
Cherokee Nation Ind Ter
Tahlequah  Sept. 24th 1889

The Commission in this case decide that Charles A. Jay age 36 yrs. and his son Joseph P. Jay age 4 yrs. are not Cherokees by blood.

See decision in case of William A. Pugh Docket 2157, B.E. Page 3.  P.O. Kokomo, Indiana.

|  |  |
|---|---|
| | Will.P. Ross |
| Attest | Chairman |
| D.S. Williams | J.E. Gunter   Com |
| Asst  Clk  Com. | |

## JAY

**DOCKET #2149**

CENSUS ROLLS

APPLICANT FOR CHEROKEE CITIZENSHIP

| POST OFFICE: Kokomo, Indiana | | ATTORNEY: Forwarded from Washington City | |
|---|---|---|---|
| **NO** | **NAMES** | **AGE** | **SEX** |
| 1 | Gilbert D.M.M. Jay | 34 | Male |

ANCESTOR: Bathsheba Jay

Rejected Sept. 24th 1889

Office Commission on Citizenship
Cherokee Nation Ind Ter
Tahlequah Sept. 24th 1889

The Commission in this case decide that Gilbert D.M.M. Jay age 34 yrs. is not a Cherokee by blood.

See decision in case of William A. Pugh Docket 2157, B.E. Page 3.
P.O. Ko-komo, Indiana

Will.P. Ross
Attest                                                   Chairman
   D.S. Williams                           J.E. Gunter   Com
   Asst  Clk  Com.

## JONES

**DOCKET #2150**

CENSUS ROLLS

APPLICANT FOR CHEROKEE CITIZENSHIP

| POST OFFICE: Greeley, Kansas | | ATTORNEY: Forwarded from Washington City | |
|---|---|---|---|
| **NO** | **NAMES** | **AGE** | **SEX** |
| 1 | Mary C. Jones | 49 | Female |
| 2 | Robert C. Jones | 29 | Male |
| 3 | Leander D. Jones | 24 | " |
| 4 | John E. Jones | 23 | " |
| 5 | Flora Jones | 19 | Female |

216

# Cherokee Citizenship Commission Docket Books
## (1880-84, 1887-89) Volume V
## Tahlequah, Cherokee Nation

| 6 | Eva Alexander | 17 | " |
|---|---|---|---|
| 7 | Ernest Jones | 13 | Male |
| 8 | Myrtle Jones | 8 | Female |

**ANCESTOR:** Elizabeth Dunbar

Rejected Sept. 21st 1889

> Office Commission on Citizenship
> Cherokee Nation Ind Ter
> Tahlequah Sept. 21st 1889

The Commission in this case decide that Mary C. Jones age 49 yrs. and her children, Robert C. Jones age 20[sic] yrs. Leander D. Jones age 24 yrs. John E. Jones age 23 yrs. Flora Jones age 19 yrs. Eva Alexander age 17 yrs. Ernest Jones age 13 yrs. Myrtle Jones age 8 yrs. and her grand Daughter Edith Hendricks age 5 yrs. are not Cherokees by blood. See decision in case of Thomas C. Dunbar Docket 2131, B.D. Page 617. P.O. Greeley, Kansas

                                        Will.P. Ross
Attest                                    Chairman
    D.S. Williams              J.E. Gunter   Com
    Asst  Clk  Com.

---

## JONES

**DOCKET #2151**

CENSUS ROLLS

APPLICANT FOR CHEROKEE CITIZENSHIP

| POST OFFICE: Des Moines, Iowa | | ATTORNEY: Forwarded from Washington City | |
|---|---|---|---|
| NO | NAMES | AGE | SEX |
| 1 | Thomas N. Jones | 44 | Male |
| 2 | Alfred M. Jones | 21 | " |
| 3 | Lindley M. Jones | 18 | " |
| 4 | Lucinda Jones | 16 | Female |
| 5 | John J. Jones | 14 | Male |
| 6 | Hattie Jones | 12 | Female |
| 7 | Mary Jones | 7 | " |

**ANCESTOR:** Millicent Nixon

Rejected Sept. 20th 1889

# Cherokee Citizenship Commission Docket Books
## (1880-84, 1887-89) Volume V
## Tahlequah, Cherokee Nation

Office Commission on Citizenship
Cherokee Nation Ind Ter
Tahlequah Sept. 20[th] 1889

The Commission in this case decide that Thomas N. Jones age 44 yrs. and his children viz. Alfred M. Jones age 21 yrs. Lindley M. Jones age 18 yrs. Lucinda Jones 16 yrs. John J. Jones age 14 yrs. Hattie Jones age 12 yrs. and Mary Jones age 7 yrs are not Cherokees by blood. See decision in the case of David Elmore et. al. Docket 2279, B.E. Page 141. P.O. Des Monies[sic] Iowa.

|  | Will.P. Ross |
| --- | --- |
| Attest | Chairman |
| D.S. Williams | J.E. Gunter   Com |
| Asst   Clk   Com. | |

---

## YOUNG

**DOCKET #2152**
CENSUS ROLLS

APPLICANT FOR CHEROKEE CITIZENSHIP

| POST OFFICE: Caseyville, Ky. | | ATTORNEY: Forwarded from Washington City | |
| --- | --- | --- | --- |
| NO | NAMES | AGE | SEX |
| 1 | Andrew J. Young | 48 | Male |
| 2 | Miles D. Young | 18 | " |
| 3 | Mary S. Young | 16 | Female |
| 4 | Julia Young | 13 | " |
| 5 | Virgil L. Young | 12 | Male |
| 6 | Mulie H. Young | 10 | |
| 7 | Hugh J. Young | 7 | Male |
| 8 | Sylvaners[sic] B. Young | 6 | " |
| 9 | Emily E. Young | 4 mos | Female |

**ANCESTOR:** Christian Young

Rejected Sept. 23[rd] 1889

218

# Cherokee Citizenship Commission Docket Books
## (1880-84, 1887-89) Volume V
## Tahlequah, Cherokee Nation

Office Commission on Citizenship Cher. Nat. Ind. Ter.
Tahlequah  Sept. 23$^{rd}$ 1889

The application in the above case is refered[sic] here from the Department of the Interior.   The claimant in his declaration made on the 30$^{th}$ day of September A.D. 1885 before H.? Morton Notary Public of Union County State of Kentucky deposes that he is a person of Cherokee Indian descent that he is forty eight (48) years of age and was born in said county and state.  That he is the son of one Thomas Young a person of Cherokee Indian descent who was born in Jefferson County, Kentucky in the A.D. 1799 and died in Union County some time in the year A.D. 1863.  That Thomas Young was the son of one Christain[sic] Young a Cherokee Indian who it is said was born on the Cherokee reservation and died in Union County, Kentucky in the year A.D. 1850.  At the same time and before the same Notary Public Louis L. Smith aged 60 years and Joseph C. Dodge aged 70 years in affidavit exparte swear to the facts alleged by the Declaratr. Louis L. Smith signs his name with a X and which is attached by Daniel C. Finn who the Commission believes was the Attorney engaged in getting up this and a large number of similar claims to citizenship and who had doubtless an interest in their successfull[sic] prosecution.  It will also be observed that the claimant was born in the year A.D. 1837, that his Father died in 1860 and his grand Father in 1850, and that one or all of their names should be enrolled on one or more of the census rolls of Cherokees by blood taken by the United States in the years 1835-48-51-52, if they [sic] of Cherokee Indian descent, but such is not the fact.  The Commission therefore decide that the claimant Andrew J. Young 48 years of age an[sic] his children viz.  Miles D. Young age 18 yrs. Mary S. Young 16 yrs. Julia Young 13 yrs. Virgil L. Young 12 yrs. Mulie H. Young 10 yrs. Hugh J. Young 7 yrs. Sylvaners B. Young 6 yrs. Emily E. Young four months are not of Cherokee blood and not entitled to citizenship in the Cherokee Nation.  P.O. Caseyville, Ky.

Will.P. Ross
Attest                                             Chairman
    D.S. Williams                         J.E. Gunter    Com
    Asst  Clk  Com.

219

## UPDEGRAFF

**DOCKET #2153**
CENSUS ROLLS

APPLICANT FOR CHEROKEE CITIZENSHIP

| POST OFFICE: Lane, Kansas | | ATTORNEY: Forwarded from Washington City | |
|---|---|---|---|
| **NO** | **NAMES** | **AGE** | **SEX** |
| 1 | Louisa E. Updegraff | 50 | Female |
| 2 | Abigal M. Ellis | 28 | " |
| 3 | Sarah E. Downing | 24 | " |
| 4 | Ella F. Dunbar | 22 | " |
| 5 | William O. Dunbar | 20 | Male |
| 6 | Alice M. Dunbar | 14 | Female |
| 7 | Laura F. Updegraff | 11 | " |
| 8 | Clara B. Updegraff | 7 | " |

(et al)

**ANCESTOR:** Millicent Jones

Rejected Sept. 20th 1889

Office Commission on Citizenship Cher. Nat. Ind. Ter.
Tahlequah Sept. 20th 1889

The Commission in this case decide that Louiza[sic] E. Updegraff age 50 yrs. and the following children, Abigal M. Ellis age 28 yrs. Sarah E. Downing age 24 yrs. Ella F. Dunbar age 22 yrs. William O. Dunbar age 20 yrs. and Alice M. Dunbar age 14 yrs. Laura S. Updegraff age 11 yrs. Clara B. Updegraff age 7 yrs. and grand children, Arthur C. Ellis age 11 yrs. Maud Ellis age 9 yrs. John F. Ellis age 7 yrs. Adda G. Ellis age 5 yrs. Harriet Ellis age 2 yrs. Effie Ellis age 3 months, Ketty[sic] D. Downing age 4 yrs. and Rosa E. Downing age 2 yrs. are not Cherokees by blood.

See decision in the case of David Elmore et. al. Docket 2279, B.E. Page 141.

Will.P. Ross
Attest                                          Chairman
    D.S. Williams                   J.E. Gunter   Com
    Asst  Clk  Com.

# Cherokee Citizenship Commission Docket Books
## (1880-84, 1887-89) Volume V
### Tahlequah, Cherokee Nation

## NORDYKE

**DOCKET #2154**
CENSUS ROLLS

APPLICANT FOR CHEROKEE CITIZENSHIP

| POST OFFICE: Richland, Iowa | ATTORNEY: Forwarded from Washington City | |
|---|---|---|
| NO | NAMES | AGE | SEX |
| 1 | Amanda E. Nordyke | 34 | Female |
| 2 | Minnie A. Nordyke | 14 | " |

ANCESTOR: Prudence Johnson

Rejected Sept. 20$^{th}$ 1889

Office Commission on Citizenship
Cherokee Nation Ind Ter
Tahlequah Sept. 20$^{th}$ 1889

The Commission in this case decide that Amanda E. Nordyke age 34 yrs. and her children Minnie A. Nordyke Daughter age 14 yrs. are not of Cherokee blood.

See decision Docket 2279, B.E. Page 141 case David Elmore et. al. P.O. Richland, Iowa.

Will.P. Ross
Attest                                            Chairman
    D.S. Williams                    J.E. Gunter    Com
    Asst  Clk  Com.

---

## PITTS

**DOCKET #2155**
CENSUS ROLLS

APPLICANT FOR CHEROKEE CITIZENSHIP

| POST OFFICE: Fountain City, N.C. | ATTORNEY: Transferred from Interior Department Washington City | |
|---|---|---|
| NO | NAMES | AGE | SEX |
| 1 | Harmon Pitts | 61 | Male |
| 2 | Oliver Pitts | 38 | " |
| 3 | William Pitts | 36 | " |

221

| 4 | Bulah Pitts | 34 | Female |
|---|---|---|---|
| 5 | Thomas Pitts | 31 | Male |
| 6 | Benjamin Pitts | 28 | " |
| 7 | Isaac Pitts | 28 | " |
| 8 | George Pitts | 25 | " |
| 9 | Sarah Pitts | 22 | Female |

ANCESTOR: David Meredith

Rejected July 2nd 1889

Office Commission on Citizenship Cher Nat Ind Ter Tahlequah July 2nd 1889

The applicant in this case in his declaration taken the 3rd day of February 1885, before W.L. Schlater, Clerk of Wayne County Indiana. Alleges that he is 61 yrs. old and was born in Guilford County, State of North Carolina and is the son of one Martha Pitts who was born in said county and state the 27th day of February A.D. 1799 and died in 1876. Martha Pitts was of Cherokee descent and was the daughter of one David Meredith who was born in Bedford County State of Virginia in 1770 and died in Wayne County Indiana in 1864 and that he was the son of one Mary Crews a Cherokee woman, who was born in the Cherokee Nation in 1752 and died in Stokes County North Carolina in the year 1820. In support of this declaration there are presented the affidavits of Mary Meredith 85 yrs. of age taken by affirmation before J.M. Guyer[sic] Justice of the Peace of Forsyth County North Carolina and of Lydia Meredith 84 yrs. of age before Jno. H. Payne Clerk of the Western District of North Carolina. These witnesses corroborate the statements of facts alleged in the Declaration of the claimant Mary Meredith, claims to be of Cherokee descent, and it is probable that both witnesses are related to the claimant. It will be sure that claimant was 61 years old at the time of making his declaration and that Martha Meredith his Mother did not die until the year 1864. It does not appear that either of them resided at any time within the limits of the Cherokee Nation or that at any time claimed any of the rights, benefits and privileges of citizens of the Cherokee Nation. It is further admitted that neither the name of claimant nor that of an ancestor is to be found on the census rolls of Cherokees taken and made by the United States and enumerated in the 7th Sec. of the Act of Dec. 8th 1886, and the amendments thereto for the guidance of this Commission in determining questions of admission to citizenship in the Cherokee Nation. The Commission therefore decide that Harman Pitts and children are not of Cherokee blood. The children of said Pitts as named in his declaration are Oliver Pitts age 38 years,

222

# Cherokee Citizenship Commission Docket Books (1880-84, 1887-89) Volume V
## Tahlequah, Cherokee Nation

William Pitts age 36 years, Bulah Pitts age 34 years, Thomas Pitts age 31 years, Benjamin Pitts age 28 years, George Pitts age 25 years, Sarah J. Pitts age 22 years. Address Fountain City, N.C.

Will.P. Ross    Chairman

Attest
    D.S. Williams                              J.E. Gunter    Com
    Asst    Clk  Com.

---

## PERKINS

**DOCKET #2156**
CENSUS ROLLS

APPLICANT FOR CHEROKEE CITIZENSHIP

| POST OFFICE: Caseyville, Kentucky | | ATTORNEY: Forwarded from Interior Department Washington City | |
|---|---|---|---|
| NO | NAMES | AGE | SEX |
| 1 | America F. Perkins | 35 | Female |
| 2 | James L. Collins | 15 | Male |
| 3 | William T. Perkins | 13 | " |
| 4 | John L. Perkins | 11 | " |
| 5 | Sarah J. Perkins | 7 | Female |
| 6 | Boland E. Perkins | 3 | Male |
| 7 | Nancy E. Perkins | 6 mos | Female |

ANCESTOR: Sarah E. Collins

Rejected Sept. 23$^{rd}$ 1889

Office Commission on Citizenship
Cherokee Nation Ind Ter
Tahlequah  Sept. 23$^{rd}$ 1889

The Commission in this case decide that America F. Perkins age 35 yrs. and the following children James L. Collins age 15 yrs. William T. Perkins age 13 yrs. John L. Perkins age 11 yrs. Sarah J. Perkins age 7 yrs. Boland E. Perkins age 3 yrs. and Nancy E. Perkins age 6 months, are not Cherokees by blood.

See decision in case of Andrew J. Young Docket 2152 B.D. Page 638.  P.O. Caseyville, Kentucky.

223

# Cherokee Citizenship Commission Docket Books
## (1880-84, 1887-89) Volume V
## Tahlequah, Cherokee Nation

Will.P. Ross

Attest                         Chairman

D.S. Williams           J.E. Gunter   Com

Asst  Clk  Com.

---

## PUGH

**DOCKET #2157**

CENSUS ROLLS

APPLICANT FOR CHEROKEE CITIZENSHIP

| POST OFFICE: Rushville, Indiana | | ATTORNEY: Forwarded from Washington City | |
|---|---|---|---|
| NO | NAMES | AGE | SEX |
| 1 | William A. Pugh  et al | 55 | Male |
| 2 | Kate P. Wilson | 32 | Female |
| 3 | Fenley B. Pugh | 30 | |
| 4 | Louisa Kate Pugh (grand child) | 2 | Female |
| 5 | Anna L. Pugh (   "      "   ) | 5 mos | " |
| 6 | Renella Wilson (   "      "   ) | 1 | |

ANCESTOR: Ren Pugh

Rejected Sept. 24th 1889

Office Commission on Citizenship

Cherokee Nation Ind Ter Tahlequah Sept. 24th 1889

This application was refered[sic] here from the Interior Department at Washington. The claimant made her Declaration by affirming the 28th day of August 1884, before James W. Brown, Clerk of the Circuit Court in and for the County of Rush & State of Indiana. He alleges that he is 55 years of age the he is a person of Cherokee Indian descent, is the son of Ren Pugh also of Indian (Cherokee) descent who it is said was born in *(Illegible)* County and State of South Carolina on the 6th day of April A.D. 1794 and died in Rush County & State of Indiana on the 1st day of August 1857. That the said Ren Pugh was the son of Rachel Pugh a halfbreed Cherokee Indian woman who it is said was born in the Cherokee Nation the 15th day of December 1761 and died in Rush County Indiana the 11 day of July 1854 and that she was the daughter of one Lish Wright a Cherokee woman who is said to have been born in the Cherokee Nation in the year 1741 and died in the state of North Carolina in the year A.D. 1817. In support of the above claim two affidavits affirmed to are presented

224

# Cherokee Citizenship Commission Docket Books (1880-84, 1887-89) Volume V Tahlequah, Cherokee Nation

both being exparte and both affiants claiming to be of Cherokee Indian descent, one of them is that of Rebecca Borden 73 years of age and who was born in Marion County State of Indiana and whose affidavit was made on the 27th day of September A.D. 1884, before Moses G. McLane Clerk of Circuit Court for before named county and state, and the other of Leah P. Small 66 years of age, taken on the 27th day of September A.D. 1884, before Joseph G. Keys Notary Public in Warren County State of Ohio. These witnesses corroborate almost word for word, the statement of the declarant. As it does not appear that the claimant or his immediate ancestor at any time resided among the Cherokee Indians or that the name of either is found on either of the census rolls of Cherokee Indians by blood taken in the years 1835-48-51-2, the Commission decide that William A. Pugh and his children, viz. Kate P. Wilson age 32 years, Finly B. Pugh 30 years, and his grand children Louisa Kate Pugh 2 yrs. and Anna C. Pugh 6 months and Renella Wilson age one year are not entitled to citizenship in the Cherokee Nation because of alleged Cherokee blood.

Will.P. Ross    Chairman

Attest
   D.S. Williams
   Asst  Clk  Com.

------

## PUGH

**DOCKET #2158**
CENSUS ROLLS

APPLICANT FOR CHEROKEE CITIZENSHIP

| POST OFFICE: Rushville, Indiana | | ATTORNEY: Forwarded from Washington City | |
|---|---|---|---|
| NO | NAMES | AGE | SEX |
| 1 | Edward D. Pugh | 24 | Male |
| 2 | Amy L. Pugh | | |
| 3 | Lewis D. Pugh | | |

ANCESTOR: David W. Pugh

Rejected Sept. 24th 1889

Office Commission on Citizenship<br>Cherokee Nation Ind Ter<br>Tahlequah  Sept. 24th 1889

225

# Cherokee Citizenship Commission Docket Books
## (1880-84, 1887-89) Volume V
### Tahlequah, Cherokee Nation

The Commission in this case decide that Edward D. Pugh age 24 yrs. and his children Andy[sic] L. Pugh age 21 yrs. and Lewis D. Pugh age 18 yrs. are not Cherokees by blood.

See decision in the case of William A. Pugh Docket 2157, B.E. Page 3. P.O. Rushville Indiana.

|  |  |
|---|---|
|  | Will.P. Ross |
| Attest | Chairman |
| D.S. Williams | J.E. Gunter   Com |
| Asst  Clk  Com. |  |

---

## PEGRAM

**DOCKET #2159**

CENSUS ROLLS

APPLICANT FOR CHEREOKEE CITIZENSHIP

| POST OFFICE: Copeville, Texas. | | ATTORNEY: Forwarded from Washington City | |
|---|---|---|---|
| NO | NAMES | AGE | SEX |
| 1 | Harriet D. Pegram | 39 | Female |
| 2 | Ora B.L.E. Pegram | 4 | " |
| 3 | Fatima J. Pegram | 2 |  |

ANCESTOR:  Lucinda Starbuck

Rejected Sept. 20th 1889

Office Commission on Citizenship
Tahlequah C.N.  Sept. 20th 1889

This Commission in this case decide that Harriet D. Pegram age 39 yrs. and children Ora B.L.E. Pegram age ? and Fatima J. Pegram age 2 yrs. are not of Cherokee blood.  See decision in the case of Caleb Hubbard Docket 2145, B.D. Page 631.  P.O. Copeville, Texas.

|  |  |
|---|---|
|  | Will.P. Ross     Chairman |
| D.S. Williams |  |
| Clerk Commission | J.E. Gunter   Com |

---

# Cherokee Citizenship Commission Docket Books
## (1880-84, 1887-89) Volume V
## Tahlequah, Cherokee Nation

### PARKER

**DOCKET #2160**

CENSUS ROLLS

APPLICANT FOR CHEROKEE CITIZENSHIP

| POST OFFICE: Pryor Creek, Ind. Ter. | | ATTORNEY: C.H. Taylor | |
|---|---|---|---|
| No | NAMES | AGE | SEX |
| 1 | Thomas T. Parker | 39 | Male |
| 2 | Louie Parker | 6 | " |
| 3 | Harriet Parker     (Sister) | 37 | Female |

ANCESTOR: Fanny Hargis

Rejected April 24<sup>th</sup> 1889

See Decision in this case in that of William F. and Ellis H. Parker in this Book Page 7 & 8. <u>Adverse</u> to claimant.
rendered April 24<sup>th</sup> 1889

D.S. Williams
Clerk Com.

---

### PARKER

**DOCKET #2161**

CENSUS ROLLS

APPLICANT FOR CHEROKEE CITIZENSHIP

| POST OFFICE: Troy, Alabama | | ATTORNEY: C.H. Taylor | |
|---|---|---|---|
| No | NAMES | AGE | SEX |
| 1 | William F. Parker, et al. | 50 | male |

ANCESTOR: Fanny Hargis.

Rejected April 24 – 1889

Now on this the 24<sup>th</sup> day of April, 1889, comes for final hearing the above named application which was filed the 5<sup>th</sup> day of October 1887. There being no evidence presented to sustain the allegation set forth and the name of Fanny Hargis from whom plaintiff claims to have derived his Cherokee blood, not being found on the roll of Cherokees by blood made in the year 1835, the Commission adjudge that Wm F. Parker and children whose names are not given are not Cherokees by blood and are not entitled to citizenship in the Cherokee Nation.

Post Office address. Troy Alabama.

227

# Cherokee Citizenship Commission Docket Books
## (1880-84, 1887-89) Volume V
## Tahlequah, Cherokee Nation

This 24<sup>th</sup> day of April 1889.
D.S. Williams
Clerk Com.

Will.P. Ross    Chairman
R. Bunch    Com
John E. Gunter    Com

---

## PARKER

**DOCKET #2162**

CENSUS ROLLS

APPLICANT FOR CHEROKEE CITIZENSHIP

| POST OFFICE: Fountainhead, Tenn | | ATTORNEY: C.H. Taylor | |
|---|---|---|---|
| **NO** | **NAMES** | **AGE** | **SEX** |
| 1 | Ellis H. Parker | 21 | Male |
| 2 | Maggie Parker    (sister) | 18 | Female |
| 3 | Olley Parker    (brother) | 16 | Male |
| 4 | Samuel Parker    ( " ) | 15 | " |

ANCESTOR: Fanny Hargis

Rejected April – 1889

This application presented the 5<sup>th</sup> day of October 1887, not being accompanied by sufficient evidence and the name of ancestor Fanny Hargis from whom claimant alleges he derived his Cherokee blood not being found on the roll of 1835. The Commission decree that Ellis H. Parker aged 21 yrs. and his sister Maggie Parker aged 18 years and his brother Olley Parker aged 16 years and Samuel Parker aged 15 years are not Cherokee blood and not therefore entitled to Citizenship in the Cherokee Nation. This decision includes the applications of James G. Parker aged 68 yrs. James B. Parker aged 25 yrs. and his children whose names are not given, Don C. Parker age 23 yrs. Thomas G. Parker aged 39 yrs. Louis Parker aged 6 yrs. (male) Hornet Parker aged 37 yrs. Post Office address Troy Alabama.

This 24<sup>th</sup> day of April 1889
D.S. Williams
Clerk Com.

Will.P. Ross
Chairman
John E. Gunter    Com

---

228

# Cherokee Citizenship Commission Docket Books
## (1880-84, 1887-89) Volume V
## Tahlequah, Cherokee Nation

## PARKER

**DOCKET #2163**
CENSUS ROLLS

APPLICANT FOR CHEROKEE CITIZENSHIP

| POST OFFICE: Troy, Alabama | | ATTORNEY: C.H. Taylor | |
|---|---|---|---|
| NO | NAMES | AGE | SEX |
| 1 | James B. Parker      et al | 25 | male |
| 2 | James G. Parker     (father) | 68 | " |

ANCESTOR: Fanny Hargis

Rejected April – 1889

See Decision in this case in that of William F. and Ellis H. Parker this Book Page 7 & 8. Adverse to claimant.
rendered April 24[th] 1889.

D.S. Williams
Clerk Com.

## PARKER

**DOCKET #2164**
CENSUS ROLLS

APPLICANT FOR CHEROKEE CITIZENSHIP

| POST OFFICE: Troy, Alabama | | ATTORNEY: C.H. Taylor | |
|---|---|---|---|
| NO | NAMES | AGE | SEX |
| 1 | Don C. Parker | 23 | male |

ANCESTOR: Fanny Hargis

Rejected April 24 – 1889

See Decision in this case in that of William F. and Ellis H. Parker in this Book Page 7 & 8. Adverse to claimant.
rendered April 24[th] 1889.

D.S. Williams
Clerk Com.

229

# Cherokee Citizenship Commission Docket Books
## (1880-84, 1887-89) Volume V
## Tahlequah, Cherokee Nation

## REDDING

**DOCKET #2165**

CENSUS ROLLS

APPLICANT FOR CHEROKEE CITIZENSHIP

| POST OFFICE: Mount Ida, Kansas | | ATTORNEY: Forwarded from Washington City | |
|---|---|---|---|
| NO | NAMES | AGE | SEX |
| 1 | Julia A. Redding | 26 | Female |
| 2 | Nora M. Redding | 18 mos | " |

ANCESTOR: John Dunbar

Rejected Sept. 21st 1889

Office Commission on Citizenship
Cherokee Nation Ind Ter
Tahlequah Sept. 21st 1889

The Commission in this case decide that Julia A. Redding age 26 yrs. and her children[sic] Nora M. Redding age 18 months are not Cherokees by blood. See decision in case of Thomas C. Dunbar Docket 2131, B.D. Page 617. P.O. Mount Ida Kansas.

Will.P. Ross    Chairman

Attest
    D.S. Williams
    Asst Clk Com.

J.E. Gunter    Com

---

## REED

**DOCKET #2166**

CENSUS ROLLS

APPLICANT FOR CHEROKEE CITIZENSHIP

| POST OFFICE: Plainfield Indiana | | ATTORNEY: From Interior Department Washington City | |
|---|---|---|---|
| NO | NAMES | AGE | SEX |
| 1 | Nancy A. Reed | 56 | Female |
| 2 | John Reed | 28 | Male |
| 3 | James Reed | 27 | " |
| 4 | Henry Reed | 24 | " |

| 5 | George Reed | 22 | " |
| 6 | Anna B. Reed | 19 | Female |

**ANCESTOR:** Emmelia Sheftlet

### *Commission on Citizenship.*

CHEROKEE NATION, IND. TER.

*Tahlequah,* Sept. 21$^{st}$ *1889*

Nancy A. Reed
    vs             Application for Cherokee Citizenship
The Cherokee Nation

The above case is referred from this Interior Department at Washington D.C. In her declaration the claimant alleges that she is 56 years old, that she is a halfbreed Cherokee Indian woman and was born in Albermarle[sic] County State of Virginia, that she is the daughter of one Amelia Sheftlet a Cherokee Indian woman who it is said was born in said county and state in 1802 and died in Hendricks County State of Indiana in 1871, that the mother of said Amelia Sheftlet was one Dolly Greene a Cherokee Indian woman who it is said was born in the Cherokee Nation and died in Abermarle[sic] County Virginia in 1825. The proposing declaration was sworn to before W.F. Haynes Clerk of the Circuit Court of Hendricks County State of Indiana on the 20$^{th}$ day of May A.D. 1884, and is corroborated by one Alexander Clark of the same county and state in an exparte affidavit made on the same date. Witness Clark represents that he is a halfbreed Iroquois Indian 44 years old and also by one William Sandridge in an affidavit made exparte on the 30$^{th}$ of May 1884 before the said Clerk of Hendricks County State of Indiana. The latter witness says that he is 78 years of age and was born in Albermarle[sic] County State of Virginia was well acquainted with Nancy A. Reed and knows her to be of Cherokee Indian descent, knew her mother Amelia Sheftlet and grand mother Dolly Greene and that in 1824 he saw Dolly Greene on the Cherokee Reservation and *(illegible)* said Cherokee claim and acknowledge her to be a full blood Cherokee Indian woman. These statements are *(illegible)* and *(illegible)* and that to an extent which in view of their exparte character renders them untrustworthy in the opinion of the Commission and as there is nothing to show that these persons have heretofore enjoyed or claimed the rights of citizenship in the Cherokee Nation and neither the name of claimant nor that of Amelia ~~Greene~~ Sheftlet is

231

# Cherokee Citizenship Commission Docket Books
## (1880-84, 1887-89) Volume V
## Tahlequah, Cherokee Nation

found on the census rolls of Cherokees by blood taken by the United States in the years 1835-48-51-52, the Commission decide that Nancy A. Reed & her children Viz, John Reed 28 yrs. of age, James Reed 27 yrs., Harvey[sic] Reed 24 yrs. George Reed 22 yrs. and Anna B. Reed 19 years are <u>not</u> of Cherokee Indian blood. P.O. Plainfield, Indiana.

Will.P. Ross    Chairman

J.E. Gunter    Com

---

## REDDING

**DOCKET #2167**

CENSUS ROLLS

APPLICANT FOR CHEROKEE CITIZENSHIP

| POST OFFICE: Prairie Center, Kansas | | ATTORNEY: Forwarded from Washington City | |
|---|---|---|---|
| **NO** | **NAMES** | **AGE** | **SEX** |
| 1 | Abigail Redding | 38 | Female |
| 2 | Mattie E. Redding | 13 | " |
| 3 | Frank H. Redding | 12 | Male |
| 4 | Leigh T. Redding | 7 | " |
| 5 | Ora V. Redding | 4 | |

ANCESTOR: Elizabeth Dunbar

Rejected Sept. 21st 1889

Office Commission on Citizenship

Cherokee Nation Ind Ter

Tahlequah Sept. 21st 1889

The Commission in this case decide that Abigail Redding age 38 yrs. and the following children, Mattie E. Redding age 13 yrs. Frank H. Redding age 12 yrs. Leigh T. Redding age 7 yrs. and Ora V. Redding age 4 yrs. are not Cherokees by blood.

     See decision in case of Thomas C. Dunbar Docket 2131, B.D. Page 617. P.O. Prairie Center Kansas.

Will.P. Ross    Chairman

Attest

    D.S. Williams

  Asst  Clk  Com.

# Cherokee Citizenship Commission Docket Books
## (1880-84, 1887-89) Volume V
## Tahlequah, Cherokee Nation

## ROBBINS

**DOCKET #2168**
CENSUS ROLLS

APPLICANT FOR CHEROKEE CITIZENSHIP

| POST OFFICE: Alla[sic], Mo. | | ATTORNEY: Forwarded from Washington City | |
|---|---|---|---|
| NO | NAMES | AGE | SEX |
| 1 | Sarah Robbins | 42 | Female |
| 2 | William E. Robbins | 22 | Male |
| 3 | Anna M. Robbins | 17 | Female |
| 4 | Florence N. Robbins | 10 | male[sic] |

ANCESTOR: Joseph Hubbard

Rejected Sept. 20<sup>th</sup> 1889

Office Commission on Citizenship
Cherokee Nation Ind Ter
Tahlequah Sept. 20<sup>th</sup> 1889

The Commission in this case decide that Sarah Robbins age 42 yrs. and her children William E. age 22 yrs. Anna M. age 17 yrs. and Florence N. Robbins age 10 yrs. are not of Cherokee blood.

See decision in the case of Caleb Hubbard Docket 2145, B.D. Page 631. P.O. Alla[sic], Mo.

Will.P. Ross     Chairman

Attest
D.S. Williams
Asst  Clk  Com.

233

# Cherokee Citizenship Commission Docket Books
## (1880-84, 1887-89) Volume V
### Tahlequah, Cherokee Nation

## RAINS

**DOCKET #2169**

CENSUS ROLLS

APPLICANT FOR CHEROKEE CITIZENSHIP

| POST OFFICE: Jacksboro, Texas | | ATTORNEY: L.B. Bell | |
|---|---|---|---|
| **NO** | **NAMES** | **AGE** | **SEX** |
| 1 | T.A. Rains | | |

ANCESTOR:

Rejected Sept. 9<sup>th</sup> 1889

Office Commission on Citizenship
Cherokee Nation Ind Ter
Tahlequah Sept. 9<sup>th</sup> 1889

Application for Cherokee Citizenship

The above case was called three times and no response from applicant or by Attorney.

The Commission therefore decide that T.A. Rains is not a Cherokee by blood. Post Office Jacksboro Texas.

Will.P. Ross    Chairman

Attest

D.S. Williams                                      J.E. Gunter    Com
Asst   Clk   Com.

## MEREDITH

**DOCKET #2170**

CENSUS ROLLS

APPLICANT FOR CHEROKEE CITIZENSHIP

| POST OFFICE: Lynnville, Iowa | | ATTORNEY: Forwarded from Washington City | |
|---|---|---|---|
| **NO** | **NAMES** | **AGE** | **SEX** |
| 1 | Ardilla Meredith    (white) | 58 | Female |
| 2 | William J. Meredith | 21 | Male |
| 3 | Albert Meredith | 19 | " |
| 4 | Elkannah Meredith | 15 | " |

ANCESTOR:  James N Meredith

234

# Cherokee Citizenship Commission Docket Books
## (1880-84, 1887-89) Volume V
### Tahlequah, Cherokee Nation

*Commission on Citizenship.*

CHEROKEE NATION, IND. TER.

*Tahlequah,* August 22<sup>nd</sup> 1889

William J. Meredith
Albert Meredith and                    Brothers
Elkannah Meredith

  From the evidence submitted by the above applicants we find that they are brothers being the sons of James H. Meredith & Ardilla Meredith. To establish the fact the affidavits of their mother Ardilla Meredith & that of Mary Meredith are submitted. They both affirm before a Justice of the Peace in & for the State of North Carolina, that James H. Meredith ~~is~~ was said to be of Cherokee blood & the reputed son of one James Meredith who was born in the State of North Carolina in the year ~~18~~ 1792. This evidence is exparte and not sufficient in our opinon[sic] to satisfy us in deciding in applicant's favor and also the applicant's attorney L.B. Bell admits that this ancestor's name James Meredith does not appear upon any of the ~~Cherokee~~ census rolls of Cherokees taken in the years 1835, 48, 51 & 52. Therefore we decide that applicants William J. Meredith age 21 yrs. Albert Meredith age 19 yrs. & Elkannah Meredith age 15 yrs. are <u>not</u> Cherokees by blood & <u>not entitled</u> to citizenship in the Cherokee Nation. Post Office, Lynnville, Iowa.

"<u>Note</u>" The facts in this case are the same as those recorded in the case of Harman Pitts, same relations. (See decision Docket 2155, Book E, Page 1.

        Will.P. Ross
            Chairman
       John E. Gunter Com

## McINTIRE

**DOCKET #2171**
CENSUS ROLLS

APPLICANT FOR CHEROKEE CITIZENSHIP

| POST OFFICE: Caseyville, Kentucky | | ATTORNEY: Forwarded from Washington City | |
|---|---|---|---|
| **No** | **NAMES** | **AGE** | **SEX** |
| 1 | Mary G. McIntire   et al | 52 | Female |
| 2 | Jane A. Taylor | 30 | " |
| 3 | James R.Y. McIntire | 26 | Male |
| 4 | Sarah E.H. Chancelor | 18 | Female |
| 5 | George W. McIntire | 14 | Male |
| 6 | Lucy A. McIntire | 11 | Female |

**ANCESTOR:** Phillip S. Young

Rejected Sept. 23rd 1889

Office Commission on Citizenship
Cherokee Nation Ind Ter
Tahlequah  Sept. 23rd 1889

The Commission in this case decide that Mary G. McIntire age 52 yrs. and the following children, Jane A. Taylor age 30 yrs. James R.Y. McIntire age 26 yrs. Sarah E.H. Chancelor age 22 yrs. Thomas McIntire age 18 yrs. George W. McIntire age 14 yrs. Lucy A. McIntire age 11 yrs. and her grand children, Clauda T. Taylor age 4 yrs. Robert H. Taylor age 2 yrs. Virgie M. Taylor 11 months and George E. Chancelor age 5 yrs. are not Cherokees by blood. See decision in case Andrew J. Christain[sic] Docket 2152, B.D. Page 638. P.O. Caseyville Kentucky.

Will.P. Ross
Chairman

Attest
D.S. Williams
Asst  Clk  Com.

236

# Cherokee Citizenship Commission Docket Books
## (1880-84, 1887-89) Volume V
### Tahlequah, Cherokee Nation

## MILLS

**DOCKET #2172**
CENSUS ROLLS

APPLICANT FOR CHEROKEE CITIZENSHIP

| POST OFFICE: Richland, Iowa | | ATTORNEY: Forwarded from Washington City | |
|---|---|---|---|
| **NO** | **NAMES** | **AGE** | **SEX** |
| 1 | Nancy Mills    et al | 78 | Female |
| 2 | Pleasant Mills | 61 | Male |
| 3 | Elwood Mills | 56 | " |
| 4 | Rhoda A. Morgan | 54 | Female |
| 5 | Erwin Mills | 51 | Male |
| 6 | Betsey J. Morgan | 49 | Female |
| 7 | Perry Mills | 47 | Male |
| 8 | Elehue Mills | 39 | " |

ANCESTOR: David Elmore

*Commission on Citizenship.*

CHEROKEE NATION, IND. TER.

*Tahlequah,* August 19th 1889

Nancy Mills
    vs            The application for re-admission to citizenship
The Cherokee Nation

The above case is accompanied by no evidence in support of the statements set forth in the declaration of claimant and affirmed before J.D. Haworth Notary Public of Keokuk County State of Iowa. On the 5th day of March A.D. 1886, It is apparent however, that the applicant bares her claim to citizenship in the Cherokee Nation as a Cherokee by blood upon the same grounds that several other applicants have done. One of these is John R. Henly and the reasons set forth for rejecting his application are[sic] regarded by the Commission as *(illegible)* an <u>adverse</u> decision in this case. The Commission therefore decide against applicant and refer to said decision for the reasons therefore. See Docket 553, Book B, Page 266. The decision includes the children of and grandchildren of said Nancy Mills, to wit

# Cherokee Citizenship Commission Docket Books
## (1880-84, 1887-89) Volume V
## Tahlequah, Cherokee Nation

To wit –

Pleasant Mills age 61 years, Edward[sic] Mills age 56 years, Rhoda A. Morgan age 54 years, Erwin Mills age 51 years, Betsey J. Morgan age 49 years, Perry Mills age 47 years, Elehue Mills age 39 years and her grand children "To wit" Mary A. *(Illegible)* age 33 years, Henry L Mills age 25 years, Emma N. Mills age 23 years, Allen C. Mills age 19 years, Lorey L Mills age 17 years, May R. Mills age 9 years, Parthena J. Morgan age 30 years, Nancy E. Leopeal age 23 years, Oliver Morgan age 19 years, Sandford E Mills age 30 years, Alford O. Mills age 30 years, Andrew E. Mills age 28 years, Nancy A. McCulley age 27 years, Lewis C. Mills age 25 years, William N. Mills age 21 years, Rosette J. Mills age 8 years, Mabel J. Mills age 5 years, Ross W. Mills age 3 years, Mary E. McDonald age 29 years, Ida A. Morgan age 20 years, Mary J. Mills age 25 years, *(Illegible)* E. Mills, Obed E. Mills age 21 yers[sic], Albert S. Mills age 19 yers[sic], Amen C. Mills age 15 yrs., Ira G. Mills age 14 yers[sic], Almeda Mills age 9, Wynona Mills age 5 yers[sic], Eliza Mills age 3 years, Anna Mills age 1 yers[sic], *( Illegible)* Mills age 14 yers[sic], *(Illegible)* Mills age 1 yers[sic] and Ella Mills age 8 yers[sic] are not Cherokees by blood and are not entitled to Cherokee citizenship in the Cherokee Nation.

> Will.P. Ross
> Chairman
> John E. Gunter    Com[sic]
> Commissioner

---

## MOODY

**DOCKET #2173**
CENSUS ROLLS

APPLICANT FOR CHEROKEE CITIZENSHIP

| POST OFFICE: Lynnville, Iowa | | ATTORNEY: Forwarded from Washington | |
|---|---|---|---|
| NO | NAMES | AGE | SEX |
| 1 | Mary E. Moody | 32 | Female |
| 2 | Everet H. Moody | 11 | Son |
| 3 | Edna F. Moody | 7 | Female |

ANCESTOR: James H. Meredith

# Cherokee Citizenship Commission Docket Books
## (1880-84, 1887-89) Volume V
## Tahlequah, Cherokee Nation

Office Commission on Citizenship
Tahlequah Aug. 21<sup>st</sup> 1889

The above application was filed on the 5<sup>th</sup> day of October 1887, and on this day the case was called for final hearing. The applicant resides now in Jasper County State of Iowa. She was born in Henry County State of Indiana. The claimant claims to derive her Cherokee blood through her father one James H. Meredith whom she believes was a Cherokee Indian. In support of the above allegations the claimants only submits[sic] as evidence her own affidavit taken before a Notary Public in and for the State of Iowa. We do not claim this sufficient evidence to establish her claim of Cherokee blood and in addition to this the applicant fails to name any of the census rolls of Cherokees taken in the year 1835, 48, 51, 52, where her ancestors names might be found thereby not complying with Section 7<sup>th</sup> of the law that governs this Commission. In view of these facts, we are of the opinion and decide that applicant Mary E. Moody aged 32 years and her children Everet H. Moody aged 11 years and Edna F. Moody aged 7 years are <u>not</u> Cherokees by blood and are not entitled to Cherokee citizenship in the Cherokee Nation. The facts that govern this case are the same as are embodied in the opinion in the case of Hermon Pitts (See Docket 2155, Book "E", Page 1.)

|  |  |
|---|---|
|  | Will.P. Ross    Chairman |
| Attest    E.G. Ross | R. Bunch    Com |
| Clerk Commission | J.E. Gunter    Com |

---

## McGUIRE
**DOCKET #2174**
CENSUS ROLLS

APPLICANT FOR CHEROKEE CITIZENSHIP

| POST OFFICE: Rushville, Indiana | | ATTORNEY: Forwarded from Washington City | |
|---|---|---|---|
| NO | NAMES | AGE | SEX |
| 1 | Henry P. McGuire | 32 | Male |
| 2 | Finley S. McGuire | 7 | " |
| 3 | Fred C. McGuire | | |

ANCESTOR: Winford A. McGuire

Rejected Sept. 24<sup>th</sup> 1889

239

# Cherokee Citizenship Commission Docket Books
## (1880-84, 1887-89) Volume V
## Tahlequah, Cherokee Nation

Office Commission on Citizenship
Cherokee Nation Ind Ter
Tahlequah Sept. 24[th] 1889

The Commission in this case decide that Henry P. McGuire age 32 yrs. and his children Finley S. McGuire age 7 yrs. and Fred C. McGuire <u>are not</u> Cherokees by blood. See decision in case of William A. Pugh Docket 2157, B.E. Page 3.

Attest                                           Will.P. Ross   Chairman
    D.S. Williams
    Asst  Clk  Com.

---

## McDOWELL

**DOCKET #2175**
CENSUS ROLLS

APPLICANT FOR CHEROKEE CITIZENSHIP

| POST OFFICE: Kokomo, Indiana | | ATTORNEY: Forwarded from Washington City | |
|---|---|---|---|
| **NO** | **NAMES** | **AGE** | **SEX** |
| 1 | Nora A. McDowell | 28 | Female |
| 2 | Claude J. McDowell | 5 | Male |
| 3 | Gilbert M. McDowell | 3 | " |

ANCESTOR: Thomas Jay

Rejected Sept. 24[th] 1889

Office Commission on Citizenship
Cherokee Nation Ind Ter
Tahlequah Sept. 24[th] 1889

The Commission in this case decide that Nora A. McDowell age 28 yrs. and children Claude J. McDowell age 5 yrs. and Gilbert M McDowell age 3 yrs. are <u>not</u> Cherokees by blood.

See decision in case of William A. Pugh Docket 2157, B.E. Page 3. P.O. Kokomo, Ind.

# Cherokee Citizenship Commission Docket Books
## (1880-84, 1887-89) Volume V
## Tahlequah, Cherokee Nation

Will.P. Ross    Chairman

Attest
    D.S. Williams
      Asst   Clk  Com.

---

## MARTIN

**DOCKET #2176**
CENSUS ROLLS

APPLICANT FOR CHEROKEE CITIZENSHIP

| POST OFFICE: Seneca, Mo. | | ATTORNEY: Forwarded from Washington City | |
|---|---|---|---|
| NO | NAMES | AGE | SEX |
| 1 | Alexander W. Martin | 39 | Male |
| 2 | Moley Martin | 11 | " |
| 3 | Arthur L. Martin | 8 | " |
| 4 | Walker Martin | 6 | " |
| 5 | Aley Martin | 4 | " |
| 6 | Myrtle Martin | 11 mos | Female |

ANCESTOR: Jane Martin &[sic] Davis

Rejected Sept. 19th 1889.

Office Commission on Citizenship Cher. Nat. I.T.
Tahlequah  Sept. 19th 1889

The application in the above case was filed before the Department of the Interior and refered[sic] to the Commission on Citizenship.  The applicant in his declaration made and sworn to on the 12th day of October A.D. 1886, before *(Illegible)* Boyd, Notary Public in the County of Newton and State of Missouri, alleges that he is a person of Cherokee Indian descent, 39 years old and was born in Clay County State aforesaid.  That he is the son of one Jane Martin, a person of Cherokee Indian descent who was born in Amherst County Virginia in the year A.D. 1810 and died in Andrew County Missouri in 1859.  And that Matilda Davis was the daughter of Kizziah Hooker whose maiden name was Kizziah Jones who was born on said reservation and died there on in[sic] 1829.  These alleged facts are sworn to in due form and regular order on the day and date above named and before the same Notary Public by one Fandal Martin 78 years old who was born in Amherst County State of Virginia, is the husband of said Jane Martin and presumably the Father of the applicant and whose signature to his affidavit taken exparte is made with a X and attested by only one witness Mr. Robert Vasson. The Commission does not regard such statement as sufficient to prove the Cherokee descent of the claimant and in the absence of his name and that of Jane Martin, his mother who was Jane Davis from the census rolls of Cherokees by blood taken and made by the United States in the years 1835-48-51-51, they decide that the Claimant Alexander W. Martin and his children viz Moley Martin age 11 years, Arthur L. Martin age 8 years, Walker Martin age 6 yrs. Aley Martin age 4 yrs. and Myrtle Martin 11 months are not of Cherokee blood and not entitled to citizenship in the Cherokee Nation.

Will.P. Ross  Chairman

Attest
    D.S. Williams
    Asst  Clk  Com.

---

## MORGAN

**DOCKET #2177**
CENSUS ROLLS

APPLICANT FOR CHEROKEE CITIZENSHIP

| POST OFFICE: | | ATTORNEY: Forwarded from Washington City | |
|---|---|---|---|
| **NO** | **NAMES** | **AGE** | **SEX** |
| 1 | Marcia A. Morgan | 42 | Female |
| 2 | Levi O. Morgan | 13 | Male |
| 3 | Charles P. Morgan | 10 | " |
| 4 | Amy E. Morgan | 8 | Female |
| 5 | Joseph H. Morgan | 5 | Male |
| 6 | Hattie E. Morgan | 3 | Female |
| 7 | Callie M. Morgan | 8 mos | " |

ANCESTOR: John Sanders

Rejected Sept. 20th 1889

Office Commission on Citizenship
Cherokee Nation Ind Ter
Tahlequah  Sept. 20th 1889

The Commission in this case decide that Marcia A. Morgan age 42 yrs. and her children Levi O. age 13 yrs. Charles P. age 10 yrs. Amy E. age 8 yrs. Joseph H.

age 5 yrs. Hattie E. age 3 yrs. and Callie M. Morgan age 8 months are not of Cherokee blood.

See decision in the case of David Elmore et. al. Docket 2279, B.E. Page 141. P.O. Milo Iowa.

Attest

    D.S. Williams

    Asst  Clk  Com.

Will.P. Ross

    Chairman

J.E. Gunter   Com

---

## MEREDITH

**DOCKET #2178**

CENSUS ROLLS

APPLICANT FOR CHEROKEE CITIZENSHIP

| POST OFFICE: Lynnville, Iowa | | ATTORNEY: Forwarded from Washington City | |
|---|---|---|---|
| NO | NAMES | AGE | SEX |
| 1 | Thomas J. Meredith    et al | 68 | Male |
| 2 | Robert Meredith | 39 | " |
| 3 | Alfred Meredith | 23 | " |
| 4 | David Meredith | 18 | " |

ANCESTOR: David Meredith

*Commission on Citizenship.*

CHEROKEE NATION, IND. TER.

*Tahlequah,* August 22   *188*9

Thomas J. Meredith

    vs.

Cherokee Nation

      In support of the above applications claimant submits as evidence the affidavits of himself and that of Mary Meredith who both appears before a Notary Public in & for the State of Iowa that applicant is a Cherokee by blood, that he is 68 years, born in the State of North Carolina, that he is the son of James Meredith and a *(illegible)* of *(Name Illegible).* As all of this evidence is exparte and not sufficient in our opion[sic] to justify us in deciding in claimants favor and further applicant's Attorney ~~admits that~~ Mr. L.B. Bell admits that claimant's ancestor's name ~~does~~ does not appear upon any of the census rolls of Cherokees taken in the year 1835, 48, 51 & 52, which the 7th Section of the laws that govern this Commission requires. See Act dated Dec. 8[th] 1886. Therefore we decide that applicant Thomas Meredith age 68 yrs. and his children to wit: Robert Meredith age 39 yrs., Alfred Meredith age 23 yrs. David Meredith age 18 yrs. and his grand children Clara Meredith age 16 yrs. Mary Ann Meredith age 11 yrs. Rosella Meredith age 9 yrs. Harland Meredith age 6 yrs. and Lucille Meredith age 15 months, are not Cherokees by blood. Post Office Lynnville Iowa. See opion[sic] in the Harman Pitts case. Same facts. Docket 2155, Book E, Page 1.

Will.P. Ross    Chairman
John E. Gunter    Com

## MILLS

**DOCKET #2179**
CENSUS ROLLS

APPLICANT FOR CHEREKEE CITIZENSHIP

| POST OFFICE: Centerville, Indiana | | ATTORNEY: Forwarded from Washington City | |
|---|---|---|---|
| NO | NAMES | AGE | SEX |
| 1 | Susannah Mills | 58 | Female |
| 2 | Rowland Mills | 36 | Male |
| 3 | Rosetta Stewart | 28 | Female |
| 4 | Edna A. Stewart  (Grand Child) | 4 | " |

ANCESTOR: David Meredith

Office Commission on Citizenship
Cherokee Nation Ind Ter
Tahlequah  August 2[nd] 1889

The applicant in the above case states in her affidavit taken before a Notary Public in and for Mayne[sic] County, state of Indiana, that she derives her Cherokee blood through her father James Meredith that she is 58 years old and was born in the State of North Carolina and that her father was born in the

# Cherokee Citizenship Commission Docket Books
## (1880-84, 1887-89) Volume V
## Tahlequah, Cherokee Nation

same State in the year 1792. The applicant further submits as evidence in support of her claim the affidavit of Mary Meredith taken before a Justice of the Peace, in and for Forsythe County, State of North Carolina, who affirms to the same points as that of applicant. As all the evidence in this case is "exparte" and the fact that the applicant fails to state on what census rolls of Cherokees might be found her ancestor's name. Therefore we decide that applicant Susanah[sic] Mills age 58 years and her children Rowland age 36 years, Rosetta Stewart age 28 years, and her Grand child Edna Stewart age 4 years are not Cherokees by blood and not entitled to citizenship in the Cherokee Nation. The facts that govern this case are the same as those embodied in the opinion in the case of Harmon Pitts. See Docket 2155 Book E, Page 1. All of the same relatives and ancestors.

Attest                      Will.P. Ross    Chairman
     E.G. Ross
         Clerk Commission

## MEREDITH
### DOCKET #2180
CENSUS ROLLS

APPLICANT FOR CHEROKEE CITIZENSHIP

| POST OFFICE: Williamsburgh[sic], Indiana | | ATTORNEY: Forwarded from Washington City | |
|---|---|---|---|
| NO | NAMES | AGE | SEX |
| 1 | Andrew Meredith    et al | 86 | Male |
| 2 | Minerva Thomas | 60 | Female |
| 3 | Jeanetta C. Kendricks | 58 | " |
| 4 | Catharine G. Gargus | 53 | " |
| 5 | Betsey A. Mandlin | 50 | " |
| 6 | John W. Meredith | 39 | Male |
| 7 | Mary L. Broadwell | 35 | Female |

ANCESTOR: Mary Crews

Andrew Meredith                 Commission on Citizenship
     vs                         Cherokee Nation
The Cherokee Nation         Tahlequah July 5[th] 1889

245

This is one of the cases included in the motion of L.B. Bell Esqr. Attorney for applicants made before the Commission the 24[th] day June but which was over ruled to be allowed to withdraw them because it was admitted that neither the name of the applicant Caleb Hubbard nor that of an ancestor would be found on the census rolls of Cherokees by blood taken and made by the United States in the years 1835-48-51-52 and does not therefore come within the jurisdiction of the Commission. While the fact thus admitted makes it incumbent on the Commission to reject the application of Andrew Meredith it is not *(illegible)* to add that the evidence on file would not *(illegible)* it otherwise justify a different decision. Andrew Meredith claims admission to citizenship upon the ground that he is of Cherokee descent being the son of one John Meredith who was born in Bedford County State of Virginia in A.D. 1779 and died in Stokes County North Carolina in A.D. 1826. And that said John Meredith was of Indian descent and the son of one Mary Meredith nee Mary Crews who was said to have been born on the Cherokee reservation East of the Mississippi River in the year A.D. 1752, and died in the year A.D. 1823. The witnesses in are Lydia Meredith age 84 years whose deposition was taken before Jno. W. Payne Clerk of the Western District of North Carolina and Mary Meredith age 85 years taken before J.S. Ray, J.P. of Forsyth County North Carolina and both of whom affirm the correctness of the statements alleged by the applicant in her declaration. These witnesses are members of the family of Meredith of where several are applicants for admission and who rely mainly on their statements to establish their claims and is therefore to be taken with great allowance unless corroborated by other persons, whose sources of information could be ascertained by a fair cross examination. It is also evident that the applicant himself and others claiming through their descent from Mary Crews had full opportunity and *(illegible)* to if benefits Cherokee Indians by blood to have had their names placed upon the rolls of 1835 as he was 86 years in 1884 when his declaration was made or upon the other rolls referred to in the Act of 1886 and 1888 as is not the case. The Commission therefore decide that Andrew Meredith is not of Cherokee descent nor are his children viz, (at the time of filing his application) Minerva Thomas aged 63 years, Janetta[sic] C. Kindricks age 58 years, Catherine G. Gargus aged 58 years, Betsy A. Mandlin aged 50 years, John W. Meredith aged 39 years, Mary L. Broadwell aged 35 years and his grand children viz: Mary C. Kern aged 18 yrs. John W. Kern aged 13 years Clarence M Broadwell aged two years, Jophn R. Broadwell aged one month, Martha E. Meredith aged 15 yrs. William A. Meredith aged 14 years, Linus F. Meredith aged 12 years, Emma L. Meredith aged 11 years, Mary A. Meredith aged 9 years, Robert M. Meredith aged 8 years, Navy L. Meredith aged 6 years,

# Cherokee Citizenship Commission Docket Books
## (1880-84, 1887-89) Volume V
## Tahlequah, Cherokee Nation

Josephine E. Harnett aged 43 years, Henry D. Thomas aged 40 years, James R. Kendricks aged 40 years, Minerva J. Holliday aged 36 years, James A. Mandlin aged 32 years, Sarah A. Commons aged 28 years, James E. Barley aged 38 years and his great grand children viz:  Robert R. Holliday aged 4 years, Anna M. Kendricks aged 2 years, Frank Harnett 22 years, Herbert Harnett aged 20 years, George Sperbuk[sic] age 23 years, William Thomas aged 13 years, James Thomas aged 8 years, Frank B. Mandlin aged 5 years, Ernest L. Commons aged 8 years, Charles C. Commons aged 6 years, Horace J. Commons aged 4 years, Margretta[sic] Bailey aged 14 years, Daniel Bailey aged 8 years, and[sic] are not entitled to citizenship in the Cherokee Nation. to citizenship in the Cherokee Nation.

Will.P. Ross<br>
Chairman<br>
John E. Gunter    Com

---

## McCOMBS

**DOCKET #2181**

CENSUS ROLLS

APPLICANT FOR CHEROKEE CITIZENSHIP

| POST OFFICE: Fort Smith, Ark. | | ATTORNEY: L.B. Bell | |
|---|---|---|---|
| NO | NAMES | AGE | SEX |
| 1 | Lelia McCombs    et al | 20 | Female |

ANCESTOR:

Rejected Sept. 9<sup>th</sup> 1889

Office Commission on Citizenship<br>
Cherokee Nation Ind Ter<br>
Tahlequah  Sept. 9<sup>th</sup> 1889

Application for Cherokee Citizenship.

The above case was called three times and no response from applicant or by Atty and there being no evidence on file in support of claim.  Therefore the Commission decide that Lelia McCombs age 20 yrs. and 2 children about 1 & 2 yrs. old whose names are not given are not Cherokees by blood.  Post Office Fort Smith Ark.

Will.P. Ross    Chairman

Attest

     D.S. Williams            J.E. Gunter    Com

     Asst  Clk  Com.

247

# Cherokee Citizenship Commission Docket Books (1880-84, 1887-89) Volume V
## Tahlequah, Cherokee Nation

## BEARD

**DOCKET #2182**
CENSUS ROLLS

APPLICANT FOR CHEROKEE CITIZENSHIP

| POST OFFICE: Lane, Kansas | | ATTORNEY: Forwarded from Washington City | |
|---|---|---|---|
| NO | NAMES | AGE | SEX |
| 1 | Margaret E. Beard | 26 | Female |
| 2 | Frank G. Beard | 4 | Male |
| 3 | Minnie E. Beard | 1½ | Female |
| 4 | Eunice P. Lasseter    (sister) | 41 | Female |

ANCESTOR: Elizabeth Dunbar

Rejected Sept. 9th 1889

Office Commission on Citizenship
Cherokee Nation Ind Ter
Tahlequah  Sept. 21st 1889

The Commission in this case decide that Margret[sic] E. Beard age 26 and her children, Frank G. Beard age 4 yrs., Minnie E. Beard age 18 months and her sister, Eunice P. Lasseter age 41 yrs. are (invalaid[sic] who resides with said Margaret E. Beard) are not Cherokees by blood. P.O. Lane Kansas.

Will.P. Ross    Chairman

Attest
    D.S. Williams
  Asst  Clk  Com.

## BOGUE

**DOCKET #2183**
CENSUS ROLLS

APPLICANT FOR CHEROKEE CITIZENSHIP

| POST OFFICE: Spiceland, Indiana | | ATTORNEY: Forwarded from Washington City | |
|---|---|---|---|
| NO | NAMES | AGE | SEX |
| 1 | Libbie J. Bogue | 45 | Female |

248

| 2 | Cordelia Bogue | 23 | " |
| 3 | Oueda Reese | 20 | " |
| 4 | Anna K. Bogue | 17 | " |
| 5 | Alfred Bogue | 13 | Male |
| 6 | Oscar H. Bogue | 11 | " |

ANCESTOR: Mary Clark

Commission on Citizenship
July 2nd 1889

Libbie J. Bogue, Nathan H. Allen, Herman H. Allen, Nancy C. Deck, Monta E. Bogue VS. Cherokee Nation

The applicant Libbie J. Bogue alleges that she is of Cherokee descent being the daughter of one Ann Allen a Cherokee who was born in Randolph County State of North Carolina, 1796, and died in 1842 in Rush County State of Indiana that said Mary Allen was the daughter of Mary Clark, who was [sic] in ~~184~~ 1765, and died in 1854, and that she was the daughter of one Martha Sanders nee Elmore, who was born in 1735 and died in 1817 & who was also of Cherokee descent. Two affidavits one presented in support of the allegations of applicant, one dated 11th day of Sept. 1884, affirmed to before M. Summerfield, Clerk of Cist. Court for Douglas County, Kansas, made by *(Name Illegible)* 71 yrs. old & the other of Charles Starbuck age 89 yrs. affirmed to Sept. 12th 1884, before Charles N. Hill Notary Public for said county & state. These affiants corroborate the statements made in the declaration of claimant. But in view of the fact that they are "exparte" & that they do not state the *(illegible)* of their knowledge & which one *(illegible)* due to *(illegible...)* not be received as conclusive of the Cherokee blood of claimants and especially so since they have at no time resided within the limits of the Nation, not sought any of the rights & privileges of Cherokee citizenship and that neither the names of the applicants nor those of their alleged Indian ancestors are found on any of the census rolls of Cherokees taken by the United States in the years of 1835, 48, 51, 52 as *(illegible)* by the Attorney for claimants L.B. Bell Esqr. The Commission therefore decide the applicants are not Cherokees by blood.

Will.P. Ross    Chairman

249

# Cherokee Citizenship Commission Docket Books
## (1880-84, 1887-89) Volume V
## Tahlequah, Cherokee Nation

### BOGUE

**DOCKET #2184**

CENSUS ROLLS

APPLICANT FOR CHEROKEE CITIZENSHIP

| POST OFFICE: Spiceland, Indiana | | ATTORNEY: Forwarded from Washington City | |
|---|---|---|---|
| **No** | **NAMES** | **AGE** | **SEX** |
| 1 | Martha E. Bogue | 42 | Female |
| 2 | Josephine E. Bogue | 15 | " |

ANCESTOR: Mary Clark

Rejected Sept. 18th 1889

Office Commission on Citizenship
Cherokee Nation Ind Ter
Tahlequah Sept. 18th 1889

The Commission in this case decide that Martha E. Bogue age 42 yrs. and her daughter Josephine E. Bogue age 15 yrs. are not Cherokees by blood. See decision in case Libbie J Bogue, Docket 2183, Book E, Page 29. P.O. Spiceland Indiana.

Will.P. Ross    Chairman

Attest

D.S. Williams
Asst  Clk  Com.

---

### BUTLER

**DOCKET #2185**

CENSUS ROLLS

APPLICANT FOR CHEROKEE CITIZENSHIP

| POST OFFICE: Sterling, Kansas | | ATTORNEY: Forwarded from Washington City | |
|---|---|---|---|
| **No** | **NAMES** | **AGE** | **SEX** |
| 1 | Hardy H. Butler | 44 | Male |
| 2 | Alva R. Butler | 16 | Female |
| 3 | Joseph H. Butler | 14 | Male |
| 4 | Harlin J. Butler | 11 | " |

ANCESTOR: Sarah Butler

# Cherokee Citizenship Commission Docket Books
## (1880-84, 1887-89) Volume V
## Tahlequah, Cherokee Nation

Rejected Sept. 20<sup>th</sup> 1889

Office Commission on Citizenship
Cherokee Nation Ind Ter
Tahlequah Sept. 20<sup>th</sup> 1889

The Commission in this case decide that Hardy H. Butler age 44 yrs. and his children, Alva R. age 16 yrs. Joseph H. age 14 yrs. and Harlin J. Butler are not Cherokees by blood. See decision in the case of Caleb Hubbard Docket 2145, B.D. Page 631.

Will.P. Ross   Chairman

Attest
    D.S. Williams
    Asst  Clk  Com.

---

## BROWN

**DOCKET #2186**

CENSUS ROLLS

APPLICANT FOR CHEROKEE CITIZENSHIP

| POST OFFICE: Baxter Springs, Kan. | | ATTORNEY: Forwarded from Washington City | |
|---|---|---|---|
| NO | NAMES | AGE | SEX |
| 1 | James Brown | 40 | Male |
| 2 | May Brown | 6 | Female |
| 3 | Myrtie Brown | 3 | " |
| 4 | Lilly Brown | 1 | " |

ANCESTOR: Jerry Moss

Rejected Sept. 20<sup>th</sup> 1889

Office Commission on Citizenship Cher. Nat.
Tahlequah I.T. Sept. 20<sup>th</sup> 1889

The applicant in the above case refered[sic] here from the Department of the Interior Washington D.C. in his declaration sworn to the 2<sup>nd</sup> day of December A.D. 1884, Ira C. Perkins, Notary Public for Cherokee County, State of Kansas, deposes that he is a person of Cherokee Indian descent and was born in Putnam County State of Georgia and that he is 40 years of age, that he is the son of Louisa Moss a person of Cherokee Indian descent who was born in county in said state in the year 1858. That the said Louisa Moss was the daughter of one

251

Jery[sic] Moss a Cherokee Indian who it is said was born on the Cherokee reservation in 1794. The foregoing statement is supported in detail by the exparte affidavits of one Leander Armstrong 68 yrs. old sworn to on the 2$^{nd}$ day of December A.D. 1884 before Ira C. Perkins Notary Public as aforesaid and of Reuben Turner 61 yrs. of age before the same Notary Public on the 23$^{rd}$ day of January A.D. 1885. Although specific in their statements, The Commission believe that if the before named Louisa Moss who died in the state of Georgia in 1858 and her Father Jery Moss who died in 188? had been of Cherokee descent their names would appear on one of the census rolls of Cherokees by blood taken by the United States in the years 1835-48-51-52, but such not being the fact the Commission decide that James Brown 4[sic] yrs. of age and his children May Brown 6 yrs. Myrtie Brown 3 yrs. and Lilly Brown one year, are not of Cherokee blood and not entitled to citizenship in the Cherokee Nation. P.O. Baxter Springs, Kansas.

Will.P. Ross   Chairman

Attest
    D.S. Williams
    Asst   Clk   Com.

════════

## BROWN

**DOCKET #2187**
CENSUS ROLLS

APPLICANT FOR CHEROKEE CITIZENSHIP

| POST OFFICE: Cottonwood Falls, Kansas | | ATTORNEY: Forwarded from Washington City | |
|---|---|---|---|
| NO | NAMES | AGE | SEX |
| 1 | Robert B. Brown | 48 | Male |
| 2 | Marietta Haskins | 25 | Female |
| 3 | Melonia Murry | 23 | " |
| 4 | Ora E. Brown | 15 | " |

ANCESTOR:  Sarah Brown

Rejected Sept. 23$^{rd}$ 1889

Office Commission on Citizenship Cher Nat Ind. Ter. Tahlequah Sept. 23$^{rd}$ 1889

The above case is refered[sic] here from the Department of the Interior Washington D.C.

The applicant in his declaration before E.A. Kimel Clk. Dist. Court Chase County, State of Arkansas on the 27[th] day of June A.D. 1884 affirms that he is 48 years of age, that he is of Cherokee Indian descent and was born in Hancock County State of Indiana, that he is the son of one Sarah Brown of Cherokee descent who was born in Pasquotand[sic] County North Carolina in 1810 *(or 12)* and reside in Leavenworth Co. State of Kan, that she is the daughter of one Mary Morris a person of Cherokee descent who it is said was born in Muklenburg[sic] Virginia in 1778 and died in Wayne Co. Indiana in 1854, that she was the reputed daughter of one Saml Morris a Cherokee Indian who was born in Cherokee County in 1750, and died in Guilford County N.C. in 1820, and that she was the daughter of Margaret Moore nee Hicks a Cherokee woman who is said to have been born in the Cherokee Nation in 1754, and died in Pasquotank Co. N.C. in 1820. These allegations are coroborated[sic] almost word for word in the language of declaration by Sarah Brown, Mother of applicant 73 yrs. old of Leavenworth County Kans. by Jesse M Lacy of Cherokee County Kansas 45 years of age and by Margaret Blare of Hendricks County, Indiana, 80 years of age and all of whom claim to be of Cherokee blood. These affidavits are all exparte and it is not contended that the name of the applicant or either of his immediate ancestors will be found on the census rolls of Cherokees by blood taken in either of the years 1835-48-51-52, by the United States. The Commission decide that Robert B. Brown and his children viz: Marietta Haskins age 28 yrs. Melonia Murry 23 yrs. Ora E. Brown 15 years are not of Cherokee blood and not entitled to citizenship in the Cherokee Nation.

Will.P. Ross   Chairman

Attest  D.S. Williams  Asst  Clk  Com.

J.E. Gunter   Commissioner

---

## BOND

**DOCKET #2188**
CENSUS ROLLS

APPLICANT FOR CHEROKEE CITIZENSHIP

| POST OFFICE: Tarck[sic], Kansas. | | ATTORNEY: Forwarded from Washington City | |
|---|---|---|---|
| **NO** | **NAMES** | **AGE** | **SEX** |
| 1 | Sarah A. Bond | 59 | Female |
| 2 | Isham R. Bond | 40 | Male |
| 3 | Rachel A. Stout | 35 | Female |

| 4 | Martha S. Cope | 32 | " |
|---|----------------|----|----|
| 5 | Abel J. Bond | 30 | Male |
| 6 | Mary K. Hall | 27 | Female |
| 7 | John S. Bond | 21 | Male |
| 8 | Cordelia L. Bond | 16 | Female |

**ANCESTOR:** Isham Sizemore

*(No information given)*

---

## BROWN

**DOCKET #2189**

CENSUS ROLLS

APPLICANT FOR CHEROKEE CITIZENSHIP

| POST OFFICE: Chetopa, Kansas | | ATTORNEY: From Washington City | |
|---|---|---|---|
| **NO** | **NAMES** | **AGE** | **SEX** |
| 1 | John W. Brown | 46 | Male |

**ANCESTOR:** Mary Morris

Rejected Sept. 21st 1889

Office Commission on Citizenship
Spt. 21st 1889
Tahlequah C.N. Ind. Ter.

The above applicant filed his application before the Interior Department and was transmitted by the Secretary of the Interior to this Commission. There is no evidence on file in support of the above application therefore we decide that applicant in support of the application further than claimants on[sic] declaration. This alone is not sufficient. Therefore the Commission decide that applicant John W. Brown age 46 yrs. is not a Cherokee by blood. P.O. Chetopa Kansas.

Will.P. Ross   Chairman

D.S. Williams
Clerk  Commission

J.E. Gunter   Com

---

254

# Cherokee Citizenship Commission Docket Books (1880-84, 1887-89) Volume V
## Tahlequah, Cherokee Nation

### BINKLEY

**DOCKET #2190**

CENSUS ROLLS

APPLICANT FOR CHEROKEE CITIZENSHIP

| POST OFFICE: Cresline[sic], Kansas | | ATTORNEY: Forwarded from Washington City | |
|---|---|---|---|
| No | NAMES | AGE | SEX |
| 1 | Carrol M. Binkley[sic] | 57 | Male |
| 2 | Josephine Adams | 24 | Female |
| 3 | Robert Binkley[sic] | 20 | Male |
| 4 | Martha J. Binkley[sic] | 17 | Female |
| 5 | James W. Binkley[sic] | 15 | Male |
| 6 | Parlee Binkley[sic] | 12 | |
| 7 | Emma Binkley[sic] | 9 | Female |
| 8 | Sarah D. Binkley[sic] | 5 | " |
| 9 | Mathew Binkley[sic] | 2 | Male |
| 10 | Almeda Binkley[sic] | 7 mos | Female |

ANCESTOR: Sally Carr

*Commission on Citizenship.*

CHEROKEE NATION, IND. TER.

*Tahlequah,* Sept. 21st *188*9

Carrol M. Brinkley
vs.
Cherokee Nation

Application for Cherokee Citizenship

      In claimants declaration taken before a clerk of the District Court of Cherokee County State of Kansas says that he is of Cherokee Indian descent, that he derived said Cherokee blood from his mother Sally Carr who was a Cherokee woman. Applicant does not allege any of the Cherokee census rolls where might be found the name of his ancestor nor does he produce any evidence to sustain his claim of Cherokee blood. Therefore the Commission decide that applicant Carrol M. Brinkley age 57 yrs. and children Josephine Adams age 24 yrs. Robert Brinkley age 20 yrs. Martha J. Brinkley age 17 , James W. Brinkley age 15 yrs. Parlee Brinkley age 12 yrs. Emma Brinkley age 9

# Cherokee Citizenship Commission Docket Books
## (1880-84, 1887-89) Volume V
## Tahlequah, Cherokee Nation

yrs. and Sarah D. Brinkley age 5 yrs. Mathew Brinkley age 2 yrs. and Almeda Brinkley age 7 months are not Cherokees by blood.

Will.P. Ross
Chairman
J.E. Gunter    Com

---

## BECKTEL

**DOCKET #2191**

CENSUS ROLLS

APPLICANT FOR CHEROKEE CITIZENSHIP

| POST OFFICE: Carthage, Mo. | | ATTORNEY: Forwarded from Washington City | |
|---|---|---|---|
| NO | NAMES | AGE | SEX |
| 1 | Bethsheba E. Becktel | 31 | Female |
| 2 | Lelah K. Becktel | 10 | " |
| 3 | Guy J. Becktel | 8 | Male |
| 4 | Maude Becktel | 1½ | Female |

ANCESTOR: Thomas Jay

Rejected Sept. 24<sup>th</sup> 1889

Office Commission on Citizenship
Cherokee Nation Ind Ter
Tahlequah  Sept. 14<sup>th</sup> 1889

The Commission in this case decide that Bethsheba E. Becktel age 31 yrs. and her children Lelah K. Becktel age 10 yrs. Guy J Becktel age 8 yrs. Maud[sic] Becktel age 18 months are not Cherokees by blood.  See decision in case of William A. Pugh Docket 2157, B.E. Page 3. P.O. Carthage Mo.

Will.P. Ross  Chairman

Attest

D.S. Williams                         J.E. Gunter   Com
Asst  Clk  Com.

---

256

# Cherokee Citizenship Commission Docket Books
## (1880-84, 1887-89) Volume V
## Tahlequah, Cherokee Nation

### BARKER

**DOCKET #2192**

CENSUS ROLLS

APPLICANT FOR CHEROKEE CITIZENSHIP

| POST OFFICE: Lamong, Indiana | | ATTORNEY: Forwarded from Washington City | |
|---|---|---|---|
| NO | NAMES | AGE | SEX |
| 1 | Hannah J. Barker | 60 | Female |
| 2 | Amelia A. Barker | 30 | " |
| 3 | Martha E. Miligan | 27 | " |
| 4 | John G. Barker | 25 | Male |
| 5 | Arsa H. Miligan     (G.child) | 2 | Female |
| 6 | Ida J. Allen          (Niece) | 14 | " |

ANCESTOR: Mary Clark

Rejected Sept. 18th 1889

Office Commission on Citizenship
Cherokee Nation Ind Ter
Tahlequah  Sept. 18th 1889

The Commission in this case decide that case decide that Hannah J. Barker age 60 years and her children Amelia A. age 30 yrs. and Martha E. Miligan nee Barker age 27 yrs. and John G. Barker age 25 yrs. and her grand children[sic] Arsa H. Miligan age 2 yrs. and her niece Ida J. Allen age 14 yrs. are not of Cherokee blood. See decision in the case Libbie J Bogue, Docket 2183, B.E, Page 29. P.O. Lamong Ind.

Will.P. Ross   Chairman

Attest

D.S. Williams                          J.E. Gunter   Com

Asst   Clk   Com.

# Cherokee Citizenship Commission Docket Books
## (1880-84, 1887-89) Volume V
## Tahlequah, Cherokee Nation

## **BEARD**

**DOCKET #2193**

CENSUS ROLLS

APPLICANT FOR CHEROKEE CITIZENSHIP

| POST OFFICE: Lawrence, Kansas. | | ATTORNEY: Forwarded from Washington City | |
|---|---|---|---|
| NO | NAMES | AGE | SEX |
| 1 | John W. Beard | 45 | Male |
| 2 | Evalina Beard | 14 | Female |
| 3 | John Herbert Beard | 9 | Male |
| 4 | James Braxton Beard | 1 | " |

ANCESTOR: Rebecca Beard

Rejected Sept. 24[th] 1889

> Office Commission on Citizenship
> Cherokee Nation Ind Ter
> Tahlequah  Sept. 24[th] 1889

The Commission in this case decide that John W. Beard age 45 yrs. and his children Evalina age 14 yrs. John Herbert age 9 yrs. and James Braxton Beard age 1 yr. are not Cherokees by blood.  See decision in case of Augustus W.F. Beard Docket 2194 B.E. Page 40.  P.O. Lawrence Kans.

> Will.P. Ross   Chairman

Attest
> D.S. Williams          J.E. Gunter   Com
> Asst  Clk  Com.

---

## **BEARD**

**DOCKET #2194**

CENSUS ROLLS

APPLICANT FOR CHEROKEE CITIZENSHIP

| POST OFFICE: Kerneville[sic], N.C. | | ATTORNEY: Forwarded from Washington City | |
|---|---|---|---|
| NO | NAMES | AGE | SEX |
| 1 | Augustus H.F. Beard | 55 | Male |
| 2 | Charles R. Beard | 25 | " |

# Cherokee Citizenship Commission Docket Books
## (1880-84, 1887-89) Volume V
## Tahlequah, Cherokee Nation

| 3 | William S. Beard | 23 | " |
|---|---|---|---|
| 4 | Thomas S. Beard | 21 | " |
| 5 | Earnest L. Beard | 20 | " |
| 6 | Junius B. Beard | 17 | " |
| 7 | Lura A. Beard | 14 | |
| 8 | Henry C. Beard | 12 | male |
| 9 | Paul L. Beard | 9 | " |
| 10 | Marvel O. Beard | 7 | " |
| 11 | Fanny M. Beard | 4 | Female |

ANCESTOR: Rebecca Beard

Office Commission
on Citizenship
Tahlequah Sept 24<sup>th</sup> 1889

Augustus H.S. Beard
vs                          Application for Cherokee Citizenship
Cherokee Nation

The above applicant says in his ~~applic~~ declaration taken before the Clerk of Superior Court in & for the State of North Carolina that he is a Cherokee by blood & that he derives the said blood from his father William G. Beard who was born in North Carolina on the 8<sup>th</sup> of Aug. 1797. As this is all the evidence applicant provides in support of his claim we are of the opion[sic] it is not sufficient to establish claimant Cherokee blood. Therefore we decide that applicant Augustus H.S[sic]. Beard age 55 yrs. & children Charles age 25 yrs. Wm age 23 yrs. Thomas S. age 21 yrs. Earnest age 20 yrs. Junius age 17 yrs. Lura age 14 yrs. Henry age 12 yrs. Paul age 12[sic] yrs. Marvel age 4[sic] yrs. are not Cherokees by blood. P.O. Kernville[sic] N.C.

Will.P. Ross
Chairman
J.E. Gunter   Com

# Cherokee Citizenship Commission Docket Books
## (1880-84, 1887-89) Volume V
## Tahlequah, Cherokee Nation

**DOCKET #2195**

CENSUS ROLLS

APPLICANT FOR CHEROKEE CITIZENSHIP

| POST OFFICE: Plainfield, Indiana. | | ATTORNEY: Forwarded from Washington City | |
|---|---|---|---|
| NO | NAMES | AGE | SEX |
| 1 | Samuel Brown | 69 | Male |
| 2 | Mary E. Parson | 38 | Female |
| 3 | Nancy J. Brown | 36 | " |
| 4 | Sarah E. Dodson | 34 | " |
| 5 | Martha A. Brown | 32 | " |
| 6 | John T. Brown | 30 | male |
| 7 | Brazelton T. Brown | 28 | " |
| 8 | Zuma A. Brown | 26 | |
| 9 | Joseph O. Brown | 23 | male |
| 10 | Jememia E. Brown | 21 | |
| 11 | Charles E. Brown | 16 | male |

ANCESTOR: Samuel Brown

Rejected Sept. 20th 1889

Office Commission on Citizenship C.N. I.T.
Tahlequah Sept. 20th 1889

The above case was refered[sic] from the Department of the Interior and consists only of the declaration of the claimant who affirms before Wm. F. Haynes Clerk of the Circuit Court in and for Hendricks County State of Indiana that he is of Cherokee Indian descent that he is 69 yrs. of age at the making of his affidavit on the 15th day of May A.D. 1884, that he was born in Randolph County, North Carolina and is the son of one Brazelton Brown who it is said was born in said county and state if 1793, and died in Hendricks County Indiana 18th day of May 1852 and that he was the son of one Samuel Brown a Cherokee Indian born on the Cherokee Indian reservation in 1770 and died in Randolph County N.C. in the year A.D. 1846. The said declaration is not sufficient to establish the Cherokee blood of claimant, Samuel Brown, and the Commission decide that he and his children viz. Mary E. Parson age 38 years, John T. Brown 30 years, Brazelton T. Brown 28 years, Zuma A. Brown 26 years, Joseph O. Brown 23 years, Jimima[sic] E. Brown 21 years, and Charles E. Brown 16 years are not entitled to citizenship in the Cherokee Nation. P.O. Plainfield Indiana.

Will.P. Ross    Chairman

Attest

    D.S. Williams               J.E. Gunter   Com

    Asst  Clk  Com.

## BENLOW

**DOCKET #2196**

CENSUS ROLLS

APPLICANT FOR CHEROKEE CITIZENSHIP

| POST OFFICE: Oak Ridge, N.C. | | ATTORNEY: Forwarded from Washington City | |
|---|---|---|---|
| NO | NAMES | AGE | SEX |
| 1 | Susan E. Benlow | 45 | Female |
| 2 | James E. Benlow | 13 | Male |
| 3 | Ella A. Benlow | 12 | Female |
| 4 | John M.C. Benlow | 10 | Male |
| 5 | Andrew M. Benlow | 8 | " |
| 6 | Julia P. Benlow | 6 | Female |
| 7 | Susan J. Benlow | 2 | " |

ANCESTOR: Lucinda Starbuck

Adverse. See decision of Commission in ~~the~~ case John R. Henly Docket 553, Book B, Page 266.

Will.P. Ross  Chairman<br>J.E. Gunter  Com

# Cherokee Citizenship Commission Docket Books
## (1880-84, 1887-89) Volume V
## Tahlequah, Cherokee Nation

## LINDLEY

**DOCKET #2197**

CENSUS ROLLS

APPLICANT FOR CHEROKEE CITIZENSHIP

| POST OFFICE: Neoga, Illinois | | ATTORNEY: Forwarded from Washington City | |
|---|---|---|---|
| **NO** | **NAMES** | **AGE** | **SEX** |
| 1 | Anna J. Lindley | 50 | Female |
| 2 | Jesse B. Lindley | 18 | Male |
| 3 | Charles E. Lindley | 15 | " |

ANCESTOR: Jesse B. Johnson

Rejected Sept. 20th 1889

Office Commission on Citizenship
Cherokee Nation Ind Ter
Tahlequah Sept. 20th 1889

The Commission in this case decide that Anna J. Lindly[sic] age 50 yrs. and her sons Jesse B. Lindly age 18 yrs. Charles E. Lindly age 15 yrs. are not Cherokees by blood.

See decision in the case of David Elmore et. al. Docket 2279, B.E. Page 141. P.O. Neoga Illinois.

Will.P. Ross    Chairman

Attest

D.S. Williams          J.E. Gunter    Com
Asst   Clk  Com.

---

## LARRANCE

**DOCKET #2198**

CENSUS ROLLS

APPLICANT FOR CHEROKEE CITIZENSHIP

| POST OFFICE: Oskaloosa, Iowa | | ATTORNEY: Forwarded from Washington City | |
|---|---|---|---|
| **NO** | **NAMES** | **AGE** | **SEX** |
| 1 | Mary Larrance | 55 | Female |
| 2 | William A. Larrance | 23 | Male |
| 3 | Anna J. Larrance | 20 | Female |

262

# Cherokee Citizenship Commission Docket Books
## (1880-84, 1887-89) Volume V
## Tahlequah, Cherokee Nation

| 4 | Albert Larrance | 12 | Male |
|---|---|---|---|

**ANCESTOR:** Ann Allen

Rejected Sept. 18$^{th}$ 1889

Office Commission on Citizenship
Cherokee Nation Ind Ter
Tahlequah Sept. 18$^{th}$ 1889

The Commission in this case decide that Mary L. Lawrence[sic] age 55 yrs. and her children William A. age 23 yrs. Anna J. age 20 yrs. and Albert Larrence[sic] are not of Cherokee blood.

See decision in case Libbie J Bogue, Docket 2183, Book E, Page 29.

Will.P. Ross   Chairman

Attest
D.S. Williams                                    J.E. Gunter   Com
Asst   Clk   Com.

---

## LINVILLE

**DOCKET #2199**

CENSUS ROLLS

APPLICANT FOR CHEROKEE CITIZENSHIP

| POST OFFICE: Gordwell[sic] N.C. | | ATTORNEY: Forwarded from Washington City | |
|---|---|---|---|
| **NO** | **NAMES** | **AGE** | **SEX** |
| 1 | Emanuel Linville   et al | 54 | Male |
| 2 | Martha J. Linville | 34 | Female |
| 3 | David S. Linville | 33 | Male |
| 4 | Mary J. Young | 31 | Female |
| 5 | John M. Linville | 28 | Male |
| 6 | Hardee L. Linville | 21 | " |
| 7 | Columbus Linville | 19 | " |
| 8 | Elijah W. Linville | 16 | " |
| 9 | Elmira Linville | 14 | Female |
| 10 | Jennetta Linville | 10 | " |

**ANCESTOR:** David Linville

263

# Cherokee Citizenship Commission Docket Books
## (1880-84, 1887-89) Volume V
## Tahlequah, Cherokee Nation

Rejected Sept. 21[st] 1889

Office Commission on Citizenship Cher. Nat. Ind. Ter. Tah. Sept. 21[st] 1889

The above case was refered[sic] from the Department of the Interior, Washington D.C. The applicant in his declaration affirmed on the 4[th] day of October A.D. 1884, before John W. Payne Clerk of the U.S. District Court for the Western District of North Carolina alleges that he is 54 years of age and is a person of Cherokee Indian descent, that he is the son of one David Linville a person of Cherokee descent who was born in Surry County State of North Carolina in the year 1777 and died in Stokes County the said state in October 1843, that he was the reputed son of one Aaron Linville, a Cherokee Indian who is said to have been born on the Cherokee reservation in 1749 and died in Stokes County N.C. or about the 17[th] day of July 1824. Accompanying this declaration are the exparte affidavits of C.C. Ned 78 years of age and Ambrose Branson of Fosythe[sic] County State of North Carolina and purporting to be affirmed to before *(Name Illegible)* Justice of the Peace in the County of Forsythe, North Carolina 3[rd] day of Oct. 1884. They are signed with a X *(illegible)* by a single witness Daniel C. Finn the Attorney. The X is made with a pencil and the name and seal of the Justice of the Peace are also in pencil. The affiants corroborate the statement of the claimant. Aside from the charater[sic] of these instuments[sic] it does not appear that the claimant at any time lived in the Cherokee Country or that his own name or that of his Father and grand Father is enrolled on the census rolls of Cherokees by blood taken by the United States in the years 1835-48-51-52. The Commission therefore decide that Emmanuel[sic] Linville is not of Cherokee blood and that he is not entitled to citizenship in the Cherokee Nation, nor are his children and grand children, viz. Martha J. Linville age 34 years, David S. Linville 33 yrs. Mary J. Young 30 yrs. John M. Linville 28 yrs. Nancy A. Landreth 23 yrs. Hardee L. Linville 21 yrs. Columbus Linville 19 yrs. Elijah W. Linville 16 yrs. Elmina A. Linville 14 yrs. Jennetta Linville 13 yrs. and (grand children) Israel D. Linville 13 yrs. Janus E. Linville 11 yrs. Benjamin F. Linville 9 yrs. George W. Linville 7 yrs. John H. Linville 5 yrs. Milton F. Linville 3 yrs. William D. Linville 8 yrs. Jennetta J. Linville 6 yrs. Flora ? Linville 2 yrs. Mary A. Young 4 years Henry T. Young 3 yrs. John R. Young 2 years, Sallie M. Young 5 months, John E. Landreth 4 yrs. *(Illegible)* A. Landreth 2 yrs. Addie F Landreth 9 months. P.O. Gordwell[sic] N.C.

# Cherokee Citizenship Commission Docket Books
## (1880-84, 1887-89) Volume V
## Tahlequah, Cherokee Nation

Will.P. Ross    Chairman

Attest

D.S. Williams                    J.E. Gunter    Com

Asst    Clk    Com.

---

## LINVILLE

**DOCKET #2200**

CENSUS ROLLS

APPLICANT FOR CHEROKEE CITIZENSHIP

| POST OFFICE: Pond, N.C. | | ATTORNEY: Forwarded from Washington City | |
|---|---|---|---|
| No | NAMES | AGE | SEX |
| 1 | William F. Linville    et al | 55 | Male |
| 2 | John M. Linville | 52 | " |
| 3 | Romulus S. Linville | 47 | " |
| 4 | Ailey J. Whicher | 45 | Female |
| 5 | Jennetta J. Medearis | 39 | " |
| 6 | Eliza A. Jones | 34 | " |
| 7 | Julius A Linville | 31 | Male |

ANCESTOR: William Linville

Rejected Sept. 21st 1889

Office Commission on Citizenship C.N. I.T. Tahlequah Sept. 21st 1889

The above case was refered[sic] from the Department of the Interior. The Commission decide that the applicants are not of Cherokee blood. Their names are as follows, to wit. William F. Linville age 55 years, John L. Linville 52 yrs. Romulus S. Linville 47. Add.[sic] F. Whicher 45 yrs. Jeannetta[sic] J. Madeoris[sic] 37, Eliza A. Jones 34 yrs. Julius A. Linville 31 yrs. and grandchildren, Walter S. Linville 18 yrs. McDuffie Linville 16 yrs. Wm G. Linville 14 yrs. Daniel L. Linville 13 yrs. John M. Linville 9 yrs. Mattie ? Linville 11 yrs. Rickny[sic] H. Linville 5 yrs. Robert B. Linville 3 years, Jam[sic] B. Linville 16 yrs. Eugene S. Linville 14 yrs. Cyrus L. Linville 12 yrs. Julius F. Linville 6 yrs. John F. Linville 3 yrs. Elzotha[sic] N. Linville 2 yrs. Laura A. Medearis 14 yrs. Eliza M. Medearis 12, *(Illegible)* A. Medearis 9 yrs. Oscar S. Medearis 9 yrs. Webster B. Medearis 7 yrs. Parmalee C. Medearis 4 yrs. William J. Jones 10 yrs. Ann A. Jones 9 yrs. Walter S. Jones 7, Romulus Jones 5 yrs. Asa A. Jones 3 yrs. Edward W. Jones 2 yrs. P.O. Pond, N.C.

See decision in case Emmanuel Linville D. 2199, B.E. P. 46.

Will.P. Ross   Chairman

Attest
    D.S. Williams                    J.E. Gunter   Com
    Asst  Clk  Com.

## GRAVES

**DOCKET #2201**

CENSUS ROLLS

APPLICANT FOR CHEROKEE CITIZENSHIP

| POST OFFICE: Baxter Springs, Kan. | ATTORNEY: Forwarded from Washington City | |
|---|---|---|
| **NO** | **NAMES** | **AGE** | **SEX** |
| 1 | Daniel Graves | | Male |

ANCESTOR:  Sarah Graves

Rejected Sept. 23rd 1889

Office Commission on Citizenship
Cherokee Nation Ind Ter
Tahlequah  Sept. 23rd 1889

The application comes before this Commission by reference from the Department of the Interior, Washington D.C. In his declaration made on the 2nd Day of March A.D. 1886, before James A. Whitecraft Clerk of the District Court in and for Cherokee County State of Kansas, the claimant swears that he is of Cherokee Indian descent and is the son of Sarah Graves of Cherokee Indian descent, born in Randolph County State of North Carolina in 1800, and died in the State of Indiana n the year 1841, and that she was the daughter of Elizabeth Hammon nee Hooker a halfbreed Cherokee born on the Cherokee Indian reservation and died in the State of Iowa in the year A.D. 1843. No proof accompanies this claim and the Commission decide against the claimant. P.O. Baxter Springs Kansas.

Will.P. Ross   Chairman

Attest
    D.S. Williams                    J.E. Gunter   Com
    Asst  Clk  Com.

# Cherokee Citizenship Commission Docket Books
## (1880-84, 1887-89) Volume V
## Tahlequah, Cherokee Nation

---

## GILMORE

**DOCKET #2202**

APPLICANT FOR CHEROKEE CITIZENSHIP

| POST OFFICE: Caseyville, Ky. | ATTORNEY: Forwarded from Washington City | | |
|---|---|---|---|
| **NO** | **NAMES** | **AGE** | **SEX** |
| 1 | Sarah E. Gilmore | 34 | Female |
| 2 | Eurie Hardy | 10 | |
| 3 | Laura B. Hardy | 8 | Female |

ANCESTOR: Nancy Collins

Rejected Sept. 23rd 1889

> Office Commission on Citizenship
> Cherokee Nation Ind Ter
> Tahlequah  Sept. 23rd 1889

The Commission in this case decide that Sarah E. Gilmore age 34 yrs. and the following children, Eurie Hardy age 10 yrs. and Laura B. Hardy age 7 yrs. are not Cherokees by blood.
See decision in case of Andrew J. Young Docket 2152 B.D. Page 638.  P.O. Caseyville, Ky.

Attest
    D.S. Williams                          J.E. Gunter    Com
    Asst   Clk  Com.

---

## GALASPIE

**DOCKET #2203**

APPLICANT FOR CHEROKEE CITIZENSHIP

| POST OFFICE: Baxter Springs, Kan. | ATTORNEY: Forwarded from Washington City | | |
|---|---|---|---|
| **NO** | **NAMES** | **AGE** | **SEX** |
| 1 | Nancy Galaspie | 66 | Female |
| 2 | George Coffey | 44 | Male |

| 3 | Abram Ross | 42 | " |
|---|---|---|---|
| 4 | Cyrus R. Estes | 30 | " |
| 5 | Fred Estes | 24 | " |

ANCESTOR: Vincent Day

Office Commission on Citizenship
Cherokee Nation Ind Ter Tahlequah Sept. 21$^{st}$ 1889

The above case was refered[sic] from the Interior Department at Washington DC. The declarations of claimant was sworn to the 22$^{nd}$ day of February A.D. 1886 before Ira C. Perkins, a Notary Public of Cherokee County State of Kansas. In it she alleges that she is 66 yrs. of age, is a person of Cherokee Indian descent & that she is the daughter of one Vincent Day, a half breed Cherokee Indian who was born on the Cherokee reservation in the year 1791 and died in Wake County State of North Carolina in the year A.A. 1878. The exparte affidavits of Wily Lawrence of aforesaid County & State sworn to before said Ira C. Perkins Notary Public on the 12$^{th}$ day of February 1886 and of Wiley Jones of the Cherokee Nation Indian Territory before A.G. Drake Notary Public of Labette County State of Kansas on the 12$^{th}$ day of February 1886 corroborate the statements of declarant of their statements as to the Cherokee Indian descent of Nancy Galaspie & her affiants or *(illegible)* as to the facts stated the name of Nancy Galaspie.

That of her father Vincent Day, should be found on the census rolls of Cherokees by blood taken & made by the United States in the years 1835, 48, 51, 52, but such is not the case. The Commission therefore decide that Nancy Galaspie age 66 yrs. and her children George Coffey age 44 yrs., Abram Ross 42 yrs. Cyrus R. Estes 30 yrs. and Fred Estes age 24 years, are not of Cherokee Blood & not entitled to Citizenship in the Cherokee Nation. P.O. Baxter Springs, Kansas.

J.E. Gunter    Com

# Cherokee Citizenship Commission Docket Books
## (1880-84, 1887-89) Volume V
## Tahlequah, Cherokee Nation

## WHICHER

**DOCKET #2204**

CENSUS ROLLS

APPLICANT FOR CHEROKEE CITIZENSHIP

| POST OFFICE: Westfield, Indiana | | ATTORNEY: Forwarded from Washington City | |
|---|---|---|---|
| NO | NAMES | AGE | SEX |
| 1 | Abel D. Whicher    et al | 59 | Male |
| 2 | John C. Whicher | 36 | " |
| 3 | Sarah J. Boran | 33 | Female |
| 4 | Rhoda Whicher | 30 | " |
| 5 | Nora M. Whicher | 15 | " |

ANCESTOR: Samuel Whicher

Office Commission on Citizenship
Cherokee Nation Ind Ter
Tahlequah Sept. 20th 1889

The Commission in this case decide that Abel D. Whicher age 59 yrs. and his children, John C. age 36 yrs. Sarah J. age 33 yrs. Rhoda age 30 yrs. Martha age 26 yrs. and Nora Whicher age 15 yrs. and his grand children, Euline V. Whicher age 11 yrs. Cora M. Beall age 16 yrs. and Hazel S. Wood age 9 months are not of Cherokee blood. – See decision in the case of Caleb Hubbard Docket 2145, Book D. Page 631. P.O. Westfield Ind.

Attest
    D.S. Williams                          J.E. Gunter    Com
    Asst   Clk   Com.

---

## WHICHER

**DOCKET #2205**

CENSUS ROLLS

APPLICANT FOR CHEROKEE CITIZENSHIP

| POST OFFICE: Westfield, Indiana | | ATTORNEY: Forwarded from Washington City | |
|---|---|---|---|
| NO | NAMES | AGE | SEX |
| 1 | Nathan H. Whicher | 53 | Male |

| 2 | Cassius M.C. Whicher | 23 | " |
|---|---|---|---|
| 3 | William S. Whicher | 21 | " |
| 4 | John B. Whicher | 18 | " |
| 5 | Anna J. Whicher | 15 | Female |
| 6 | Linzy Whicher | 13 | Male |
| 7 | Nathan H. Whicher | 11 | " |
| 8 | Cecil Whicher | 9 | " |
| 9 | Andrew J. Whicher | 7 | " |

**ANCESTOR:** Samuel Whicher

Rejected Sept. 20th 1889

Office Commission on Citizenship
Cherokee Nation Ind Ter
Tahlequah Sept. 20th 1889

The Commission in this case decide that Nathan H. Whicher age 53 yrs. and his children, Cassius M.C. age 23 yrs. William S. age 21 yrs. John B. age 18 yrs. Anna J. age 15 yrs. Linzy age 13 yrs. Nathan H. age 11 yrs. Cecil age 9 yrs. and Andrew J. Whicher, are not of Cherokee blood. See decision in the case of Caleb Hubbard Docket 2145, B.D. Page 631. P.O. Westfield Ind.

Attest

D.S. Williams                                J.E. Gunter   Com
Asst  Clk  Com.

---

## WILLIAMS

**DOCKET #2206**

CENSUS ROLLS

APPLICANT FOR CHEROKEE CITIZENSHIP

| POST OFFICE: Fountain City, Indiana | | ATTORNEY: Forwarded from Washington City | |
|---|---|---|---|
| NO | NAMES | AGE | SEX |
| 1 | Nancy Williams | 68 | Female |
| 2 | Martha Teagle | 50 | " |
| 3 | Richard Williams | 47 | Male |
| 4 | Isaac Williams | 45 | " |

# Cherokee Citizenship Commission Docket Books (1880-84, 1887-89) Volume V
# Tahlequah, Cherokee Nation

| 5 | Franklin Williams | 43 | " |
|---|---|---|---|
| 6 | Anna E Harold | 41 | Female |
| 7 | Elyena Swain | 38 | " |
| 8 | Sarah Pease | 32 | " |
| 9 | Samuel Williams | 29 | Male |
| 10 | Mary E. Lacy | 24 | Female |
| 11 | Emma J. Coates | 23 | " |

ANCESTOR: Martha Pitts

Rejected Sept. 20th 1889

Office Commission on Citizenship
Cherokee Nation Ind Ter
Tahlequah Sept. 20th 1889

The Commission in this case decide that Nancy Williams age 68 and her children, Martha Teagle nee Williams age 50 yrs. Richard age 47, Isaac age 45, Franklin age 43 yrs. Anna E. Harold nee Williams age 41 yrs. Elyena Swain nee Williams age 29 yrs. Mary E. Lacy nee Williams age 24 yrs. and Emma J. Coates nee Williams age 23 yrs. are not of Cherokee blood.

See decision in the case of Caleb Hubbard Docket 2145, B.D. Page 631.

P.O. Fountain City Indiana.

Attest
    D.S. Williams             J.E. Gunter    Com
    Asst   Clk   Com.

---

## WALKER
**DOCKET #2207**
CENSUS ROLLS

APPLICANT FOR CHEROKEE CITIZENSHIP

| POST OFFICE: Richland, Iowa | | ATTORNEY: Forwarded from Washington City | |
|---|---|---|---|
| NO | NAMES | AGE | SEX |
| 1 | Martha R. Walker | 31 | Female |
| 2 | Miran D. Walker | 9 | M[sic] |

| 3 | Atta E. Walker | 7 | |
| 4 | Mary V. Walker | 4 | Female |
| 5 | John C. Walker | 1 | Male |

**ANCESTOR:** Providence Johnson

Rejected Sept. 18th 1889

Office Commission on Citizenship
Cherokee Nation Ind Ter
Tahlequah Sept. 18th 1889

The Commission in this case decide that Martha R. Walker age 31 yrs. and her children, Miran D. age 9 yrs. Atta E. age 7 yrs. Mary V. age 4 yrs. and John C. Walker age 1 year are not of Cherokee blood.

See decision in case Libbie J Bogue, Docket 2183, Book E, Page 29.

Will.P. Ross    Chairman

Attest
    D.S. Williams
    Asst   Clk   Com.

J.E. Gunter   Com

## WARD

**DOCKET #2208**
CENSUS ROLLS 1835-'51, & '52

APPLICANT FOR CHEROKEE CITIZENSHIP

| POST OFFICE: | | ATTORNEY: Wm A. Thompson | |
|---|---|---|---|
| NO | NAMES | AGE | SEX |
| 1 | P.W. Ward | | Male |
| 2 | John M. Ward | 5 | " |

**ANCESTOR:** Nathan Peoples

Rejected Sept. 10th 1889

Office Commission on Citizenship
Cherokee Nation Ind Ter
Tahlequah Sept. 10th 1889

There being no evidence submitted in the above case and the name of Nathan Peoples not being found on the census rolls of Cherokees by blood taken and made by the United States in the years 1835-51-52.   The Commission decide that P.W. Ward and his son John M. Ward 5 years old at the filing of the application the 22nd Day of September 1887, are not of Cherokee blood and not entitled to citizenship in the Cherokee Nation. P.O. address not given. W.A. Thompson Attorney for claimant.

Attest
    D.S. Williams                      J.E. Gunter    Com
    Asst  Clk  Com.

---

## KINZER

**DOCKET #2209**
CENSUS ROLLS

APPLICANT FOR CHEROKEE CITIZENSHIP

| POST OFFICE: Durango, Colorado | | ATTORNEY: Forwarded from Washington City | |
|---|---|---|---|
| NO | NAMES | AGE | SEX |
| 1 | Hesekiah Kinzer | 46 | Male |
| 2 | Bessie Kinzer | 18 | Female |
| 3 | John Kinzer | 14 | Male |
| 4 | Latta Kinzer | 8 | Female |
| 5 | Ella Kinzer | 2 | " |

ANCESTOR: Massey Sanders

Rejected Sept. 18th 1889

Office Commission on Citizenship
Cherokee Nation Ind Ter
Tahlequah Sept. 18th 1889

The Commission in this case decide that the applicant Hesekiah Kinzer age 46 yrs. and his children John age 14 yrs., Latta age 8 yrs. and Ella Kinzer age 2 yrs. are not of Cherokee blood.

See decision in case Libbie J Bogue, Docket 2183, Book E, Page 29.
Attest
    D.S. Williams                      J.E. Gunter    Com
    Asst  Clk  Com.

---

# Cherokee Citizenship Commission Docket Books
## (1880-84, 1887-89) Volume V
## Tahlequah, Cherokee Nation

### KINZER

**DOCKET #2210**

CENSUS ROLLS

APPLICANT FOR CHEROKEE CITIZENSHIP

| POST OFFICE: Union, Iowa | | ATTORNEY: Forwarded from Washington City | |
|---|---|---|---|
| No | NAMES | AGE | SEX |
| 1 | Adam Kinzer | 41 | Male |
| 2 | Cora Kinzer | 14 | Female |
| 3 | Myrtie Kinzer | 8 | " |
| 4 | Henry B. Kinzer | 2 | Male |

ANCESTOR: Massey Sanders

Rejected Sept. 24th 1889

> Office Commission on Citizenship
> Cherokee Nation Ind Ter
> Tahlequah Sept. 24th 1889

The Commission in this case decide that case decide that Adam Kinzer age 41 years and his children, Cora Kinzer age 14 years, Myrtie Kinzer age 8 years, and Henry B. Kinzer age 2 years, are not of Cherokee blood. See decision in the case of David Elmore et. al. Docket 2279, B.E. Page 141. P.O. Union, Iowa.

Attest
    D.S. Williams                      J.E. Gunter    Com
    Asst   Clk   Com.

---

### KINZER

**DOCKET #2211**

CENSUS ROLLS

APPLICANT FOR CHEROKEE CITIZENSHIP

| POST OFFICE: Richland, Iowa | | ATTORNEY: Forwarded from Washington City | |
|---|---|---|---|
| No | NAMES | AGE | SEX |
| 1 | William Kinzer | 39 | Male |
| 2 | Robert H. Kinzer | 10 | " |

ANCESTOR: Massey Sanders

274

# Cherokee Citizenship Commission Docket Books (1880-84, 1887-89) Volume V
## Tahlequah, Cherokee Nation

Rejected Sept. 20<sup>th</sup> 1889

> Office Commission on Citizenship
> Cherokee Nation Ind Ter
> Tahlequah Sept. 20<sup>th</sup> 1889

The Commission in this case decide that William Kinzer age 39 yrs. and his son Robert H. Kinzer are not of Cherokee blood.

See decision in the case of David Elmore et. al. Docket 2279, B.E. Page 141. P.O. Richland, Iowa.

Attest

D.S. Williams                          J.E. Gunter    Com
Asst   Clk   Com.

---

## ELLIOTT

**DOCKET #2212**

CENSUS ROLLS

APPLICANT FOR CHEROKEE CITIZENSHIP

| POST OFFICE: Lynnville, Iowa | | ATTORNEY: Forwarded from Washington City | |
|---|---|---|---|
| **NO** | **NAMES** | **AGE** | **SEX** |
| 1 | Jane N. Elliott | 39 | Female |
| 2 | John Elliott | 23 | Male |
| 3 | Perry Elliott | 17 | " |
| 4 | Amanda O. Elliott | 15 | Female |
| 5 | Henry Elliott | 13 | Male |
| 6 | Lucilla Elliott | 14 | Female |
| 7 | Bella Elliott | 8 | " |
| 8 | Orley Elliott | 4 | |

ANCESTOR: James H. Meredith

Rejected Sept. 24<sup>th</sup> 1889

> Office Commission on Citizenship
> Cherokee Nation Ind Ter
> Tahlequah Sept. 24<sup>th</sup> 1889

# Cherokee Citizenship Commission Docket Books (1880-84, 1887-89) Volume V Tahlequah, Cherokee Nation

The Commission in this case decide that Jane N. Elliott age 39 yrs. and her children, John Elliott age 23 yrs. Perry Elliott age 17 yrs. Amanda O. Elliott age 15 yrs. Henry Elliott age 13 yrs. Lucilla Elliott age 10 yrs. Belle Elliott age 8 yrs. and Orley Elliott age 4 yrs. are not Cherokees by blood.

See decision in case of Andrew J. Meredith Docket 2180, B.C. Page 376. P.O. Lynnville Iowa.

Attest
    D.S. Williams                    J.E. Gunter   Com
    Asst  Clk  Com.

## EASTERLING

**DOCKET #2213**
CENSUS ROLLS

APPLICANT FOR CHEROKEE CITIZENSHIP

| POST OFFICE: South Bend, Kansas[sic] | | ATTORNEY: Forwarded from Washington City | |
|---|---|---|---|
| **NO** | **NAMES** | **AGE** | **SEX** |
| 1 | Dinah C. Easterling | | Female |
| 2 | Guberlina Wright | 44 | |
| 3 | Martha Stout | 42 | Female |
| 4 | Sarah Hobson | 34 | " |
| 5 | Alvin B. Easterling | 29 | |

ANCESTOR: Brazelton Brown

Rejected Sept. 19[th] 1889

Office Commission on Citizenship
Cherokee Nation Ind Ter
Tahlequah Sept. 19[th] 1889

The application in the above case was refered[sic] from the Department of the Interior Washington D.C. The declaration of the applicant herself which was made on the 30[th] day of June A.D. 1885, before R.M. Armstrong Clerk of the District Morris County State of Kansas is supported by no proof. The Commission therefore decide that Dinah C. Easterling age not given, and her children viz, Guberlina Wright age 44 yrs. Martha Stout 42 yrs. Sarah Hobson

34 yrs. and Alvin B. Easterling age 29 years, are not of Cherokee Indian descent and not entitled to citizenship in the Cherokee Nation. P.O. South Bend Kansas.

Attest
    D.S. Williams                 J.E. Gunter    Com
    Asst   Clk   Com.

## TIPTON

**DOCKET #2214**
CENSUS ROLLS

APPLICANT FOR CHEROKEE CITIZENSHIP

| POST OFFICE: Plymouth, Kansas | | ATTORNEY: Forwarded from Washington City | |
|---|---|---|---|
| NO | NAMES | AGE | SEX |
| 1 | Eliza C. Tipton | 32 | Female |
| 2 | John A. Tipton | 12 | Male |
| 3 | Nelly M Tipton | 8 | Female |
| 4 | Myrtie Tipton | 6 | " |
| 5 | Grace Tipton | 3 | " |
| 6 | Dollie Tipton | 1 | " |

ANCESTOR: Landon Duffield

In the matter of the above application and her children, we the Commission fail to find any evidence whatever that would justify the applicants to citizenship in this Nation. All the evidence is of a hearsay nature. The law governing this Commission in making up ~~their~~ its decisions plainly states that applicants must name some ancestor on some one of the several rolls & from that they descend from such ancestor named: in this case we fail to find the name of Landon Duffield who the applicant alleges as her ancestor. Therefore, We the Commission on Citizenship adjudge the applicant and her six children, viz: John A., James W., Nelly M., Myrtie, Grace and Dolly[sic] Tipton are not Cherokees by blood, and are therefore intruders upon the public domain of the Cherokee Nation and not entitled to the enjoyment of any rights and privileges of the Cherokee Nation.

                  J. T. Adair     Chairman Commission
                  D.W. Lipe      Commissioner
                  H.C. Barnes   Commissioner

# Cherokee Citizenship Commission Docket Books
## (1880-84, 1887-89) Volume V
## Tahlequah, Cherokee Nation

Office Com on Citizenship
Tahlequah, I.T. Sept. 24<sup>th</sup> 1888

---

### TIPTON

**DOCKET #221**

CENSUS ROLLS

APPLICANT FOR CHEROKEE CITIZENSHIP

| POST OFFICE: Emporia, Kansas | | ATTORNEY: Forwarded from Washington City | |
|---|---|---|---|
| **NO** | **NAMES** | **AGE** | **SEX** |
| 1 | Mary E. Tipton | 47 | Female |
| 2 | Susie Tipton | 17 | " |
| 3 | Jessie Tipton | 15 | Male |
| 4 | Samuel Tipton | 13 | " |
| 5 | Eddie Tipton | 9 | " |
| 6 | Eliza Tipton | 7 | Female |
| 7 | Jane Tipton | 5 | " |
| 8 | Howard Tipton | 3 | Male |

**ANCESTOR:** Alfred Carter

See decision in this case in that of Mary E. Tipton in Book "A", Page 60 – It being docketed twice. Adverse to claimant.

Cornell Rogers
Clk Com on Citizenship

Office Com on Citizenship
Tahlequah I.T. Sept. 24<sup>th</sup> 1888

---

# Cherokee Citizenship Commission Docket Books
## (1880-84, 1887-89) Volume V
## Tahlequah, Cherokee Nation

### TAYLOR

**DOCKET #2216**

CENSUS ROLLS

APPLICANT FOR CHEROKEE CITIZENSHIP

| POST OFFICE: Emporia, Kansas. | | ATTORNEY: Forwarded from Washington City | |
|---|---|---|---|
| NO | NAMES | AGE | SEX |
| 1 | Brice Taylor | 22 | Male |

ANCESTOR: George Duffield

Rejected Sept. 19th 1889

Office Commission on Citizenship
Cherokee Nation Ind Ter
Tahlequah Sept. 19th 1889

The above application was refered[sic] from the Department of the Interior at Washington D.C.

The Commission decide against the applicants[sic] for admission to citizenship in the Cherokee Nation for reasons stated in the case of Land Duffield. See Docket 2135 Book D. Page 621. P.O. Emporia Kansas.

Attest

D.S. Williams                    J.E. Gunter    Com
Asst  Clk  Com.

### TAYLOR

**DOCKET #2217**

CENSUS ROLLS

APPLICANT FOR CHEROKEE CITIZENSHIP

| POST OFFICE: Van Buren, Ark | | ATTORNEY: A.E. Ivey | |
|---|---|---|---|
| NO | NAMES | AGE | SEX |
| 1 | Finley M. Taylor | 45 | Male |

ANCESTOR: Madison Taylor

Rejected Sept. 9th 1889

279

# Cherokee Citizenship Commission Docket Books
## (1880-84, 1887-89) Volume V
## Tahlequah, Cherokee Nation

Office Commission on Citizenship
Cherokee Nation Ind Ter
Tahlequah  Sept. 9[th] 1889

Application for Cherokee Citizenship

The above case was called and submitted by Atty A.E. Ivey without evidence. The Commission therefore decide that Finley M Taylor age 45 yrs. is not a Cherokee by blood. Post Office Van Buren Ark.

Attest

D.S. Williams                                    J.E. Gunter   Com
Asst  Clk  Com.

-------

## CUNNINGHAM

**DOCKET #2218**

CENSUS ROLLS

APPLICANT FOR CHEROKEE CITIZENSHIP

| POST OFFICE: Cherokee City, Ark. | | ATTORNEY: J.M. Bryant A.E. Ivey | |
|---|---|---|---|
| No | NAMES | AGE | SEX |
| 1 | M.J. Cunningham | 39 | female |
| 2 | Noah P. Cunningham | 17 | male |
| 3 | John T. Cunningham | 15 | " |
| 4 | James S. Cunningham | 13 | " |
| 5 | Cora Ella Cunningham | 11 | female |
| 6 | Belle Luna Cunningham | 9 | " |
| 7 | Arritia Cunningham | 7 | " |
| 8 | Loly Kindness Cunningham | 5 | " |

ANCESTOR: Mary Brown

*Commission on Citizenship.*

CHEROKEE NATION, IND. TER.

*Tahlequah,* Sept. 26[th]  *188*8

280

# Cherokee Citizenship Commission Docket Books
## (1880-84, 1887-89) Volume V
## Tahlequah, Cherokee Nation

Mrs. M.J. Cunningham, et al
   (VS)
Cherokee Nation

Now on this day the 26th day of Sept. 1888 comes the above case up for final hearing. The evidence in this case is not clear at all, and does not connect the applicant with the alleged Cherokee ancestor, Mary Brown, nor does it show who was the parents of Mrs. Cunningham. – The evidence is insufficient, supposing Mary Brown was of Cherokee blood, to justify this Commission to act otherwise than reject this case.

Therefore, Mrs. M.J. Cunningham and her seven children, viz: Noah A., John T., James S., Cora Ella, Bell[sic] L., Arritia and Loley[sic] Kindness Cunningham ~~are not~~ have not established their rights to citizenship in this Nation, and the Commission are of the opinion that they have no just claim to such and we do hereby so declare. –

    J. T. Adair    Chairman Commission
    H C Barnes   Commissioner

## COLLINS

**DOCKET #2219**
CENSUS ROLLS 185 & 2

APPLICANT FOR CHEROKEE CITIZENSHIP

| POST OFFICE: Talbotton, Ga. | | ATTORNEY: C.J. Harris | |
|---|---|---|---|
| NO | NAMES | AGE | SEX |
| 1 | Thos. Parker Collins | 26 | male |

ANCESTOR: Parker Collins

Now on this the 20th day of June 1888, comes the above case up for final hearing, and the Commission say: "We the Commission on Citizenship after "examining the testimony in the above case, and also the rolls of 1851 and 1852, "find that the applicant, Thomas Parker Collins is a Cherokee by blood, and is "hereby re-admitted to all the rights and privileges of a Cherokee citizen by "blood, is in compliance with an Act of the National Council creating the said "Commission, dated December 8th 1886."

    J. T. Adair    Chairman Commission
    John E. Gunter  Commissioner
    D.W. Lipe    Commissioner

281

## FOSTER

**DOCKET #2220**
CENSUS ROLLS 1851 & 2

APPLICANT FOR CHEROKEE CITIZENSHIP

| POST OFFICE: Talbotton, Ga. | | ATTORNEY: C.J. Harris | |
|---|---|---|---|
| No | NAMES | AGE | SEX |
| 1 | Mary Malissa Foster | 29 | Female |
| 2 | Allen Boudinot Foster | 2 | Male |

ANCESTOR: Parker Collins

Now on this the 20th day of June 1888, the above case came up for final hearing, and the Commission says, "We the Commission on Citizenship after "examining the evidence in the above case, find that the applicants Mary "Malissa Foster and her son, Allen Boudinot Foster, are Cherokees by blood, "and are hereby re-admitted to all the rights and privileges of Cherokee citizens "by blood, which is in compliance with an Act of the National Council creating "the said Commission dated the 8th day of December 1886."

              J. T. Adair     Chairman Commission
              John E. Gunter   Commissioner
              D.W. Lipe        Commissioner

## McDANIEL

**DOCKET #2221**
CENSUS ROLLS 1851 & 1852

APPLICANT FOR CHEROKEE CITIENSHIP

| POST OFFICE: Talbotton, Ga. | | ATTORNEY: C.J. Harris | |
|---|---|---|---|
| No | NAMES | AGE | SEX |
| 1 | Martha Hall McDaniel | 38 | Female |
| 2 | Joseph Lassel McDaniel | 10 | Male |
| 3 | Mary Hattie McDaniel | 12 | Female |
| 4 | Luner Malissa McDaniel | 8 | " |
| 5 | Tommie Ioler McDaniel | 6 | " |
| 6 | Parker McDaniel | 4 | " |

# Cherokee Citizenship Commission Docket Books
## (1880-84, 1887-89) Volume V
## Tahlequah, Cherokee Nation

| 7 | Mattie Stella McDaniel | 18 mos | Female |
|---|---|---|---|

ANCESTOR: Parker Collins

Now on this the 20[th] day of June 1888, comes the above case up for final hearing, and the Commission say: "We the Commission on Citizenship after "examining the testimony in the above case, and also the rolls of 1852, find that "the applicant, Martha Hall McDaniel and her six children, Joseph Lassil – Mary "Hattie – Luner Malissa – Tommie Iola – Parker and Mattie Stella McDaniel are "Cherokees by blood, and are hereby re-admitted to all the rights & privileges of "Cherokee citizens by blood, which is in compliance with an Act of the National "Council dated Dec. 8[th] 1886."

J. T. Adair     Chairman Commission
John E. Gunter     Commissioner
D.W. Lipe     Commissioner

## MORGAN

**DOCKET #2222**
CENSUS ROLLS

APPLICANT FOR CHEROKEE CITIZENSHIP

| POST OFFICE: Sequoyah District C.N. | | ATTORNEY: | |
|---|---|---|---|
| **NO** | **NAMES** | **AGE** | **SEX** |
| 1 | Cherokee Nation | | |
| 2 | (VS) | | |
| 3 | J.S. Morgan & family | | |

ANCESTOR: Malacha Watts

Now on this the 20[th] day of April, 1888, comes the above case up for final hearing. They having been cited to appear before the Commission on the 16[th] day of April 1888, and failing to appear at the appointed time, Hon. R.F. Wyly, Nations Atty, moves the Commission to declare ~~them~~ J.S. Morgan & family intruders upon the public domain of the "Cherokee Nation".

See decision in the W.J. Watts case on page 68 of this book. –    Rejected –

J. T. Adair     Chairman Commission
John E. Gunter     Commissioner

# Cherokee Citizenship Commission Docket Books (1880-84, 1887-89) Volume V
## Tahlequah, Cherokee Nation

## WATTS

Cherokee Nation          Office Commission on Citizenship
    (VS)                Tahlequah, I.T. April 20[th] 1888.
W. J. Watts, et.al.

We deem it best to give a synopsis of the history of this case from its inception down to the present time.

Under the provisions of an Act, approved February 7[th] 1888, amending an Act, entitled "An Act providing for the appointment of a Commission to try and determine applications for Cherokee Citizenship approved December 8[th] 1886, W.J. Watts and others were accordingly notified to appear before this Commission on the 16[th] day of April, 1888, then and there to establish their rights to citizenship in the Cherokee Nation, and having been called on three several days at the Court-house door in the town of Tahlequah, and no answer being made either in person or by Attorney, now comes R.F. Wyly, Nations Attorney, and moves the Commission to declare these parties as "intruders upon the Cherokee public domain."

Motion was sustained by the Commission for these reasons; first, that W.J. Watts, did, sometime during the year 1872, appear before Chief Justice, John S. Vann, of the Supreme Court of this Nation, and submitted the evidence of his claim to citizenship for approval or rejection, the same to be reported to the National Council for the final action under the law.      Now the law under which Mr. Vann was then acting, was based upon a joint resolution of the National Council, approved December 10[th] 1869, entitled, "Joint Resolution of "the National Council in regard to the North Carolina Cherokees."      This resolution was passed upon petition from the Cherokees then living in the state of North Carolina, asking to be admitted into the Cherokee Nation, as members thereof.

The Act referred to, entitled "An Act relating to the North Carolina "Cherokees", under which the Chief Justice of the Supreme Court of the Cherokee Nation made his report of this case, was as follows: "Be it enacted by "the National Council, that all such Cherokees (North Carolina Cherokees) as "may hereafter remove into the Cherokee Nation and permanently locate therein

## Cherokee Citizenship Commission Docket Books
## (1880-84, 1887-89) Volume V
## Tahlequah, Cherokee Nation

"as citizens thereof, shall be deemed as Cherokee citizens; - Provided said
"Cherokees shall enroll themselves before the Chief Justice of the Supreme
"Court within two months after their arrival in the Cherokee Nation and make
"satisfactory showing to him of their being Cherokees, and the said Chief Justice
"is hereby required to report the number, names, ages and sex of all persons
"admitted by him to be entitled to Cherokee citizenship, and also the number,
"names, ages and sex of the persons denied the rights of Cherokee citizenship to
"the annual session of the National Council in each year."

Approved November 20th 1870.

     Mr. Vann heard the evidence in this case, under the foregoing quoted law,
at Fort Gibson, Cherokee Nation, and made a report, ~~in this case~~, in which he
says: "This certifies that during my sitting as Chief Justice of the ~~Supreme~~
"Supreme Ct. Cherokee Nation, to take evidence in case of applications for
"Cherokee Citizenship at Fort Gibson, C.N. some time in April, 1872 as a
"Court of Commission" authorized by National Council for the same, one W.J.
"Watts, son of Malacha Watts, filed his application, then & there for Cherokee
"Citizenship, with sufficient proof to entitle him to said rights according to the
"best of my judgment; which I forwarded to the Senate with my
"recommendation and classed "B".
John S. Vann
"This Nov. 5th 1874                A. J. S. C.
C.N."

The recommendation of Mr. Vann, as Chief Justice, was placed before the
Senate of the Cherokee Nation, and a bill granting the Watts citizenship passed
that body, but failed to pass the lower branch of the National Council,
consequently, their claim was last before that body. Second. We next hear of
these parties being cited to appear before the "Chambers Court"; this notice was
duly served on the 24th day of February 1879, and failing to appear at the
appointed time, judgment was rendered against A.J. Watts on motion of John F.
Lyons, Nations Attorney, by default.

     This is the history of these parties as concerns their citizenship, up to the
present time.

Third. The evidence of these parties shows that some of them or their ancestors
should appear upon the census rolls of Cherokees taken in the Old Nation in the

285

year 1835, if in Tennessee, as alleged. The rolls fail to show the names of any of these parties, or their ancestors, though there are persons on them by the name of Watts, who are enrolled thereon as full blooded Cherokees.

W.J. Watts and others have to establish a lineal descent from some person whose name must appear on ~~any~~ some of the rolls, to wit: rolls of 1835, 1848, 1851 and 1852. They have ignored the right and privilege tendered them to try and prove their descent from some one on those rolls, which if proven, would entitle them to Cherokee citizenship. This is their affair, and not ours.     It will be seen at once by reference to the Act, approved Nov. 20th 1870, that the Chief Justice of the Supreme Court had no authority to admit or reject applicants for Cherokee citizenship:   only make report with his recommendation in the premises.

W.J. Watts, J.S. Morgan, Tom Blackard, John Blalock, Thomas Hope, Matt Nicholson, Mrs. Mayberry, one Patterson, one Nord, Mrs. Boyd, one Blalock[sic], A.J. Watts, William Watts, Marion Watts, Mrs. Soloman Watts, and Mc Watts, and their families, are hereby declared by this Commission to be intruders upon the public domain of the Cherokee Nation.

J. T. Adair    Chairman Commission
John E. Gunter    Commissioner

## BLACKARD

**DOCKET #2224**
CENSUS ROLLS

APPLICANT FOR CHEROKEE CITIZENSHIP

| POST OFFICE: Sequoyah District, C.N. | | ATTORNEY: | |
|---|---|---|---|
| NO | NAMES | AGE | SEX |
| 1 | Cherokee Nation | | |
| 2 | (VS) | | |
| 3 | Tom Blackard & family | | |

ANCESTOR: Malacha Watts

Now on this the 20th day of April 1888, the above case comes up for final hearing. They having been cited to appear before the Commission on the 16th day of April 1888, and failing to appear at the appointed time, Hon. R.F. Wyly,

Nations Atty. moves the Commission to declare Tom Blackard & family "intruders upon the public's domain of the Cherokee Nation".

See decision in W.J. Watts case, on page 68 of this book. Adverse ~~to cla~~

J. T. Adair      Chairman Commission
John E. Gunter     Commissioner

## BLAYLOCK

**DOCKET #2225**
CENSUS ROLLS

APPLICANT FOR CHEROKEE CITIZENSHIP

| POST OFFICE: Sequoyah District, C.N. | | ATTORNEY: | |
|---|---|---|---|
| No | NAMES | AGE | SEX |
| 1 | Cherokee Nation | | |
| 2 | (VS) | | |
| 3 | John Blaylock & family | | |

ANCESTOR: Malacha Watts

Now on this the 20th day of April 1888, comes the above case up for final hearing. They having been cited to appear before the Commission on the 16th day of April 1888, and failing to appear at the appointed time, Hon. R.F. Wyly, Nations Atty. moves the Commission to declare John Blaylock & family "intruders upon the public's domain of the Cherokee Nation".

See decision in W.J. Watts case, upon page 68 of this book. – Adverse –

J. T. Adair      Chairman Commission
John E. Gunter     Commissioner

287

# Cherokee Citizenship Commission Docket Books
## (1880-84, 1887-89) Volume V
## Tahlequah, Cherokee Nation

## HOPE

**DOCKET #2226**
CENSUS ROLLS

APPLICANT FOR CHEROKEE CITIZENSHIP

| POST OFFICE: Sequoyah District, C.N. | | ATTORNEY: | |
|---|---|---|---|
| No | NAMES | AGE | SEX |
| 1 | Cherokee Nation | | |
| 2 | (VS) | | |
| 3 | Thomas Hope & family | | |

ANCESTOR: Malacha Watts

Now on this the 20[th] day of April 1888, comes the above case up for final hearing, they having been cited to appear before the Commission on the 16[th] day of April 1888, and failing to appear at the appointed time, Hon. R.F. Wyly, Nations Atty. moves the Commission to declare Thomas Hope & family "intruders upon the public domain of the Cherokee Nation".

See decision in W.J. Watts case, upon page 68 of this Docket. – Adverse –

J. T. Adair    Chairman Commission
John E. Gunter    Commissioner

## NICHOLSON

**DOCKET #2227**
CENSUS ROLLS

APPLICANT FOR CHEROKEE CITIZENSHIP

| POST OFFICE: Sequoyah District, C.N. | | ATTORNEY: | |
|---|---|---|---|
| No | NAMES | AGE | SEX |
| 1 | Cherokee Nation | | |
| 2 | (VS) | | |
| 3 | Matt Nicholson & family | | |

ANCESTOR: Malacha Watts

Now on this the 20[th] day of April 1888, comes the above case up for final hearing, they having been cited to appear before the Commission on the 16[th] day of April 1888, and failing to appear at the appointed time, Hon. R.F. Wyly,

288

Nations Atty. moves the Commission to declare Matt Nicholson & family "intruders upon the public domain of the Cherokee Nation".

See decision upon page 68 of this Docket in the W.J. Watts case.
– Adverse –

J. T. Adair     Chairman Commission
John E. Gunter   Commissioner

## MAYBERRY

**DOCKET #2228**
CENSUS ROLLS

APPLICANT FOR CHEROKEE CITIZENSHIP

| POST OFFICE: Sequoyah District, C.N. | | ATTORNEY: | |
|---|---|---|---|
| NO | NAMES | AGE | SEX |
| 1 | Cherokee Nation | | |
| 2 | (VS) | | |
| 3 | Mrs. May-Berry & family | | |

ANCESTOR: Malacha Watts

Now on this the 20th day of April 1888, comes the above case up for final hearing, they having been cited to appear before this Commission on the 16th day of April 1888, and failing to appear at the appointed time, Hon. R.F. Wyly, Nations Atty. moves the Commission to declare Mrs. Mayberry & family "intruders upon the public domain of the Cherokee Nation".

See decision in W.J. Watts case, on page 68 of this Docket. – Adverse –

J. T. Adair     Chairman Commission
John E. Gunter   Commissioner

## PATTERSON

**DOCKET #2229**
CENSUS ROLLS

APPLICANT FOR CHEROKEE CITIZENSHIP

| POST OFFICE: Sequoyah District, C.N. | | ATTORNEY: | |
|---|---|---|---|
| **No** | **NAMES** | **AGE** | **SEX** |
| 1 | Cherokee Nation | | |
| 2 | (VS) | | |
| 3 | Patterson & family | | |

ANCESTOR: Malacha Watts

Now on this the 20th day of April 1888, comes the above case up for final hearing, they having been cited to appear before this Commission on the 16th day of April 1888, and failing to appear at the appointed time, Hon. R.F. Wyly, Nations Atty. moves the Commission to declare one Patterson & family "intruders upon the public domain of the Cherokee Nation". See decision in W.J. Watts case, found upon page 68 of this Docket. – Adverse –

J. T. Adair    Chairman Commission
John E. Gunter    Commissioner

## NORD

**DOCKET #2230**
CENSUS ROLLS

APPLICANT FOR CHEROKEE CITIZENSHIP

| POST OFFICE: Sequoyah District, C.N. | | ATTORNEY: | |
|---|---|---|---|
| **No** | **NAMES** | **AGE** | **SEX** |
| 1 | Cherokee Nation | | |
| 2 | (VS) | | |
| 3 | Nord & family | | |

ANCESTOR: Malacha Watts

Now on this the 20th day of April 1888, comes the above case up for final hearing, they having been cited to appear be[sic] the Commission on the 16th day of April 1888, and failing to appear at the appointed time, Hon. R.F. Wyly, Nations Atty. moves the Commission to declare one Nord & family as "intruders upon the public domain of the Cherokee Nation".

# Cherokee Citizenship Commission Docket Books
## (1880-84, 1887-89) Volume V
## Tahlequah, Cherokee Nation

See decision in the W.J. Watts case, found on page 68 of this Docket. – Adverse –

J. T. Adair    Chairman Commission
John E. Gunter    Commissioner

---

## BOYD

**DOCKET #2231**
CENSUS ROLLS

APPLICANT FOR CHEROKEE CITIZENSHIP

| POST OFFICE: Sequoyah District, C.N. | | ATTORNEY: | |
|---|---|---|---|
| NO | NAMES | AGE | SEX |
| 1 | Cherokee Nation | | |
| 2 | (VS) | | |
| 3 | Mrs.    Boyd & family | | |

ANCESTOR: Malacha Watts

Now on this the 20th day of April 1888, comes the above case up for final hearing, they having been cited to appear before the Commission on the 16th day of April 1888, and failing to appear upon the appointed time, Hon. R.F. Wyly, Nations Atty. moves the Commission to declare Mrs. Boyd & family as "intruders upon the public domain of the Cherokee Nation".

See decision in the W.J. Watts case, upon page 68 of this Docket. – Adverse –

J. T. Adair    Chairman Commission
John E. Gunter    Commissioner

---

## BLAYLOCK

**DOCKET #2232**
CENSUS ROLLS

APPLICANT FOR CHEROKEE CITIZENSHIP

| POST OFFICE: Sequoyah District, C.N. | | ATTORNEY: | |
|---|---|---|---|
| NO | NAMES | AGE | SEX |
| 1 | Cherokee Nation | | |
| 2 | (VS) | | |

| 3 | Blaylock & family | | |
|---|---|---|---|

**ANCESTOR:** Malacha Watts

Now on this, the 20[th] day of April 1888, comes the above case up for final hearing, they having been cited to appear before the Commission upon the 16[th] day of April 1888, and failing to appear upon the day appointed, Hon. R.F. Wyly, Nations Atty. moves the Commission to declare one Blaylock & family as "intruders upon the public domain of the Cherokee Nation".

See decision of the Commission in the W.J. Watts case on page 68 of this Docket. – Adverse –

J. T. Adair    Chairman Commission
John E. Gunter    Commissioner

## WATTS

**DOCKET #2233**
CENSUS ROLLS

APPLICANT FOR CHEROKEE CITIZENSHIP

| POST OFFICE: Sequoyah District, C.N. | | ATTORNEY: | |
|---|---|---|---|
| NO | NAMES | AGE | SEX |
| 1 | Cherokee Nation | | |
| 2 | (VS) | | |
| 3 | A.J. Watts & family | | |

**ANCESTOR:** Malacha Watts

Now on this, the 20[th] day of April 1888, comes the above case up for final hearing, they having been cited to appear before the Commission upon the 16[th] day of April 1888, and failing to appear upon the appointed time, Hon. R.F. Wyly, Nations Atty. moves the Commission that to declare A.J. Watts & family as "intruders upon the public domain of the Cherokee Nation".

See decision in the W.J. Watts case, found upon page 68 of this Docket. – Adverse –

J. T. Adair    Chairman Commission
John E. Gunter    Commissioner

# Cherokee Citizenship Commission Docket Books
## (1880-84, 1887-89) Volume V
## Tahlequah, Cherokee Nation

## WATTS

**DOCKET #2234**

CENSUS ROLLS

APPLICANT FOR CHEROKEE CITIZENSHIP

| POST OFFICE: Sequoyah District, C.N. | | ATTORNEY: | |
|---|---|---|---|
| No | NAMES | AGE | SEX |
| 1 | Cherokee Nation | | |
| 2 | (VS) | | |
| 3 | William Watts & family | | |

ANCESTOR: Malacha Watts

Now on this, the 20$^{th}$ day of April 1888, comes the above case up for final hearing, they having been cited to appear before the Commission upon the 16$^{th}$ day of April 1888, and failing to appear at the appointed time & place, Hon. R.F. Wyly, Nations Atty. moves the Commission to declare William Watts and family as "intruders upon the public domain of the Cherokee Nation".

See decision in the W.J. Watts case, found on page 68 of this Docket. Adverse –

J. T. Adair     Chairman Commission

John E. Gunter     Commissioner

## WATTS

**DOCKET #2235**

CENSUS ROLLS

APPLICANT FOR CHEROKEE CITIZENSHIP

| POST OFFICE: Sequoyah District, C.N. | | ATTORNEY: | |
|---|---|---|---|
| No | NAMES | AGE | SEX |
| 1 | Cherokee Nation | | |
| 2 | (VS) | | |
| 3 | Marion Watts & family | | |

ANCESTOR: Malacha Watts

Now on this, the 20$^{th}$ day of April 1888, comes the above case up for final hearing, they having been cited to appear before the Commission on the 16$^{th}$ day of April 1888, and failing to appear at the appointed time & place, Hon. R.F. Wyly, Nations Atty. moves the Commission to declare Marion Watts & family as "intruders upon the public domain of the Cherokee Nation".

# Cherokee Citizenship Commission Docket Books
## (1880-84, 1887-89) Volume V
## Tahlequah, Cherokee Nation

See decision in the W.J. Watts case, found on page 68 of this Docket.
– Adverse –

J. T. Adair    Chairman Commission
John E. Gunter   Commissioner

---

## WATTS

**DOCKET #2236**
CENSUS ROLLS

APPLICANT FOR CHEROKEE CITIZENSHIP

| POST OFFICE: Sequoyah District, C.N. | | ATTORNEY: | |
|---|---|---|---|
| NO | NAMES | AGE | SEX |
| 1 | Cherokee Nation | | |
| 2 | (VS) | | |
| 3 | Mrs. Soloman Watts & family | | |

ANCESTOR: Malacha Watts

Now on this, the 20th day of April 1888, comes the above case up for final hearing, they having been cited to appear before the Commission on the 16th day of April 1888, and failing to appear at the appointed time and place, Hon. R.F. Wyly, Nations Atty. moves the Commission to declare Mrs. Solomon Watts & family as "intruders upon the public domain of the Cherokee Nation".

See decision in the W.J. Watts case, found on page 68 of this Docket.
– Adverse –

J. T. Adair    Chairman Commission
John E. Gunter   Commissioner

---

## WATTS

**DOCKET #2237**
CENSUS ROLLS

APPLICANT FOR CHEROKEE CITIZENSHIP

| POST OFFICE: Sequoyah District, C.N. | | ATTORNEY: | |
|---|---|---|---|
| NO | NAMES | AGE | SEX |
| 1 | Cherokee Nation | | |
| 2 | (VS) | | |

| 3 | Mc Watts & family | | |
|---|---|---|---|

**ANCESTOR:** Malacha Watts

Now on this, the 20th day of April 1888, comes the above case up for final hearing, they having been cited to appear before the Commission on the 16th day of April 1888, and failing to appear at the appointed time and place. Now R.F. Wyly, Nations Atty. moves the Commission to declare Mc Watts & family as "intruders upon the public domain of the Cherokee Nation".

See decision in the W.J. Watts case, found on page 68 of this Docket. Adverse –

J. T. Adair    Chairman Commission
John E. Gunter    Commissioner

## GEE

**DOCKET #2238**
CENSUS ROLLS

APPLICANT FOR CHEROKEE CITIZENSHIP

| POST OFFICE: Vinita, Ind. Ter. | | ATTORNEY: | |
|---|---|---|---|
| No | NAMES | AGE | SEX |
| 1 | John R. Gee | | Male |
| 2 | Charles W. Gee | | " |
| 3 | James J. Gee | | " |
| 4 | – Dead –    Emma Gee | | Female |
| 5 | Alice Gee | | " |
| 6 | Mary Gee | | " |
| 7 | John Gee | | Male |
| 8 | Gordon Gee | | " |
| 9 | Frederick Gee | | " |
| 10 | Lilly Gee | | Female |
| 11 | Ella Gee | | " |

**ANCESTOR:** Lewis Stowers

This case was originally, by this Commission, set for the 3rd day of May 1888, and was postponed by the Court until the 17th day of May 1888, and the parties appearing. The case was again put off upon request of Mrs. Gee until the 2nd day of July 1888.

## Office Commission on Citizenship

Tahlequah, Ind. Ter. July 2nd 1888.

John R. Gee, et al.
(Vs)
Cherokee Nation

This case was one that was tried by the Hon. Commission on Citizenship in January 1884, and was decided adversely to claimant.

It is now before this Commission under an amendment to the Act creating this Court, approved February 7th 1888. The parties being duly notified under date of the 30th of March 1888, to appear at Tahlequah, C.N., on the 3rd day of May, 1888, and establish their right to citizenship in this Nation under the 7th Sec. of the Act of December 8th 1886 creating the Commission on Citizenship of an Act, approved December 8th 1886, in relation to Citizenship. Mr. Gee appeared on the 3rd of May, the day set for trial and the case was postponed until to day, the 2nd day of July 1888 – when it was taken up and the testimony read and submitted.

All the evidence addressed in favor of Mr. Gee goes to show that he claimed Cherokee blood from his mother, whose name was Barbara Gee, who was the daughter of Lewis Stowers and Susan Stowers, nee Hill, who once lived in the state of Tennessee, and removed from there to the state of Ohio. The Rolls mentioned in the 7th Sec. of the Act creating this Commission approved Dec. 8th 1886, were submitted as evidence on part of the Nation, by Hon. R.F. Wyly, Nations Attorney – Now in summing up this case, it is only necessary to ascertain the fact, whether or not, Mr. Gee's mother, Barbara Gee, or his grand-parents, Lewis Stowers and or Susan Stowers – nee Hill, appear upon any of the authenticated census or pay rolls mentioned in the 7th Sec. of the before mentioned law.

The evidence is a complete claim, showing that Mr. Gee and his children are the descendants of Lewis & Susan Stowers, but it does not establish the fact that they are Cherokee Indians, even *(illegible)* the rolls of Cherokees, spoken of, not considers.

# Cherokee Citizenship Commission Docket Books
## (1880-84, 1887-89) Volume V
## Tahlequah, Cherokee Nation

The names of Lewis & Susan Stowers and the name of Susan Hill, and the name of Barbara Gee, fail to appear upon any of the certified rolls of Cherokees made by the United States, in the state of Tennessee. Therefore:

We the Commission on Citizenship, after duly and carefully examining said rolls for Mr. Gee's ancestors, who even may have resided within the state of Tennessee, fail to find their names enrolled thereon as Indians, or even as whites, heads of families. We are of the opinion that, John R. Gee, and his children, viz: Charles W. Gee, James J. Gee, Alice Welch nee Gee, May High, nee Gee, John Gee, Gordon Gee, Frederick Gee, Lilly Gee, and Ella Gee, are not Cherokees, neither are they entitled to the rights, privileges and immunities of such by virtue of such blood – and further, they are declared to be intruders upon the public domain of the Cherokee Nation.

J. T. Adair     Chairman Commission

D.W. Lipe     Commissioner

## REPROGLE

**DOCKET #2239**

CENSUS ROLLS

APPLICANT FOR CHEROKEE CITIZENSHIP

| POST OFFICE: Canadian Dist. C.N. | | ATTORNEY: | |
|---|---|---|---|
| NO | NAMES | AGE | SEX |
| 1 | Tempa E. Reprogle & family | | |

ANCESTOR:

Cherokee Nation
    VS
Tempa E. Reprogle et al

This case is one of several that comes within the provision[sic] of the provisions of an Act approved February 7[th] 1888 amending a law, approved December 8[th] 1886, entitled, "An Act providing for the appointment of a Commission to try and determine applications for Cherokee Citizenship".

It seems that Tempa E. Reprogle has been residing within the limits of the Cherokee Nation in Canadian District from, and prior to the year 1878, not as acknowledge citizen of the Cherokee Nation, for on the 19[th] day of July 1878, her application for Cherokee Citizenship was taken up and disposed of by the "Chambers Court", a Commission to try and determine such applicants,

297

adversely to claimant. Since which time she has been protected in this Nation under which is commonly termed among such persons as "Protection papers" and very effectually too, by the United States Indian Agent under instruction to do so, form the Hon. Commission of Indian Affairs, if such persons presented to have [the Agent] prima facia a just claim to Cherokee Citizenship.

Also Tempa E. Reprogle was under the authority of the above mentioned Act approved Feby. 7th 1888, duly notified on the 10th day of April 1888 to appear before this Commission in the Town of Tahlequah, Cherokee Nation, on the 16th day of May, 1888, then and there to establish her rights to citizenship in this Nation under the 7th Section of the before mentioned law approved December 8th 1886. Her name was accordingly called three times upon three several days at the door of the Commission room at Tahlequah Cherokee Nation. Commencing upon the 16th day of May 1888, the day set upon which she was lawfully notified to appear, and no answer being returned either in person or by Attorney or otherwise: Now comes Hon. R.F. Wyly, Nations Attorney and moves the Commission to declare Tempa E. Reprogle and family as "Intruders upon the public domain of the Cherokee Nation." The motion was sustained by the Commission and Tempa E. Reprogle and family are accordingly declared as Intruders upon the domain of the Cherokee Nation.

J. T. Adair    Chairman Commission
D.W. Lipe    Commissioner

This the 19th day
of May AD 1888
Tahlequah I.T.

## COBB

**DOCKET #2240**
CENSUS ROLLS

APPLICANT FOR CHEROKEE CITIZENSHIP

| POST OFFICE: Muskogee, Ind. Ter. | | ATTORNEY: | |
|---|---|---|---|
| NO | NAMES | AGE | SEX |
| 1 | John O. Cobb & family | | |

ANCESTOR:

Now on this the 23rd day of May 1888, comes the above case for final hearing. Mr. John Cobb and others being duly served with a process from this

298

# Cherokee Citizenship Commission Docket Books
## (1880-84, 1887-89) Volume V
## Tahlequah, Cherokee Nation

Commission under authority of an amendment of the National Council approved Feby 7th 1888. Amending an Act entitled "An Act providing for the appointment of a Commission to try and determine applications for Cherokee Citizenship" approved Dec. 8th 1886. On the 9th day of April 1888 to appear before this Commission in the Town of Tahlequah Cherokee Nation. (See Sec. 18th of Act approved Dec. 8th 1886. Then and there to answer why the decree of a former Commission admitting them to citizenship should not be set aside on account of fraud and bribery having been practiced in obtaining the same. So far at the merits of this case is concerned, it is the same as that of Mrs. Martha A. Payne. Mr. Cobb's wife (died) being a sister of Mrs. Payne. Mr. Cobb was called at the door of the rooms of the commission on three several days, and failing to appear either in person or by Attorney or otherwise.

Now comes Hon R.F. Wyly, Nations Attorney and moves the Commission to declare John O. Cobb and his children, Intruders upon the Public Domain of the Cherokee Nation. The motion was sustained and John O. Cobb and his children by his wife Eudona Cobb nee Moffet now deceased are hereby declared to be Intruders and not entitled to any of the rights and privileges of a Cherokee citizen.

J. T. Adair    Chairman Commission

D.W. Lipe    Commissioner

---

## CHASTIAN

**DOCKET #2241**

CENSUS ROLLS        APPLICANT FOR CHEROKEE CITIZENSHIP

| POST OFFICE: | | ATTORNEY: | |
|---|---|---|---|
| **NO** | **NAMES** | **AGE** | **SEX** |
| 1 | Rainy Chastian | | |
| 2 | and family | | |

ANCESTOR:

Now on this the 23rd day of May 1888, comes the above case up for final hearing. Mr. Chastian having been duly served with a notification from this Commission under the provisions of an amendment of the National Council approved Feby 7th 1888, amending an Act entitled "An Act of providing for the appointment of a Commission to try and determine applications for Cherokee Citizenship", approved Dec 8th 1886 on the 20th day of March 1888, to appear before the Commission in the Town of Tahlequah Cherokee Nation, I.T. on the

# Cherokee Citizenship Commission Docket Books
## (1880-84, 1887-89) Volume V
## Tahlequah, Cherokee Nation

1$^{st}$ day of May 1888. Then and there to establish his rights to Cherokee citizenship under the 7$^{th}$ section of the above mentioned law, approved Dec 8$^{th}$ 1886. Mr. Chastain's application for Cherokee citizenship was on file before the "Chambers Court" a duly authorized commission to try and determine applications for Cherokee citizenship in the year 1879 and was upon motion of John F. Lyons then Nation's Attorney for said Court decided against by default Her[sic] failing to appear. Mr. Chastian did not move out of the Nation after he was decided against but contained to reside within its borders and was as stated before notified on this account to appear and establish his claim to citizenship in the Cherokee Nation. This he has the 2$^{nd}$ time refused to do and if he has a just claim at all, he has ignored the Commission and *(illegible)* upon his rights. Mr Chastian was called three times on three several days at the door of the rooms of this Commission in the Town of Tahlequah I.T. and failing to answer either in person or by Attorney, or otherwise. Now comes Hon. R.F. Wyly, Nations Atty and moves the Commission to declare Rainey[sic] Chastian et al Intruders upon the public domain of the Cherokee Nation. The motion was sustained and Rainey Chastian & his children by Judy E. Chastian (dec'd) formerly the daughter of *(Illegible)* Watts not Cherokees and are hereby declared to be Intruders within the limits of the Cherokee Nation.

J. T. Adair   Chairman Commission
D.W. Lipe   Commissioner

---

## Cases coming under the 6$^{th}$ Sec. of an Amendment approved Feby. 7$^{th}$ 1888

### BLACK

**DOCKET #2242**
CENSUS ROLLS

APPLICANT FOR CHEROKEE CITIZENSHIP

| POST OFFICE: Echo, Ind. Ter. | | ATTORNEY: Isaac Mode | |
|---|---|---|---|
| **NO** | **NAMES** | **AGE** | **SEX** |
| 1 | John Black | 53 | Male |
| 2 | Willie Black | 15 | " |
| 3 | George Black | 13 | " |
| 4 | Coon Black | | " |
| 5 | Ida Black | 3 | Female |
| 6 | May Black | 2 | " |

# Cherokee Citizenship Commission Docket Books
## (1880-84, 1887-89) Volume V
## Tahlequah, Cherokee Nation

| 7 | Burt Davie (Grandchild) | 2 | Male |
|---|---|---|---|

**ANCESTOR:** Randolph & Fanny Carter and Ruth Black

John Black, et al          Office Com on Citizenship
   (vs)                 Tahlequah I.T. June 5<sup>th</sup> 1888
Cherokee Nation

The above case comes before this Commission under the 6<sup>th</sup> Section of an Act, approved February 7<sup>th</sup> 1888, amending an Act entitled "An Act providing for the appointment of a Commission to try and determine applications for Cherokee Citizenship", approved December 8<sup>th</sup> 1886.

Mr. Black was duly notified to appear on the 14<sup>th</sup> day of May 1888 before this Commission in the town of Tahlequah, Cherokee Nation, then and there to establish his rights to citizenship in this Nation under the Seventh (7) Section of the before mentioned law, approved Dec. 8<sup>th</sup> 1886. The case was put off by consent of both parties until the 4<sup>th</sup> day of June 1888, when Mr. Black did appear with the Rev. Isaac Mode as Attorney, and the case was duly docketed and heard in accordance with law. Mr. Black alleged as his ancestors, from whom he proposed to prove a descent that would entitle him to Cherokee citizenship, one Randolph Carter and his wife Fanny Carter.

The testimony of the Plaintiffs in this case goes to show that Randolph Carter moved from the state of Tennessee to the state of Arkansas about the year 1837, and from there, about the year 1838, moved into McDonell[sic] County in the state of Missouri, and lived about six (6) miles from the Cherokee line for about twenty (20) years, until his death, which took place some three (3) years prior to the late Rebellion. This placed Randolph Carter and his family contiguous to the Cherokee Indians for a period of some twenty years, and in all that time he nor his family ever set up any claims or pretensions that they were Cherokee Indians. The evidence of claimants also show that Randolph Carter and his family were in the State of Tennessee in the year 1835, and as a matter of course, if Cherokees as alleged, would appear as such upon the census rolls of Cherokees taken in that year by the United States in the states of North Carolina, Georgia, Tennessee and Alabama. The evidence on part of the Plaintiffs further shows, that these parties never in any way ever received any of the benefits arising from any of the treaties between the Cherokee Nation and the United States. This is in substance the evidence upon which these parties rely to obtain citizenship in the Cherokee Nation.

301

# Cherokee Citizenship Commission Docket Books
## (1880-84, 1887-89) Volume V
## Tahlequah, Cherokee Nation

The evidence on part of the Nation goes to show that these parties, Randolph & Fanny Carters' names do not appear upon the rolls of 1835 in any manner, as the rolls show. The evidence further shows, and conclusively[sic] too, that these parties were of the African case of people, and were known and recognized in the community in which they lived and were known, as part negroes, and never set up claim, or pretended in any way, that they were Cherokees.

After a careful and impartial review of this case, we are of the opinion that these parties John Black, Willie Black, Ida Black, Mary Black, Coon Black, George Black and Burt Davie, are not Cherokees by blood, and do hereby declare that they are not Cherokees by blood. entitled to any of the franchises, rights, privileges and immunities of Cherokees by blood, and are intruders upon the public domain of this Nation.

J. T. Adair    Chairman Commission

John E. Gunter    Commissioner

---

## Case coming up under the 6<sup>th</sup> Sec. of an Amendment to Act of Dec. 8-'86 ap<sup>ed</sup> Feby. 7<sup>th</sup> '88

### GEE

**DOCKET #~~2243~~[sic]**

CENSUS ROLLS

APPLICANT FOR CHEROKEE CITIZENSHIP

| POST OFFICE: Vinita, Ind. Ter. | | ATTORNEY: Self | |
|---|---|---|---|
| **NO** | **NAMES** | **AGE** | **SEX** |
| 1 | John R. Gee | 58 | Male |
| 2 | Charles W. Gee | 32 | " |
| 3 | James J. Gee | 30 | " |
| 4 | Alice Gee   married Welch | 26 | " |
| 5 | Mary Gee    "    High | 24 | " |
| 6 | John Gee | 22 | Male |
| 7 | Gordon Gee | 20 | " |
| 8 | Frederick Gee | 19 | " |
| 9 | Lilly Gee | 15 | |

| 10 | Ella Gee | 13 | |
|----|----------|-----|--|

**ANCESTOR:** Lewis Stowers & his wife whose maiden name was

Susan Hill

Look on page 84 of this docket.

---

**Case coming up under the 6<sup>th</sup> Sec. of the Act approved Febry. 7<sup>th</sup> '88**

## BALES

**DOCKET #2243**

CENSUS ROLLS

APPLICANT FOR CHEROKEE CITIZENSHIP

| POST OFFICE: Muskogee, I.T. | | ATTORNEY: David Bales   Self | |
|-----|-----|-----|-----|
| **NO** | **NAMES** | **AGE** | **SEX** |
| 1 | David Bales | 48 | Male |
| 2 | James Bales | 15 | " |
| 3 | Juley Bales | 13 | Female |
| 4 | Clercy Bales | 12 | " |
| 5 | Owen Bales | 9 | Male |
| 6 | Safronia Bales | 5 | Female |
| 7 | Jefferson Bales | 1 | Male |

**ANCESTOR:** From his Grand-mother, the wife of John Craig –

David Bales, et al
   (VS)
Cherokee Nation

    The above case coming up for final hearing on this the 4<sup>th</sup> day of July 1888.

    The first witness on part of the Plaintiffs, W.A. Lewis, claims that he knew this Bales family in the state of Arkansas and that they were said to be Cherokees, but did not know it of his own personal knowledge, only by hearing others say so.    Annie Carr, the second witness states that she is acquainted with David Bales and knew also, his father & mother, but did not know them to be Cherokees, but that they pass as such when she knew them.

# Cherokee Citizenship Commission Docket Books
## (1880-84, 1887-89) Volume V
## Tahlequah, Cherokee Nation

Nathaniel Lish goes to show from his testimony that from what he had heard, that John Craig and his wife, grandfather & grandmother of David Bales and his sisters & brothers, were white people.

The statement of Geo. Wilkinson shows that he was a little acquainted with John Craig & his wife, but did not know whether this woman, his wife, was a Cherokee or not, but that she looked like one.

All the testimony taken in Independence County, Arkansas, is of a hearsay nature; all the witnesses testifying to what the Craigs told them.

After summoning up the evidence in this case on behalf of applicants, the Commission is forced to give but little evidence to it, on account of it being of a hearsay character. The testimony of Mrs. Nancy Martin, who is now 88 years old, shows that she knew one Sam Craig, who married Eliza Harlin, A Cherokee woman, and that he had one bachelor brother named Jim, and that Sam Craig had two sons named John and Robert when he left the Old Nation about the time of the general emigration, and that John was about the age of her son James who is now about 60 years old.

It will be seen at once that the John Craig mentioned by Mrs. Harlin, as the son of Sam Craig, cannot be a grandparent of David Bales and his brothers & sisters, for he, if living, would only be about 60 years old, and the age of David Bales now is 48 years, which would make this John Craig 48 years age, about 12 years old. He was not any ones grandfather then.

The census rolls of Cherokees taken in the Old Nation in the year 1835, prior to the removal of the Cherokees to this Nation; show only the names of Sam Craig, a white man, head of an Indian family.

Now it will be remembered that none of the testimony in these cases goes to show who, or even the names, the wife of John Craig was, the alleged ancestor of these parties. After duly considering all the testimony in this case and carefully examining the census rolls of Cherokees taken by United States Agents in the state of Tennessee, Alabama, Georgia and North Carolina, in the year 1835, we fail to find the names of the alleged Cherokee ancestors of these parties.

# Cherokee Citizenship Commission Docket Books
## (1880-84, 1887-89) Volume V
## Tahlequah, Cherokee Nation

Therefore, We the Commission on Citizenship do hereby declare that David Bales and his children, viz: James, Juley, Clercy, Owen, Safronia and Jefferson Bales, and Francis M. Bales and his children, viz: John, Isaac, Mary, Maranda, Jacob F. and Cornelius Bales, and Willis B. Bales and his children, viz: Willie, Sarah, George, & Mary Bales, and one other, name not knows and Celey I. Comer, sister of David Bales, and her children, viz: Robert, Elvira, Melvina, John and Andrew Comer and some other children, names not remembered, are not Cherokees by blood and are not entitled to the rights, privileges and immunities of such by virtue of Cherokee blood, and are also intruders upon the public domain of the Cherokee Nation.

J. T. Adair    Chairman Commission

D.W. Lipe    Commissioner

---

**Case coming up under the 6<sup>th</sup> Sec. of the Act amending Act of Dec. 8<sup>th</sup> '86**

## BALES

**DOCKET #2244**
CENSUS ROLLS

APPLICANT FOR CHEROKEE CITIZENSHIP

| POST OFFICE: Muskogee, I.T. | | ATTORNEY: David Bales<br>For F.M. Bales & family | |
|---|---|---|---|
| **NO** | **NAMES** | **AGE** | **SEX** |
| 1 | Francis M. Bales | 46 | Male |
| 2 | John Bales | | " |
| 3 | Isaac Bales | | " |
| 4 | Mary Bales | | Female |
| 5 | Maranda Bales | | " |
| 6 | Jacob Fall Bales | | Male |
| 7 | Cornelius Bales | | " |

ANCESTOR: From his Grand-mother, the wife of John Craig –

Decision in this case will be found on page 102 of this Docket in the David Bales case.

Cornell Rogers

Clerk Com. on Citizenship

---

# Cherokee Citizenship Commission Docket Books
## (1880-84, 1887-89) Volume V
## Tahlequah, Cherokee Nation

### Case coming up under the amendment of Febry 7th 88 – amending Act of Dec. 8th '86

### COMER

**DOCKET #2245**

CENSUS ROLLS

APPLICANT FOR CHEROKEE CITIZENSHIP

| | POST OFFICE: Muskogee, I.T. | ATTORNEY: David Bales<br>For Celey I. Comer & family | | |
|---|---|---|---|---|
| No | NAMES | | AGE | SEX |
| 1 | Celey I. Comer | | 30 | Female |
| 2 | Robert Comer | | | |
| 3 | Elvira Comer | | | |
| 4 | Melvina Comer | | | |
| 5 | John Comer | | | |
| 6 | Andrew Comer, and | | | |
| 7 | other children, names not | | | |
| 8 | known by Mr. Bales, who | | | |
| 9 | gave this family in | | | |

ANCESTOR: From her grand-mother, the wife of John Craig

Decision in the case of David Bales on page 102 of this Docket governs this case.

Cornell Rogers
Clerk Com. on Citizenship

306

# Cherokee Citizenship Commission Docket Books
## (1880-84, 1887-89) Volume V
## Tahlequah, Cherokee Nation

### Case coming up the amendment of Febry 7<sup>th</sup> '88, amending Act of Dec. 8<sup>th</sup> 1886

### BALES

**DOCKET #2246**

CENSUS ROLLS

APPLICANT FOR CHEROKEE CITIZENSHIP

| POST OFFICE: | | ATTORNEY: David Bales, For Willis B. Bales & family | |
|---|---|---|---|
| **No** | **NAMES** | **AGE** | **SEX** |
| 1 | Willis B. Bales | | |
| 2 | Willie Bales | | |
| 3 | Sarah Bales | | |
| 4 | George Bales | | |
| 5 | Mary Bales, and one | | |
| 6 | other, whose name is not | | |
| 7 | remembered by Mr. David Bales | | |
| 8 | who gave this family in. | | |

ANCESTOR: From his grandmother, the wife of John Craig

Decision in this case will be found on page 102 of this Docket in the David Bales case.

Cornell Rogers
Clerk Com. on Citizenship

307

# Cherokee Citizenship Commission Docket Books
## (1880-84, 1887-89) Volume V
## Tahlequah, Cherokee Nation

### Case coming up under the 6[th] Sec. of the Act approved Febry 7[th] '88, amending Act of Dec. 8[th] '86

### GRIGGS

**DOCKET #2247**

CENSUS ROLLS

APPLICANT FOR CHEROKEE CITIZENSHIP

| POST OFFICE: | | ATTORNEY: J.M. Bryan Boudinot & Rasmus | |
|---|---|---|---|
| **NO** | **NAMES** | **AGE** | **SEX** |
| 1 | Polly Griggs | | |
| 2 | Sally Griggs    - Brown - | | |
| 3 | John R. Griggs | | |
| 4 | Dora Griggs    - Hawkins - | | |
| 5 | Henry Griggs | | |
| 6 | Nancy L Griggs    - Brown - | | |
| 7 | Mary E. Griggs | | |
| 8 | Charles Griggs | | |
| 9 | Albert Griggs | | |

ANCESTOR: Betsy Woods, nee Hubbard

Office Commission on Citizenship
Cherokee Nation Ind Ter
Tahlequah  August 20[th] 1889

The applicant in this case alleges in her application that *(cut off page)* is the daughter of Betsy Woods nee Hubbard who was a Cherokee Indian by blood and whose name would be found on the Census roll of 1851. In support of this declaration she offered the testimony of Martha Crittenden who states that she a Cherokee Indian by blood and a recognized citizen of the Cherokee Nation and that Polly Griggs is her double first cousin, their fathers and mothers were brothers and sisters and that Betsy Woods was *(cut off page)* mother of applicant and a sister to Wick Hubbard, and drew *(cut off page)* old settler money. This statement is corroborated by the testimony of Aaron Crittenden and on examination of the Old Settler rolls of 185*(cut off page)* the Commission finds the name of Betsy Woods, nee Hubbard en*(cut off page)* as a Cherokee Indian. Therefore the Commission decides that claimant and her children, Sally, John R,

308

# Cherokee Citizenship Commission Docket Books (1880-84, 1887-89) Volume V
## Tahlequah, Cherokee Nation

Dora, Henry, Nancy L, Mary E, Charles and Albert Griggs are of Cherokee blood, and entitled to all the rights of Cherokee Citizenship.
Attest
    E.G. Ross
          Clerk Commission          J.E. Gunter   Com

---

## Case coming up under the 6$^{th}$ Sec. of the Act approved Febry 7$^{th}$ '88, amending Act of Dec. 8$^{th}$ 1886

### BATTELLE
**DOCKET #2248**
CENSUS ROLLS

APPLICANT FOR CHEROKEE CITIZENSHIP

| POST OFFICE: | | ATTORNEY: | | |
|---|---|---|---|---|
| NO | NAMES | | AGE | SEX |
| 1 | Willis Battelle | | | Male |

ANCESTOR:

This case comes before this Commission under the provisions of an amendment approved Febry. 7$^{th}$ 1888, amending the Act of the National Council creating this Commission, approved Dec. 8$^{th}$ 1886. Mr. Battelle was accordingly served with a process emanating from this Commission, dated the 17$^{th}$ day of May 1888, to appear upon the 2$^{nd}$ day of July of this year, and establish his citizenship in this Nation.

Mr. John R. Gee, who is a relation of the Mr. Battelle, and from whom both claim the same ancestry, appeared and at his request, this together with his own case was deferred until the 2$^{nd}$ day of July 1888, as aforesaid. Mr. Willis Battelle's name was called on thee several days at the door of the Commission Court Room in the town of Tahlequah, C.N., and no answer being returned in person or by Attorney, the Commission on Citizenship declare that Willis Battelle has ignored the privileges tendered him by this Commission to prove his rights to citizenship in this Nation under the 7th Sec. of the Act approved Dec. 8$^{th}$ 1886, in relation to "citizenship", and is therefore an Intruder upon the public domain of the Cherokee Nation.

# Cherokee Citizenship Commission Docket Books
## (1880-84, 1887-89) Volume V
## Tahlequah, Cherokee Nation

J. T. Adair    Chairman Commission
D.W. Lipe    Commissioner

Office Commission on Citizenship.
Tahlequah, Ind. Ter.  July 6[th] 1888.

---

### Case coming up under the 6[th] Sec. of the Act apd Febry 7[th] '88, amending Act Dec. 8[th] 1886

### BOND

**DOCKET #2249**
CENSUS ROLLS

APPLICANT FOR CHEROKEE CITIZENSHIP

| POST OFFICE: | | ATTORNEY: | |
|---|---|---|---|
| No | NAMES | AGE | SEX |
| 1 | Sarah A Bond | | |

ANCESTOR:

Error.  Docketed once –

---

### Case coming up under the 6[th] Act[sic] Sec. of Act appd Febry 7[th] '88, amending Act Dec. 8[th] 1886

### GOODWIN

**DOCKET #2249**
CENSUS ROLLS

APPLICANT FOR CHEROKEE CITIZENSHIP

| POST OFFICE: | | ATTORNEY: | |
|---|---|---|---|
| No | NAMES | AGE | SEX |
| 1 | S.S. Goodwin | | |
| 2 | & family | | |

ANCESTOR:

Now on this the 9[th] day of July 1888, comes the above case up for final hearing, it is adjudged and determined, in view of the fact that S.S. Goodwin and family were duly notified to be present on July 3[rd] 1888, and establish their rights to citizenship in this Nation, and Mr. Goodwin being called on three several days at the door of the rooms of the Commission, in the town of

310

# Cherokee Citizenship Commission Docket Books
## (1880-84, 1887-89) Volume V
## Tahlequah, Cherokee Nation

Tahlequah Cherokee Nation, and failing to appear either in person or by Attorney, that the said S.S. Goodwin and his family Emaline Goodwin, his wife, have ignored the privilege tendered them, and are not Cherokees by blood, and not entitled to the rights and privileges of Cherokee citizens by virtue of such blood.

D.W. Lipe     Acting Chairman Commission

John E. Gunter    Commissioner

---

**Case coming up under the 6<sup>th</sup> Sec. of the Act amending Act of Dec. 8<sup>th</sup> 1886**

### GILLIS

**DOCKET #2250**

CENSUS ROLLS 1835-48-51&52

as well as Old Settler rolls    APPLICANT FOR CHEROKEE CITIZENSHIP

| POST OFFICE: | | ATTORNEY: Boudinot & Rasmus | |
|---|---|---|---|
| **NO** | **NAMES** | **AGE** | **SEX** |
| 1 | Elizabeth Gillis | 58 | Female |
| 2 | Martin Shoemake | 28 | Male |
| 3 | Alice Shoemake | 15 | Female |
| 4 | Ida Gillis     Grandchild | 3 | |

ANCESTOR: Wm Reid

The above case is are[sic] coming before the Commission on Citizenship under the provisions of an Act of Febry 7<sup>th</sup> 1888 amending an Act of Dec. 8<sup>th</sup> 1886, in relation to citizenship. Elizabeth Gillis, et al, *(cut off page)* duly notified under date of May 28<sup>th</sup> 1888, to appear before this Commission at Thalequah, Cherokee Nation, on the 9<sup>th</sup> day of July 1888, then and there to establish their right to citizenship in said Nation under the 7<sup>th</sup> Sec. of said Act of Dec. 8<sup>th</sup> 1886. The above applicant alleges as their Cherokee ancestor, one Wm Reid, who they claim is of Cherokee descent, and whose name will appear on some of the rolls mentioned in the 7th Sec. of the Act approved Dec. 8<sup>th</sup> 1886. Such however, turns out to be not true, for the name of Wm Reid fails to appear on the rolls as set up.     It is useless to recount the testimony in this case, for in the absence of corroborating evidence shown by these rolls already mentioned, this Commission cannot grant citizenship to anyone.    We, therefore declare, Elizabeth Gillis, Martin Shoemake, Alice Shoemake and Ida Gillis not to be Cherokees by blood, and not entitled to any of the rights and privileges of

# Cherokee Citizenship Commission Docket Books
## (1880-84, 1887-89) Volume V
## Tahlequah, Cherokee Nation

Cherokee citizens on account of their blood, and are intruders upon the public domain of the Cherokee Nation.

J. T. Adair    Chairman Commission

H.C. Barnes  Commissioner

Office Commission on Citizenship
Tahlequah I.T. Oct. 4<sup>th</sup> 1888

---

## NEAL

**DOCKET #2251**

CENSUS ROLLS

APPLICANT FOR CHEROKEE CITIZENSHIP

| POST OFFICE: Camp Creek, I.T. | | ATTORNEY: | |
|---|---|---|---|
| NO | NAMES | AGE | SEX |
| 1 | Jake Neal & family | | |

ANCESTOR: Malishi Watts

OFFICE COMMISSION ON CITIZENSHIP.

*Tahlequah, Ind. Ter.*

Jake Neal
J.L. Payne
Wm Payne
John Boyd and
Wiley Taylor
    (VS)
Cherokee Nation

Now on this the 16<sup>th</sup> day of July 1888, comes Hon. R.F. Wyly, Nations Attorney and moves the Commission to declare Jake Neal, J.L. Payne, Wm Payne, John Boyd and Wiley Taylor, intruders upon the public domain of the Cherokee Nation.

These parties live in Sequoyah District and claim a relationship with the Watts of that District, whose case was decided by default on the 20<sup>th</sup> day of April 1888. The above parties, Jake Neal, et al, were according to the summons returned, notified to appear before the Commission on the 11<sup>th</sup> day of June 1888, then and there to establish their rights to citizenship in this Nation, under the 7th Section of the Act approved Dec. 8<sup>th</sup> 1886, as set forth in notification of service. This case was postponed by request of W.J. Watts, who wrote this Commission

312

and asked a continuance to get ready in producing testimony. The case was then put off until the 10<sup>th</sup> day of July 1888, when the above parties constituting this cause were called on these several days. and no answer being returned, motion was made as before stated, to declare these parties intruders. They have ignored the privilege tendered them by this Commission to establish their rights to Cherokee citizenship in the Cherokee Nation. Therefore, by virtue of authority vested in this Commission by law, Jake Neal, J.L. Payne, Wm Payne, John Boyd and Wiley Taylor and their families are hereby declared not to be entitled to any of the rights and privileges of Cherokee citizens, and are intruders upon the public domain of the Cherokee Nation.

> D.W. Lipe    Actg Chairman Commission
> John E. Gunter   Commissioner

Office Commission on Citizenship
  Tahlequah Ind. Ter.  July 16<sup>th</sup> 1888.

---

## BOYD

**DOCKET #2252**
CENSUS ROLLS

APPLICANT FOR CHEREKEE CITIZENSHIP

| POST OFFICE: Camp Creek, Ind. Ter. | | ATTORNEY: | | |
|---|---|---|---|---|
| **NO** | **NAMES** | | **AGE** | **SEX** |
| 1 | John Boyd & family | | | |

ANCESTOR: Malachi Watts

See decision in the Jake Neal case on this Book, page 111 – Docket 2251 – By Default.

> Cornell Rogers
> Clk. Com. on Citizenship

Office Com on Citizenship
  Tahlequah I.T.  July 16<sup>th</sup> 1888

---

## TAYLOR

**DOCKET #2253**

CENSUS ROLLS

APPLICANT FOR CHEROKEE CITIZENSHIP

| POST OFFICE: Camp Creek, I.T. | | ATTORNEY: | |
|---|---|---|---|
| No | NAMES | AGE | SEX |
| 1 | Wiley Taylor & family | | |

ANCESTOR: Malachi Watts

See decision in the Jake Neal case on this Book – page 111 – Docket 2251 – By default.

Cornell Rogers
Clerk Com. on Citizenship

Office Com on Citizenship
Tahlequah I.T. July 16th 1888

## PAYNE

**DOCKET #2254**

CENSUS ROLLS

APPLICANT FOR CHEROKEE CITIZENSHIP

| POST OFFICE: Camp Creek, I.T. | | ATTORNEY: | |
|---|---|---|---|
| No | NAMES | AGE | SEX |
| 1 | J.L. Payne & family | | |
| 2 | Wm Payne & family | | |

ANCESTOR: Malachi Watts

See decision in the Jake Neal case in this Book – page 111 – By Default – This July 16th 1888.

Cornell Rogers
Clk. Com. on Citizenship

Office Com on Citizenship
Tahlequah I.T. July 16th 1888

314

**Cases coming before this Commission under the amendment of**
**Febry 7<sup>th</sup> '88, amending Act of Dec. 8 '86**

### CRAWFORD

**DOCKET #2255**
CENSUS ROLLS

APPLICANT FOR CHEROKEE CITIZENSHIP

| POST OFFICE: Saline Dist. I.T. | | ATTORNEY: | |
|---|---|---|---|
| NO | NAMES | AGE | SEX |
| 1 | William Crawford | | |
| 2 | Jasper Crawford | | |

ANCESTOR:

The above case is brought to the notice of this Commission by Hon. R.F. Wyle, Nations Attorney, filing motion on part of the Nation to declare William and Jasper Crawford intruders upon the public domain of the Cherokee Nation, they having been duly served with a notification from this Commission, under date of the 25<sup>th</sup> day of May 1888, to appear upon the 16<sup>th</sup> of July 1888 in the town of Tahlequah, then and there to establish their rights to citizenship in the Cherokee Nation under the 7<sup>th</sup> Sec of Act approved Dec. 8<sup>th</sup> '86 in relation to citizenship. Now therefore; in view of the fact that William and Jasper Crawford have ignored the privilege tendered them to establish their rights if they have any, in this Nation, and the Hon. R.F. Wyly, moves this Commission to act in the premises, William Crawford and Jasper Crawford are hereby declared to be intruders upon the public domain of the Cherokee Nation, as they have failed to establish rights and privileges of Cherokee citizen by virtue of such blood.

D.W. Lipe    Actg Chairman Commission
John E. Gunter   Commissioner

Office Commission on Citizenship
  Tahlequah I.T.  July 19<sup>th</sup> 1888

# Cherokee Citizenship Commission Docket Books
## (1880-84, 1887-89) Volume V
## Tahlequah, Cherokee Nation

### GOINS

**DOCKET #2256**

CENSUS ROLLS

APPLICANT FOR CHEROKEE CITIZENSHIP

| POST OFFICE: Sequoyah Dist | | ATTORNEY: | |
|---|---|---|---|
| NO | NAMES | AGE | SEX |
| 1 | Taylor Goins & family | | |
| 2 | Matt Goins & family | | |

ANCESTOR:

Now on this the 21$^{st}$ day of July 1888, this case comes up for final hearing on motion of Hon. R.F. Wyly, Nations Atty, to declare the above named parties and their families intruders upon the public domain of the Cherokee Nation. They having been called three times in three several days at the door of the Commission in the town of Tahlequah, C.N. and no answer being returned either in person or by Attorney or otherwise.

The Commission is of the opinion that they have no just claim or they would have presented the[sic] themselves and tried their cause in the usual manner as stated forth in the notification of service, duly served and citing them to appear before this Commission on the 19$^{th}$ day of July 1888, then to establish their claim to Cherokee citizenship.

The motion of the Nations Attorney is sustained, and Taylor Goins and Matt Goins and their families are declared not to have any of the rights and privileges of Cherokee citizens by blood, and are therefore intruders upon the public domain of the Cherokee Nation.

      D.W. Lipe  Actg. Chairman Commission

      John E. Gunter Commissioner

Office Commission on Citizenship
 Tahlequah Ind Ter July 21$^{st}$ 1888.

316

# Cherokee Citizenship Commission Docket Books
## (1880-84, 1887-89) Volume V
## Tahlequah, Cherokee Nation

## SHANNON

**DOCKET #2257**

APPLICANT FOR CHEROKEE CITIZENSHIP

| POST OFFICE: | | ATTORNEY: | |
|---|---|---|---|
| **No** | **NAMES** | **AGE** | **SEX** |
| 1 | Alice Shannon | | |
| 2 | Louisa Shannon | | |

ANCESTOR:

Now on this the 21$^{st}$ day of July 1888, comes Hon. R.F. Wyly Nations Attorney, and files motion to declare the above named parties as intruders upon the public domain of the Cherokee Nation. They having been duly served with a summons emanating from this Commission, on the 7$^{th}$ day of June 1888, to appear before the Commission on Citizenship on the 19$^{th}$ day of July 1888, there to establish their rights to citizenship in the Cherokee Nation, and their names being called three times on three several days and no answer being returned either in person or by Attorney or otherwise. The motion of Hon. R.F. Wyly Nations Attorney, was sustained and Alice Shannon and Louisa Shannon are therefore declared to be intruders upon the public domain of the Cherokee Nation, and are not, in our opinion, entitled to any of the rights and privileges of Cherokee citizens by blood.

D.W. Lipe    Actg Chairman Commission

John E. Gunter    Commissioner

---

**Case coming up under the amendment to the Act of Dec. 8$^{th}$ 1886**

## SMITH

**DOCKET #2258**

APPLICANT FOR CHEROKEE CITIZENSHIP

| POST OFFICE: Delaware Dist. | | ATTORNEY: | |
|---|---|---|---|
| **No** | **NAMES** | **AGE** | **SEX** |
| 1 | William Smith & family | | |

ANCESTOR:

# Cherokee Citizenship Commission Docket Books
## (1880-84, 1887-89) Volume V
## Tahlequah, Cherokee Nation

This case is one that comes before the Commission on Citizenship under the amendment of Febry. 7th 1888, to the Act creating and empowering this court. Mr. Smith was duly certified to appear before this Commission in the town of Tahlequah, Ind. Ter. on the 21st day of July 1888, then and there to establish his right to citizenship in the Cherokee Nation, under the 7th Sec. of the Act of Dec. 8th 1886. Mr. Smith was called three times on three several days and failing to appear either in person or by Attorney or otherwise; Now comes Hon. R.F. Wyly, Nations Attorney and moves the Commission to declare William Smith & family intruders upon the public domain of the Cherokee Nation. Mr. Smith has ignored the Commission on Citizenship and treated with contempt the authority of the Cherokee Nation. Therefore; the motion of Nations Atty. R.F. Wyly, is sustained and William Smith & family are hereby declared to be intruders upon the public domain of the Cherokee Nation public domain of the Cherokee Nation with no rights of citizens of the Cherokee Nation.

J. T. Adair    Chairman Commission
H.C. Barnes  Commissioner

Office Com on Citizenship
  Tahlequah, Ind. Ter. July 23 '88

---

## Case coming up under the amendment of Febry 7th '88, to original Act of Dec. 8th '86

### GUINN

**DOCKET #2259**
CENSUS ROLLS

APPLICANT FOR CHEROKEE CITIZENSHIP

| POST OFFICE: Siloam Springs, Ark. | | ATTORNEY: Boudinot & Rasmus | |
|---|---|---|---|
| NO | NAMES | AGE | SEX |
| 1 | Bob Guinn | 58 | Male |
| 2 | Elizabeth Splitlog – nee Guinn | 28 | Female |
| 3 | Paralee Davidson – nee Guinn | 27 | " |
| 4 | James Guinn | 23 | Male |
| 5 | Ada Guinn | 21 | Male |
| 6 | Martha A. Graham – nee Guinn | 20 | Female |
| 7 | John Guinn | 18 | Male |
| 8 | Jasper Guinn | 6 | " |

| 9 | Abraham Guinn | 4 | " |
|----|----------------|----|--------|
| 10 | Sarah Guinn | 2 | Female |
| 11 | Marion Guinn | 1 | Male |

ANCESTOR: Almon Guinn

*Commission on Citizenship.*

CHEROKEE NATION, IND. TER.

*Tahlequah,* September 20<sup>th</sup> *188*9

Bat Guinn
    vs              Application for Cherokee Citizenship
The Cherokee Nation

      The claimant in the above case alleges that he is ~~of~~ 58 years old and that he is the son of one Almon Guinn from whom he claims to derive his Cherokee Indian blood. From the ~~evidence~~ statement of the claimant in his own case before the Commission on Citizenship July 28<sup>th</sup> 1888 it appears that Almon Guinn left Polk County State of Tennessee in 1850 and died if he is not mistaken in Polk County State of Arkansas in the year 1856. The right of this family to citizenship on account of their Cherokee blood was made the subject of investigation by the "Tehee Commission" on Citizenship in the year 1883 in the case of Asa Guinn the brother of the claimant and was then decided against them. Nuronia Mitchell a sister of Bat Guinn and Asa Guinn claimed ~~to have~~ before that Commission to have been admitted to citizenship by *(Illegible)* Vann of the Supreme Court of the Cherokee Nation and presented a proper *(illegible)* to be a copy of a certificate to that affect signed by W.H. Turner Clerk of the Court issued in 1871. These proceedings have caused us to examine the case as now presented to this Commission with proper care and consideration. The witnesses examined on the part of the claimant are Bat Guinn himself, his sister Nurania Mitchell <u>nee</u> Guinn, Nathaniel Fish, Watt Sanders and on the part of the Nation Nancy Poor and J.M. Hildebrand, all before the Adair Commission in 1888 and Nancy Martin sister of Bat Guinn before the Commission on the 7<sup>th</sup> *(illegible)* in the case of Mary N. Webb daughter of Asa Guinn who is now an applicant for citizenship. Capt. Nathaniel Fish 88 yrs. of age claims to have known Almon Guinn on the *(Illegible)* river in the Old Nation now in the state of Georgia about the year 1817 and says that he was a Cherokee and spoke Cherokee but does not know his family and lived about two days journey from

Guinn, the statements of this witness are derived chiefly from ~~communications~~ interviews with the Guinn (Asa) since his arrival in the Cherokee Country as is shown by his cross examination. He did not know the claimant. The witness Watt Sanders knew nothing of the grandparents of applicant. He lived several miles from Almon Guinn and knows that he spoke the Cherokee language. He had not seen claimant for many years and would not have known him but for information received from himself. J.M. Hildebrand *(illegible)* of Canadian District, lived on the Ocoee River in Tennessee & He is 68 years of age. He knew Almon and Joshua Guinn who were said to be brothers. Almon lived about 3 miles from his fathers, also knew his family. He never knew or heard Almon Guinn set up any claims to be Cherokee but had every chance to do so if he were one. He was there when the Treaty of 1835 was made. Almon Guinn's daughters were frequently at his Father's. He remembers the names of Mary and Tilda, but the others he had forgotten. He also remembers Asa and Bat Guinn as his sons have heart them called Cherokees. These statements are corroborated in every material point by those of Mrs. Nancy Poor a sister of the last witness. The preponderance of evidence is against the claimant and it is made conclusive on the mind of the Commission from two considerations, viz: If Almon Guinn and family had been of Cherokee blood they would certainly have been enrolled as were the Cherokees living on *(Illegible)* and in other parts of the Cherokee Nation by the Agents of the United States in 1835, 48, 52. But ~~they~~ a careful examination of those folls fails to reveal their names. The Commission therefore decide that the claimant Bat Guinn aged 58 years at the date of filing his application and his children Elizabeth Splitlog nee Guinn 28 yrs, Paralee Davis nee Guinn 26 yrs., James Guinn 23 years, Asa Guinn 21 years, Martha Ann Graham, nee Guinn 20 years, John Guinn 18 yrs., Jasper Guinn 6 yrs., Abraham Guinn 4 yrs., Sarah Guinn 2 years and Marion Guinn 1 year old, are not entitled to citizenship in the Cherokee Nation. P.O. Siloam Arkansas.

> Will.P. Ross
> Chairman
> J.E. Gunter    Com

# Cherokee Citizenship Commission Docket Books
## (1880-84, 1887-89) Volume V
### Tahlequah, Cherokee Nation

**Case coming before this Com, under the amendment of Feby 7th '88, to Act of Dec. 8th 1886**

## WARD

**DOCKET #2260**
CENSUS ROLLS

APPLICANT FOR CHEROKEE CITIZENSHIP

| POST OFFICE: Going Snake Dist. | | ATTORNEY: | |
|---|---|---|---|
| NO | NAMES | AGE | SEX |
| 1 | John Ward & family | | |

ANCESTOR:

The above case is brought to the notice of the Commission by Hon. R.F. Wyly Nations Attorney filing motion to *(cut off page)* the above parties intruders upon the public domain of the Cherokee Nation. John Ward family having had notice served on them June 11th 1888 according to law, to appear before the Commission on Citizenship on the 25th day of July 1888 in the town of Tahlequah I.T. then and there to establish their rights to Cherokee Citizenship in the Cherokee Nation under the 7th Sec. of the Act creating this Commission dated Dec. 8th 1886 as all applicants for citizenship in the Cherokee Nation <u>must do</u> before they can be re-admitted to such privileges & benefits by this Commission.

John Ward family having been was called three times on three several days and failing to appear either in person or by Attorney or otherwise several days at the door of the Rooms of the Commission on Citizenship, after the time of his motion to appear and no answer being returned either in person or by Attorney or otherwise; he having treated with contempt the authority of the Cherokee Nation in not obeying summons to appear before this Commission. Therefore, We the Commission on Citizenship sustain the motion of Hon. R.F. Wyly, Nations Atty and declare John Ward and his family, now residing in Going Snake District Cherokee Nation, to be intruders upon the ~~lands of~~ public lands of the Cherokee Nation, and not entitled to the rights and privileges of citizens thereof.

J. T. Adair    Chairman Commission
H.C. Barnes   Commissioner

Office Commission on Citizenship
  Tahlequah I.T. July 27th 1888

# Cherokee Citizenship Commission Docket Books
## (1880-84, 1887-89) Volume V
## Tahlequah, Cherokee Nation

### Case coming up under the amendment of Febry 7<sup>th</sup> '88, of Act of Dec. 8<sup>th</sup> '86

### HUMPHREYS

**DOCKET #2261**
CENSUS ROLLS

APPLICANT FOR CHEROKEE CITIZENSHIP

| POST OFFICE: Going Snake District | | ATTORNEY: | |
|---|---|---|---|
| NO | NAMES | AGE | SEX |
| 1 | Mrs. D. Humphreys & family | | |
| 2 | Henry Humphreys | | |
| 3 | James Humphreys | | |
| 4 | Louisa Humphreys | | |

ANCESTOR:

The above case is brought to the notice of this Commission by Hon. R.F. Wyly Nations Attorney, filing motion to declare Mrs. D. Humphreys and her family intruders upon the public domain of the Cherokee Nation, they having had notice served on them June 18<sup>th</sup> 1888, according to law, to appear before the Commission on Citizenship on the 25<sup>th</sup> day of July 1888, in the town of Tahlequah, I.T. then and there to establish their rights to Cherokee citizenship in the Cherokee Nation under the 7th Sec. of the Act creating this Commission, dated Dec. 8<sup>th</sup> 1886, as all applicants for citizenship in the Cherokee Nation must do before they can be re-admitted to such privileges & benefits by this Commission.

Mrs. D. Humphreys, et al, being called three times on three several days at the door of the Rooms of the Commission on Citizenship, after the time of their motion to appear, and no answer being returned either in person or by Attorney or otherwise, it is adjudged and determined that Mrs. D. Humphreys, et al, have treated with contempt the authority of the Cherokee Nation. Therefore, We the Commission on Citizenship in view of these facts above recited sustain the motion of Hon. R.F. Wyly, Nations Atty. and declare Mrs. D. Humphreys, Henry Humphreys, James Humphreys and Louisa Humphreys, now residing in Going Snake District, Cherokee Nation, to be intruders upon the public lands of the Cherokee Nation, and are not entitled to the rights and privileges of citizens thereof.

# Cherokee Citizenship Commission Docket Books
## (1880-84, 1887-89) Volume V
### Tahlequah, Cherokee Nation

J. T. Adair   Chairman Commission
H.C. Barnes   Commissioner

Office Commission on Citizenship
Tahlequah I.T.  July 27$^{th}$ 1888

---

## Case coming up under the amendment of Febry 7$^{th}$ '88, of Act of Dec. 8$^{th}$ '86

### WARD

**DOCKET #2262**
CENSUS ROLLS

APPLICANT FOR CHEROKEE CITIZENSHIP

| POST OFFICE: Going Snake Dist. | | ATTORNEY: | |
|---|---|---|---|
| NO | NAMES | AGE | SEX |
| 1 | Elizabeth Ward & family | | |

ANCESTOR:

The above case is brought to the notice of this Commission by Hon. R.F. Wyly Nations Attorney, filing motion to declare Elizabeth Wards family intruders upon the public domain of the Cherokee Nation, they having had notice served on them June 12$^{th}$ 1888, according to law, to appear before the Commission on Citizenship on the 25$^{th}$ day of July 1888, in the town of Tahlequah, I.T. then and there to establish their rights to Cherokee citizenship in the Cherokee Nation under the 7th Sec. of the Act creating this Commission, dated Dec. 8$^{th}$ 1886, as all applicants for citizenship in the Cherokee Nation must do before they can be re-admitted to such privileges & benefits by this Commission.

Elizabeth Ward & family, having been called three times on three several days at the door of the Rooms of the Commission on Citizenship, after the time of their motion to appear, and no answer being returned either in person or by Attorney or otherwise, it is adjudged and determined by that Elizabeth Ward & family, have treated with contempt the authority of the Cherokee Nation. Therefore, We the Commission on Citizenship in view of these facts above recited, sustain the motion of Hon. R.F. Wyly, Nations Atty. and declare Elizabeth Ward & family, now residing in Going Snake District, to be intruders upon the public domain of the Cherokee Nation, and they are not entitled to the rights and privileges of citizenship in the Cherokee Nation.

# Cherokee Citizenship Commission Docket Books
## (1880-84, 1887-89) Volume V
## Tahlequah, Cherokee Nation

J. T. Adair    Chairman Commission

H.C. Barnes   Commissioner

Office Commission on Citizenship

Tahlequah I.T.  July 27<sup>th</sup> 1888

---

## Case coming up under the amendment of Febry 7<sup>th</sup> '88, of Act of Dec. 8<sup>th</sup> '86

## BRAUGHT

**DOCKET #2263**

CENSUS ROLLS

APPLICANT FOR CHEROKEE CITIZENSHIP

| POST OFFICE: Delaware Dist. C.N. | | ATTORNEY: | |
|---|---|---|---|
| NO | NAMES | AGE | SEX |
| 1 | C.G. Braught & family | | |

ANCESTOR:  Wife, daughter <u>Rainey</u> Chastian.

The above case is brought to the notice of the Commission on Citizenship by Hon. R.F. Wyly Nations Attorney, filing motion to declare the above parties intruders upon the public domain of the Cherokee Nation.  Mr. Braught having had notice served on him the 19<sup>th</sup> day of June 1888, according to law, to appear before the Commission on Citizenship in the town of Tahlequah, Cherokee Nation, on the 26<sup>th</sup> day of July 1888, then and there to establish his rights to Cherokee citizenship in the Cherokee Nation under the 7<sup>th</sup> Sec. of Act of Dec. 8<sup>th</sup> 1886, creating and empowering this Commission, and failing to do so, though his name was was called three times on three several days and failing to appear either in person or by Attorney or otherwise several days at the door of the Rooms of the Commission in this town, after the day set for his appearance, and no answer being returned either in person or by Attorney or otherwise, it is adjudged and determined by the Commission on Citizenship, that Mr. Braught has treated with contempt the authority of the Cherokee Nation, and has no case of citizenship to try, hence his non-appearance. – The motion of Nations Atty is for the above reasons, sustained and CG. Braught  family are declared to be intruders upon the public domain of the Cherokee Nation without the rights and privileges of Cherokee citizens.  C.G. Braught's wife is the daughter of Rainey Chastian, who has been decided against by a former Commission.

# Cherokee Citizenship Commission Docket Books
## (1880-84, 1887-89) Volume V
## Tahlequah, Cherokee Nation

J. T. Adair    Chairman Commission
H.C. Barnes   Commissioner

Office Commission on Citizenship
Tahlequah I.T. July 30<sup>th</sup> 1888

---

### Case coming up under the amendment of Febry 7<sup>th</sup> '88, of Act of Dec. 8<sup>th</sup> '86

## CHICKENBEARD

**DOCKET #2264**
CENSUS ROLLS

APPLICANT FOR CHEROKEE CITIZENSHIP

| POST OFFICE: Delaware Dist. | | ATTORNEY: | |
|---|---|---|---|
| **No** | **NAMES** | **AGE** | **SEX** |
| 1 | One – Chickenbeard & family | | |

ANCESTOR:

The above case is brought to the notice of the Commission by Hon. R.F. Wyly Nations Atty, filing motion to declare – Chickenbeard & family intruders upon the public domain of the Cherokee Nation, he having been served with a process from this Commission to appear before it in the town of Tahlequah, Cherokee Nation, on the 30<sup>th</sup> day of July 1888, then and there to establish his rights to Cherokee citizenship in the Cherokee Nation under the 7<sup>th</sup> Sec. of the Act of Dec. 8<sup>th</sup> 1886, and failing to do so after his name had been was called three times on three several days at the door of the Rooms of the Commission – therefore the motion of Nations Atty – it is adjudged and determined by the Commission on Citizenship, that Chickenbeard has treated with contempt the authority of the Cherokee Nation, and ignored the privilege tendered him to establish his rights to Cherokee Citizenship. Therefore: We the Commission on Citizenship, sustain motion of Nations Atty. and declare one Chickenbeard & family, now residing in Delaware Dist. to be intruders upon the public domain of the Cherokee Nation, and are not entitled to citizenship in the Cherokee Nation. to the rights and privileges of Cherokee citizens.

J. T. Adair    Chairman Commission
H.C. Barnes   Commissioner

Office Commission on Citizenship
Tahlequah I.T. July 30<sup>th</sup> 1888

# Cherokee Citizenship Commission Docket Books
## (1880-84, 1887-89) Volume V
## Tahlequah, Cherokee Nation

**Case coming up under the amendment of Febry 7th '88, of Act of Dec. 8th '86**

### HACKNEY

**DOCKET #2265**

CENSUS ROLLS

APPLICANT FOR CHEROKEE CITIZENSHIP

| POST OFFICE: | | ATTORNEY: | |
|---|---|---|---|
| **NO** | **NAMES** | **AGE** | **SEX** |
| 1 | Isaac Hackney & family | | |

ANCESTOR:

The above case is brought to the notice of the Commission by Hon. R.F. Wyly Nations Atty, filing motion to declare Isaac Hackney & family intruders upon the public domain of the Cherokee Nation, he having been served with a process from this Commission to appear before the Commission on Citizenship in the town of Tahlequah, Cherokee Nation, on the 30th day of July 1888, then and there to establish their rights to Cherokee citizenship in the Cherokee Nation under the 7th Sec. of Act of Dec. 8th 1886, and failing to do so after they had been called three times on three several days at the door of the rooms of the Commission – therefore the motion of Nations Atty – it is adjudged and determined by the Commission on Citizenship, that Isaac Hackney & family have treated with contempt the authority of the Cherokee Nation, and ignored the privilege tendered them to establish their citizenship in the Cherokee Nation. Therefore: We the Commission on Citizenship, sustain motion of Nations Atty. and declare Isaac Hackney & his family to be intruders upon the public domain of the Cherokee Nation, they now residing in Delaware Dist. and are not entitled to the rights and privileges of citizens of the Cherokee Nation.

J. T. Adair    Chairman Commission
H.C. Barnes    Commissioner

Office Commission on Citizenship
  Tahlequah I.T. Aug. 2nd 1888

# Cherokee Citizenship Commission Docket Books
## (1880-84, 1887-89) Volume V
## Tahlequah, Cherokee Nation

### Case coming up under the amendment of Febry 7th '88, to original Act of Dec. 8th 1886

### OSBORN

DOCKET #2266

CENSUS ROLLS

APPLICANT FOR CHEROKEE CITIZENSHIP

| POST OFFICE: Coo-y-yah, Ind. Ter. | | ATTORNEY: | |
|---|---|---|---|
| NO | NAMES | AGE | SEX |
| 1 | Frank Osborn | | |
| 2 | Florence Osborn | | |
| 3 | Gratia Osborn | | |
| 4 | Babu Osborn | | |

ANCESTOR:

Commission on Citizenship Tahlequah Ind. Ter. Aug. 6th 1888

The above case is called to the notice of the Commission on Citizenship by the Nations Atty of the Nation[sic], filing motion to declare Frank Osborn, et al, intruders upon the public domain of the Cherokee Nation, they having been duly summoned on the 16th day of June 1886 to appear before this Commission in the town of Tahlequah, Cherokee Nation, on the 20th day of July 1888, then and there to establish their rights to Cherokee citizenship under the 7th Sec. of Act of Dec. 8th 1886 in relation to citizenship, and failing to do so it is adjudged and determined and declared by the Commission on Citizenship, that Frank Osborn, Florence Osborn, Gratia Osborn and Babu Osborn, now residing in *(Illegible)* Dist, Cherokee Nation, have ignored the privilege tendered them to prove their citizenship in the Cherokee Nation, and that they have treated with contempt the authority of the Cherokee Nation. The motion of Hon. R.F. Wyly, Nations Atty. is sustained and Frank Osborn, Florence Osborn, Gratia Osborn and Babu Osborn are declared intruders upon the public domain of the Cherokee Nation.

J. T. Adair    Chairman Commission
H.C. Barnes  Commissioner

# Cherokee Citizenship Commission Docket Books
## (1880-84, 1887-89) Volume V
## Tahlequah, Cherokee Nation

### Case coming up under the amendment of Febry 7th 1888, to Act of Dec. 8th 1886

### YATES

**DOCKET #2267**

CENSUS ROLLS

APPLICANT FOR CHEROKEE CITIZENSHIP

| POST OFFICE: Coo-y-gah, Ind. Ter. | | ATTORNEY: | |
|---|---|---|---|
| NO | NAMES | AGE | SEX |
| 1 | Mrs. M.A. Yates | | |
| 2 | J.W. Yates | | |
| 3 | J.L. Yates | | |
| 4 | Ernest Yates | | |
| 5 | Earl Yates | | |
| 6 | Pete Yates | | |

ANCESTOR:

Commission on Citizenship Tahlequah Ind. Ter. August 6th 1888

The above case is brought to the notice of the Commission on Citizenship by the Nations Atty, filing motion to declare the above named parties to this cause intruders upon the public domain of the Cherokee Nation, having been duly summoned on the 16th day of June 1886 to appear before this Commission in the town of Tahlequah, Cherokee Nation, on the 23rd day of July 1888, then and there to establish their rights to Cherokee citizenship under the 7th Sec. of Act of Dec. 8th 1886, in relation to citizenship, and failing to do so it is adjudged and determined and declared by the Commission on Citizenship, that Mrs. M.A. Yates, J.W. Yates, J.L. Yates. Ernest Yates, Earl Yates and Pete Yates, now residing in *(Illegible)* Dist, Cherokee Nation, have ignored the privilege tendered them by this Commission to establish, or prove, their citizenship in the Cherokee Nation, and that they have treated with contempt the authority of the Cherokee Nation. The motion of Hon. R.F. Wyly, Nations Atty. is therefore sustained the above and foregoing named persons are declared <u>intruders</u> upon the public domain of the Cherokee Nation.

J. T. Adair    Chairman Commission

H.C. Barnes    Commissioner

# Cherokee Citizenship Commission Docket Books
## (1880-84, 1887-89) Volume V
## Tahlequah, Cherokee Nation

### PHIPPS

**DOCKET #2268**

CENSUS ROLLS

APPLICANT FOR CHEROKEE CITIZENSHIP

| POST OFFICE: Gibson Station, I.T. | | ATTORNEY: Gideon Morrgo | |
|---|---|---|---|
| NO | NAMES | AGE | SEX |
| 1 | Elizabeth Phipps | 66 | female |
| 2 | Columbus Phipps | 28 | male |
| 3 | Nancy Hanford, nee Phipps | 30 | female |
| 4 | Joe Phipps | 24 | male |
| 5 | Dora Phipps   orphan | 7 | female |
| 6 | James Phipps | 3 | male |

ANCESTOR:

Citation waved in the above case, and time set by consent of parties, which is the 30$^{th}$ day of August, 1888.

Cornell Rogers
Clerk Com. on Citizenship

*Commission on Citizenship.*

CHEROKEE NATION, IND. TER.

*Tahlequah,* Sept. 8$^{th}$ 1888

Elizabeth Phipps, et al
(VS)
Cherokee Nation

Now on this the above written date, comes the above case up for final hearing, all the evidence being in and fully and carefully examined, also the census & pay rolls of Cherokees taken in the Old Nation in the years 1835, 1851 & 1852.      The testimony of James Simpson goes to show that "Old Man" Matoy was the father of James Matoy, and that he was an Indian, but that he does not know that he was a Cherokee Indian, and that there were both Catawba and Natches'[sic] Indians living among the Cherokees in the Old Nation, all speaking the Cherokee language, and that Jim Matoy was the eldest son of "Old Man" Matoy, and that he had other sons. Further that he knew the mother of James Matoy and that her name was "Nancy" and that she was not a Cherokee, and that "Old Man" Matoy had Rutha Helton for a wife, the mother of Rebecca Ellege, and that he does not know that she was a Cherokee.

Arch McDaliels' statement shows that he came to this country in the year 1832, and that he knew the Matoys in the Old Nation from his first recollection, and that he knew Jim Matoy, the father of claimant and also his wife, Nelly Skitt, also Sally Helton, the mother of Elizabeth Phipps, the claimant, and that Sally, the mother of Mrs. Phipps has several children in the Old Nation, and no two had the same father, and that the names of her children were, Polly, Jim and Elizabeth, and that they were "out children" and that Rutha and Elizabeth Helton were sisters and Catawba Indians, and that Mrs. Phipps married prior to the year 1834, in the Old Nation and remained there until after the war.        The census and pay rolls of Cherokees taken and made of Cherokees[sic] in the Old Nation in the years 1835, 1851 and 1852, fail to exhibit the names of Elizabeth Phipps or that of her mother, Sally Helton, in consequence of which, We the Commission on Citizenship find (under the law of Dec. 8$^{th}$ '86) that Elizabeth Phipps ~~and her five children, viz:~~ Columbus Phipps, Nancy Hanford, nee Phipps, Joe Phipps, Dora Phipps and James Phipps are not Cherokees by blood and not entitled to the rights and privileges of such by virtue of their blood and are hereby declared to be intruders upon the public domain of the Cherokee Nation.

> D.W. Lipe    Actg Chairman Commission
> H.C. Barnes    Commissioner

## GARDENHIRE

**DOCKET #2269**
CENSUS ROLLS

APPLICANT FOR CHEROKEE CITIZENSHIP

| POST OFFICE: Metz, Ind. Ter. | | ATTORNEY: J.M. Bryan | |
|---|---|---|---|
| No | NAMES | AGE | SEX |
| 1 | G.W. Gardenhire | 46 | Male |
| 2 | Jacob I. Gardenhire | 19 | " |
| 3 | Clyde Gardenhire | 17 | "<br>~~Female~~ |
| 4 | Charles Gardenhire | 15 | " |
| 5 | Albert S. Gardenhire | 13 | " |
| 6 | Estelle Gardenhire | 11 | Female |

# Cherokee Citizenship Commission Docket Books
## (1880-84, 1887-89) Volume V
## Tahlequah, Cherokee Nation

| 7 | James Gardenhire | 9 | Male |
|---|---|---|---|

**ANCESTOR:** ~~Martha Welch~~  Martha Gardenhire, nee Welch

*Commission on Citizenship.*

CHEROKEE NATION, IND. TER.

*Tahlequah,* September 19[th] 1888

G.W. Gardenhire, et al
(VS)
Cherokee Nation

The above case is one that has for a long time "hung fire" in the Courts and Councils of this Nation.

The first notice that we have of this case if from a memorial under date of Nov. 15[th] 1877, in which Mr. George W. Gardenhire petitions the National Council of the Cherokee Nation for citizenship, accompanied by the affidavits of Lutitia Still, R.W. Hawkins, P.S. Hawkins, Wm Vinson, Esther J. Edwards and H.D. Reese, all of which were in favor of the petitioner.    The Council saw fit not to pass the claim of Mr. Gardenhire upon his petition for citizenship, for their own reasons.

This case was then brought before the "Chambers Court" and duly tried on the 10[th] day of July, 1878, and the Commission the said "We have looked carefully into the case, and find no satisfactory evidence to show Cherokee blood in Martha Welch, the claimants' alleged mother.  Mr. Gardenhire is therefore declared not to be a Cherokee by blood x x x."

We take cognizance ~~of this case~~ of this case under the amendment of February 7[th] 1888, to the original Act creating and empowering this Commission, of December 8[th] 1886. – Citation waived – Mr. Gardenhire, through his Attorney, Mr. J.M. Bryan, came forward, and had his case set for hearing on the 17[th] day of September 1888, and was on the following day, Sept. 18[th], taken up and formally tried upon the following testimony.

Summary of Evidence.

331

## Cherokee Citizenship Commission Docket Books
## (1880-84, 1887-89) Volume V
## Tahlequah, Cherokee Nation

The testimony of Mr. Gardenhire taken before this Commission under date of Sept. 17[th] 1888, goes to show that his father was Jacob Gardenhire, and his mother Martha Gardenhire, nee Welch, who was a daughter of Arthur Welch, who once lived in the state of North Carolina, but afterwards removed into the state of Tennessee on a stream called Running-Water, and from there into the state of Arkansas, and that this, last move was made before the general emigration of Cherokees from the Old Cherokee Nation to this Country, but fails to exactly state how long; Must have been prior to the year 1835. Mr. John P. Edwards says that he married into the Gardenhire family in the year 1859, and that he is a citizen of the Cherokee Nation by adoption, and that at the time he was married – 1859 – the applicant lived in the state of Arkansas, and that he first became acquainted with him in the year 1862, and that he then claimed to be a Cherokee Indian, and that Mr. Edwards' wife claims him as her relative and a Cherokee, and that he understood from his wife's mother, that the reason that Jacob Gardenhire, the father of the applicant, left Tennessee and went to Arkansas, was that he had married a Cherokee woman, and that his folks very much disapproved of his marriage, and that his wife's relationship to Mr. George W. Gardenhire is wholly from the white side and that Jacob Gardenhire and James L. Gardenhire are cousins.

Mr. H.D. Reese says, that about the year 1853 he was living on the Tennessee river[sic], not far from where Chattanooga now stands, and that about this time, a William Gardenhire moved to a place near him and continued to live there until he (Reese) left that country in the year 1837, and that this Wm Gardenhire had several children, all, or nearly all of whom were married to Cherokees. That Judge Gardenhire was married to a daughter of Path Killer, another son also had a Cherokee wife – but fails to mention his name – and that two of his daughters also married Cherokees. Lutitia Gardenhire married a Mr. Eldridge and Almyra[sic] Gardenhire married George McPherson.

The testimony of Vinson only shows that Jacob Gardenhire married Martha Welch – really nothing more or nothing else.

Esther Edwards says that she had her rights to citizenship established in the Cherokee Nation, and that she is acquainted with the applicant, and that Martha Welch, who was the wife of Jacob Gardenhire, was known as a Cherokee among the Cherokees. On cross examination she says that she knew Jacob Gardenhire, the father of the applicant, and that she lived in East Tennessee and came here about six years ago – statement made May 12[th] 1878 –

and that she never knew Martha Welch, the mother of the applicant, and that Jacob Gardenhire was a white man.

R.W. Hawkins says that he use[sic] to live near the applicant in the state of Arkansas, and that the Gardenhires were known in that neighborhood as Cherokees, but his only knowledge of the applicant's family being Cherokees, is from hearsay.

Lutitia Still says that she first knew Martha Welch in Arkansas, about two years after the emigration – 1836 or 1837 – and that she spoke the Cherokee language, as well as resemble them and claimed to be a Cherokees, and that Jacob Gardenhire was her first cousin. Mrs Still further says under date of the 12[th] of September 1888, in a statement that she made before the Clerk of Cooweescoowee[sic] District, in this case, that four of the Gardenhires married Cherokees, as follows:

Judge Gardenhire married a Pathkiller.

Elmyra " " George McPherson.

Lutitia " " Jesse Edridge[sic] and

Jacob " " Martha Welch, and that she knows these persons who married Gardenhires to be Cherokees, and that Martha Welch was the mother of George W. Gardenhire, the applicant.

A.F. McCabb says that his grandfather was a Gardenhire and married a Path Killer, and that Jacob Gardenhire was a cousin of his grandfather, James T. Gardenhire, and that his relationship to the applicant is wholly on the white side.

In summing up the evidence in this case, the Commission on Citizenship have done so, and taken into consideration the proof in this cause in all its bearings.     The greatest effort that seems to have been exerted by the demandants was to establish as relationship with the Cherokee Gardenhires, that is, descendants from parties by this name with Cherokee women, for the Gardenhires originally were white folks, as was the father of the applicant, Jacob Gardenhire.

There seems to be but little stress placed outside of the fact that as yet the plaintiffs have only connected themselves with those who have a right to citizenship in the Cherokee Nation. This cannot admit, or if Cherokees re-admit such parties to citizenship in the Cherokee Nation, for the fact is still patent that the relationship of the plaintiffs as descended from some one on the Rolls of

# Cherokee Citizenship Commission Docket Books
## (1880-84, 1887-89) Volume V
## Tahlequah, Cherokee Nation

Cherokees mentioned in the 7th Sec. of the Act of Dec. 8th 1886, is still wanting.

The only evidence that would lead one to believe that Martha Gardenhire, nee Welch, was a Cherokee, is that of Mrs. Still whom she made her supplemental statement before the Clerk of Cooweescoowee Dist. all the out of the whole, is of a hearsay nature, and cannot be given that evidence, that would follow if the parties testified to something that they knew of personally. The meager statement of Mrs. Still in the face of so much other unsatisfactory testimony, and the fact of the rolls of Cherokees not containing the name of the alleged Cherokee ancestor, or that of the applicants themselves in this case, it is therefore declared and adjudged by the Commission on Citizenship, that George W. Gardenhire, Jacob I. Gardenhire, Clyde Gardenhire, Charles Gardenhire, Albert S. Gardenhire, Estelle Gardenhire and James Gardenhire are not Cherokees by blood, and are intruders upon the public domain of the Cherokee Nation.

J. T. Adair    Chairman Commission
D.W. Lipe    Commissioner
H.C. Barnes  Commissioner

## SIZEMORE

**DOCKET #2270**
CENSUS ROLLS

APPLICANT FOR CHEROKEE CITIZENSHIP

| POST OFFICE: Vian, Illinois Dist, Ind. Ter. | | ATTORNEY: C.H. Taylor | |
|---|---|---|---|
| No | NAMES | AGE | SEX |
| 1 | Mrs. Malinda Sizemore | 64 | Female |
| 2 | Robert Sizemore | 38 | Male |
| 3 | Columbus C. Sizemore | 36 | " |
| 4 | Mary Sizemore | 34 | Female |
| 5 | Lizzie Sizemore | 32 | " |
| 6 | Sarah Sease | 22 | " |
| 7 | Harriett Goins | 30 | " |
| 8 | Rhoda Sizemore | 28 | " |
| 9 | Rachel Sizemore | 26 | " |
| 10 | Emily Russell | 24 | " |

334

| 11 | Allen Sizemore | 20 | Male |
|----|----------------|----|------|
| 12 | William Sizemore | 18 | " |
| 13 | Ephraim Sizemore | 16 | " |
| 14 | Winnie Sizemore | 14 | Female |

ANCESTOR: Ah-yea-kah

*Commission on Citizenship.*

CHEROKEE NATION, IND. TER.

*Tahlequah,* Oct. 4<sup>th</sup> *1888*

Malinda Sizemore, et al
(VS)
Cherokee Nation

The above case comes before this Commission under an Act of the National Council of February 7[th] 1888, amending an Act, approved December 8[th] 1886 in relation to citizenship. The parties having been duly notified on the 5[th] day of June 1888, to appear before the Commission on Citizenship at Tahlequah, Cherokee Nation on the said day of July 1888, then and there to establish their rights to citizenship in said Nation under the 7[th] Section of said Act, approved December 8[th] 1886. For some cause the case was continued until the 4[th] day of Oct 1888, when, after the case was duly submitted, and fully considered, it is adjudged and determined by the Commission on Citizenship, that Malinda Sizemore, and her children, viz: Robison Sizemore, Christopher C. Sizemore, Eliza Ann Davis, nee Sizemore, Harriett M. Goins, nee Sizemore, Rhoda E. Still, nee Sizemore, Rachel R. Davis, nee Sizemore, Sarah J. Sease, nee Sizemore, Allen T. Sizemore, William A. Sizemore, Ephraim Sizemore, Winnie Sizemore and Emily Russell, nee Sizemore, are not Cherokee by blood and are not entitled to any rights and privileges of the citizens of the Cherokee Nation on account of their blood, and, with the exception of those who may be married in accordance as the law governing intermarriage, if any, are intruders upon the public domain of the Cherokee Nation for these reasons, that the name of Ah-yea-kah, from whom these partiers, just named, claim a Cherokee descent fail to appear on any of the rolls laid down in the 7th Sec. of the Act of Dec. 8[th] 1886, in relation to Citizenship, neither do they contain the names of the parties themselves.

# Cherokee Citizenship Commission Docket Books
## (1880-84, 1887-89) Volume V
## Tahlequah, Cherokee Nation

J. T. Adair     Chairman Commission
H.C. Barnes    Commissioner

### BRAY

**DOCKET #2271**

CENSUS ROLLS

APPLICANT FOR CHEROKEE CITIZENSHIP

| POST OFFICE: | | ATTORNEY: | |
|---|---|---|---|
| **No** | **NAMES** | **AGE** | **SEX** |
| 1 | Charles Bray | | |
| 2 | Ida Faries, nee Bray | | |

ANCESTOR:

*Commission on Citizenship.*

CHEROKEE NATION, IND. TER.

*Tahlequah,* Sept. 26[th] *188*8

Charles Bray and
Ida Faries
    (VS)
Cherokee Nation

Now on this the 26[th] day of Sept. 1888, the above parties, son and daughter of John B. Bray, dec'd, who having been regularly summoned under the provisions of an Act in relation to citizenship, approved Febry 7[th] 1888, to be and appear before this Commission on the 19[th] day of July 1888, and failing to do so, tho' their names were called on three several days at the door of the Commission rooms in the town of Tahlequah, Cherokee Nation, and no answer being returned either in person or by Attorney, now comes Hon. R.F. Wyly, Nations Atty, and moves the Commission to take judgment against Charles Bray and his sister Ida Faries, nee Bray, son & daughter of John B. Bray, dec'd. – The Commission sustain the motion of Nations Atty. and Charles Bray and Ida Faries are hereby declared to be intruders upon the public domain of the Cherokee Nation, with no interest in common with the Cherokee people.

J. T. Adair     Chairman Commission

336

# Cherokee Citizenship Commission Docket Books
## (1880-84, 1887-89) Volume V
## Tahlequah, Cherokee Nation

H.C. Barnes   Commissioner

## TRUETT

**DOCKET #2272**
CENSUS ROLLS

APPLICANT FOR CHEROKEE CITIZENSHIP

| POST OFFICE: Afton, I.T. | | ATTORNEY: I.B. Hitchcock | |
|---|---|---|---|
| **NO** | **NAMES** | **AGE** | **SEX** |
| 1 | Mary E. Truett | 49 | Fem |
| 2 | Lillie May Allen | 8 | " |
| 3 | James S. Truett | 20 | Male |
| 4 | Charles W.  " | 19 | " |
| 5 | Z. Allen | 5 | Fem |
| 6 | James I  " | 2 | Male |

ANCESTOR:  Wm & Matilda Pyeatt[sic]

Citation waived by Claimant Oct 2 A.D. 1888
in the above entitled case.

In the matter of Mary E. Truett, et al, applicants for readmission to citizenship in the Cherokee Nation – The above case having come up for final hearing and all the evidence bearing on said case having been duly examined. The Commission find that there is an insufficient amount of evidence necessary to establishment[sic] of such a claim to warrant its adoption.

In the statement of John M. Taylor, as well as R.M. Walkins[sic] it is observed that the affiant was so situated as to know and he testifies pointedly that Wm and Matilda Pyatt, the ancestors of the applicants, were considered white folks by the Cherokees in that section of the country, and ~~before~~ upon examination of the rolls, it is found that they do not appear as alleged in the evidence. Hence it is concluded by the Commission on Citizenship that Mary E. Truett, James S. Truett, Charles W. Truett, and Lilly May Allen, and James I. Allen and G. Allen are not Cherokees by blood and are not entitled to any of the rights and privileges of such Cherokees and are hereby declared to be Intruders upon the public domain of the Cherokee Nation Public Domain of the Cherokee Nation.

337

# Cherokee Citizenship Commission Docket Books
## (1880-84, 1887-89) Volume V
## Tahlequah, Cherokee Nation

J. T. Adair    Chairman Commission
H.C. Barnes   Commissioner

Office Com on Citizenship
  Tahlequah I.T. Oct. 3rd 1888

---

### One of the cases mentioned in law of Dec. 8th 1886

### KELLY

**DOCKET #2273**
CENSUS ROLLS

APPLICANT FOR CHEROKEE CITIZENSHIP

| POST OFFICE: Echo, Ind. Ter. | | ATTORNEY: | |
|---|---|---|---|
| No | NAMES | AGE | SEX |
| 1 | Muta Angelina Kelly | 54 | Female |
| 2 | Thedor[sic] Kelly | 32 | Male |
| 3 | John D. Kelly | 30 | " |
| 4 | Mary F. Monroe, nee Kelly | 27 | Female |
| 5 | Robert E. Kelly | 24 | Male |
| 6 | William Kelly | 23 | " |
| 7 | Joseph P. Kelly | 20 | " |
| 8 | Franklin Kelly | 17 | " |
| 9 | Charles Kelly | 13 | " |

**ANCESTOR:** James Davis

Thedon Kelly married a Dorcus Duncan, a Cherokee
John D. Kelly    "    " Susan Carey,    "    "
Mary F. Monroe  "    " James Monroe,  "    "
Robert E. Kelly  "    " Miss *(Illegible)*, claims Cherokee blood but not
                                recognized
William Kelly    "    Abb[sic] Harlaw's daughter, a Cherokee

Charged with obtaining citizenship through fraud & bribery

338

Cherokee Citizenship Commission Docket Books
(1880-84, 1887-89) Volume V
Tahlequah, Cherokee Nation

# Office Commission on Citizenship

*Tahlequah, Ind. Ter.* Oct. 31$^{st}$  *1888*

Cherokee Nation
(VS)
Angelina Kelly & family
charged with obtaining citizenship in the Cherokee Nation
through fraud and bribery

The above entitled case is one of the eight mentioned in the 18$^{th}$ Sec. of an Act the National Council of the Cherokee Nation, approved Dec. 8$^{th}$ 1886 in relation to citizenship. The parties defendants in this cause, being charged with having obtained citizenship in the Cherokee Nation through fraud and bribery.

Now it will be remembered that the Supreme Court known as the "Bob Daniels Court" was acting as a Commission on Citizenship, to try and determine certain citizenship cases, and that the law authorizing it was approved Dec. 3$^{rd}$ 1869, and that the Court as a "Commission on Citizenship" closed its labors as such, and adjourned Sine Die on the 21$^{st}$ day of June 1871 (See minutes of Special "Court of Commission" Supreme Court, 1871). On the 10$^{th}$ day of Dec. 1869, the Nation Council passed a Joint resolution in regards to the North Carolina Cherokees coming or removing to the Cherokee Nation. This resolution was passed upon sundry petitions having been presented to the National Council from said Cherokees and also a communication from the Hon. Commissioner of Indian Affairs on the subject of their removal to this Nation, and upon this, was passed an Act of the National Council approved Nov. 20$^{th}$ 1870, authorizing and empowering the Chief Justice of the Supreme Court to enroll said North Carolina Cherokees who might remove into the Cherokee Nation and make application to him within two months after their arrival, and then it became the duty of said Chief Justice to make report of such cases. as provided for under the law, to the next session of the National Council of each year. "And the said Chief Justice, is hereby required to report the number, "names, ages and sex of all persons readmitted by him to be entitled to Cherokee "citizenship and also the number, names, ages and sex of all the persons denied "the rights of Cherokee citizenship to the annual session of the National Council "in each year." (See Act of Nov. 20$^{th}$ 1870 in relation to citizenship - The records of the Supreme Court, or the records of that Office, while John S. Vann may have been acting in *(illegible)* with above quoted law, does not show that any cases were reported to the National Council in accordance with the requirements of this act.

Mr. Henry C. Barnes who was Deputy Sheriff of Tahlequah District at this time, and ex officio Sheriff of the Supreme Court, says, that in Nov. 1871, Muta A. Kelly, wife of J.D. Kelly made an application for citizenship, and from the evidence she produced – the Court granted Muta A. Kelly citizenship, she having proven to the satisfaction of the Court that she was a daughter of James Davis.

Mr. Barnes was certainly mistaken about the Court hearing and receiving testimony in any citizenship case at the time of the granting of the certificate held by these parties, in November 1871, as the Commission when it consisted of the Supreme Court Judges, ceased its labors as such, on the 21$^{st}$ of June 1871, some five months prior to the date of this certificate.

(See Minutes of Special Court of Commission Supreme Court 1871 page 87) The Chief Justice of the Supreme Court, John S. Vann at this time, may have been often engaged in hearing evidence on the subject of citizenship during the intervals of the sitting of the Supreme Court, as he was an Officer filling functions under two laws, and it may have been that Mr. Barnes got these things somewhat confused, as was probably an easy matter under the then existing affairs of this subject of citizenship, and then too, Mr. Barnes' statement was in Dec. 1884, some (13) years or more afterwards.

We the Commission on Citizenship have fully investigated this case, and from the laws governing the same, are of the opinion that Angelina Kelly & her family received their citizenship in the Cherokee Nation, if it can be construed that they ever had any, through fraud – for these reasons, to wit:

The Chief Justice of the Supreme Court has as authority to exceed the law (Act of Nov. 20$^{th}$ 1870) in the matter of citizenship in enrolling for report, persons other than those who may have come from the state of North Carolina.

Mrs. Muta A. or Angelina Kelly does not set up any claim that she was from North Carolina. The pretended certificate of W.H. Turner, Clerk of the Supreme Court, for Judge Jno S. Vann, is "I certify Muta A. Kelly (formerly Davis) has proven to the satisfaction of Chief Justice Jno. S. Vann that she is of

# Cherokee Citizenship Commission Docket Books
## (1880-84, 1887-89) Volume V
### Tahlequah, Cherokee Nation

Cherokee blood; and thereby entitled to all rights and privileges of other Cherokees and now on record in Office of Supreme Court. November 10th 1871

W.H. Turner, Clk
Supreme Court for Judge
Jno. S. Vann.

We say pretended certificate of citizenship for even if it had been signed by Mr. Vann himself, as Chief Justice of the Supreme Court, which he was at the daate of this paper, the law under which he was acting (Act Nov. 20th 1870) did not confer the right on him to grant citizenship, only to report the case with his findings to the National Council, for its definite action. It will be *(illegible)* that the law says "All persons admitted by him to be entitle to Cherokee citizenship." This does not give the Chief Justice under the law, the right to determine the question of citizenship, only to *(illegible)* for formable action by the National Council such cases as he should deem to be entitled to the rights of citizenship in the Cherokee Nation, after hearing the evidence in the case. The fact that a person is in the Cherokee Nation with simply a certificate of this kind in his possession, showing that he or she had proven to the satisfaction of an Officer, whose duties are specifically defined by law, with no such authority or power as the granting of citizenship contained therein, is a fraud on the Cherokee Nation, if used for any other purpose that that for which it was granted, to establish his or their claim for citizenship before the National Council, with no binding force whatever on part of said Nation. – We do not say that Chief Justice John S. Vann, dec'd. exceeded his authority in issuing these certificates, of entitlement as given by him in conformity with the law under which he was then acting.

They are not certificates of citizenship, only certificates of persons whom the Chief Justice thought entitled to receive citizenship as the hands of the National Council under the law? Therefore; Muta Angelina Kelly, Theodore Kelly, John D. Kelly, Mary F. Monroe nee Kelly, Franklin Kelly and Charles Kelly are not citizens of the Cherokee Nation by virtue of Cherokee blood, as the fact has not been established before the proper authorities of the Cherokee Nation.

J. T. Adair      Chairman Commission
D.W. Lipe      Commissioner
Commissioner

H.C. Barnes   Commissioner dissenting

# Cherokee Citizenship Commission Docket Books
## (1880-84, 1887-89) Volume V
## Tahlequah, Cherokee Nation

### Case coming up under amendment of Febry. 7th 1888

### VAUGHN

**DOCKET #2274**
CENSUS ROLLS

APPLICANT FOR CHEROKEE CITIZENSHIP

| POST OFFICE: Cooweescoowee Dist. | ATTORNEY: no Atty – | | |
|---|---|---|---|
| No | NAMES | AGE | SEX |
| 1 | Bill Vaughn & family | | |

ANCESTOR:

The above case comes before this Commission under an amendment of Febry 7th 1888, to an Act of Dec. 8th 1886 in relation to citizenship. Mr. Vaughn had motion duly served on him on the 12th day of Sept, 1888, to appear before the Commission on Citizenship in the town of Tahlequah, Cherokee Nation, on the 15th day of Oct. 1888, then and there to establish his citizenship in said Nation, and failing to do so, thought his name was called three time in three several days. Now comes R.W. Walker for R.F. Wyly, Nations Attorney, and moves he Commission to take judgment against said Vaughn & family, they having treated with contempt the authorities of the Cherokee Nation, and ignored the privileges given them to establish their rights to citizenship in said Nation. The motion was sustained, and the Commission on Citizenship declare Bill Vaughn & family intruders upon the public domain of the Cherokee Nation.

J. T. Adair    Chairman Commission
H.C. Barnes    Commissioner

### Case coming up under amendment of Febry. 7th 1888

### HARRIS

**DOCKET #2275**
CENSUS ROLLS

APPLICANT FOR CHEROKEE CITIZENSHIP

| POST OFFICE: Cooweescoowee Dist. | ATTORNEY: No Atty | | |
|---|---|---|---|
| No | NAMES | AGE | SEX |
| 1 | John Harris & family | | |

ANCESTOR:

The above case comes before this Commission under an amendment of Febry. 7[th] 1888, to the Act of Dec. 8[th] 1886 in relation to the question of citizenship. John Harris having had notice served on him on the 12[th] day of Sept. last to appear before the Commission on Citizenship in the town of Tahlequah, Cherokee Nation, on the 15[th] day of Oct. 1888, then and there to establish his rights to citizenship in said Nation, and failing to do so, though his name was called three times on three several days. Now comes R.W. Walker for R.F. Wyly, Nations Attorney, and moves the Commission to take judgment against said Harris & family, they having treated with contempt the authorities of the Cherokee Nation, and ignored the right tendered them to establish their citizenship in the Cherokee Nation.    The motion was sustained, and the Commission on Citizenship declare John Harris & family intruders upon the public domain of the Cherokee Nation.

J. T. Adair    Chairman Commission

H.C. Barnes    Commissioner

---

**Case coming up ~~under amendment also~~ mentioned in Law of Dec. 8[th] 1886**

## DOLLYHITE

**DOCKET #2276**
CENSUS ROLLS

APPLICANT FOR CHEROKEE CITIZENSHIP

| No | POST OFFICE: | | ATTORNEY: | | |
|----|----|----|----|----|----|
| | Cherokee Nation (vs) | | AGE | SEX | |
| 1 | Samuel Dollyhite & family | | | | |
| 2 | charged with obtaining citizenship | | | | |
| 3 | through fraud & bribery  (See Act | | | | |
| 4 | Dec. 8[th] 1886) | | | | |

ANCESTOR:

Case Re-opened for hearing on the 2[nd] ~~30[th]~~ of ~~Oct. 1888~~ April 1889 on motion of Dollyhite's Atty. Hon. L.B. Bell

Cornell Rogers
~~Clk. Com.~~

343

## Cherokee Citizenship Commission Docket Books
## (1880-84, 1887-89) Volume V
## Tahlequah, Cherokee Nation

April 2 <sup>th</sup>[sic] '89
~~Oct. 20 '88~~
this Jan 22 '89
D.S. Williams
   Asst Clk
     Com

Office Com on Citizenship, Tahlequah I.T. Oct. 23<sup>rd</sup> 1888

Now on this, the above written date comes the Atty. for the Nation, through R.W. Walker, and moves the Commission to enter judgment against Samuel Dollyhite & family, they having been duly notified under date of Sept. 19<sup>th</sup> 1888, to appear before the Commission on Citizenship, in the town of Tahlequah, Cherokee Nation, on the 19<sup>th</sup> day of Oct, 1888, then and there to answer why the decree of a former Commission should not be declared null and void on account of fraud having been practiced in obtaining Citizenship in said Nation. The case was duly was called three times on three several days at the door of the Commission rooms in the town of Tahlequah, and no answer being returned either in person, by Attorney or otherwise: Now comes R.W. Walker for Hon. R.F. Wyly, Nations Atty, and moves the Commission to declare Saml Dollyhite & family intruders upon the public domain of the Cherokee Nation, and further to declare, null & void the decree of Commission granting them citizenship, they having treated with contempt the authorities of said Nation and ignored the privilege tendered them to prove to the satisfaction of the authorities of said Nation to establish their rights to citizenship in the same. – The motion was sustained for the above reasons, and Samuel Dollyhite & family, and one Bettie Brown, nee Dollyhite are declared to be intruders upon the public domain of the Cherokee Nation with no interest in common with the Cherokee tribe of Indians.

        J. T. Adair    Chairman Commission
        H.C. Barnes  Commissioner
        D.W. Lipe    Commissioner

          Office Commission on Citizenship
               Cherokee Nation
           Tahlequah  October 21<sup>st</sup> 1889

Cherokee Nation
     vs                Fraud in acquiring admission
Samuel Dollyhite & Family    to Cherokee Citizenship

# Cherokee Citizenship Commission Docket Books
## (1880-84, 1887-89) Volume V
## Tahlequah, Cherokee Nation

The above case comes before the Commission on Citizenship under the 18th Section of the Act approved December 7th 1886 creating the Commission, and is one of long which has heretofore been the subject of investigation and decision. Its history is briefly states. By the 5th Section of an Act providing for taking the census of the Cherokee Nation approved December 3rd 1869, the Supreme Court was constituted a Commission Court and authorized and directed to *(illegible)* the right to citizenship such persons as might be *(illegible)* to them as intruders by the census takers and *(illegible)* of the several Districts. Samuel Dollyhite and his wife Margaret Ann, then was domiciled in Cooweescoowee District were so reported by the Solicitor. Mr and Mrs Dollyhite had recently moved into the Nation from Arkansas where they had, on their arrival from Texas, bought and resided for a year on a farm within a short distance of the Cherokee line. Mrs. Dollyhite prepared a claim to their right of Citizenship in the Nation upon the ground that she was a person of Cherokee Indian descent. The Supreme Court on the 7th day of April 1871 had the following proceedings and decision on the case, viz. Case of Samuel Dollyhite and wife Margaret Ann taken of and from affidavits produced together with marriage license granted Dollyhite by Clk of District Court for Flint District and the certificate of W.A. Thompson Duncan, Minister of Gospel. The Court decide that claimants are entitled to citizenship, wife by blood and husband by compliance with the marriage law. "But on allegations of that fraud had been practiced in obtaining this decision the National Council by an Act approved November 29, 1873, among other provisions looking to an inquiry into these allegations of fraud directed" the Chief Justice of the Supreme Court as early as practicable in 1874 to try the causes or claims of the individuals herein referred to in the Supreme Court room in Tahlequah and said suits shall be by summons directed by said Judge to the Sheriff of any of the Dist*(smudge)* this Nation to be served at least thirty days before the day of trial and any person failing to obey such summons shall be *(illegible)* against the same as if the said persons were present." Samuel Dollyhite and family *(illegible)* among others were included in that act. Chief Justice Keys held his court and on the 3rd day of October 1874 presented to the National Council his report as follows "The Court is of the opinion that in the case of Samuel Dollyhite and family of Cooweescoowee District C.N. the parties have failed to establish rights to Cherokee Citizenship from the evidence submitted and that the claims of the persons named in the Act were fraudulent and without foundation in the law or in fact. The National Council therefore on the 6th December 1874 by public enactment declared these persons including by name Samuel Dollyhite and family the defendants in this case, to be intruders and asking for their removal as such by the authorities of the United States

## Cherokee Citizenship Commission Docket Books
## (1880-84, 1887-89) Volume V
## Tahlequah, Cherokee Nation

beyond the limits of the Cherokee Nation. By no subsequent act of competent authority have these proceedings been *(illegible)* or the persons named recognized as lawful citizens. Indeed this Commission is not *(illegible)* that there were further proceedings *(illegible)* them until the before named Act of December 8th 1886 became a law and specifically directed the Commission to reinvestigate these cases of alleged fraud and bribery and if found to be true to declare the Acts and decrees of the Courts and Commission admitting them to citizenship to be null and void.

Accordingly summons were issued to Samuel Dollyhite and family to appear before the Commission and answer in the *(illegible)*. It was *(smudge)* as of common notoriety that Samuel Dollyhite and his wife Margaret Ann had *(illegible)* several years since *(smudge)* the Cherokee Country and were both now deceased, but that their family of two daughters, Cornelia married to a man named Long Brown, who claims no right of citizenship and Bettie who also married a Brown, are living in Cooweescoowee District. The case was called for final hearing before this Commission on the 24th day of June and was *(illegible...)* by R.M. Wolf for the Nation and L.B. Bell and R.F. Wyly Esqrs. for the Defendants.

The question involved in this case and to be determined by the Commission is whether fraud in the *(illegible...)* was the means by which the Supreme Court was induced to make the decision which they rendered on the 7th day of April 1871, that Samuel Dollyhite and wife Margaret Ann were entitled to citizenship. "The wife by blood and husband by compliance with the marriage law." It is not important whether the fraud if any were resorted to was brought to bear upon the members of the Court through corrupt personal motives only the *(illegible...)*. The former supposition has not been entertained by any one, the character of the judges being above reproach or suspicion. How many of the papers upon which the opinion of the Court was based, if any at all, have been lost or mislaid this Commission has not the means of learning. But such as are now found and before it would not warrant their action. So far as now known, Mrs. Dollyhite was admitted upon a letter dated Jan. 10, 1871 and *(illegible)* General Stand Watie to the judges of the Court by request of Mrs. Dollyhite stating that she claimed to be the daughter of Eliza Bible, nee Eliza Green, a Cherokee woman then deceased and that if Eliza Green was her mother as she represented and the granddaughter of one Betsy Took, she was unquestionably a Cherokees as Betsy Took was almost a full blood Cherokee. And this was the ground upon which her admission was made as will appear

346

from the statement of one of judges of the Court made to J.W. Alberty who was a member of the National Council in 1873 or 4, when action was had in *(illegible)* to these defendants & other intruders. There is no evidence on file in support of the above application therefore we decide that applicant that Eliza Bibles nee Eliza Green was the ~~daughter~~ mother of Margaret Ann Dollyhite, a fact if one that was easily *(illegible)* of proof through her children George Bible and other persons of respectable standing in Cooweescoowee District. The testimony of this same witness proves that Dollyhite ~~and wife~~ bought and settled on a farm in the County of Washington and state of Arkansas immediately on the Cherokee line in 1870, that he repeatedly expressed a wish to get a right in the Country that he sold his farm in twelve months for a wagon and four mules which he offered to give to Judge Alberty for a right in the Cherokee Nation. Lewis *(Illegible)* swore before Chief Justice Keyes that Dollyhite claimed that his wife was related to the Fallings family into which a *(Illegible)* had married and said he would give his mule for evidence to establish her right. He was refered[sic] to *(Illegible)* Cordry who had married a Falling in Texas, but he declined to appear as a witness. John H. Wolfe late District Judge of Tahlequah District swears that neither Dollyhite nor his wife claimed to be Cherokees when they arrived at Tahlequah from Arkansas and not until after it had mentioned to him by way of a joke. C.H. Taylor Esqr. swears that Mrs. Dollyhite and one Vincent then living on 14 Mile Creek, near Tahlequah were full ~~brothers~~ sister and brother and that she refered[sic] to *(illegible)* him to prove his right altho[sic], she had been admitted by the Supreme Court because it would work as hardship or interfere with her rights. She would not even testify in his behalf and failing this he sold out and returned to Texas. She then claims her Cherokee descent from the Bible Family. The statement of Wm *(Illegible)* shows that neither Dollyhite nor Mrs. Dollyhite was regarded as of Indian descent by a cousin of his in Texas and from where they moved to Arkansas. These facts justify this Coimmission in ~~declar~~ finding that Samuel Dolly[sic] and ~~family~~ wife Margaret Ann obtained admission to citizenship in the Cherokee Nation through fraud. ~~and~~

Will.P. Ross
Chairman
Rabbit Bunch
J.E. Gunter    Com

# Cherokee Citizenship Commission Docket Books
## (1880-84, 1887-89) Volume V
### Tahlequah, Cherokee Nation

## BARKER

**DOCKET #2277**
CENSUS ROLLS

APPLICANT FOR CHEROKEE CITIZENSHIP

| POST OFFICE: Cooweescoowee Dist. | | ATTORNEY: | |
|---|---|---|---|
| No | Cherokee Nation NAMES (vs) | AGE | SEX |
| 1 | A. Barker & family | | |
| 2 | charged with obtaining | | |
| 3 | citizenship through fraud | | |
| | and bribery | | |

ANCESTOR:

The above case is brought to the notice of this Commission on Citizenship by R.W. Walker for Hon. R.F. Wyly, Nations Atty, filing motion to declare A. Barker & family intruders upon the public domain of the Cherokee Nation, upon the grounds, that they were duly notified under date of Sept. 20th 1888, to appear before the Commission in the town of Tahlequah Cherokee Nation on the 20th day of Oct. 1888, then and there to answer why a decree of a former Commission granting them citizenship should not be declared null and void on account of fraud having been practiced in obtaining the same, in said Nation.

The case was duly called on three several days at the door of the rooms of the Commission in Tahlequah, and no answer being returned in person or by Attorney or otherwise. Now comes Hon. R.F. Wyly, Nations Atty. through R.W. Walker and moves the Commission to declare A. Barker & family intruders upon the public domain of the Cherokee Nation and further to declare null & void the decree of former Commission granting their citizenship, they having treated with contempt the authorities of said Nation if ignored the privileges tendered them to establish their rights to citizenship to the satisfaction of the Cherokee Nation. The motion is sustained for the above reasons, and A. Barker and his family declared to be intruders upon the public domain of said Nation, without any rights or privileges in common with the citizens of the same.

J. T. Adair    Chairman Commission
D.W. Lipe    Commissioner
H.C. Barnes    Commissioner

348

# Cherokee Citizenship Commission Docket Books
## (1880-84, 1887-89) Volume V
## Tahlequah, Cherokee Nation

Office Com on Citizenship
Tahlequah I.T. Oct. 23<sup>rd</sup> '88.

---

## BELL

**DOCKET #2278**
CENSUS ROLLS

APPLICANT FOR CHEROKEE CITIZENSHIP

| No | POST OFFICE: Cherokee Nation (vs) | ATTORNEY: R.W. Walker | |
|---|---|---|---|
| | | AGE | SEX |
| 1 | Robert N. Bell | | |
| 2 | Susan E. Crawford, nee Bell | | |
| 3 | J.W. Bell | | |
| 4 | Martha W. Morgan, nee Bell | | |
| 5 | John E. Bell | | |
| 6 | M.M. Bell | | |
| 7 | Sarah O. Scott, nee Bell | | |
| 8 | Phillip Bell | | |
| 9 | Jesse N. Bell | | |

ANCESTOR:

This case was tried by Hon. J.T. Chairman of Com. and Henry C. Barnes Commissioner. Mr. D.W. Lipe Commissioner having been objected to on the grounds of relationship by offinity. – The Commission could not agree as to a finding in this case – It was so reported.

Cornell Rogers
Clk Com. on Citizenship

Office Com on Citizenship
Tahlequah I.T. Nov. 1<sup>st</sup> 1888.

Office Commission on Citizenship
Cherokee Nation
Tahlequah June 5<sup>th</sup> 1889

349

Cherokee Citizenship Commission Docket Books
(1880-84, 1887-89) Volume V
Tahlequah, Cherokee Nation

The Cherokee Nation
vs
Moses Bell and Family

The above named case comes before this Commission through a difference of opinion between Hons. J. T. Adair Chairman Commission, President, and Henry C. Barnes, members of the Commission on Citizenship created by the Act of December 8<sup>th</sup> 1886. The Hon. D.W. Lipe, the other member of the Commission, not sitting. The history of the case is briefly as follows; The Cherokee Nation in the ~~See.~~ 18<sup>th</sup> Sec. of the above named Act. after reciting that Moses Bell and Family and other persons therein named, having been charged with obtaining by fraud and bribery the decrees of the Commissioners or Courts granting them citizenship in the Cherokee Nation directs the Commission to summons said persons to appear before it and show cause why the decree of said Commissions or Courts shall not be declared null and void on account of such fraud practiced and upon investigation, should such fraud be proven, the Commission is hereby directed to declare such decrees null and void, and the above named parties shall be, by the Principal Chief, declared to be intruders and removed from the limits of the Cherokee Nation.

In reply to these allegations the Defendants enter a general denial and present a certificate dated November 13<sup>th</sup> 1871, ~~which purported to be~~ purporting to be signed by John S. Van, Chief Justice of the Supreme Court and Wm H. Turner, Clerk of the Supreme Court of the Cherokee Nation declaring Mrs. Sarah J. Bell, wife of Dr. M. Bell, to be entitled to all rights and privileges of other Cherokees in the Cherokee Nation, it having been proven to the satisfaction of the Chief Justice by affidavits of Dr. S.H. Payne and wife, Martha A. Payne, made before Ellis Sanders, Clerk of the Dist. Court for Sequoyah District, that she is a full sister of said Martha A. Payne and Eudonia Cobb, who established their Cherokee rights before the Court of Commission at its sitting and dated May 29, 1871, by blood.

It is contended by Plaintiff that this Act ~~of atherefore~~ admitting of Mrs. Bell to citizenship is illegal and fraudulent, and to the point upon which the case rests the attention of the Commission will be given.

By the 5<sup>th</sup> Sec of the Act approved the 3<sup>rd</sup> day of December 1869, the Supreme Court ~~of the~~ was specially empowered to act as a Court of Commission on behalf of the Nation for the hearing and determination of all cases of doubtful citizenship which shall be reported to them by the persons to be appointed to

# Cherokee Citizenship Commission Docket Books
## (1880-84, 1887-89) Volume V
## Tahlequah, Cherokee Nation

take the census of the Nation under the provisions of that Act only *(illegible...)*. The Supreme Court closed its session as a Commission on Citizenship on the 21st day of June 1871, and adjourned <u>sine die</u>. Dr. Bell & family, if in this country did not appear before that Commission. Hon. Robert B. Daniel the Chief Justice having died, Associate Justice John S. Vann became Acting Chief Justice.

By a joint resolution of the National Council approved December 10th 1869, "In regard to the North Carolina Cherokees", the North Carolina Cherokees, "were invited to emigrate west and become identified into the Cherokee Nation as citizens thereof." The term "North Carolina Cherokees" fully and clearly defines the class of Cherokees *(illegible)* by it. In ~~for~~ anticipation of the acceptance of the invitation by the North Carolina Cherokees, the Act entitled "An Act relating to the North Carolina Cherokees was passed and approved November 18th 1870, making it the duty of such Cherokees coming into the Country and permanently *(illegible...)* themselves before the Chief Justice within two months and ~~making it~~ the duty of the Chief Justice to report to the National Council the number, names, age and sex of all persons admitted by him and also the number, names, age and sex of the persons denied the right of Cherokee citizenship in such year." This Act was limited to "the North Carolina Cherokees" and confirmed the authority of the Chief Justice to admit persons to citizenship under the conditions named, to the "North Carolina Cherokees", and as belonging to which class there is no contention on the part of defendants. That such was the full scope of the Act referred to, so far as the power of the Chief Justice ~~was~~ went is made apparently the Act approved November 22nd 1871. *(Illegible)* of the Act of Nov. 18th 1870, which required "the Chief Justice of the Cherokee Nation to receive and hear the petitions of all persons claiming the rights of Cherokee citizenship and to take evidence with regard to the same ~~and~~ and to transmit the petitions of such petitions, with all the evidence relating thereto, with such remarks *(illegible...)* of each petitioner so he may deem proper, to the National Council during the first week of such regular session, for final action nor shall the *(illegible)* of the said Chief Justice extend any further than to receive the petitions and take evidence as aforesaid."

It must then be apparent that the Chief Justice had no authority to issue the certificate of citizenship to Mrs. Sarah J. Bell, wife of Dr. M. Bell, as claimed, on the 13th day of November 1980, under the provisions of the Act of November 18th 1870. Such ~~act~~ issuance of the certificate was clearly illegal and to that extent void. Was it also fraudulent? The answer to that question rests upon less tangible grounds but such as may be relied upon as sufficient to

351

answer the question in the affirmative. It is quite clearly shown that the certificate with both the signatures of the Chief Justice and the Clerk was written by the same person and that person the clerk, that the Supreme Court was not in session on the 13[th] day of November 1871. The Chief Justice J.S. Vann and associate Justice Sixkiller both being sick, and that Mr. Vann was ~~that day~~ in the afternoon of that day elected both associate and Chief Justice of the Supreme Court. And that the only persons present when the certificate was issued was Chief Justice Vann, Clerk W.H. *(Illegible)*.

That the views here *(illegible)* have been entertained by the several branches of the government is evident from their actions in the provisions. The Act of Nov. 29[th] 1873 required the Chief Justice of the Supreme Court as early as practicable in 1874 to try the causes, or claims of *(illegible...)*

This Commission therefore declares the decree *(illegible)* to have been made by John S. Vann, Chief Justice admitting Moses Bell and family (to wit; Sarah J. Bell (now deceases), Robert H. Bell, Susan E. Crawford nee Bell, J.W. Bell, Martha W. Morgan nee Bell, John C. Bell, M.M. Bell, Sarah O. Scott nee Bell, Phillip Bell and Jesse H. Bell, dated November 13[th] 1871, null and void.

> Will.P. Ross
> Chairman
> *(Cherokee Letters)*
> John E. Gunter    Com

---

## DAVIS

**DOCKET #2279**
CENSUS ROLLS 1835-1851 & 52

APPLICANT FOR CHEROKEE CITIZENSHIP

| POST OFFICE: Tahlequah, Ind. Ter. | | ATTORNEY: Boudinot & Rasmus | |
|---|---|---|---|
| NO | NAMES | AGE | SEX |
| 1 | Benjamin M. Davis | 31 | Male |

ANCESTOR: Matilda Davis nee Guinn

Rejected Sept 9[th] 1889

> Office Commission on Citizenship
> Cherokee Nation Ind Ter
> Tahlequah  Sept. 9[th] 1889

Application for Cherokee Citizenship.

The Commission decide that in the above named case that Benjamin M Davis age 31 years at the date of filing his application the 3rd of October 1887, is not of Cherokee blood and is not entitled to citizenship in the Cherokee Nation. See decision in the case of David C. Davis Docket 2280 Book E Page 89. P.O. Tahlequah C.N.

Attest
D.S. Williams — J.E. Gunter Com
Asst Clk Com.

---

## DAVIS

**DOCKET #2280**
CENSUS ROLLS 1835, '48, '51 & '52

APPLICANT FOR CHEROKEE CITIZENSHIP

| POST OFFICE: Tahlequah Ind. Ter. | | ATTORNEY: Boudinot & Rasmus | |
|---|---|---|---|
| NO | NAMES | AGE | SEX |
| 1 | David C. Davis | 40 | male |

ANCESTOR: Matilda Davis, nee Guinn

*Commission on Citizenship.*

CHEROKEE NATION, IND. TER.

*Tahlequah*, Sept 9th *188*9

David C. Davis
vs — Application for Cherokee Citizenship
The Cherokee Nation

The claimant in the above case alleges that he is the son of Matilda Davis, whose maiden name was Matilda Guinn, the daughter of one Almon Guinn ~~and~~ from whom he derives his Cherokee blood and whose name he believes is enrolled on the census rolls of Cherokees by blood taken and made by the United States in the years 1835, 51, 52. The witnesses in this case are John Martin and Asa Guinn. John Martin testifies that he is fifty years old and gets his Cherokee blood from his father Wm Martin and he from <u>his</u> father, Samuel

Martin and that he does not know that he derives any any[sic] by hearsay, from his grand Mother Matilda Martin nee Guinn, and who was ~~the~~ also Matilda Martin nee Guinn and who was ~~the~~ also Matilda Davis. He knew his grand Father ~~Also~~ Almon Guinn about 40 years before in Polk County Tennessee and that he died about the year 1855 and left Tennessee before 1848. The father of applicant Young Davis was a white man. Asa Guinn the other witness before the Commission testifies that he is 62 yrs. old, knows applicants to be sons of Matilda Davis, nee Guinn, sister of witness and claims to be of Cherokee descent, derived from his father Almon Guinn who lived on Ocoee river[sic] in Polk County, Tennessee, and died in 1851 or 52 and was living in Polk County Tennessee in 1835. He identifies claimants as ~~the~~ his relatives. The name of Matilda Davis is not found on the census rolls of 1835, 51 & 51 nor is that of Almon Guinn, as it would have been if he was recognized of Indian blood and participated in the payments being made those Cherokees entered upon these rolls. The Commission then decide that David C. Davis and his daughters Sally age 13 years. Hester 15 yrs. and Gipsy S. 6 yrs. and *(Illegible)* Young 10 yrs., Jack 8 yrs. and Boss Davis 3 years are not of Cherokee blood and not entitled to citizenship in the Cherokee Nation. P.O. Tahlequah, Ind. Ter.

Will.P. Ross
Chairman
J.E. Gunter    Com

## LUKE

**DOCKET #2281**
CENSUS ROLLS 1848-51-52-35-
Old Settler                    APPLICANT FOR CHEROKEE CITIZENSHIP

| POST OFFICE: Muskogee, Ind. Ter. | | ATTORNEY: Boudinot & Rasmus | |
|---|---|---|---|
| **NO** | **NAMES** | **AGE** | **SEX** |
| 1 | Tennessee Mc A. Luke | 39 | Fem |
| 2 | Jeff Luke | 18 | Male |
| 3 | Elizabeth Luke | 13 | Fem |
| 4 | Thomas Luke | 12 | Male |
| 5 | Mattie Luke | 9 | Female |
| 6 | Eugene Luke | 3 | Male |

**ANCESTOR:** Giles McAnnulty

Rejected Sept. 9[th] 1889

# Cherokee Citizenship Commission Docket Books
## (1880-84, 1887-89) Volume V
## Tahlequah, Cherokee Nation

Office Commission on Citizenship
Cherokee Nation Ind Ter
Tahlequah  Sept. 9<sup>th</sup> 1889

Application for Cherokee Citizenship

The above applicant was called 3 times & no answer & there being no evidence on file in support of the application the Commission decide adversely to applicants, Tennessee Mc A. Luke age 39 yrs., and his children viz:  Jeff Luke age 18 yrs., Elizabeth Luke age 13 yrs., Thomas Luke age 12 yrs. Mattie Luke age 9 yrs. & Eugene Luke age 3 yrs. P.O. Muskogee, Ind. Ter.

Attest
      D.S. Williams                    J.E. Gunter    Com
      Asst  Clk  Com.

## LANDRUM

**DOCKET #2282**
CENSUS ROLLS '35-'51-'52

APPLICANT FOR CHEROKEE CITIZENSHIP

| POST OFFICE: Vinita, I.T. | | ATTORNEY: L.B. Bell | |
|---|---|---|---|
| No | NAMES | AGE | SEX |
| 1 | Nannie V. Landrum | 25 | Female |

ANCESTOR: Daniel Landrum

Re-admitted Sept. 9<sup>th</sup> 1889

Office Commission on Citizenship
Cherokee Nation Ind Ter
Tahlequah  September 9<sup>th</sup> 1889

Application for Cherokee Citizenship

The applicant in the above case alleges that she is the daughter of one Daniel Landrum alias Daniel Hass whose names she believes will be found on the census rolls of Cherokees by blood taken and made by the United States in the years 1835, 51, 52.  The applicant having been identified by Mrs. Anna Ballard 51 years as the daughter of Daniel Landrum sometimes called Daniel Hass and Anna Haskins both of whom were of Cherokee blood and the name of the said Daniel Hass being found on the census roll of 1852.  The Commission

355

decide that Nannie V. Landrum 22 yrs. old is of Cherokee blood and entitled to readmission to citizenship in the Cherokee Nation. P.O. Vinita In. Ter.

Attest
    D.S. Williams                      J.E. Gunter   Com
    Asst  Clk  Com.

---

## THRIFT

**DOCKET #2283**
CENSUS ROLLS

APPLICANT FOR CHEROKEE CITIZENSHIP

| POST OFFICE: Fairmount, Ind. | | ATTORNEY: L.B. Bell | |
|---|---|---|---|
| NO | NAMES | AGE | SEX |
| 1 | Jane Thrift | | |

ANCESTOR:

The Commission decide against claimant. See decision in case John R. Henly Docket 553, Book B, Page 266.

J.E. Gunter   Com

---

## McDANIEL

**DOCKET #2284**
CENSUS ROLLS

APPLICANT FOR CHEROKEE CITIZENSHIP

| POST OFFICE: Grape Creek, N.C. | | ATTORNEY: C.H. Taylor | |
|---|---|---|---|
| NO | NAMES | AGE | SEX |
| 1 | Mary McDaniel | 40 | Female |

ANCESTOR: Polly Taylor

Readmitted Sept. 25$^{th}$ 1889

Office Commission on Citizenship
Cherokee Nation Ind Ter
Tahlequah Sept. 25$^{th}$ 1889

The testimony of John M. Taylor of Tahlequah establishes the fact that the applicant is the daughter of his sister Catharine McDaniel and whose first

356

husband and the Father of applicant was Felix Panther, and as the name of Catharine McDaniel and Mary McDaniel are enrolled on the census rolls of Cherokees by blood taken and made by the United States in the years 1851-52. The Commission decide that Mary McDaniel 40 years of age is of Cherokee descent and entitled to re-admission to citizenship in the Cherokee Nation under the Constitution and laws thereof. Post Office Grape Creek North Carolina.

Attest
    D.S. Williams                  J.E. Gunter   Com
    Asst  Clk  Com.

## WINSLOW

**DOCKET #2285**
CENSUS ROLLS

APPLICANT FOR CHEROKEE CITIZENSHIP

| POST OFFICE: Fairmount, Indiana | | ATTORNEY: | |
|---|---|---|---|
| **NO** | **NAMES** | **AGE** | **SEX** |
| 1 | Jane W. Winslow | 64 | Female |
| 2 | Mary M. Bog?? | 43 | " |
| 3 | Thomas L. Winslow | 38 | Male |
| 4 | Martha Shugart | 35 | Female |
| 5 | John N. Winslow | 34 | Male |
| 6 | Joseph A. Winslow | 29 | " |
| 7 | Delana E Winslow | 25 | Female |
| 8 | William C. Winslow | 33 | Male |
| 9 | Jonathan Winslow | 3 | " |
| 10 | Lara Bog?? | 7 | Female |
| 11 | Robert W. Shugart | 14 | Male |
| 12 | Mary E. Shugart and other grandchildren | 11 | Female |

ANCESTOR: Sarah Elmore

Adverse. See decision of the Commission in case John R. Henly Docket 553, Book B, Page 266.

                      J.E. Gunter   Com

# Cherokee Citizenship Commission Docket Books
## (1880-84, 1887-89) Volume V
## Tahlequah, Cherokee Nation

## HUNT

**DOCKET #2279**[sic]

CENSUS ROLLS

APPLICANT FOR CHEROKEE CITIZENSHIP

| POST OFFICE: | | ATTORNEY: | |
|---|---|---|---|
| **NO** | **NAMES** | **AGE** | **SEX** |
| 1 | Jounnah Hunt | | Female |

**ANCESTOR:** Caleb Hubbard

Rejected Sept. 20<sup>th</sup> 1889

Office Commission on Citizenship
Cherokee Nation Ind Ter
Tahlequah Sept. 20<sup>th</sup> 1889

The Commission in this case decide that Jounnah Hunt is not of Cherokee blood.

See decision in the case of Caleb Hubbard Docket 2140 B.D. Page 631.

Attest
D.S. Williams                          J.E. Gunter   Com
Asst   Clk   Com.

---

## ELMORE

**DOCKET #2280**[sic]

CENSUS ROLLS

APPLICANT FOR CHEROKEE CITIZENSHIP

| POST OFFICE: Saint Joseph Mo. | | ATTORNEY: Forwarded from Washington City | |
|---|---|---|---|
| **NO** | **NAMES** | **AGE** | **SEX** |
| 1 | Robert Elmore | | |
| 2 | David Elmore | | |
| 3 | Abigal Stillwell | | |
| 4 | Sarah A. Curry | | |
| 5 | Catherine V. Smith | | |

**ANCESTOR:** Anderson Elmore

358

# Cherokee Citizenship Commission Docket Books (1880-84, 1887-89) Volume V Tahlequah, Cherokee Nation

Office Commission on Citizenship
Cherokee Nation, Ind Ter
Tahlequah, Sept 19th 1889

In support of the above application referred from the Department of the Interior Washington D.C. is found the affidavit of one Sarah J. Pemberton 58 years of age who affirmed on the 18th day of October 1886 before Eugne[sic] Agnes, Notary Public for Buchanan County State of Missouri, that she is well acquainted with the before named applicants and has been from their births, and knows that they are the children of one Anderson Elmore who was born in Jefferson County, State of Tennessee on the 13th day of September A.D. 1817, and died in Dekalb County State of Missouri the 28th day of march A.D. 1877, that said Anderson Elmore was a son of one David Elmore, a person of Cherokee Indian descent who told affiant that he was born in Guilford County, North Carolina in 1782 and who died in Anderson County State of Missouri the 16th day of August A.D. 1847, and that the said David Elmore was the affiants father, and who said that he was the son of one Abijal[sic] Elmore a Cherokee Indian who was born on the Cherokee Indian reservation and died in Guilford County and State of North Carolina. The exparte affidavit of a single witness who is closely related to the applicants and directly interested in the favorable decision of the case is not deemed sufficient evidence to establish the facts alleged. Besides the evidence shows that David Elmore died in 1847 and Anderson Elmore father of applicants in 1877 and whose names should appear if they were Cherokees on one or more of the census rolls of Cherokees by blood taken by the United States in 1835, 48, 51, 52 but do not. The Commission therefore decide that the before named claimants viz, David Elmore, Robert Elmore, Abijal J. Stillwell, Sarah A Curry and Catharine V. Smith are not of Cherokee blood.   P.O. Saint Joseph Buchanan County, Missouri.
Attest

    E.G. Ross                             J.E. Gunter   Com
      Clerk Commission

## FARRO

**DOCKET #2281**[sic]
CENSUS ROLLS 1835-1852

APPLICANT FOR CHEROKEE CITIZENSHIP

| POST OFFICE: Van Buren Ark | | ATTORNEY: A.E. Ivey | |
|---|---|---|---|
| NO | NAMES | AGE | SEX |
| 1 | Louise Farro | 30 | Fem |

ANCESTOR: Margaret Botico

Rejected Sept. 16th 1889

Office Commission on Citizenship
Cherokee Nation Ind Ter
Tahlequah  Sept. 16th 1889

The above case was called three times and no response from applicant or by Atty and there being no evidence on file in support of claim the Commission decide that Louise Farro age 30 yrs. is not a Cherokee by blood. P.O. Vanburen Arkansas.

Attest
   D.S. Williams
   Asst  Clk  Com.

J.E. Gunter   Com

360

# Index

375

# Index

www.ingramcontent.com/pod-product-compliance
Lightning Source LLC
Chambersburg PA
CBHW020239030426
42336CB00010B/536